Music and Musicians in Renaissance Cities and Towns

This interdisciplinary collection examines musical culture in urban centres in Renaissance Europe and the New World. Although musicologists have already investigated such topics, lack of familiarity with (urban) historical methodologies has often resulted in failure to explore fully the ways in which the urban environment had an impact on musical activity of all kinds; neither is this question adequately addressed by urban historians. This book thus aims to integrate musicological and urban-historical approaches. To urban historians it shows the range of work undertaken by music historians; to musicologists it presents some different approaches, questions and perspectives which suggest new lines of enquiry for future investigations.

FIONA KISBY is Research Fellow at the Department of Music, Royal Holloway College, University of London.

Music and Musicians
in Renaissance Cities and
Towns

Edited by Fiona Kisby

CAMBRIDGE
UNIVERSITY PRESS

PUBLISHED BY THE PRESS SYNDICATE OF THE UNIVERSITY OF CAMBRIDGE
The Pitt Building, Trumpington Street, Cambridge, United Kingdom

CAMBRIDGE UNIVERSITY PRESS
The Edinburgh Building, Cambridge CB2 2RU, UK
40 West 20th Street, New York, NY 10011-4211, USA
10 Stamford Road, Oakleigh, VIC 3166, Australia
Ruiz de Alarcón 13, 28014 Madrid, Spain
Dock House, The Waterfront, Cape Town 8001, South Africa

http://www.cambridge.org

First published 2001

Printed in the United Kingdom at the University Press, Cambridge

Typeface Adobe Minion 10/13pt   *System* QuarkXpress® [SE]

A catalogue record for this book is available from the British Library

Library of Congress Cataloguing in Publication data

Music and musicians in Renaissance cities and towns / edited by Fiona Kisby.
    p.   cm.
Includes index.
ISBN 0 521 66171 4
1. Music – 15th century – History and criticism. 2. Music – 16th century – History and
criticism. 3. Cities and towns, Renaissance – Europe. I. Kisby, Fiona.
ML172.M86 2001   00-062177
780′.9173′2–dc21

ISBN 0 521 66171 4 hardback

CONTENTS

Contents

ILLUSTRATIONS

NOTES ON CONTRIBUTORS

SOTERRAÑA AGUIRRE RINCÓN is Assistant Professor at the University of Valladolid. She is the author of *Ginés de Boluda (c. 1545 – des 1604). Biografía y obra musical* (Valladolid, 1995) and *Un manuscrito para un convento: el 'Libro de Música' de Sor Luisa de la Ascensión* (Valladolid, 1998).

EGBERTO BERMÚDEZ is a tenured professor at the Instituto de Investigaciones Esteticas of the National University in Bogotá, Colombia, and has published a number of works on Latin-American and Colombian music history. He is the founder and co-founder respectively of *Canto* and the Fundacion de Musica, an ensemble and institution dedicated to performing and researching the Spanish and Latin-American musical past.

BARRA BOYDELL is Senior Lecturer in Music at the National University of Ireland, Maynooth. He has written articles and books on the history of music in Ireland and music iconography, including *Music at Christ Church Before 1800: Documents and Selected Anthems* (Dublin, 1998) and *The Crumhorn and Other Renaissance Windcap Instruments* (Buren, 1982).

IAIN FENLON is Reader in Historical Musicology, University of Cambridge, and Fellow of King's College. He is the author of a number of books and articles on music and culture in early modern Italy including *Music and Patronage in Sixteenth-Century Mantua* (Cambridge, 1980–82) and (with James Haar) *The Italian Madrigal in the Early Sixteenth Century* (Cambridge, 1988). He is currently completing a book on *Music, Ceremony and Self-Identity in Renaissance Venice*.

BARBARA HAGGH is Associate Professor of Music at the University of Maryland at College Park. She has published numerous articles on a wide range of topics relating to the history of medieval sacred music, including music at the Sainte-Chapelle of Paris and Cambrai Cathedral; she has also written extensively on music in Brussels and Ghent in the fifteenth century.

FIONA KISBY completed a Ph.D. on the household chapels of the early Tudor kings at the University of London in 1996. She then held a British Academy Postdoctoral Research Fellowship at Royal Holloway College, University of London. She is a Fellow of the Royal Historical Society and has published a number of articles on the early Tudor court and the cultural life of late medieval London and Westminster in music and history journals.

JOACHIM KREMER is a lecturer at the Hochschule für Musik und Theater, Hanover. He is the author of two books, *Das norddeutsche Kantorat im 18. Jahrhundert. Untersuchungen am Beispiel Hamburgs* (Kassel, 1995) and *Joachim Gerstenbüttel (1647–1721) im Spannungsfeld von Oper und Kirche. Ein Beitrag zur Musikgeschichte Hamburgs* (Hamburg, 1997).

BEAT KÜMIN is Lecturer in Early Modern European History at the University of Warwick. He is the author of *The Shaping of a Community: the Rise and Reformation of the English Parish c. 1400–1560* (Aldershot, 1996) and is currently working on the social history of inns and taverns in early modern Europe.

BETH ANNE LEE-DE AMICI is Visiting Assistant Professor of Music at the University of Michigan at Ann Arbor. She recently completed her doctorate in musicology at the University of Pennsylvania with a dissertation on sacred ceremony and music in the academic colleges of medieval Oxford. She is the joint author of an article on the medieval rondeau, which will be published in a forthcoming volume, *Binchois Studies*, edited by Andrew Kirkman and Dennis Slavin.

JOHN J. MCGAVIN is Senior Lecturer in English at the University of Southampton. He has published articles on Chaucer, rhetoric, English and Scottish medieval drama and is the author of *Chaucer and Dissimilarity* (Fairleigh Dickinson University Press, 2000). He is currently editing the provincial records of early drama, ceremonial and secular music in Scotland for the Records of Early English Drama series.

GRETCHEN PETERS holds a Ph.D. in musicology from the University of Illinois at Urbana-Champaign. She is currently Assistant Professor of Music History at the University of Wisconsin-Eau Claire and is the author of 'Private Notarial Contracts as a Valuable Source of Evidence for Urban Musical Culture in Late Medieval Southern France', *Early Music* 25 (1997), pp. 403–10.

JAMES SAUNDERS recently completed a Cambridge University Ph.D. thesis which examined the impact of religious change on the choirmen of English cathedrals between 1558 and 1649. He is currently a Church of England ordinand at Cranmer Hall, Durham.

REINHARD STROHM is Heather Professor of Music at the University of Oxford. He is the author of six books and numerous articles on music history from the later Middle Ages to the nineteenth century, including *Music in Late Medieval Bruges* (Oxford, 1985) and *The Rise of European Music, 1380–1500* (Cambridge, 1993).

MAGNUS WILLIAMSON is Lecturer in Music at the University of Newcastle upon Tyne. His doctoral thesis (Oxford University, 1995) was on the institutional background, codicology and ritual use of the Eton choirbook and he has published several articles and record reviews on the music and history of this and related sources.

PREFACE

A large number of scholars have kindly helped in the preparation of this volume. I am particularly grateful to Caroline Hibbard for support and encouragement during the early stages of research. Also Caroline Barron, Peter Clark, Gary Gibbs, Beat Kümin, Andrew Pettegree, Richard Rodger, Tony Thompson and Bob Tittler have all made helpful comments. Julian Cole and Magnus Williamson have provided helpful editorial assistance and Richard Hallas processed one of the maps. Ian Biddle, Geoffrey Chew, Jenny Dames, Tess Knighton, Ken Kreitner, Miguel Angel Marín and David Wells-Cole have also helped considerably in translating foreign-language contributions.

I am indebted to Penny Souster at Cambridge University Press for her patience and advice during the many months it took to bring this volume to fruition. A special thanks must go to the British Academy for their generous support during my tenure of a Postdoctoral Research Fellowship in the Department of Music at Royal Holloway College, University of London, when this book was prepared. It has been a great pleasure and a privilege to be a part of this department and all colleagues there have provided a congenial and stimulating atmosphere in which to work; Tim Carter, David Charlton, Geoffrey Chew, Katharine Ellis and Andrew Wathey have been particularly helpful during work on this book. The progress of the present volume has also been aided considerably by the work of the archivists and librarians in the institutions used during its writing who never fail to provide a first-class service. I would also like to thank John Walmsley for his generous help and inspiring teaching, and my husband Charles Darwin Littleton for his patience and support.

ABBREVIATIONS

ADB	Archives Départementales des Bouches-du-Rhône, Marseilles
ADH	Archives Départementales de l'Hérault, Montpellier
AGI	Archivo General de Indias, Seville
AGN	Archivo General de la Nación, Bogotá
AH	Archives of the Collegiate Church of St Pieter, Anderlecht, at the Erasmushuis, Brussels
AMA	Archives Municipales d'Avignon
AMMo	Archives Municipales de Montpellier
AMT	Archives Municipales de Toulouse
AMV	Archivo Municipal de Valladolid
ARB	Archivo Regional de Boyacá, Tunja
ARBH	Kerkarchief van Brabant/Archives ecclésiastiques de Brabant, Algemeen Rijksarchief/Archives générales du Royaume, Brussels (see A. d'Hoop, *Inventaire générale des archives ecclésiastiques du Brabant*, 6 vols. (Brussels, 1905–32), vols. I and II)
ASCA	Oxford, Bodleian Library, MSS d.d. All Souls College
ASG	Kerkarchief van Brabant, Archief Sint-Goedele (see P. De Ridder, *Inventaris van het oud archief van de kapittelkerk van Sint-Michiel en Sint-Goedele te Brussel*, 3 vols. (Brussels, 1987–8))
ASV	Venice, Archivio di Stato
BL	London, British Library
BNM	Venice, Biblioteca Nazionale Marciana
CPR	*Calendar of the Patent Rolls Preserved in the Public Record Office*
CWA 1	R. C. Dudding (ed.), *The First Churchwardens' Book of Louth 1500–1524* (Oxford, 1941) (a transcription of Lincoln, Lincolnshire Archives, MS Louth, St James's Parish 7/1 (1500–24))
CWA 2	Lincoln, Lincolnshire Archives, MS Louth, St James's Parish 7/2 (1526–59)
CWA 3	Lincoln, Lincolnshire Archives, MS Louth, St James's Parish 7/3 (1560–1624)
DCD	Muniments of the Dean and Chapter of Durham Cathedral, Durham
Dom. Acc.	J. M. Fletcher and C. A. Upton (eds.), *The Domestic Accounts of Merton College, Oxford 1 August 1482 – 1 August 1494* Oxford Historical Society Publications new series 34 (Oxford, 1996)

EDC	Muniments of the Dean and Chapter of Ely Cathedral, Cambridge University Library
Grove	S. Sadie (ed.), *New Grove Dictionary of Music and Musicians*, 20 vols. (London, 1980)
HMLC	B. Haggh, 'Music, Liturgy and Ceremony in Brussels, 1350–1500', Ph.D. thesis, University of Illinois at Urbana-Champaign (1988)
LA	Lincolnshire Archives, Lincoln
LG	Lincolnshire Archives, Lincoln, MS Monson 7/1 (Compotus Book, Lady Guild, 1473–1504)
LOCR	R. W. Goulding, *Louth Old Corporation Records* (Louth, 1891)
LPFD	J. Gairdner, R. H. Brodie and J. S. Brewer (eds.), *Letters and Papers, Foreign and Domestic, of the Reign of Henry VIII*, 21 vols. (London, 1862–1910)
MagCA *Lib. comp.*	Oxford, Magdalen College Archives, *Libri computi*
MCV	Venice, Museo Correr
MerCA *B1*	Oxford, Merton College Archives, First Bursar's Account (Aug.–Nov.)
MerCA *B2*	Oxford, Merton College Archives, Second Bursar's Account (Nov.–Mar.)
MerCA *B3*	Oxford, Merton College Archives, Third Bursar's Account (Mar.–Aug.)
MerCA *SA*	Oxford, Merton College Archives, Subwarden's Account
MMB	Frank Ll. Harrison, *Music in Medieval Britain*, 2nd edn (London, 1963)
NAS	National Archives of Scotland, Edinburgh
NCA	New College Archives, Oxford
PCM	Muniments of the Dean and Chapter of Peterborough Cathedral, Cambridge University Library
RCB	Representative Church Body Library, Dublin
RIA	Royal Irish Academy, Dublin
SoA	E. Duffy, *The Stripping of the Altars: Traditional Religion in England c. 1400–c. 1580* (New Haven, 1992)
TCD	Trinity College, Dublin
TG	Lincolnshire Archives, Lincoln, MS Monson 7/2 (compotus book, Trinity Guild, 1489–1528)
VCH Lincs	W. Page (ed.), *The Victoria County History of Lincoln* (London, 1906), vol. II
WA I	M. Luther, *D. Martin Luthers Werke: Kritische Gesamtausgabe (Weimarer Ausgabe)*, series I (*Werke*), 64 vols. (Weimar, 1883–1990)
WA II	M. Luther, *D. Martin Luthers Werke: Kritische Gesamtausgabe (Weimarer Ausgabe)*, series II (*Tischreden*), 6 vols. (Weimar, 1912–21)
WA III	M. Luther, *D. Martin Luthers Werke: Kritische Gesamtausgabe (Weimarer Ausgabe)*, series III (*Die Deutsche Bibel*), 12 vols. (Weimar, 1906–61)
WA IV	M. Luther, *D. Martin Luthers Werke: Kritische Gesamtausgabe (Weimarer Ausgabe)*, series IV (*Briefwechsel*), 18 vols. (Weimar, 1930–85)
WAM	Muniments of the Dean and Chapter of Westminster Abbey, London
WSRO	West Sussex Record Office, Chichester

Editorial symbols

Italicised letters in document quotations indicate expanded abbreviations.
< ... > denotes text reconstructed from damaged documents.
[ ] denotes authorial insertion of a word or letter.

A note on monetary values and other terms

The monetary values used in the following essays refer to money of account, the system of counting which, subject to certain regional modifications, had become established in Europe by late medieval times. One 'pound' (*libra* etc.) was equal to twenty coins (shillings; *solidus* etc.); and one shilling denoted twelve coins (pennies; *denarius*). The regional variations and different systems of reckoning are given in P. Spufford, *Handbook of Medieval Exchange* (London, 1986), pp. xx–xxi.

As there is no real consensus as to the definition of 'town' and 'city' in the scholarly literature of Europe and North America, these two terms are used interchangeably throughout this book (C. R. Friedrichs, *The Early Modern City 1450–1750* (New York, 1995), p. x).

CHAPTER ONE

INTRODUCTION: URBAN HISTORY, MUSICOLOGY AND CITIES AND TOWNS IN RENAISSANCE EUROPE

FIONA KISBY

It was only in the nineteenth century that the sharply demarcated, centrally administered states of Europe in existence today developed. At the first millennium Western Europe consisted of hundreds of principalities, bishoprics, city states, empires and conglomerates of dynastically linked monarchies which together constituted Latin Christendom. Cultural and political interpenetration resulted, for in many cases languages spoken, religions, trading systems, and political and governmental jurisdictions intertwined.[1] The early Middle Ages was an era of predominantly rural existence in most parts of the region. Many urban centres were small – most had populations of less than 5,000 and virtually none had reached 50,000.[2] From 1000 until the 1340s urban expansion, accompanied by general population growth, occurred; after this, owing to a succession of plague epidemics, food shortages and warfare, development dramatically decreased throughout Europe until the beginning of the sixteenth century.[3] However, despite this demographic decay, urban populations as a whole declined no more than 5–10 per cent in the long term while rural communities diminished by around 27–35 per cent. Thus by 1500 a larger proportion of Europe's population lived in urban societies than in 1300.[4] The sixteenth and early seventeenth centuries witnessed another period of urban growth and the associated technological advances and wealth creation gave rise to Europe's exploration, conquest and colonisation of the New World.[5]

---

[1] C. R. Friedrichs, *The Early Modern City 1450–1750* (New York, 1995), p. x; C. Tilly and W. Blockmans (eds.), *Cities and the Rise of States in Europe, A.D. 1000–1800* (Oxford, 1989), pp. 7, 14; for detailed maps see G. Barraclough (ed.), *The Times Atlas of World History* (London, 1984); G. Parker, *The Dutch Revolt* (London, 1990), p. 31 (The Netherlands) and R. E. Dickinson, *The Regions of Germany* (London, 1945) (German territories).

[2] E. A. Gutkind, *International History of City Development*, 8 vols. (London and New York, 1964–72), vol. III, p. 234; D. Nicholas, *The Later Medieval City 1300–1500* (London, 1997), pp. 1–2. Tilly and Blockmans (eds.), *Cities and the Rise of States*, p. 13. Urban communities in this period were not necessarily distinguished by size; any community that had occupationally heterogeneous populations and that was the focus of communications for considerable regions and locus of specialised production, distribution and administration had urban characteristics.

[3] For population statistics see J. Cox Russell, *British Medieval Population* (Albuquerque, 1948); E. A. Wrigley and R. S. Schofield, *The Population History of England 1541–1871: a Reconstruction* (London, 1981); P. Bairoch, J. Batou and P. Chèvre, *The Population of European Cities: Data Bank and Short Summary of Results* (Geneva, 1988); T. Chandler and G. Fox, *Four Thousand Years of Urban Growth* (New York, 1987); J. Cox Russell, *Medieval Regions and their Cities* (Newton Abbot, 1972), pp. 23, 122; C. M. Cipolla, *The Middle Ages: the Fontana Economic History of Europe*, 6 vols. (New York, 1976), vol. I, pp. 34–41; Tilly and Blockmans (eds.), *Cities and the Rise of States*, p. 13; Nicholas, *Later Medieval City*, p. 50.

[4] Nicholas, *Later Medieval City*, p. 70.

[5] L. N. McAlister, *Spain and Portugal in the New World 1492–1700* (London, 1984).

These developments did not occur uniformly across the whole of Europe. In 1000 the world's cultural, political and economic epicentre lay around the Indian Ocean, and Córdoba (in Iberia) and Constantinople (capital of the Byzantine Empire) were the great metropolises located on routes of communication that connected to large non-European cities such as Cairo and Baghdad. The prosperity of regions and size of cities in Western Europe were strongly affected by their relations to, and centrality in, this great Asian-based system of trade.[6] Thus by the mid-fourteenth century until *c.* 1500 the city-states of Italy – on trade routes which linked centres like Constantinople to south-west Germany, Flanders and northern France – rose to prominence.[7] During the sixteenth century the dominance of the southern communities waned and the cities of The Netherlands, west Germany, northern France and southern England were in the ascendant.[8] These trends are shown in Table 1.1.

Despite this general trend in urban growth, most people's experience of Western Europe in Renaissance times was still a rural one, for only around 10–15 per cent of the population lived in towns and cities of any description.[9] Yet this does not mean that urbanisation was beyond their experience. Cities were a constant presence in rural life and their influences on patterns of consumption, modes of thought, religious practice and trade reached out far beyond their physical boundaries and thus had an impact on, at one time or another, the lives of most rural dwellers.[10] Quite clearly, towns played an important role in the economic, political, social and cultural history of early modern Europe and are therefore legitimate objects of study.

The central importance of urban centres in the development of Renaissance Europe is reflected by the long tradition of civic histories written by city chroniclers, both ecclesiastical and lay, and the interest in the city shown by architects, military historians and cartographers since late medieval times.[11] In fact, one of three great cartographic achievements of the sixteenth century was the *Civitates Orbis Terrarum* published by Georg Braun and Frans Hogenberg, the first serious attempt to provide graphic representations of the main cities of the world.[12] Since the early nineteenth century, researchers have shown a growing interest in the town to such an extent that a sub-field of historical scholarship, urban history, has now developed. Owing to different traditions and varying agendas of research affected by archival, political and other factors, important differences in national historiographies have evolved and lively debate, innovative teaching and fruitful international research collaborations have resulted.[13]

---

[6] Tilly and Blockmans (eds.), *Cities and the Rise of States*, pp. 7, 13, 14; P. M. Hohenberg and L. H. Lees, *The Making of Urban Europe 1000–1994* (London, 1995), p. 10. Medieval trade routes are illustrated in Barraclough (ed.), *The Times Atlas*, pp. 40–1, 58–9.   [7] Russell, *Medieval Regions*, pp. 50, 67, 74, 75.

[8] J. de Vries, *European Urbanization 1500–1800* (London, 1984), pp. 28–9, 158–66.

[9] Russell, *Medieval Regions*, p. 15; Hohenberg and Lees, *The Making of Urban Europe*, p. 8.

[10] A. Cowan, *Urban Europe, 1500–1700* (London, 1998), pp. v–vi.   [11] Nicholas, *Later Medieval City*, pp. 297–8.

[12] Published in six volumes between 1572 and 1617: R. A. Skelton and A. O. Vietor (eds.), *Braun and Hogenberg Civitates Orbis Terrarum. Towns of the World, 1572–1618* with an introduction by R. A. Skelton (Cleveland and New York, 1966). These maps show the physical topography of the towns and the landscape of the urban hinterland; aspects of local society are also represented by figures engaged in a variety of activities, see pp. v–viii. Together the volumes contain 363 plates, including images of most of the cities mentioned in the present book.

[13] For historiographical overviews of literature on continental Europe see R. Rodger, *Urban History: Prospect and Retrospect* (Leicester, 1993); P. Clark, 'The Early Modern Town in the West: Research Since 1945', in P. Clark (ed.), *The Early Modern Town: a Reader* (New York, 1977), pp. 1–42. R. Reulecke and G. Juck, 'Urban History Research in Germany: its Development and Present Condition', *Urban History Yearbook* (1981), pp. 39–54; for Britain see S. Reynolds, 'The Writing of Medieval Urban History in England', *Theoretische Geschiedenis* 19 (1992), pp. 43–57; P. Burke, 'The Early Modern Town – its History and Historians', *Urban History Yearbook* (1981), pp. 55–8; I. Hammarström, 'Urban History in Scandinavia: a Summary of Recent Trends', *Urban History Yearbook* (1978), pp. 46–55.

Table 1.1 *Approximate populations of select European cities, 1000–1600*

Centre	Population (1,000s)[a]					
	1000	1200	1300	1400	1500	1600
(Baghdad)	125	100	40	90	—	30
(Constantinople)	300	150	100	75	200	700
Genoa	15	30	100	100	58	63
Milan	—	—	100	90	100	120
Naples	30	30	60	45	125	275
Rome	35	35	30	33	55	100
Venice	45	70	110	100	100	151
Dublin	4	9	11	15	8	5
Edinburgh	—	—	1	2	18	15
London	25	25	35	45	50	200
Oxford	—	—	—	—	5	5
Avignon	—	13	6	30	18	26
Montpellier	1	13	35	17	6	15
Rouen	12	15	35	35	40	70
Toulouse	10	20	30	21	30	40
Paris	20	110	150	275	225	300
Córdoba	450	60	60	40	35	31
Seville	90	80	90	70	45	135
Valladolid	6	—	25	—	30	41
Antwerp	—	15	17	5	30	47
Bruges	12	25	40	125	35	27
Brussels	1	—	18	26	33	50
Ghent	8	25	—	56	55	31
Innsbruck	—	—	1	—	4	6
Vienna	—	12	20	20	20	50
Brunswick	10	21	12	18	18	16
Hamburg	—	2	8	22	15	40
Hanover	—	2	5	5	6	7
Lübeck	—	6	28	25	25	23
Bogotá	—	—	—	—	20	—
Cuzco	—	—	—	24	50	24
Lima	—	—	—	—	—	14
Mexico City	—	—	—	—	80	58

Note:

[a] For urban centres in Latin America, plus Baghdad and Constantinople, see Chandler and Fox, *Four Thousand Years*; for all other centres see Bairoch, Batou and Chèvre, *The Population of European Cities*.

Scholars in Britain have played a leading role in these developments. In the 1960s and 1970s a principal spokesman was Professor H. J. Dyos, based at the University of Leicester.[14] Dyos argued that urban history should seek to understand 'urbanisation itself, a process involving concentrations of populations at certain densities and shifts in their occupation and social structures'. He also stressed that it should focus on 'cities themselves and not . . . the historical events and tendencies that have been purely incidental to them'. According to him, it would only be through investigating the different characteristics of cities and 'the ways in which their components fitted together or impinged on other things' that would distinguish urban historians from those who may be said merely to be 'passing through' urban history's territory.[15]

To a certain extent Dyos expanded the agenda of European urban history scholarship in his call for it to address, as far as possible, the 'totality' of the urban experience and unite the concepts of a historical process (urbanisation) and its outcome (an urbanised place). However, if the aims and objectives of the urban historian were relatively straightforward, the techniques and methodologies used to reach them – and thus establish urban history as a distinct 'discipline' – were more difficult to determine. For Dyos the issue could be resolved if urban history was considered a 'focus for a variety of forms of knowledge, not a form of knowledge in itself' and was 'not a single discipline in the accepted sense, but a field in which many disciplines converge, or . . . are drawn upon'.[16] More recently, this view has been reiterated by a number of other urban historians. For Richard Rodger (editor of *Urban History*)[17] urban history is not the sum of a town's 'constituent parts – cultural, physical, organisational and behavioural – but . . . an analysis of their interaction in a unique spatial setting'. Thus urban historians were to commit themselves first to the city and only occasionally to a particular methodology; they were to be more eclectic in their disciplinary approaches and 'sample the methodological and theoretical delights drawn from a wide range of available interdisciplinary possibilities'.[18]

In their attempts to study the process of urbanisation and the site of its development – the city and town – urban historians have tended to focus on three areas: the origins of cities (their constitutional, legal and archaeological history); the activities taking place in cities (especially economic and demographic processes that characterise urban populations); and the social consequences of urban life (including psychological and cultural effects of urban living, material culture, the routines of daily life, sensory experience, social and occupational structure).[19] The work they have produced usually falls into two camps: that of the 'annalists' provides descriptive, narrative histories, often

---

[14] The institution has subsequently become a focal point of international research through the creation of its Centre for Urban History in 1985 (www.le.ac.uk/urbanhist). The proceedings of an early conference at Leicester, addressing the materials and methods of urban history, were published in H. J. Dyos (ed.), *The Study of Urban History* (London, 1968).

[15] H. J. Dyos, 'Urbanity and Suburbanity', in D. Cannadine and D. Reeder (eds.), *Exploring the Urban Past: Essays in Urban History by H. J. Dyos* (Cambridge, 1982), pp. 32, 36.

[16] Dyos, 'Urbanity and Suburbanity', pp. 31, 36. H. J. Dyos, 'Editorial', *Urban History Yearbook* (1974), p. 3; (1977), p. 3; (1978), p. 3. This proposal was not without its critics: R. Rodger, 'Urban History: Prospect and Retrospect', *Urban History* 19 (1992), p. 10; S. Glynn, 'Approaches to Urban History: the Case for Caution', *Australian Economic History Review* 10 (1970), pp. 218–95.

[17] *Urban History* was a continuation of the *Urban History Newsletter* (1963–) which became *Urban History Yearbook* (1974–91).

[18] R. Rodger, 'Urban History', p. 4; R. Rodger, 'Theory, Practice and European Urban History', in *European Urban History: Prospect and Retrospect* (Leicester, 1993), pp. 1–18, here p. 3.

[19] Hohenberg and Lees, *The Making of Urban Europe*, p. 2. Some recent examples include: F. Braudel, *Capitalism and Material Life 1400–1800* (New York, 1973); P. Clark (ed.), *Small Towns in Early Modern*

of a single place; while 'analysts' have taken a more international, systematic and comparative approach.[20] The development of the historiography for both the pre- and post-industrial eras is reflected in the *c.* 20,000 entries of the 1996 *Consolidated Bibliography of Urban History*.[21] Interestingly, detailed analysis of its contents reveals a striking lack of interest in one particular area: only around 6 per cent of the citations refer to urban 'culture' in any form, and virtually none concerns music in towns and cities in pre-industrial Europe or indeed that of any time or place.[22]

Clearly, at the beginning of the twenty-first century, urban history tends to be restricted largely to the 'essentially infrastructural' and is still 'a matter of demography, distributive economics and consequential social arrangements and re-adjustments'.[23] However, this lack of interest – in culture and particularly music – is disappointing, especially because, as shown above, urban historians themselves have set an interdisciplinary agenda for their studies in their aim to explore the 'totality' of the urban experience.

Urban historians' reluctance to embrace musicological scholarship may be owing to a fear of the perceived incomprehensibility of its historiography resulting from the technicality of its methodologies; and the assumption that music played only a marginal role in any urban communities and is consequently irrelevant to their concerns. Admittedly, the history of music has most often traditionally charted the rise and decline of particular styles or forms. Also, the musical medium has often been characterised as a set of compositional techniques used by 'great male composers' to write pre-composed – as opposed to improvised – mensural, polyphonic music. This is sometimes thought to be most effectively and appropriately understood by structural analysis using technical language only intelligible to the highly trained, musically literate. However, certain musicologists have more recently reorientated their approaches and have endeavoured to focus equally on the context as well as the content of musical works and have characterised the music of history – particularly of late medieval and early modern times – more as a series of 'responses to social, economic and political circumstances and to religious and intellectual stimuli'.[24] For them, Renaissance music is not a medium spreading evenly over the landscape but something which grew from the concentration of artistic talents in particular times and places. Urbanisation is seen as the process which produced the social, economic, religious and political matrices in which musical culture could flourish and therefore the music history of towns and cities in Europe has most often been the subject of their enquiry.[25] Such work is mostly of a 'non-technical' nature and

Europe (Cambridge, 1995); P. Clark and B. Lepetit (eds.), *Capital Cities and their Hinterlands in Early Modern Europe* (Aldershot, 1996); P. Clark and A. Aerts (eds.), *Metropolitan Cities and their Hinterlands in Early Modern Europe* (Leuven, 1990); H. Schmal (ed.), *Patterns of European Urbanisation since 1500* (London, 1981); P. Bairoch, *Cities and Economic Development: from the Dawn of History to the Present* (London, 1988); D. Abrams and E. A. Wrigley (eds.), *Towns in Societies* (Cambridge, 1979); R. Rörig, *The Medieval Town* (London, 1967); G. Sjoberg, *The Pre-Industrial City* (New York, 1960); R. Holt and G. Rosser (eds.), *The Medieval Town* (London, 1990); J. Barry (ed.), *The Tudor and Stuart Town* (London, 1990).

[20] Rodger, 'Theory', pp. 1–2.
[21] R. Rodger (ed.), *Consolidated Bibliography of Urban History* (Aldershot, 1996), p. xiv.
[22] *Ibid.*, pp. xi–xvii.
[23] P. Collinson and J. Craig (eds.), *The Reformation in English Towns, 1500–1640* (Basingstoke, 1998), p. 3.
[24] M. Everist (ed.), *Models of Musical Analysis: Music Before 1600* (London, 1990), pp. vii–xii; I. Fenlon (ed.), *The Renaissance* (London, 1989), pp. ix, 1. This debate is the subject of polemical discussion in J. Kerman, *Musicology* (London, 1985).
[25] Several hundred items will be analysed in F. Kisby, 'Musical Culture in European Urban Societies to *c.* 1650: a Bibliographical Survey', in preparation; L. Lockwood, *Music in Renaissance Ferrara, 1400–1505* (Oxford, 1984), p. 7.

more 'historical' in its methodologies. It has demonstrated that music was not at the periphery of the pre-industrial townscape but rather was a central and significant aspect of the urban experience. Accordingly it has begun to show how music shaped space and time within the urban environment and how the various institutions, organisations, associations and social structures which developed in towns and cities in response to the process of urbanisation had an impact on musical activity of various kinds. In the light of this, musicology must now be legitimised as one of those disciplines upon which, in their purported intellectual promiscuity, urban historians draw.

Yet if disciplinary co-operation is to occur, it must be a two-way process; and if urban historians have been reluctant to embrace musicological work, so too have musicologists who have focused on music in towns been unwilling to learn from urban history and investigate the widest possible arena for the production, consumption and performance of music in Renaissance towns. For example, many exploiting the 'music in . . .' model have often used the concept only as a convenient label for geographical location; particular genres, or the music of elite institutions or individuals (composers, performers and patrons) that simply happened to be based/produced/heard *in* particular urban centres are merely placed in a context the impact of which is thereafter mostly neglected.[26] As Tim Carter has argued, by focusing on the role of a leading patron *in* the urban context scholars are perpetuating the notion of the 'great composer' present in the older historiography of musical style. By fetishising genres or institutions – with little further imaginative examination of how that context had a bearing on musical activity in the broadest sense – they have merely offered 'anthropomorphic versions' of the very same thing.[27]

In the light of this, if music offers another medium through which to view the city, and the diverse methodologies of its study – not all of them 'technical' – offer additional interpretative frameworks of understanding upon which, it has been argued, urban historians could usefully draw, future musicological work must move towards reconceptualising music's multi-faceted role in urban contexts. Only then will all the arenas in which music was heard, produced, patronised and performed be uncovered and musicology will take its legitimate place as one of the many disciplinary tools used to decode the 'urban variable'.[28] Music must be viewed as a sound-world embedded in and explicable through reference to a framework of devotional, spiritual, social, political, economic and artistic activity.[29] In the first instance, anthropological approaches could prove useful. Thus, 'place' consists of much more than a physical setting; it also embodies locale – the social worlds which provide settings for social interaction; and the sense of place or identification with a place engendered by living in it.[30] Second, ethnomusicological

---

[26] E.g. see the articles by C. Monson and J. Haar in Fenlon (ed.), *The Renaissance*, pp. 251, 315; and Lockwood, *Music in Renaissance Ferrara*. It is perhaps no coincidence that in the title of one of the most successful recent examples of this genre of work (M. Feldman, *City Culture and the Madrigal at Venice* (Berkeley, 1995)), the culture of the city is given a prominent place.

[27] T. Carter, 'The Sound of Silence: Models for an Urban Musicology', Tagung der Fachgruppe für Soziologie und Sozialgeschichte der Musik, Berlin-Schmökwitz, November 1999. I am grateful to Professor Carter for allowing me to read his unpublished typescript.

[28] Rodger, 'Theory', pp. 16–18; S. B. Warner, 'The Management of Multiple Urban Images', in D. Fraser and A. Sutcliffe (eds.), *The Pursuit of Urban History* (London, 1983), pp. 383–94; C. Geertz, 'Ideology as a Cultural System', in D. E. Apter (ed.), *Ideology and Discontent*, International Yearbook of Political Behaviour Research 5 (London, 1964), p. 73 n. 19.

[29] B. Wilson, *Music and Merchants: the Laudesi Companies of Republican Florence* (Oxford, 1992), pp. 1–4.

[30] J. A. Agnew, *The Power of Place: Bringing Together Geographical and Sociological Imaginations* (Boston, 1989), pp. 1–8.

perspectives, which investigate how music was integrated with other sensory aspects of life (moving away from the legacy of the post-Romantic Western Art tradition which has characterised music as a mono-sensorial experience), may also help. These approaches can only be successful if music is characterised as a pluralistic medium so that musicologists investigate not only the notated, pre-composed, mensural polyphony of elite 'high culture' but also the improvised, monophonic, non-mensural material that infrequently survives in written form. More importantly, they should observe how these two cultures interacted and overlapped, if at all.[31]

The perspectives advocated here may involve interpreting patterns of source-survival in different ways and possibly searching for evidence of musical culture *even* if no music survives.[32] In the latter case, sound must be reconstructed from the silence of the archives, which must be used imaginatively and viewed as texts to be interpreted rather than objective records of past events.[33] They will require the reinterpretation of conventional terms such as consumer, producer, patron, player and performer and as much emphasis/effort should be placed on rediscovering the outward effects of music in this period as well as on its internal substance. They will involve looking equally at how music was woven into the fabric of daily life as well as special occasions and investigating how, when, where and why music was made available to ordinary citizens.[34] Musicians will have to be viewed as acoustical and visual symbols as well as performers. Music could be regarded as sound ('good' *and* 'bad') which was an index of politics and a focus for tensions and social contest, as a medium which was subject to power-play by emerging interest groups through its control and provision and as a tool of subversion and parody in the face of institutionalised power.[35]

It is the aim of this collection of essays – which examines urban communities in different locations in Renaissance Europe and the New World – to begin to address some of these issues and bring musicology within the sphere of urban history, just as some of its closest sister disciplines, such as art history and literature, already are. Its comparative approach is particularly significant for, in the face of patchy or arbitrary survival of music and historical sources, this facilitates a greater variety of related questions concerning the role and function of music in urban contexts to be comprehensively addressed.

Collectively, the essays focus on the relationships between music production, performance, education, patronage and civic structures and environments *of all kinds*.[36] Not only does this approach allow authors to highlight difference and similarity in the production, performance, sponsorship, forms, dissemination, function and 'meanings' of musical activity in specific towns and cities, but it also begins uniquely to facilitate a greater understanding of musical cultures in comparable/generic urban contexts upon

---

[31] For a discussion of this issue, see C. Story, 'GB-Lbl Harley MS 2942: Music in Context', M.Mus. thesis, Royal Holloway College, University of London (1998).

[32] A. Wathey, 'Musicology, Archives and Historiography', in B. Haggh, F. Daelemans and A. Vanrie (eds.), *Archives et Bibliothèques de Belgique. Musicology and Archival Research: Colloquium Proceedings, Brussels 22–23 April 1993*, Archives et Bibliothèques de Belgique 46 (Brussels, 1994), p. 6; J. Milsom, 'Songs and Society in Early-Tudor London', *Early Music History* 16 (1997), pp. 235–94.

[33] Carter, 'The Sound of Silence'; Wathey, 'Musicology', p. 6.

[34] H. M. Brown, 'Minstrels and their Repertory in Fifteenth-Century France: Music in an Urban Environment', in S. Zimmerman and R. Weissman (eds.), *Urban Life in the Renaissance* (London, 1989), p. 142.

[35] See E. Cockayne, 'Cacophony; or, Vile Scrapers on Vile Instruments. Bad Music in Early-Modern English Towns', *Urban History (Special Music Issue)*, forthcoming.

[36] For information on individual cities covered in this volume see Gutkind, *International History of City Development*; for their locations, see Illustration 1.1.

Boundary of
Holy Roman Empire

Republic of Venice

1.1   Select urban centres in Renaissance Europe.

which future studies can build. Thus, Reinhard Strohm examines three Austrian cities, two of which (Vienna and Innsbruck) grew in political importance with their selection as residences by the Habsburgs from the fourteenth and fifteenth centuries respectively. Iain Fenlon investigates Venice, a wealthy city-state republic and one of the largest territorial powers of late medieval Italy.[37] John McGavin studies Haddington, an incorporated Scottish burgh;[38] and Barra Boydell looks at Dublin, a regional port and the administrative headquarters of English colonisation of Ireland.[39] The colonial theme is

[37] W. H. McNeill, *Venice: the Hinge of Europe 1081–1797* (Chicago and London, 1974), pp. xiii, xvi, xvii, 46, 51, 69, 72.

[38] M. Lynch, 'Towns and Townspeople in Fifteenth-Century Scotland', in J. A. F. Thomson (ed.), *Towns and Townspeople in the Fifteenth Century* (Gloucester, 1988), pp. 173–89; M. Lynch, M. Spearman and G. Stell (eds.), *The Scottish Medieval Town* (Edinburgh, 1988).

[39] C. Lennon, *The Lords of Dublin in the Age of Reformation* (Blackrock, 1989), pp. 19–39; R. A. Butlin, 'Irish Towns in the Sixteenth and Seventeenth Centuries', in R. A. Butlin (ed.), *The Development of the Irish Town* (London, 1977), p. 61.

pursued by Egberto Bermúdez who surveys musical life in Spanish America, the urban centres of which became the base for colonisation in the New World for they were the communities which offered the most stability and scope for the reproduction of European civilisation.[40] Valladolid, a city which was, in the first half of the sixteenth century, at its peak of prosperity as the capital and main court residence of the king of Spain (a country newly united under Charles I/V, Holy Roman Emperor) is discussed by Soterraña Aguirre Rincón.[41] Beth Anne Lee-De Amici studies a university town and Joachim Kremer deals with several members of the Hanseatic League, an association of some 200 towns active during the late fourteenth to mid-sixteenth centuries in protecting trading interests in the North Sea and Baltic areas.[42] Magnus Williamson investigates Louth, one of the 500–600 small market towns of pre-industrial Britain, which channelled trade in farm produce from the surrounding countryside.[43] Gretchen Peters describes Montpellier and Toulouse which, in demographic terms, figured amongst the thirty or so first-rank towns in late medieval Europe;[44] she also focuses on Avignon which experienced a great influx of wealth and population during the fourteenth century when it became the seat of the papacy.[45] Barbara Haggh looks at Brussels, one of the largest cities north of the Alps which became the northern capital of the Dukes of Burgundy throughout the fifteenth century and, owing to the accession of Charles V (son of Philip the Fair of Burgundy) in the sixteenth century, was also the centre of the Holy Roman Empire.

Through his extensive survey of the musical life of Vienna, Innsbruck and Bolzano in late medieval times, Reinhard Strohm introduces a whole range of topics which then receive further detailed examination in subsequent essays on other urban contexts. His observations cover music produced in both the public and private domains and sacred and secular spaces; and the data he presents relate to the music produced by singers and instrumentalists working in or patronised by secular churches, parishes, cathedrals, monasteries, local guilds and fraternities, universities, schools, domestic/noble households or courts, municipal governments, taverns and town thoroughfares. He identifies the urban rituals and describes the liturgical calendar in these Austrian towns which stimulated musical activity and examines the repertories, both extant and lost, to which these gave rise. He also describes how certain forms of music were partly financed by private benefactors or through the public purse. Most importantly he highlights the interrelationships between the musical cultures of the various institutions in each town and points out that their musical forces were often co-ordinated and harnessed for the greater civic ceremonies of common interest.

---

[40] M. A. Burkholder and L. L. Johnson, *Colonial Latin America* (Oxford and New York, 1998), pp. 36–7, 46, 160, 183, 184.

[41] Clark, *The Early Modern Town*, p. 15; B. Bennassar, *Valladolid au siècle d'Or: Une ville de Castile et sa Campagne au XVIe siècle*, Civilisations et Sociétés, 4 (Paris, 1967), pp. 124–7.

[42] P. Dellinger, *The German Hansa*, trans. and ed. D. S. Ault and S. H. Steinberg (London, 1970), pp. xvii–xxi, 282–3.

[43] A. Dyer, 'Small Market Towns', in P. Clark (ed.), *Cambridge Urban History of Britain II: 1540–1840* (forthcoming); P. Clark (ed.), *Country Towns in Pre-Industrial England* (Leicester, 1981), pp. 2, 13.

[44] J. Caille, 'Urban Expansion in Languedoc from the Eleventh Century to the Fourteenth', in K. Reyerson and J. Drendel (eds.), *Urban and Rural Communities in Medieval France: Provence and Languedoc 1000–1500* (Leiden, 1998), pp. 23–50.

[45] J. Rollo-Koster, 'Mercator Florentinensis and Others: Immigration in Papal Avignon', in Reyerson and Drendel, *Urban and Rural Communities*, pp. 73–95; A. Tomasello, *Music and Ritual at Papal Avignon* (Ann Arbor, 1983), pp. 1, 21, 30–31, 150, 153.

The significance and development of the physical spaces in which civic ceremonial occurred and the variety of musical and ritual elements used during such public occasions form the subject of the chapter by Iain Fenlon. His work describes some of the processions and ceremonies that marked the annual religious calendar, the victories and treaties of the Venetian state and the election of its doge. All contributed in various ways to 'the myth of Venice' – the politico-religious rhetoric which, among other things, perpetuated the notion of Venice as the perfect city-state through its outstanding beauty, religiosity and republicanism.[46] Fenlon describes the shaping of the main theatre in which much of the urban ritual and ceremonial occurred, the piazza of the basilica of St Mark (the saint appropriated by the urban community and identified as the special protector of the city). He also draws attention to the topographical variety of Venice and explores the other settings for ceremonial and devotional events and investigates the interconnections between them. The participants and audiences of what he shows to be very differentiated types of celebration and the contrasting modes of musical performance experienced by them during the celebrations are considered. This evidence is then used to reassess the reception of the 'myth of Venice'. Rather than viewing it as an ideology that received 'wholesale societal attachment', Fenlon suggests that the myth itself was a vital aspect of the attempt at patrician control over 'the population of a city which certainly contained heretical and dissenting elements'.

Both Gretchen Peters and John McGavin examine more closely the role of municipalities as patrons of music in late medieval and early modern times. McGavin analyses the language used to describe minstrel activity which appears in Haddington's municipal records and also considers the significance of the 'silence' or lack of evidence preserved in these documentary sources. He shows how Haddington's burgh minstrels contributed to the ritual noises of the town and were a prominent element of public display, and demonstrates how the regulation of their behaviour by various interest groups within the town became a focus for group rivalry and an index of power politics within this particular urban context. Peters found that, in late medieval times, the autonomous governing councils of Montpellier and Toulouse maintained a civic ensemble which participated in a whole variety of secular and sacred ceremonials connected with urban rule. Containing five members performing on trumpets, reeds and percussion, the Montpellier group which was established by the mid-fourteenth century was one of the largest and earliest to be founded in Europe and, as Peters argues, probably reflected the city's prosperity and wealth. That references to it continued to occur during the late fourteenth and early fifteenth centuries indicates that musical patronage remained a high priority even when Montpellier, like other European cities mentioned above, was experiencing economic and demographic decline. In contrast, although by the mid-fourteenth century Avignon – the principal residence of the papal court – had a population almost as large as Montpellier's, the civic support of music was far more limited there and no civic-subsidised wind band appears to have existed until the mid-fifteenth century. As Peters points out, this development occurred after the papal departure when the city council had begun to gain more autonomy.

Certain contributions focus on contrasting 'communities' within urban societies. This examination of music from the perspective of religious, social, economic, administrative, educational or political groupings (e.g. guilds, fraternities, colleges, courts or

---

[46] For more on this topic see E. Muir, *Civic Ritual in Renaissance Venice* (Princeton, 1981), pp. 1–23.

parishes) allows a closer examination than ever before of music's place and function in the various 'worlds within worlds' that characterised urban communities throughout pre-industrial Europe. Beat Kümin examines the music occurring in the English parish, the basic ecclesiastical and administrative unit in which men and women conducted their public spiritual lives and the focal point of local identity. His investigation of the preconditions for music at the local level demonstrates how these parochial communities played an important role in the cultural life of the nation as a whole. Not only does this essay draw attention to the role of lay benefaction in the gradual elaboration of parochial liturgy which had such a large impact on the development of English polyphony in the century before the Reformation, but it also highlights the extensive secular pursuits that gave rise to musical activity in the various neighbourhoods. Moreover, this author's comparison of both urban and rural communities highlights the different ways in which music functioned in each local context. Magnus Williamson discusses in greater detail one particular association which figured large in the English parish life before the Reformation: the local guild or fraternity. As the accounts of these organisations – which existed to provide intercessory Masses for the dead and pastoral support and conviviality (through feast-day celebrations) for the living – have rarely survived, their role as patrons of music has seldom been considered. However, through a detailed case-study of the parish of St James's in the town of Louth, whose local guild accounts are extant, Williamson highlights the diverse ways in which guild sponsorship helped to enrich the musical life of this provincial centre.

Beth Anne Lee-De Amici and Soterraña Aguirre Rincón investigate two types of community which have tended to be viewed by musicologists as self-enclosed entities which maintained little contact with the urban societies within which they were located: the academic colleges in late medieval Oxford and the royal court in sixteenth-century Valladolid. By focusing on the links between town and gown and court and community not only do both authors uncover new details concerning these institutions' musical lives, but they also shed new light on the cultural histories of the respective towns. In Oxford, Lee-De Amici shows that the academic colleges used sacred liturgy and its associated music as a means by which to interact with fellow members of the university, scholars from sister colleges and the Oxford townsfolk. In Valladolid, Aguirre Rincón demonstrates that the repeated presence of the court of Charles I of Spain, Holy Roman Emperor, was the catalyst for the metamorphosis of the cultural life of the town and modified the uses to which music was put by its citizens.

One of the most prominent topics in the historiography of early modern Europe – the Reformation – is the main focus of contributions by Joachim Kremer and Barra Boydell. Hitherto, musicological studies of religious reforms have tended to focus on the impact of change on liturgy, doctrine and style. However these authors considerably expand this perspective and relate musical culture (in the broadest sense) to its 'total' setting and one of its primary contexts – towns at the local level; additionally they consider the 'long' sixteenth century in its entirety and examine the various (dis)continuities in musical culture both before, during and after the main reforms. Kremer, for example, questions the very meaning of the term 'reformation' as it is commonly understood in the older musicological historiography. By examining the pace of religious change as it affected the musical life of and personnel employed in various institutions in a number of urban centres in north Germany throughout the sixteenth and early seventeenth centuries, he shows how the Reformation – although indeed an important historical turning point – was not a 'sudden' event. Thus, with respect to musical reform, geographical and chronological unity existed to only a limited extent. Boydell shows how the provision and development of music within Christ Church cathedral priory, Dublin, during the century of reform was subject to the competing authorities of Church, city and state. In the late fifteenth century the cathedral's music was intimately associated with its urban context, as its boy choristers whose voices embellished the liturgy were supported by an endowment made by a prominent local citizen. With the establishment of Protestantism by the late sixteenth century these civic associations were severely curtailed and the characteristics of the cathedral's musical life were redefined. Thus, while Dublin became an increasingly recusant city the cathedral developed closer links with the Anglican government and state. Among other things, musicians from cathedrals in England were appointed and on occasions the musicians of the Lord Deputy of Ireland joined Christ Church's choir in musical performances on certain feast days.

The thematic focus is further broadened by the articles of Barbara Haggh and James Saunders which examine the personal and professional experiences of particular groups of musicians in various towns. Through a detailed survey of the titles and functions of personnel in the secular churches of Brussels, Haggh identifies those individuals who played a major role in the development and performance of chant and liturgical polyphony in this flourishing Burgundian capital. In his study of cathedral choirmen, Saunders investigates the socio-economic contexts within which they operated in England after the earliest religious reforms until the Civil War. This prosopographical essay draws attention to the fact that, in the period under consideration, most choirmen interacted with the economy of the urban communities in which many of their institutions were located and took a wide range of additional jobs whose remuneration supplemented that earned from their singing careers. Owing to this, Saunders convincingly argues that it is highly unlikely that most choirmen were the penurious professionals that certain contemporaries of the later sixteenth and seventeenth centuries (with their own partisan agenda) described. Neither does this evidence support the belief, often expressed in older scholarship, that high-calibre musicians were unlikely to require employment in institutions whose remuneration appeared, at face value, to be so low. If income from supplementary jobs was a common form of moonlighting for choirmen of the period, then quality musicians may not only have been found at the larger, richer institutions.

If cities were important social and administrative centres in mainland Europe such settlements played an even greater role in the formation of the new colonies in Latin America in the late fifteenth and early sixteenth centuries. The highly developed urban-based political order already established by the native peoples was usurped by the earliest Spanish explorers and remodelled to provide the base for powerful royal and ecclesiastical administration in the new lands. Provision was also more easily made in the urban centres (either those previously founded by the indigenous tribes or newly built by the explorers) for the familiar amenities of European civilisation that the first settlers endeavoured to reproduce wherever they went. This volume would therefore not be complete without a consideration of music in the cities and towns of the New World. This is provided by Egberto Bermúdez who explores many of the themes highlighted in earlier essays in relation to the transplantation of European musical culture to the American colonies. He describes the new opportunities for Spanish musicians created by the Church when it established its institutions in the newly discovered lands; he also outlines the various ways in which the indigenous peoples were exposed to European musical traditions through the Church's bid to indoctrinate in the Catholic faith. The music performed during various civic ceremonials, religious festivities and other kinds of spectacle is investigated and Bermúdez explores the ways in which Amerindian elements were assimilated to these European-modelled events. This author also points out that Spaniards and indigenous Indians were not the only racial groups present in the urban colonies; others were present, in particular African slaves brought to the New World to work for the Spanish settlers. All these groups thus had an impact on music in the urban environment and the opportunities for interaction between their various artistic cultures were numerous. Finally, Bermúdez indicates how the possession of musical instruments and books or the performance of certain kinds of music was an indication of status in both the private and public spheres.

The research represented here is an offering to those working within at least two disciplines. To urban historians it shows the range of work beginning to be undertaken by music and other historians. To musicologists it presents some of the different approaches, questions and perspectives which may lead to new lines of enquiry for future investigations of the 'music in . . .' type. It provides no definitive paradigms, but simply aims to make a start in the right direction. By doing this it is hoped that not only will more contributions to the interdisciplinary 'field of knowledge' on the urban history agenda since the 1960s be made, but a fuller understanding of the processes and circumstances which shaped late medieval and early modern musical forms in urban contexts will eventually be obtained.

CHAPTER TWO

MUSIC AND URBAN CULTURE IN AUSTRIA: COMPARING PROFILES

REINHARD STROHM

The following study attempts to develop a few preliminary ideas and distinctions with regard to the institutional context of music in three late medieval Austrian cities: Vienna, Innsbruck and Bolzano.[1] Along with other studies in this book which are of a similar kind but on different subjects, these pages may be read as a sampling of more general patterns or typologies. But I am aiming not so much at a general typology as at small-scale comparisons and at the interpretation of differences. I attempt to explore 'types' ('court music', for example) as well as 'cases' (biographic detail, for example). These concur in many different ways to form local histories. In a particular local history, the typical or standard observations and the characteristic or unique features form a conglomerate which might be called a 'profile'. This profile is, of course, something that changes over time.

When these rather elementary matters are explored, we shall need to re-establish another balance. Music of the European Middle Ages is often considered to be more a product of institutional patterning than is music of the modern age, which is believed to have become more aesthetically independent. Admittedly, the relationship between music and institutions seems to have shifted over the centuries. We have come, for example, from 'socially constituted' musical performances in front of courtiers who were present because they were courtiers, to 'aesthetically constituted' performances in front of people who are present because they wish to hear the music. But the grand historical narrative of a development from the first to the second type has been overdone. I suggest that both types have occurred in all eras and that the aesthetic impulses for medieval music-making have been underestimated. Our present emphasis on social and institutional contexts arises from a poor state of transmission: the further we go back in history, the more we know about institutions and the less about individual and aesthetic motivations. A proper perspective is necessary, which refrains from conjecturing institutional and social parameters across all those spaces where transmission has simply denied us the details of life and thought. We really do not know what originally filled those spaces.

Vienna in the fourteenth and fifteenth centuries was a seat of government of the Habsburg dukes of Upper and Lower Austria, who had ruled there since 1278. It was a comparatively large city (see Illustration 2.1), with c. 20,000 inhabitants, and the largest

[1] The term 'Austria' is used here in its modern sense, and also includes the German-speaking Tyrol.

2.1 View of Vienna; G. Bruin, S. Novellanus, F. Hogenburgius, [*Civitates orbis terrarum*] *Theatri praecipuarum totius mundi urbium liber sextus* (Cologne, 1618), plate 21.

in its region after Prague.[2] The court had been responsible for the patronage of secular musicians and *Minnesang* since the time of the Babenberger dynasty and the city was the home of the earliest minstrels' company in the Holy Roman Empire, the fraternity of St Nicholas, constituted apparently in 1288 and based at the parish church of St Michael.[3] Neither of these secular institutions, however, was as yet concerned with musical education, mensural music or music theory. Typically for Austria, this was the task of monasteries. Most musically active in Vienna were the Benedictine Abbey '*zu den Schotten*' (*Schottenstift*), the friaries of the Austin Hermits, Franciscans and Dominicans and from 1414 the Habsburg foundation of the Abbey of St Dorothy (Austin Canons). By the late fifteenth century, nevertheless, music theory, education and other forms of musical practice were cultivated mostly in the court chapel, the university, the cathedral and the civic music school.

Vienna is one of those cities where the castle of the territorial overlord – the *Burg* – was integrated in the city area just inside the walls, forming a kind of extra fortified bastion. It stood on the same ground-level as, and fully communicated with, the other parts of the city. This spatial arrangement (also found, for example, at Innsbruck, Trent, Ingolstadt and Munich, but not at Merano, Landshut, Passau or Prague) significantly enabled interactions between the feudal and urban cultural practices.

The Habsburg rulers had employed individual court chaplains and choirboys in their castle-chapel (*Burgkapelle*) since the thirteenth century, although this type of tradition must not be confused with a continuous musical organisation as would later be implied by the term 'chapel'. The term 'cappella' still only referred to a private place of worship and it did not come to refer to 'an organisation of musical clerics' until the late fifteenth century.[4] The *Burgkapelle* was the private chapel of the courtiers, served by resident clergy including *cantores* and choirboys.[5] It was of course distinct from the household retinue of the itinerant rulers which always included chaplains and often singers, but was not a resident urban institution. In 1359, Duke Rudolph IV ('the Founder') endowed a collegiate foundation of secular canons in his private chapel in the *Burg*; in 1365 he transferred the foundation to the church of St Stephen which was to be rebuilt. In the same year he inaugurated the University of Vienna, following Emperor Charles IV's example of a court university in Prague (established 1348).[6] With these three institutions of monarchic origin – the castle chapel, the collegiate foundation, the university – the practice and study of music in Vienna became thoroughly transformed within a few generations.

The collegiate church of St Stephen, which was exempt from episcopal jurisdiction (and was elevated to cathedral status in 1469), became Vienna's centre of sacred musical practice. Its architectural dominance of the town, even today, is symbolic and was

---

[2] J. C. Russell, *Medieval Regions and their Cities* (Newton Abbot, 1972), pp. 98–101.

[3] On medieval music in Vienna generally, see R. Flotzinger and G. Gruber, *Musikgeschichte Österreichs*, 2 vols. (Graz, 1977), vol. I, pp. 59–172; J. Mantuani, *Die Musik in Wien: Von der Römerzeit bis zur Zeit des Kaisers Max I* (Vienna, 1907).

[4] See R. Strohm, *The Rise of European Music, 1380–1500* (Cambridge, 1993), pp. 270–81.

[5] C. Wolfsgruber, *Die k.u.k. Hofburgkapelle und die k.u.k. geistliche Hofkapelle* (Vienna, 1905), p. 20 and *passim*. On the Vienna-based chapels of the Habsburgs, see also Strohm, *The Rise of European Music*, pp. 311–13, 503–6.

[6] On musical learning in both universities see T. R. Ward, 'Music and Music Theory in the Universities of Central Europe During the Fifteenth Century', in A. Pompilio *et al.* (eds.), *Trasmissione e recezione delle forme di cultura musicale. Atti del XIV Congresso della Società Internazionale di Musicologia*, 3 vols. (Turin, 1990), vol. I, pp. 49–57. For Vienna, see also Mantuani, *Die Musik in Wien*, pp. 281–4.

intended to be. Through its foundation, it was attached both to the court and the university: it served as the university church where Masses and other ceremonies for academic feasts and obits were held.[7] The choir-school at St Stephen's was called the 'citizens school' (*Bürgerschule*) and was served by academic members of the university. The musical provision at St Stephen's rested on this choir-school and its boarding-house for poor singing pupils with a school building near the church, the *cantorey* (rebuilt in the 1440s).[8] The pupils were required by the statute of foundation to sing in Mass and Vespers services; forms of collaboration between university masters, 'old students' and young schoolboys were clearly specified. The *cantorey* was also a civic institution, legally and financially under the control of the city magistrate.[9] Considering that the collegiate foundation was under the special protection of the dukes of Austria, that the city's patriciate was vitally interested in the religious and cultural services of the choir-school which also supervised the other urban schools, that many leading members of the university belonged to the mendicant orders and thus to urban religious communities and that the collegiate (secular) clergy tended to be recruited from the regional aristocracy, this institutional conglomeration united all the dominant groups of society in a network of mutual protection and patronage. This network had come about by a series of acts of foundation and statutes, which of course were criss-crossed by disputes over financial management, status rivalries and by disciplinary or political conflicts.

Financial support for ceremonies functioned – as was typical – on the basis of rental incomes from estates and other investments (endowments), in return for which the clergy and musicians had to perform religious services. The prototype of what is called a 'service' here is the anniversary (*jartag*): an annual religious service, often an obit, with a fixed programme of Mass and Vespers to which processions and/or other prayers were added as required. In this period there was no clear division between the programmes and repertories of public and private ceremonies, except that obits had their own, more austere, status. The celebration of Mass (*officium, Amt*) was a prototype accompanying all civic functions of any significance. Sacred spaces were reserved for Mass in many civic buildings: in schools, palaces, citizens' houses, city gates and of course in the city hall, where the schoolboys of St Stephen's regularly appeared under their cantor. For example, they had to sing annually on *Reminiscere* Sunday (the second Sunday in Lent) for the renewal of the magistrate, a type of ceremony common to many European cities. A particularly successful ritual was the Corpus Christi procession endowed by King Frederick III in the early 1440s in several towns of the realm, in which instrumentalists as well as (at Vienna) the choristers of St Stephen's performed.

Instrumentalists were usually rewarded with salaries, fees and gratuities from the public purse, rather than endowments. Musicians salaried by the magistrate from 1426 onwards included two city trumpeters and a timpanist, a city organist attached to the *cantorey* and pipers.[10] They usually appeared at the regular festivities of the city magistrate

---

[7] See Mantuani, *Die Musik in Wien*, pp. 281–4, and G. Pietzsch, *Zur Pflege der Musik an den deutschen Universitäten bis zur Mitte des 16. Jahrhunderts* (Hildesheim, 1971), pp. 12–17, 26–36, 185.

[8] Several statutes are printed in Mantuani, *Die Musik in Wien*, pp. 282–9. See also H. Brunner, *Die Kantorei bei St. Stephan in Wien* (Vienna, 1948). The term 'cantorey' (*Kantorey*) referred first to the building, then to the people organised in it; city accounts of the 1440s already use both meanings. For the distinction between the collegiate dignitary of 'cantor' (*Sangherr*) and the cantor as musical leader of the school, see Mantuani, *Die Musik in Wien*, pp. 287–8 n.   [9] A. Mayer, *Die Bürgerschule zu St. Stephan in Wien* (Vienna, 1880).

[10] The bulk of the archival material is held in Stadtarchiv Wien, *Stadtrechnungen/Oberkammeramtsrechnungen*. See also A. Mayer *et al.*, *Quellen zur Geschichte der Stadt Wien*, 10 vols. (Vienna, 1895–1937).

and the court, both of which would rival each other in their financial support when the king or emperor or important nobles were visiting; they also often performed on princely birthdays or similar occasions, when civic musicians might play in secular surroundings and for dancing.

There is an element of ambiguity about Vienna's institutional profile, even by comparison with the complex conditions of, for example, the Burgundian court. There is, for example, the mutual subsidizing of court, church and city in the running of public ceremonies: when city or court minstrels, choirboys, succentors, monastic choirs and collegiate clergy performed in honour of noble visitors or for public holidays, the salaries and gratuities were most often paid by the city magistrate regardless of the status and purpose of the musical services rendered. On the other hand, the funding of public music for dynastic occasions from tax owed to the ruler seems to have been frequent. Also ambiguous (and hardly reducible to a type) is the biographic profile of Hermann Edlerawer, Cantor of St Stephen's from 1440 to 1449. His regular duties for the choir-school included the direction of Masses and processions for the civic authorities, in which he or his deputy conducted the schoolboys. But he was a layman, a composer of polyphony, a university member and an honoured citizen and diplomat.[11] In 1445, Edlerawer sustained an academic dispute with the famous court secretary of King Frederick III, the Italian humanist Enea Silvio Piccolomini.

Ambiguity also affects the whole question of a musical 'repertory' in Vienna's institutions at the time, ranging from chant and extemporised polyphony in the monasteries via organ music – popular everywhere – to mensural polyphony, sacred and secular. An international polyphonic repertory, sacred and secular, is found in choirbook fragments from the citizens' school at St Stephen's (*c.* 1410–1420)[12] and in the famous 'St Emmeram Codex' (*c.* 1440) assembled at the university or citizens' school by Hermann Poetzlinger.[13] Further music books (*cantionalia*) are documented at St Stephen's[14] and several smaller fragments preserve organ music and mensural song which might have been heard at the *Schottenstift* abbey and the fashionable Augustinian monasteries.[15] The abbey was not only a musical centre but also a centre of the Benedictine reform promoted by the congregation of S. Giustina of Padua in this period (*c.* 1420–1460).[16] At the choir-school of St Stephen's, mensural polyphony (*cantus figurativus*) was taught and practised by the 1440s; the statutes of the *cantorey* of 1460 distinguish between the general repertory which all schoolboys performed on high feasts ('*cantus gregorianus, conducten* and other song which is appropriate to each festivity') and 'cantus figurativus', which only the gifted boys had to learn.[17] Some of these *conducten* and other festal songs were probably extra-liturgical sacred songs for processions and Christmas ceremonies.

---

[11] For his biography, see I. Rumbold, 'The Compilation and Ownership of Munich, Clm 14274', *Early Music History* 2 (1982), pp. 169–76.

[12] R. Strohm, 'Native and Foreign Polyphony in Late Medieval Austria', *Musica Disciplina* 38 (1984), pp. 215–16.   [13] Rumbold, 'The Compilation'.

[14] According to the church warden's inventory of St Stephen's of 1476, the music books kept in the 'cantorey' were: 'two graduals, two antiphonals, three large cantionals of Herman, one large cantional of Jacob, six small cantionals, one red cantional with several sexterns, one red cantional of Jacob, one old cantional with several sexterns, small books with prophecies, the cantor's register . . .' (missals are listed separately). See K. Uhlircz, *Die Rechnungen des Kirchmeisteramtes von St. Stephan zu Wien über die Jahre 1404 (. . .) 1535* (Vienna, 1902), p. 477.   [15] Strohm, 'Native and Foreign Polyphony'.

[16] Mantuani, *Die Musik in Wien*, p. 289 n.; J. F. Angerer, *Die liturgisch-musikalische Erneuerung der Melker Reform. Studien zur Erforschung der Musikpraxis in den Benediktinerklöstern des 15. Jahrhunderts* (Vienna, 1974).   [17] Mantuani, *Die Musik in Wien*, p. 286 n.

The relationship between Vienna, the Habsburg courts and the polyphonic collection of the famous Trent Codices is puzzling. These seven large books of fifteenth-century polyphony found at the Cathedral of Trent in northern Italy (a territory then ruled by a prince-bishop under Habsburg influence) contain local, regional and international repertories.[18] Even when nationalist hypotheses are discarded, this music collection remains connected with the Imperial court through personalities based at or related to Vienna, such as the humanist and friar Johannes Hinderbach, Bishop of Trent, the possibly Viennese magister Johannes Wiser, School Rector of Trent Cathedral, or Enea Silvio Piccolomini, a friend of Hinderbach and possibly a promoter and collector of the music of the Dufay circle (notwithstanding the fact that he dismissed Viennese music in his much-quoted description of the city).[19]

Extant archival documentation indicates that the Viennese liked to spend money on public, ceremonial events in which musicians appeared, whether schoolboys, collegiate *cantores*, or civic minstrels and ducal trumpeters, or all of them together. All the available institutional forces were often co-ordinated and harnessed for the greater ceremonies of common interest. These ceremonies were partly financed by private benefactors through endowments or through the public purse. The Viennese considered themselves in need of conspicuous rituals, for they strengthened, in the eyes of citizens, Vienna's status as territorial capital – a position not firmly established until the sixteenth century. Some of this practice may have arisen more spontaneously, perhaps attracting voluntary subsidies only as it became more habitual. In the city accounts, for example, the annual gratuities for singers in the magistrate's anniversary Mass are cautiously recorded as 'non-recurrent' outgoings (*zeaintzigs ausgebn*) throughout the 1440s and 1450s. Occasional and permanent funding, however, are but different forms of the same type of social practice, i.e. that of buying specialised services as is characteristic of a merchant city. Buying musical services from each other – city from court, court from church and so on – and thus subsidising each other's music, was part of the same ambiguity that existed between the major institutions in terms of statute and status.

Musical life at Vienna may appear to have been over-complicated. That the Viennese also loved just to sing and dance in their houses and streets has never been reasonably doubted (Enea Silvio Piccolomini grudgingly confirms it), but apparently their socio-political situation called for public rituals that involved money, committed a variety of representative forces, and strengthened collective identities.

The County of Tyrol was acquired by the Habsburg dynasty in 1363.[20] Innsbruck became its seat of government only in 1420, when Duke Frederick, Count of Tyrol, moved his administration from the ancient castle of Tyrol above Merano to the northern part of the

[18] See, most recently, P. Wright (ed.), *I codici musicali Trentini. Nuove scoperte e nuovi orientamenti della ricerca* (Trent, 1996); R. Strohm, 'Trienter Codices', in L. Finscher (ed.), *Die Musik in Geschichte und Gegenwart*, 2nd edn, vol. IX, (Kassel, 1999), cols. 801–12.

[19] A. Lhotsky, *Die Wiener Artistenfakultät 1365–1497*, Österreichische Akademie der Wissenschaften, Philosophisch-Historische Klasse, Sitzungsberichte 247/2 (Vienna, 1965), pp. 137–9; on Piccolomini's possible involvement with the Aosta Codex, see M. Cobin, 'The Compilation of the Aosta Codex: a Working Hypothesis', in A. Atlas (ed.), *Dufay Quincentenary Conference. Brooklyn College, 1974* (New York, 1976), pp. 83–7; on the question of his own interests, see R. Strohm, 'Music, Humanism and the Idea of a "Rebirth" of the Arts', in *The New Oxford History of Music*, vol. III, 2nd edn (Oxford, forthcoming).

[20] Tyrol was a self-contained Habsburg territory on a par with Upper Austria, Lower Austria, Styria, the territories on the upper Rhine and other possessions which were, from generation to generation, newly distributed among the members of the dynasty who all carried the title of Duke of Austria.

2.2   View of Innsbruck; G. Bruin, S. Novellanus, F. Hogenburgius, [*Civitates orbis terrarum*] *De praecipuis, totius universi urbibus, liber secundus* (Antwerp, 1575), plate 42.

county and took residence within Innsbruck's walls (see Illustration 2.2). His new court (*Neuhof*) and later added buildings called the 'middle court' (*mitterhof*) formed a self-contained precinct within the town walls; it comprised the necessary living rooms, stables and private chapels (with Mass endowments attached to them) and was adjacent to the parish church of St Jacob, which was used by the members of the court. The new residence was ideally located, for it was situated on the River Inn and was close to the main trade routes across the Brenner Pass and towards the north.

Whatever liturgical and musical traditions the Habsburg rulers may have brought with them to Innsbruck, they had to accommodate them within a narrow institutional set-up. The church of St Jacob was able to provide Mass and at least some Offices; since 1303 it had had a school with a *rector scholarum*, to which were later added the posts of succentor (*junkmaister*), assistants (*astanten*) and about twenty-five schoolboys available for singing. However all major endowments and indeed the supervision of the cure of souls rested with the local Praemonstratensian abbey of Wilten, just south of the town.[21]

[21]   The late medieval history of the parish church and school has been surveyed in L. Streiter, 'Der Gottesdienst in Alt-Innsbruck', *Pfarrblatt für Innsbruck, Hötting und Mühlau* 8/1 (October 1926), pp. 3–4; 8/2 (November 1926), pp. 4–6; 8/4 (January 1927), pp. 5–7; 8/7 (April 1927), pp. 3–5; 8/9 (May 1927), pp. 5–6; L. Streiter, 'Die Innsbrucker Pfarrschule', *Pfarrblatt für Innsbruck, Hötting und Mühlau* 9/1 (October 1927), pp. 5–7; 9/2 (November 1927), pp. 6–7; 9/3 (December 1927), pp. 3–5; 9/4 (January 1928), pp. 5–6; 9/5 (February 1928), pp. 8–9; and L. Streiter, 'Der Innsbrucker Weltklerus in alter Zeit', *Pfarrblatt für Innsbruck, Hötting und Mühlau* 9/2 (November 1928), pp. 10–12; 9/3 (December 1928), pp. 5–6. See also J. Weingartner, *Die Pfarrei*

The town council had also achieved a certain influence on the parish priests and school by the fifteenth century. Civic support came through confraternities (of the Assumption of Our Lady and a few others) and merchant families (the Kuchelmeister, the Tänzl and others); they endowed sumptuous anniversaries benefiting the schoolmaster, succentor and boys when they sang in obits and confraternity Masses. Even trumpeters were employed in some of these civic anniversary celebrations. But within a few decades, the political and financial weight of the court entirely changed this cultural balance.

The financial power of the Tyrolean court was the result of a rare historical contingency – the discovery of rich silver mines in the north Tyrol (near Schwaz) which, together with copper and salt supplies in the same area, provided the rulers and their merchant collaborators with spectacular wealth for about three generations. By 1490, when Count Sigmund of Tyrol was deposed by his cousin Maximilian I, the income was drying up and the reserves had been squandered, partly on music.

The fifteenth-century history of Tyrolean court music[22] cannot be recapitulated here, but a profile of its status within the urban context may be sketched. Sigmund, Duke of Austria, began his rule in 1446 as Count of Tyrol after a seven-year spell at the royal court of Graz under the wardenship of King Frederick III (the later emperor). Although Sigmund's father, Frederick of Tyrol (*d.* 1439), had developed a courtly ceremonial life at Innsbruck, this seems to have been much disrupted by 1446. Whereas important repertories of mensural polyphony assembled in the Aosta and earliest Trent Codices were accessible to the chaplains of both Frederick of Tyrol and King Frederick III,[23] even the existence of an official court chapel at Innsbruck is in doubt. The idea that Sigmund had a '*Hofkantorei*', or that this institution was established in 1463 and had chaplains, choirboys and an organist,[24] is not a correct reading of the sources. The court records only speak of individual chaplains and of an exuberant musical life in other contexts. With respect to terminology, no fifteenth-century court had a *cantorey*; this was the name of an ecclesiastical institution, a singing-school attached to a church, as at St Stephen's, Vienna.[25] And, if we wish to speak of a 'court chapel', let us remember that the term 'chapel' in the sense of 'an organised group of musicians' did not yet exist.

So how was the court music organised? We learn about this from the account books and from many court ordinances (*Hofordnungen*), drawn up as the liberality of the prince spiralled out of control and expenses for personnel had to be restrained. Several draft ordinances in a chancery manuscript of 1471–2, for example, reflect negotiations between the duke and his councillors about the number of household servants and the horses required for them (in one draft, the total number of horses required is eighty-eight). The list of chaplains, secretaries and musicians is given in Table 2.1.

Magister Niclas was Niclas Krombsdorfer, who first appears in the court accounts in 1463. Having served the Este court of Ferrara from 1436 to 1462 as a singer and

und die Pfarrkirche von St. Jakob. Festschrift zum 200 jährigen Weihejubiläum (Innsbruck, 1924); H. Lentze, *Die St. Jakobskirche in Innsbruck im Lichte der Rechtsgeschichte* (Innsbruck, 1957), pp. 4–10; K. Schadelbauer, 'Das Kalendarium Wernheri als tirolische Chronik', *Studien zur Geschichte des Stiftes Wilten* 1, Innsbruck, n.d. (*c.* 1940), on an obit- and anniversary-book of St Jacob (Innsbruck, Landesmuseum Ferdinandeum, MS F.B. 2627) which contains much information on endowed services and their performers.

[22] W. Senn, *Musik und Theater am Hof zu Innsbruck* (Innsbruck, 1954), pp. 1–18; M. Schneider, 'Vom Musikleben am Hof Herzog Sigmunds des Münzreichen', in G. Ammann (ed.), *Der Herzog und sein Taler*, Exhibition Catalogue (Innsbruck, 1986), pp. 57–66; Strohm, *The Rise of European Music*, pp. 518–21.

[23] Strohm, *The Rise of European Music*, pp. 253–5.

[24] Senn, *Musik und Theater*, p. 11; Schneider, 'Vom Musikleben', p. 57.

[25] The name *Hofkantorei* seems to appear first in sixteenth-century Saxony.

Table 2.1 *Officers of Duke Sigmund of Austria, 1471–2: summary of draft ordinances of the Innsbruck court*

Chaplains	
Dr Berchtold Han	2 horses
Herr Linhart Kaiser (confessor)	1 horse, 2 people
Herr Michel Sigwein	1 horse
Herr André Makh	1 horse
Chancery scribes	
Wilhalm Costentzer	1 horse
Wolfgang Sumer	1 horse
Hanns Wiser[a]	1 horse
Others	
Dr Heller, notary	1 person
Mag. Hanns, physician	2 horses
Mag. Niclas, organist	2 horses, 4 people
An alchemist	2 people
2 trumpeters, 1 trombonist (*Basawner*), 3 pipers	6 horses
Paule, lutenist	1 person[b]

Notes:

[a] Hanns Wiser of Rheinfelden (*d.* 1486), Duke Sigmund's private secretary. He is not identical with the Trent musician and schoolmaster Johannes Wiser who was made the duke's (honorary?) chaplain in 1471.

[b] Innsbruck, Tiroler Landesarchiv, Hs. 208a, fols. 5v–24v.

instrumentalist, he was subsequently employed by Duke Sigmund as a court organist with a 'salary' 100 li plus 2 guilders per year, usually disbursed in four or five instalments a year.[26] He was not obviously connected to the 'chaplains', whose names are unknown to music history: they were priests, primarily occupied with the reading of Mass in the prince's domestic chapels at Innsbruck or in his many castles. Like other courtiers they often travelled with the Duke; Krombsdorfer was in his retinue from time to time. In records of the 1460s, he is usually styled 'organist' and sometimes '*maister*' (i.e., magister), but never 'chaplain'. He was not responsible for the chaplains, who were apparently not connected with the court music.[27] His duties included the care of 2–4 singing boys whom he taught secular song and lute-playing, who were expected to sing at court.[28] Krombsdorfer was also associated with trumpeters, trombonists, pipers, lutenists and harpers many of whom were servants of the court or casual visitors. The location of his organ(s) is uncertain; he probably used the positive and even portable organs which the court did possess for secular music; his participation in services in the tiny castle chapel is also likely. A close colleague of Krombsdorfer from 1464 onwards was Wilhalm Perger, usually cited as 'singer'; he left in 1471 or 1472, took holy orders

[26] Innsbruck, Tiroler Landesarchiv, Raitbuch vol. 2 (1461–2), fol. 282r–v, 8 September 1463. On Krombsdorfer's biography, see also Strohm, *The Rise of European Music*, pp. 519–20.

[27] An inventory of the possessions of chaplain André Mak, 1463, lists valuable household items and two horses; the only book is a volume of 'Decretales, with a decent commentary' (Tiroler Landesarchiv, Inventare, E 21).

[28] Girls served the court as well, both in the chambers of the countess and as singers for entertainment.

and then joined the Sforza chapel of Milan. Krombsdorfer's successor as court organist was the famous Paul Hofhaimer, employed by 1478; among Hofhaimer's extant compositions (vocal as well as organ settings), sacred pieces are a small minority. It thus appears that 'Maister Niclas' was in the 1460s the leader of a group of secular court musicians which also included singing children and instrumentalists; these probably contributed to the lavishly funded entertainments of this court.

In addition to the regular court servants, visiting musicians were also amply rewarded for their occasional services. The climax of this musical culture is probably to be seen in the wedding festivities which Duke Sigmund ordered for his second marriage to Katharina, Princess of Saxony, in February 1484. In that year, Arnolt (Schlick?) and Henricus Isaac also served the court as 'composers' (thus styled in the records), and the humanist Hans Fuchsmagen organised the presentation or even the musical performance of humanistic Latin poems in honour of the bride.[29]

The account books of the court also record large payments to priests and to musicians for sacred rituals. These, however, took place not in the castle chapel but in the church of St Jacob. The courtiers endowed, subsidised and attended them, but were not responsible for them. One of the most popular ceremonies was the Corpus Christi service and procession, endowed by King Frederick III, for which the king himself had read the gospel at its inception in Innsbruck in 1442. The performers in such circumstances were not the court musicians but the schoolmaster with the members of the choir-school.[30] In fact, a number of associations developed between the court and the nearby parish church. For example, the organist Krombsdorfer and the court singing boys often performed in St Jacob's. Also, some of the court's boys were actually taught grammar (and, quite probably, music) by the parish schoolmaster. The singers of the choir-school also performed in the court and in the streets or in other secular locations to entertain nobles; this well-paid musical practice (known as 'ansingen') was not court- but school-generated.[31] In Innsbruck, girls often sang for the nobility; possibly, the church-school collaborated with a local nunnery and offered musical instruction to young girls there.

What do we know about the musical repertory of St Jacob in this period? In 1993 I suggested that the large collection of sacred polyphony in the so-called Nikolaus Leopold Codex which in 1511 was owned by the Innsbruck schoolmaster Nikolaus Leopold but had been assembled from individual fascicles copied since c. 1466, was the repertory used by successive schoolmasters of St Jacob.[32] Their names are known and their careers can be researched with the help of the Innsbruck court archives.[33] The Leopold Codex has clear repertorial and codicological similarities with the later Trent Codices (Tr 88, 89 and 91), choir-school manuscripts used at Trent cathedral school which assemble all-European polyphony in recent styles; their dates of compilation span the years c. 1462 to c. 1476. Thus the 'court music' of Innsbruck, as far as it is 'church music', is largely to be found in those European manuscript collections which originated as 'school music' in two major church schools of the region.

In 1472 Niclas Krombsdorfer went to the bishop's court in Brixen to become a

---

[29] Senn, *Musik und Theater*, pp. 2–12, 29; Strohm, *The Rise of European Music*, p. 538.

[30] Innsbruck, Tiroler Landesarchiv, Raitbuch (1460/61), fol. 227r (Wednesday after 12 May 1461).

[31] See below, pp. 25–6.   [32] Bavarian State Library, Munich, Mus. MS 3154.

[33] Schoolmaster Valentin Unger, for example, became a chaplain of Philip the Handsome of Spain. See also Strohm, *The Rise of European Music*, pp. 519–22.

priest; he then returned to Innsbruck to serve as court chaplain and from 1479 he was parish rector of St Jacob. In those years he may have conducted singers both in the court chapel and in the parish church – although the performing group of schoolmaster, succentor, assistants and schoolboys, whom Krombsdorfer did not direct, remained a functioning musical ensemble at the disposal of both the church and court. Krombsdorfer did have a hand in musical services – for example, he often received and disbursed the court's payments for a certain festal ceremony – and he lent occasional assistance to the duke himself, for example at the wedding in February 1484 when he 'readied' the visiting singers whom the duke had invited to participate in the festivities.[34]

The merchant town of Bolzano (*Bozen*) in the county of Tyrol, situated at the confluence of the rivers Eisack, Etsch and Talfer, controlled the trade-routes across the Brenner and Reschen passes, as well as the eastward connections with Carinthia, Styria and Carniola. Bolzano also had successful manufacturing guilds, including those of the basket-makers, vat-makers and metal-workers; agriculture was based on wine-growing in the valleys and on grange-farming in the upper regions. The town had become prosperous by 1443 when it was half-destroyed by fire; it quickly recovered but some of its administrative documents seem to have been lost. No earlier record survives, for example, which refers to an office of town mayor; perhaps the ducal district judge at nearby Gries acted in this capacity. Also the Prince-Bishop of Trent had his representative in the town.[35] Bolzano was the largest German-speaking parish in the diocese of Trent; the ecclesiastical district to which it belonged also included the wealthy parishes of Caldaro (*Kaltern*), Eppiano (*Eppan*) and Termeno (*Tramin*). By the time Bolzano's town and church records had begun in the 1460s, a fully fledged political structure and a rich ceremonial life centred on the town's only parish church and school of St Mary was established.[36] The town council had an unusually strong influence on the church, for the church overseer (*kirchprobst*) was a civic officer. In many administrative matters, however, the overlordship of the Count of Tyrol was decisive, although sometimes checked by that of the bishop. The count had acquired the right of presentation concerning the church rector as well as certain connected benefices.[37]

Among the latter, the chapel of St Jacob in the cemetery of the parish church interests us. On 27 May 1431, Frederick IV, Count of Tyrol, presented to this benefice his personal chaplain, Johannes Lupi (Wolf) of Bolzano; in 1447 Lupi also acquired the rectorship of Caldaro and a chaplaincy at Trent Cathedral, where he is named cathedral organist in 1452.[38] By identifying Lupi's autograph will of *c.* 1455, Peter Wright has shown that Lupi was the main scribe and owner of the two earliest Trent Codices (Tr 87 and 92), compiled between *c.* 1434 and *c.* 1445. From 1439, Lupi's career was

[34] Innsbruck, Tiroler Landesarchiv, Raitbuch vol. 17 (1484), fol. 33r: 'zevertigen die cantores so auff meins g.h. hochzeit her ervordert waren'.

[35] The earliest mayor named in the archives, Hainrich Praitenperger (1465), had in 1456 held the position of episcopal *vicarius* and magistrate (*Statrichter*). Bayerisches Hauptstaatsarchiv Munich, HL Trient, 1a, vol. VI (copy-book of Bishop Georg), 1.1.56.

[36] K. T. Hoeniger, 'Das älteste Bozner Ratsprotokoll vom Jahr 1469', [*Bozner*] *Jahrbuch für Geschichte, Kultur und Kunst*, 1931/34, ed. K. M. Mayr (Bolzano, 1934), pp. 7–111.

[37] K. Atz and A. Schatz, *Der deutsche Antheil des Bistums Trient* (Bozen, 1903), vol. I, especially pp. 21–44.

[38] R. Lunelli, 'La patria dei codici musicali tridentini', *Note d'Archivio per la Storia Musicale* 4 (1927), p. 121; summarised, with further documents, in P. Wright, 'On the Origins of Trent 87/1 and 92/2', *Early Music History* 6 (1986), pp. 255–7.

partly spent at the court of King Frederick III where he was a chaplain in the service of the young Duke Sigmund, Count of Tyrol, until 1447.[39] It can therefore be suggested that the international polyphonic repertory of Trent Codices 87 and 92 was known to the chaplains of Frederick IV of Tyrol (*d.* 1439), of King Frederick III (who ruled the Tyrol from 1439 to 1446) and of Duke Sigmund, Count of Tyrol (who ruled from 1446).

That Johannes Lupi was a wealthy and expert musician is demonstrated by his will.[40] To colleagues at Trent, Teseno and Caldaro, he bequeathed lutes and keyboard instruments; to the fabric (i.e. the overseer's office) of the parish church of Bolzano he donated his six *cantionalia*, or books of *cantus figuratus*. Lupi appointed the church overseer, Christoph Hasler, as executor for his Bolzano assets which were mostly bequeathed to the parish church and its chapel of St Jacob. Most of the beneficiaries of Lupi's will were either canons of Trent Cathedral, or protégés of Duke Sigmund like Lupi himself, acting in some official capacity in the Bolzano–Trent area.[41] Thus, less than twenty years after their compilation, the six manuscripts of polyphonic music (not yet of bibliophile value) were given to the Bolzano church probably in order to be used 'ad laudem dei omnipotentis'.

Research on Bolzano's musical life in this period has hardly begun.[42] My own studies suggest that civic support for music in all its forms was unusually strong, although focused on the sacred ritual provided by the parish church and church school. The latter was organised in the usual way, with a schoolmaster – governed concurrently by the school wardens of the town council and by the parish rector – and a succentor with assistants and schoolboys.[43] The town regularly paid gratuities to the trumpeters and pipers of the duke (suggesting that they played in the town when the court visited or passed through); it also financed apparently magnificent *Salve* services for which the priests, schoolmaster with singing boys, church overseers and verger (*Mesner*) together earned around 40–50 li annually. The church organist was paid around 30 li per year by the overseer and received clothing from the council. To these public payments for musicians must be added the income from anniversaries and pious foundations made by the court and the nobility (the Liechtenstein family, for example), and by craft guilds and confraternities such as the basket-makers (*Cotzenpinter*). The latter were constituted at the chapel of St Jacob; Lupi had intended to leave them money.[44]

Other typical church expenses connected with music were the copying and repairing of liturgical books; organ-building and repairs; expenses for blackboards in the school with painted musical staves for the teaching of music; extra gratuities for the schoolboys to sing for sick people with the holy host on the ember days and during the wine harvest;

---

[39] Wright, 'On the Origins'; P. Wright, 'The Compilation of Trent 87–I and 92–II', *Early Music History* 2 (1982), pp. 237–71.

[40] See Wright, 'On the Origins', pp. 265–70. Since Lupi died only in 1467, most of the bequests may ultimately not have been carried out.

[41] C. Hasler, for example, who was expected to succeed Lupi to the benefice of St Jacob, became Duke Sigmund's secretary by *c.* 1470.

[42] For previously published research, see H. Obermair, 'Die liturgischen Bücher der Pfarrkirche Bozen aus dem letzten Viertel des 15. Jahrhunderts', *Der Schlern* 59/9 (1985), pp. 516–36 (based on three surviving church inventories); Strohm, *The Rise of European Music*, pp. 289–90, 507–8.

[43] J. Ladurner, 'Das Schulwesen in Botzen im 15. Jahrhundert', *Bothe für Tirol und Vorarlberg* (1847), pp. 264, 268; Obermair, 'Die liturgischen Bücher', p. 521 n. A civic school is known through its statutes of 1424, but does not figure much later on.

[44] When this guild was amalgamated with the confraternity of Corpus Christi in 1463 (charter in the Archivio Comunale, Bolzano), a sung anniversary for 1 li per year was endowed.

clothing, food and drinks for the singers when singing in public; gratuities for organists, schoolmasters, succentors and their assistants when they applied for positions and were spending probationary periods.[45] All these budgetary items grew continuously.

The most conspicuous financial factor for the youngest Bolzano musicians was a different one. Annually at Christmas time (and later on other feasts), a special singing group directed by the schoolmaster earned between 70 li and 110 li for processional tours around the town and to outlying mansions to sing serenades. These earnings were in addition to regular payments covering their expenses for refreshments; they are documented from 1475 but had probably been received since the early 1460s. The schoolmaster's personal basic salary might at that time be estimated at 15–18 li, plus gratuities for anniversaries. The performances, called 'ansingen', were customary in the area and have remained the hallmark of schoolboy activities in later centuries known as the 'Kurrende'. In the fifteenth century much of the repertory was probably sacred – Christmas carols and motets, for example – and much of it was polyphonic.[46] The practice was in one sense related to those of the minstrels of the Middle Ages who performed at the dinner tables of the wealthy for spontaneous gratuities. In another sense it was an outlet for the musical skills accumulated in the church school, where extra-liturgical repertories, which could not be used in the ordinary church ritual, were collected and rehearsed. Indirect evidence that mensural music (*cantus figuratus*) was taught is provided by the fact that already in *c.* 1455 Johannes Lupi had bequeathed his books of *cantus figuratus* to the parish church, although it was at the cathedral school of Trent that the same manuscripts and repertories were further expanded. Unfortunately we do not know the name of the Bolzano schoolmaster who would have used Lupi's *cantionalia* with his singers.

Public performances easily developed into theatre as well. In 1475, an Easter play was performed during a churchwarden's dinner. As early as 1472, church accounts from Bolzano mention a mystery play of Corpus Christi (*spill an Korpus Kristy*), for which a dragon (*worm*), crowns and other items were being prepared or repaired for 4 li 3 d. The play was already an elaborate, extra-liturgical affair and the 'worm' was moved around town in procession. It was again performed in 1475 and continued in later years.[47] The Bolzano mystery plays performed around 1500 have been comprehensively researched.[48] They were acted by the schoolboys with their masters, financed by the parish church and town council and designed and directed by the schoolmasters. The custom had spread across the Tyrol through a network of urban institutions. Several extant play manuscripts from *c.* 1500 are copies of each other or related to common originals; in 1493 the town council of Bolzano sent a scribe to Vipiteno/Sterzing to copy passion plays.[49] Already in 1488, the church overseer Hanns Runngkär recorded in his accounts: 'I have given a painter who let me copy three passions for the play, . . . 3 li 6d'. The church accounts of

[45] There were many debates between town council and parish rector over the church music. In 1475 Albrecht Weinreich (a schoolmaster recommended by the duchess) was rejected by the priest but accepted by the council who urged him to continue providing the music for the town to earn his public salary; see Strohm, *The Rise of European Music*, p. 508.   [46] See Strohm, *The Rise of European Music*, pp. 294–6, 508.

[47] Archivio Comunale Bolzano, no. 640 (Kirchprobstrechnungen, 1472), fol. 6r; no. 641 (1475), fol. 14v, and further.

[48] J. Eduard Wackernell, *Altdeutsche Passionsspiele aus Tirol* (Graz, 1897); N. R. Wolf, 'Bozner Passionsspiele', in K. Ruh (ed.), *Die deutsche Literatur des Mittelalters, Verfasserlexikon*, 2nd edn (Berlin, 1975); E. Kühebacher (ed.), *Tiroler Volksschauspiel. Beiträge zur Theatergeschichte des Alpenraums* (Bozen, 1976); in this last volume, see especially W. Lipphardt, 'Musik in den spätmittelalterlichen Passionsspielen und Osterspielen von Bozen, Sterzing und Brixen', pp. 127–66.   [49] Lipphardt, 'Musik', pp. 158–9.

1494/5 specify, among many other details, that passion plays were copied from Sterzing originals by 'students'.[50] The play-manuscripts of Bolzano schoolmaster Benedikt Debs (*d.* 1515), which he probably used for teaching, also contain many older and shorter play-texts assembled over generations; some of them became integrated in the new, longer plays, the performance of which lasted up to seven days.[51]

Having formed our profiles from a number of typical or standard notions (public ceremonies, endowments, schoolmasters, organists, etc.), tempered by distinctions of quantity, historical contingencies or the impact of individuals (silver mines, mystery plays, Edlerawer, Krombsdorfer, Lupi, Duke Sigmund, etc.), we might now ask how this all hangs together and is situated in history. The relationship between contingency and structure is enigmatic: general notions such as 'court', 'urban community', 'performance' may or may not have a meaning that is transferable from one context to another. We ought to be aware that our use of these general notions is unlikely to be 'objective' and is rather guided by individual interests and established rhetorics. Even the term 'community' seems inseparable from a certain twentieth-century ideology for which the key-word of a 'mass society' and surely also the notion of 'individualism' are synonymous with modern decline. In central Europe, the concept of 'community' (*Gemeinschaft*) is heavily politically contaminated as it has been used for too long to disguise powerful interests. Analogously, we must reckon that the discourse of 'the Church' or 'the Court' in the late Middle Ages was a loaded one, identifying intentions and interests as well as structures. If this argument can be accepted, then the uses of all the standard notions and structural terms in the preceding pages remain *sub judice.* We do not really know yet whose language our description of a historical structure reinforces. The only thing we can safely assume is that we are continuing to write the history of the winning side.

[50] Archivio Comunale Bolzano, no. 652 (Kirchprobstrechnungen, 1488–9), fol. 30v; no. 654 (1494–5), fols. 71v–76r.   [51] Lipphardt, 'Musik', 128.

CHAPTER THREE

MAGNIFICENCE AS CIVIC IMAGE: MUSIC AND CEREMONIAL SPACE IN EARLY MODERN VENICE

IAIN FENLON

The public rituals of early modern Venice, particularly those that relate to the state and its figurehead, the doge, were invariably religious before they were political. In its more developed form, as practised at least from the thirteenth century, Venetian political theology assigned to the elected head of the Venetian polity a role that was analogous to that of the pope in Rome. Ceremonies which surrounded the doge, and in which he participated, emphasised his position as an intermediary, one that became particularly crucial at moments of crisis. It was then that the doge was placed in the role of prime agent of intercession, the true representative of St Mark on earth.[1] Critical to the historical development of this concept was the legend of the arrival in Venice of the body of St Mark in the ninth century; from this flowed an identification with the saint as the special protector of the city, which in turn determined the character of much Venetian ritual and of the spaces in which it was performed. Some sense of this relationship is already present in the earliest visual representation of the *translatio*, in the Chapel of St Clement in St Mark's basilica. Here an important amplification of the traditional narrative is introduced; the Evangelist's body is received not only by the Bishop of Castello, but also by those of the other five dioceses of the lagoon, as well as by the doge accompanied by the people and clergy of Venice. The St Clement mosaic not only depicts the Venetian church and state in its totality, but also emphasises the benefits and consequences of possession. Mark was no longer the property of Aquilea or Grado, as he had been previously, but of Venice itself. This was in turn simply the first stage of a lengthy historical process in which Mark became increasingly both more Venetian and more ducal.[2]

In the early stages of this gradual process of appropriation, the construction of a sufficiently imposing structure to house the Evangelist's body, which on its arrival had been temporarily housed 'ad ducis palatium', became something of a priority. The area selected, transformed out of the ancient *castrum*, had the practical merit of being close to the existing palace of the doge;[3] the decision to build had liturgical and ceremonial consequences. The present basilica, the third to be put up on the site, was begun in 1063

I am grateful to the British Academy for the award of a Research Readership during the years 1996–98, and to the University of Cambridge and King's College for their continued support.

[1] E. Muir, 'The Doge as *primus inter pares*: Interregnum Rites in Early Sixteenth-Century Venice', in S. Bertelli and G. Ramakus (eds.), *Essays Presented to Myron P. Gilmore*, 2 vols. (Florence, 1978), vol. I, pp. 145–60; see also E. Muir, *Civic Ritual in Renaissance Venice* (Princeton, 1981).

[2] O. Demus, *The Mosaics of San Marco in Venice*, 4 vols. (Chicago, 1984), vol. I, pp. 65–9.

[3] M. Agazzi, *Platea Sancti Marci* (Venice, 1991), p. 13.

but was not finally consecrated until 1094. Many details of the external decoration, including columns of marble and porphyry, figured reliefs and the four horses placed above the main portico, came from the shiploads of trophies brought to Venice after the conquest of Constantinople during the Fourth Crusade.[4] The south façade is particularly rich in triumphal motifs including the so-called 'Pillars of Acre', the famed porphyry tetrachs and the Pietra del Bando from which official proclamations were made. These spoils constitute an impressive ensemble, a reminder that the main entrance to the square throughout the Middle Ages was from the lagoon itself, and that this façade was the first part of the basilica to be seen. More importantly, it also draws attention to the fact that the south door, framed by the 'Pillars of Acre', was, before it was closed off by the construction of the Cappella Zen, the main entrance to the basilica from the doge's palace. As such it was possibly an important juncture in the ceremonial route followed by the doge on important occasions. The pillars, believed at the time to have come from the Holy Land, formed part of a symbolic interpretation of the basilica into the New Jerusalem.[5] This parallel, expressed through architectural and decorative detail, was also incorporated into ritualistic practice, principally through the Easter morning ceremonies in St Mark's when the doge processed to the Easter Sepulchre in the basilica.[6] There the 'Quem queritis' dialogue was sung according to a local practice, determined by the participation of the doge as principal witness to the Resurrection, and the role of San Marco as both private chapel and state church, the 'sacral, political and economic centre of the empire'.[7]

These interrelated functions are made even more explicit in the main western façade, where the iconography of the scriptural reliefs follows a carefully planned scheme. It serves not only as a visual preface to the interior, but also as a magisterial expression of dominion achieved through the display of trophies and the images of local saints, crucially punctuated by the sculptural programme of the Last Judgement. In something of a minor key the incorporation of the virtues provides a religious and ethical element, while the introduction of the labours and the months serves to emphasise the importance of civic duty. The six plaques which sit in the spandrels are a mixture of old and new. Three come from Constantinople, while the remaining three were carved as matching pieces in Venice. As a series they make constant reference to the origins of Venice, through images of the Archangel Gabriel and the Virgin (and so to the myth of the city's foundation on Ascension Day), and to the two warrior-saints George and Demetrius.[8] It has been argued that this rich iconographical mixture of elements from both popular and learned traditions would have been understood, if only in part, by a wide audience.[9]

During the second half of the twelfth century, while the third and final church was being built, the area around San Marco began to take on a more formal appearance. By this date the space immediately surrounding the church included a tower, originally built

[4] Demus, *The Mosaics*, vol. I, pp. 1–17.
[5] M. Vickers, 'Wandering Stones: Venice, Constantinople and Athens', in K.-L. Selig and E. Sears (eds.), *The Verbal and the Visual: Essays in Honor of William Sebastian Hecksher* (New York, 1990), pp. 225–47.
[6] S. Rankin, 'From Liturgical Ceremony to Public Ritual: "Quem queritis" at St Mark's', in G. Cattin (ed.), *Da Bisanzio a San Marco* (Venice, 1997), pp. 137–91.   [7] Muir, *Civic Ritual*, p. 132.
[8] O. Demus, 'La decorazione scultorea duecentesca delle facciate', in *Le sculture esterne di San Marco* (Milan, 1995), pp. 12–23.
[9] A. Niero, 'Simbologia dotta e popolare nelle sculture esterne', in B. Bertoli (ed.), *La basilica di San Marco, arte e simbologia* (Venice, 1993), pp. 125–48.

as a fortification but subsequently transformed into a campanile, a hospice for pilgrims and the doge's palace itself. The enlargement of the orchard in front of San Marco brought to the area to the west a new sense of spaciousness and order; it involved filling in a narrow canal which originally ran across the middle of the present piazza, and the demolition of the church of San Geminiano. With these changes San Marco became, for the first time, the focal point of what was now a genuine piazza, which functioned as an imposing forecourt to the church to which it was both visually and ceremonially connected.[10] Its total area, which has been calculated at 12,000 square metres, made the piazza and piazzetta together larger than any of the mainland squares, even those of Bologna or Siena. Finally paved in 1266, the new ensemble was now complete. Further changes made in the course of the sixteenth century not only amplified it but also made it more scenographic: the basilica was now more centrally located along the eastern side of the square and the campanile became a more obviously free-standing structure. Until the end of the Republic it served as the main theatre for religious and civic ritual in Venice, for the processions and ceremonies that marked the annual calendar, as well as victories, treaties, the election of the doge and other public events. As one of the earliest central piazzas in Italy, it has been construed as marking the transition to a less feudal style of government.[11]

The appearance of the Piazza San Marco at the beginning of the sixteenth century is shown in two famous views of more or less the same date: Gentile Bellini's painting of 1496 and Jacopo de' Barbari's detailed bird's-eye view of the city published in 1500. The latter shows, on both the north and south sides of the piazza, a mixture of buildings of different periods and styles – gothic, Romanesque and fifteenth-century – united by the porticoes which had been such a feature of the area since the space had been enlarged in the twelfth century.[12] With one exception, this was how the square looked until Jacopo Sansovino's neo-Vitruvian remodelling of the piazza began in the 1530s, the exception being the remodelling of the north side of the square by Bartolommeo Bon, clearly visible in Bellini's painting and even more completely shown in de' Barbari's woodcut.[13] Bon's building, sometimes described as prosaic and even anachronistic, deliberately enforces a sense of continuity with Venetian traditions and institutions.[14]

Sansovino's vision was different. He was appointed *proto* to the procurators in 1529, with responsibility for the construction and maintenance of San Marco and the buildings in the piazza and the piazzetta, and in consequence became architect to the wealthiest patrons of new building works in the city, the procurators of St Mark. According to legend, it was the construction and decoration of the ducal church as a repository for the sacred relics of St Mark that had originally led to the establishment of the post of procurator; one of the most ancient in the Venetian constitution, it was conferred for life. At an early stage the holder was the doge's nominee, but during the first half of the thirteenth century the procurator was made responsible to the Great Council, which also assumed the power of election. This important change in the constitutional arrangements is a clear indication of the changing nature of the office which in the mean-

---

[10] J. Schulz, 'Urbanism in Medieval Venice', in A. Molho (ed.), *City States in Classical Antiquity and Medieval Italy* (Stuttgart, 1991), pp. 432–7.   [11] Agazzi, *Platea Sancti Marci*, p. 145.

[12] J. Schulz, 'J. de Barbari's View of Venice', *Art Bulletin* 60 (1978), pp. 425–74.

[13] *Ibid.*; P. F. Brown, *Venetian Narrative Painting in the Age of Carpaccio* (New Haven and London, 1988), pp. 144–52.

[14] M. Tafuri, '*Memoria et Prudentia*: Mentalità patrizie e res aedificatoria', in M. Tafuri (ed.), *Venezia e il Rinascimento: Religione, scienza, architettura* (Turin, 1985), pp. 10–11.

time, largely because of bequests, had grown into the most important financial authority of the state; his responsibilities now included those of maintaining a depository for
the specie of both the commune and of individual citizens, of administering estates and
perpetual trusts and of running a lending bank.[15] The number of procurators was
increased; from the moment when they had first been responsible to the Great Council,
the potential had existed for curtailing ducal jurisdiction over the affairs of the basilica.
Henceforward it was not the ecclesiastical authorities that provided the ultimate check
in the affairs of San Marco, of which the doge was both *patronus* and *gubernator*, but a
civic magistracy which had gradually evolved into one of the most powerful offices of the
Venetian state.

From the beginning of their history the procurators had made decisions of artistic
importance. It was the procurators who chose the *proto*, the procurators who supervised
the mosaic decorations of the interior of the church, and the procurators who chose the
officials who administered the liturgy within it except for the primicerio (a senior eccle-
siastic who was appointed by the doge); these included not only the clerics but also the
organists and the *maestro di cappella*. Involvement in the operations of the liturgy inside
the basilica extended to the appointment of singers and canons. The early development
of the procuratorship from its original dual role of doge's deputy and guardian of San
Marco, is paralleled by the transformation of the church itself from the private chapel of
the doge to that of the state church of Venice. This transformation, which inevitably
shaped artistic decisions of all kinds, is reflected in the character and iconography of the
mosaics as they were executed from the late twelfth century onwards; in the architectural developments in the piazza and the piazzetta during the fifteenth and sixteenth centuries, and in the development of ceremonial arrangements that were evolved for use
both inside and outside San Marco during the same period. In this sense the evolution
of music and ritual, as it gradually passed from the private liturgical sphere to the public
one, was just one element in a lengthy process of civic self-fashioning which can be
charted in detail from the thirteenth century onwards, and in which the procurators were
the main agents.

The wholesale remodelling of the piazza, the piazzetta and their surrounding buildings marks a crucial moment in this process, which also involved a considerable enlargement of the main ceremonial space as well as new construction (see Illustration 3.1).
Sansovino's task was not merely to complete Bon's building, but rather to inaugurate the
first phase of a grandiose scheme to line the remaining sides of the piazza and the piazzetta together with the eastern end of the *molo* with new ones in the classical style.[16]
According to the account of Sansovino's son Francesco, his father had realised that the
piazza was the most noble public space of any Italian city, and had resolved that it should
be dignified with buildings that, following ancient practice, were to be adorned with Doric
and Ionian orders 'full of columns, friezes and cornices'.[17] The effect was to superimpose
an evocation of ancient Rome upon the existing Byzantine elements, whose meaning had
been strengthened by the neo-Byzantine revival of the late fifteenth and early sixteenth

[15] R. C. Mueller, 'The Procurators of San Marco in the Thirteenth and Fourteenth Centuries: a Study of the
Office as a Financial Trust', *Studi veneziani* 13 (1971), pp. 105–220.

[16] D. Howard, *Jacopo Sansovino: Architecture and Patronage in Renaissance Venice* (New Haven and London,
1987), pp. 8–61.

[17] For discussion see Howard, *Jacopo Sansovino*, pp. 10–16, and J. Onians, *Bearers of Meaning: the Classical
Orders in Antiquity, the Middle Ages, and the Renaissance* (Princeton, 1988).

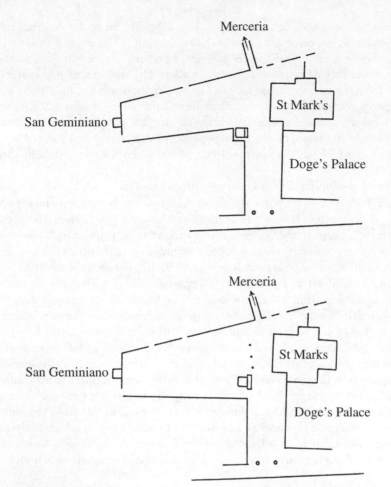

3.1   Sketch-plans of Piazza San Marco at the beginning and end of the sixteenth
       century; D. Howard, *Jacopo Sansovino: Architecture and Patronage in
       Renaissance Venice* (New Haven and London, 1987), p. 11. Reproduced by
       permission.

centuries. In the years after the League of Cambrai, the notion of Venice as *altera Roma*
became a noticeable presence in the 'myth of Venice'.[18] By the time of his death, Sansovino
had completed the loggetta at the foot of the campanile, the library facing the ducal palace
and the mint. His overall conception has been seen not only as a conscious attempt to
evolve, in architectural terms, the 'myth of Venice' through the use of a distinctive classicising language, but also as a courageous reinterpretation, on a monumental scale, of the
typology of the ancient Roman forum as described by Vitruvius. As such it has been
placed at the centre of a sustained *renovatio urbis*, inaugurated during the dogeship of

---

[18] J. Ackerman, 'Observations on Renaissance Church Planning in Venice and Florence, 1470–1570', in
Florence and Venice: Comparisons and Relations, 2 vols. (Florence, 1979–80), vol. II, pp. 291–2; M. Tafuri,
'*Pietas repubblicana*, neobizantismo e umanesimo. San Salvador: un tempio *in visceribus urbis*', in Tafuri,
Venezia e il Rinascimento, pp. 24–78.
[19] M. Tafuri (ed.), '*Renovatio urbis*': *Venezia nell' età di Andrea Gritti (1523–1538)* (Rome, 1984).

Andrea Gritti (1523–38) and carried out with his active encouragement.[19] It was during this period that Adrian Willaert was employed, presumably with the intention of extending the general policy of enhancement to the functions of the *cappella marciana* and of the repertory that they performed.[20] In relation to Vespers in particular, Willaert's development of the *cori spezzati* style was based on the existing *alternatim* tradition in which the music of the liturgy was provided by the canons, some chanting and the remainder singing simple improvised polyphony.[21] The result, monumentalised in Willaert's contribution to the first published collection of double-choir psalms, *I salmi appertinenti alli vesperi . . . a uno et a duoi chori* (Venice, 1550), may be thought of as a classicising of ancient tradition, an equivalent in music to Sansovino's architecture.

The function of the piazzetta as a ceremonial gateway to the square, and to the official buildings which surrounded it, is proclaimed by the two marble columns which stand at its southern edge; on one stands a statue of St Theodore, the first patron of the city, on the other the winged lion of St Mark, his successor. At the other end of the piazzetta stood the loggetta, a meeting place for patricians called to the square on government business. This function was also carried over to Sansovino's new structure, which was also used by the procurators for transactions relating to the nearby shops and markets which lay under their jurisdiction. With its unmistakable invocation of the rhetoric of the classical triumphal arch, Sansovino's loggetta provided a more dignified setting for these activities. It has been described as 'the most complete surviving visual representation of the "myth of Venice" – that is, the Venetian view of their own state as the perfect republic'.[22] The loggetta emphatically proclaims both patrician control of the square and its surrounding buildings as well as the authority of the procurators. More pragmatically the terrace provided a vantage-point from which the processions in the square beneath, frequent by the end of the sixteenth century, could be viewed.

The heightened theatricality with which state processions, with all their ritual, ceremonial, liturgical and musical components, could be organised in the piazza had been almost immediately realised as a consequence of the decision to demolish the church of San Geminiano in the late twelfth century. According to Francesco Sansovino, this aroused papal displeasure which was only finally assuaged by contrition and a series of compensatory measures. These included the undertaking that an annual ducal procession (*andata*) was to be made in perpetuity to a new church of San Geminiano, to be built further to the west.[23] Whether or not Sansovino's anecdote is credible, state ceremonial life must have taken on a new dimension as a result of this early remodelling of the piazza. Certainly the Easter morning procession described by Martin da Canal in the thirteenth century is an early forebear of the ducal *andata* illustrated as described in ceremony books and elsewhere from the sixteenth century onwards. Canal describes the order of procession, which included the doge, the primicerio of St Mark's and the canons of the basilica as well as a number of patricians splendidly dressed, and notes the presence of the *trionfi*. One of these, the six silver trumpeters, would have been an important element in the soundscape; Canal also mentions cymbal players, who are not recorded in the visual and documentary records of the *andata* in its sixteenth-century form. Having

[20] For the appointment see G. Ongaro, 'Willaert, Gritti e Luppato: miti e realtà', *Studi musicali* 17 (1988), pp. 55–70.

[21] I. Fenlon, 'Strangers in Paradise: Dutchmen at St Mark's in 1525', in P. Dalla Vecchia and D. Restani (eds.), *Trent'anni di ricerche musicologiche: Studi in onore di F. Alberto Gallo* (Rome, 1996), pp. 323–37.

[22] Howard, *Jacopo Sansovino*, p. 34.

[23] Jacopo Sansovino, *Venetia città nobilissima e singolare . . . con nove e copiose aggiunte di D. Giustinian Martinioni* (Venice, 1663), pp. 496–7.

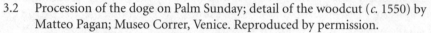

3.2   Procession of the doge on Palm Sunday; detail of the woodcut (*c.* 1550) by
Matteo Pagan; Museo Correr, Venice. Reproduced by permission.

walked to the church of San Geminiano the procession then returned to the basilica. In
the middle of the square all came to a halt, and three of the canons of St Mark's sang a
responsory. On arriving inside the basilica there was more chanting by the canons, and
then three of their number began an extended version of the *Laudes regiae*. Mass, celebrated by the primicerio, brought the proceedings to an end. According to Canal, this
basic formula was followed in ducal processions on major feast days.[24]

By the sixteenth century the *andata*, which in its most elaborate version included
all the principal office-holders together with some minor officials, the ambassadors of
foreign states, the canons of San Marco, the Patriarch and, at the physical core of the procession, the doge himself, had become the most elaborate processional form in Venice.
As such it became an image of the city itself, through Matteo Pagan's monumental series
of eight woodcuts (see Illustration 3.2) as well as in maps and engravings of scenes from
Venetian life, presumably produced for pilgrims, tourists and bibliophiles rather than for
Venetians (see Illustration 3.3).[25] While the hierarchical ordering of the procession was
fixed, the personnel were constantly changing; all the individuals who walked did so as
the temporary holders of official positions. In addition to these the *andata* also displayed
the ducal *trionfi*. As Sansovino remarked, 'When walking in triumph and with solemnity,
[the doge] carries with him, among others, seven things worthy of consideration, which
show us his pre-eminence. These things he received from the first princes of the world,
that is, from the popes and emperors.'[26] This refers to the gift of symbolic objects including eight banners, six silver trumpets, a candle, a cushion, a faldstool and a sword, to
Doge Sebastiano Ziani by Pope Alexander III, during his famous visit to Venice to seek
reconciliation with Federico Barbarossa in 1177. Ziani's determination on this occasion

---

[24] A. Limentani (ed.), *Martin da Canal: Les escritoires de Venise, Cronaca veneziana in lingua francese dalle
origini al 1275* (Florence, 1972), pp. 246–8. For the *Laudes regiae*, which the Venetians imposed on their over-
seas possession as an expression of allegiance, see E. H. Kantorowitz, *Laudes regiae* (Berkeley and Los
Angeles, 1946), pp. 147–56. A three-part setting by Hugo de Lantins, probably written for the coronation of
Francesco Foscari, survives; see G. Fasoli, 'Liturgia e ceremoniale ducale', in A. Pertusi (ed.), *Venezia e il
Levante fino al secolo XV*, 3 vols. (Florence, 1983), vol. I, pp. 261–95, and F. A. Gallo (ed.), *Il codice musicale
2216 della Biblioteca Universitaria di Bologna*, 2 vols. (Bologna, 1968–70), vol. I, pp. 60–1.

[25] The entire series is reproduced in Muir, *Civic Ritual*, pp. 193–7.

[26] Sansovino, *Venetia città nobilissima*, p. 479.

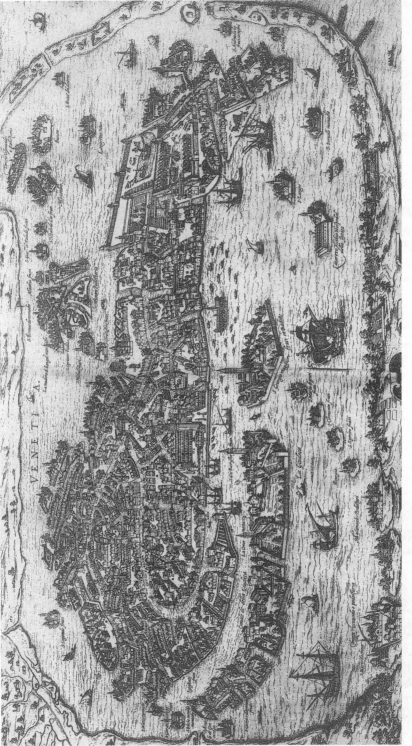

3.3　Map of Venice; G. Bruin, S. Novellanus, F. Hogenburgius, *Civitates orbis terrarum Liber primus* (Cologne, 1582), plate 43.

to protect the pope and to mediate in the dispute was rewarded by the gift of *trionfi*, each of which came to be interpreted as the symbol of a distinct ducal privilege. These seven gifts, which as Sansovino recognised empowered the doge as a princely equal of popes and emperors, were carried in the ducal procession on all the major occasions in the ceremonial year, which by the end of the sixteenth century numbered about forty. They were both historical relics and emblems of status and authority.[27] The canons of San Marco also walked in the ducal procession and it was through their participation that the *patriarchino*, the rite peculiar to San Marco, could be transposed from one place to another.[28] In consequence, when Mass was celebrated as part of the ducal procession to a particular church or convent, it was done so according to a liturgy that since 1456 had been exclusively associated with the basilica. In this symbolic practice the use of the *patriarchino*, elaborated by the *cappella marciana*, served to emphasise the doge's authority; in effect the *patriarchino* was a liturgy of state.[29]

Although the *andata* was both exclusive and hierarchical,[30] its basic arrangement was supplemented on occasion by the addition of other social groupings such as the *scuole grandi* (confraternities), the trade guilds or even a particular parish; this broadened participation, and was presumably intended to underline the allegedly harmonious corporate organisation of the city, another basic underpinning of the myth of Venice. While the *scuole* represented the notion of communal devotion and charity, the guilds symbolised the complementary idea of commerce as the foundation of civic concord.[31] At the same time the *andata* often expanded its frame of reference by including various additional musical and religious elements. On many of the more important feasts in the Venetian calendar, the *cappella marciana* walked in the *andata*, so did the singers employed by some of the wealthier *scuole*, as their participation in the public ceremonial of the city became even more pronounced in the course of the sixteenth century.[32] In Bellini's painting showing the Scuola di San Giovanni carrying their prized relic of the True Cross in the procession on the feast day of St Mark, a group of five singers is shown accompanied by an instrumental ensemble.[33] In expanded form, these processions amplified the liturgy outside the basilica by making use not only of the central civic space of the city, but other areas as well. In this way, civic and liturgical acts which were usually associated with ducal authority were able to broaden their audience, which could participate not only passively (by observing) but also actively by walking in the procession, chanting litanies and singing laude. At the same time, the wide geographical dispersal of the *andata* knitted together *sestieri* (districts into which the city was divided for administrative purposes), parishes, *scuole* and guilds in a closely woven fabric of religious and civic observance.

[27] A. Pertusi, 'Quaedam regalia insignia: Ricerche sulle insegne del potere ducale a Venezia durante il Medioevo', *Studi veneziani* 7 (1965), pp. 3–123; Muir, *Civic Ritual*, pp. 103–19, 204–11.

[28] G. Fasoli, 'Liturgia e ceremoniale ducale', pp. 261–95.

[29] G. Cattin, *Musica e liturgia a San Marco. Testi e melodie per la liturgia delle ore dal XII al XVII secolo. Dal graduale tropato del duecento ai graduali cinquecenteschi*, 4 vols. (Venice, 1990–92).

[30] For a discussion, arguably too schematic, see E. Muir, 'Images of Power: Art and Pageantry in Renaissance Venice', *American Historical Review* 84 (1979), pp. 16–52; Muir, *Civic Ritual*, pp. 189–204.

[31] Tafuri, '*Memoria et Prudentia*', pp. 1–3.

[32] For the *cappella*, see J. H. Moore, *Vespers at St Mark's: Music of Alessandro Grandi, Giovanni Rovetta and Francesco Cavalli*, 2 vols. (Ann Arbor, 1981), vol. I, p. 184; for the *scuole*, see J. Glixon, '"Far una bella processione": Music and Public Ceremony at the Venetian Scuole Grandi', in T. Charteris (ed.), *Altro Polo: Essays on Italian Music in the Cinquecento* (Sydney, 1990), pp. 190–220.

[33] Brown, *Venetian Narrative Painting*; H. M. Brown, 'On Gentile Bellini's Processione in San Marco (1496)', in *International Musicological Society Congress Report XII* (Berkeley, 1977), pp. 649–58.

Venetian ceremonies were also able to incorporate a wider audience, such as the visitors for whom the city itself was a place of pilgrimage as well as the principal European staging-post on the journey to and from the Holy Land. The Venetian celebration of Corpus Christi is perhaps the most spectacular example of state appropriation of an event of universal spiritual significance, for a mixture of economic, political and devotional reasons.[34] On this occasion pilgrims joined in the traditional procession in the piazza and each one, accompanied by a member of the Venetian nobility, carried a candle which was subsequently placed in front of the Holy Sepulchre in Jerusalem.[35] The result, characteristic of much Venetian ritual, transformed the universally Christian into the specifically Venetian, by appropriating a feast, celebrated with public processions throughout Catholic Europe, and investing it with local significance. In this process the city became a psychological and symbolic extension of the sacred space of Jerusalem itself, and the ceremonies in the piazza and the basilica, carried out in the presence of the doge, an official benediction of a great Catholic enterprise. The Corpus Christi procession is a reminder that while the motivations for Venetian civic and religious rituals were complex and interlocking, the audience for them was certainly not uniform, but expanded and contracted for different occasions.

It is equally characteristic that the most important ceremonies marking a change of doge – funerals and coronations – were also public occasions.[36] Although predominantly religious in form and content, both contained distinctive civic elements. They were also public and were centred on the basilica, the doge's palace and the surrounding ceremonial spaces. On the death of a doge, nine doubles, sounded from the bell-tower of St Mark's, were taken up by all the *scuole* and churches of the city. Bells were the common coinage of the city soundscape. This time not only did they announce the death to the population, but they also warned the members of the Great Council, the sovereign assembly of the Republic, that the election of a new doge was about to begin. Having accompanied the corpse to the head of the Scala dei Giganti, that is to the very spot where the deceased doge had taken his oath and been crowned, the Signoria retired to continue the election; its absence from both the Requiem in the basilica and the funeral procession which took place prior to interment is a further symbolic underlining of the principle of continuity, 'In segno', as Sanudo put it, 'si è morto il Doxe non è morta la Signoria'.[37] This moment also marked the passing of the funeral rites from the domain of religious and government elites into a more public sphere. The long procession which now escorted the body around St Mark's Square included not only members of the family but also all the *scuole piccole*, the monastic orders and the nine clerical congregations of the city. All of the *scuole grandi* walked in their normal positions in the procession except one, usually that of which the doge had been a member, which walked behind the body carried by a contingent of sailors from the Arsenal. In front of the basilica the procession

---

[34] For the general phenomenon of the Corpus Christi procession see M. Rubin, *Corpus Christi: The Eucharist in Late Medieval Culture* (Cambridge, 1991), pp. 243–71.

[35] Muir, *Civic Ritual*, pp. 223–30; I. Fenlon, 'Music, Ceremony and Self-Identity in Renaissance Venice', in F. Passadore and F. Rossi (eds.), *La cappella musicale di San Marco nell' età moderna* (Venice, 1998), pp. 8–9.

[36] The most important contemporary accounts of dogal coronations and funerals are those recorded at the end of the sixteenth century in ASV, Collegio Ceremoniali I and II, and that drawn up for the *maestro del cerimoniale* in BNM Lat. III–172 (2276), fols. 67v–71r. See also Marino Sanudo, *I diarii*, R. Fulin *et al.* (eds.), 58 vols. (Venice, 1879–1903), vol. XXX, cols. 479–90, and vol. XXXI, cols. 7–11. For modern accounts see A. Da Mosto, *I Dogi di Venezia con particolare riguardo alle loro tombe* (Venice, 1939), pp. xxiii–xxxi; Muir, 'The Doge as *primus inter pares*'. [37] Sanudo, *I diarii*, vol. XXX, col. 389.

stopped and the corpse was raised on its stretcher nine times, while the members of the accompanying Scuola Grande cried out 'Iddio habbia misericordia!' and the bells rang out nine doubles. The procession then continued through the narrow streets to the church where the burial was to take place, in the sixteenth century usually one of the two great mendicant churches. Just as the breaking of the insignia of ducal power that took place on death represented the end of political authority,[38] so too these rites, in which the body was accompanied by members of the three Venetian 'estates', symbolised the severance of the man from his office.

The investiture ceremonies which followed the election of a doge, while presenting him in an almost monarchical light, also emphasised his obligation to follow the duties and restrictions on his power laid down by a Republican patriciate. These too were public. Entering San Marco by the south door leading from the ducal palace, the doge-elect mounted the *pulpitum magnum*, in front of the iconostasis and from there was presented to the crowds massed below in the nave by the senior elector. The formula used stresses the role of the state in the election of the new doge, 'the virtues and worthy condition of whom are such that, through divine grace, he will fervently strive for the good and conservation of the state, and every public as well as private interest', a reminder of his historical and legal obligations.[39] After this the doge, having made a brief statement promising justice, plenty, peace and the protection of the Venetian empire, descended from the pulpit and, having walked the short distance to the high altar, where he was embraced by the primicerio, kissed it. This simple gesture, normally made by the celebrant at both the beginning and the end of Mass, is a reminder of the priestly aspects of the dogeship. Facing the primicerio and placing his hand on a copy of the Gospels, the doge-elect then swore an oath to protect the honour and patrimony of San Marco 'bona fide et sine fraude', a direct reference not only to the basilica's substantial holdings of land, property and trusts, but also to the doge's fundamental traditional role as the principal guardian of the Evangelist's relics. It was at this moment in the Mass that the *Oration di San Marco*, of which a number of large-scale musical settings by the Gabrielis and other composers working in Venice have survived, was performed.[40] Then, his final act in the investiture, the primicerio took one of the eight red ceremonial banners bearing the image of the Lion of St Mark that were normally carried at the head of the ducal *andata* from the admiral of the Arsenal, and presented it to the doge-elect, saying 'We consign to your Serenity the banner of Saint Mark as a sign of true and perpetual dogeship', to which the doge-elect replied 'I accept' and then passed the standard back to the admiral of the Arsenal. At the entrance to the choir, the doge-elect stepped into a portable wooden pulpit together with two male members of his family and the admiral of the Arsenal, who was still holding the ceremonial standard of St Mark. Carried aloft by a squad of sailors from the Arsenal, they moved through the square throwing coins to the crowd. In this way the liturgical ceremonies with their civic insertions were seamlessly joined to popular celebration (see Illustration 3.4).

The final phase of the investiture ceremonies, for a more elite public, was the coronation itself, which took place in the loggia at the top of the Scala dei Giganti, framed

---

[38] Muir, 'The Doge as *primus inter pares*', pp. 147–8.

[39] ASV, Collegio Ceremoniale I, fol. iv. MCV, Cicogna PD 381b (unfoliated). 'Pietro Lando' reports a different version in which the doge-elect is presented with the words 'we have elected a doge and hope that he is pleasing to you', to which the reply was shouted 'Marco! Marco!'

[40] Fenlon, 'Music, Ceremony and Self-Identity', pp. 13–14.

3.4   The election of the doge, from Giacomo Franco, *Habiti d'huomini* (1609).

by Sansovino's giant marble statues of Mars and Neptune. First a written declaration (*promissione ducale*) was handed by the Grand Chancellor to the oldest councillor, and the doge-elect publicly swore to obey its provisions.[41] To the sound of church bells, drums and the noise of the crowds, the white cloth skullcap (*camauro*) was placed on his head by the youngest ducal councillor, then the oldest, pronouncing the formula 'Accipe coronam Ducatus Venetiarum' ('accept the ducal crown of Venice'), crowned the doge with the ceremonial *corno*. It was believed that the unusual form of this distinctive piece of headgear was intended to parallel the papal mitre, while that of the *camauro* was, according to Sansovino, 'quasi come insegna di persona sacra';[42] here, as in so much else relating to the figure of the doge, the analogy between the successor of St Mark and that of St Peter is made explicit. To the applause of the onlookers the doge then moved to the third arch of the loggia of the ducal palace where, having called for silence, he repeated the promises that he had made earlier in the basilica before entering the palace itself and going, still accompanied by the banner of St Mark, to the Sala dei Pioveghi where he took his place for the first time on the ducal throne. To the assembled company he then repeated his election promises for the third time. In following this sequence of ceremonial procedures, the coronation moved from public and religious rituals in the basilica, to political and elite ones in the doge's palace, an inversion of the symbolic structure of the funeral which had preceded it a few days earlier.

A more comprehensive use of the city and its ceremonial spaces occurred on other occasions, when the topographical variety of the city became a feature of spectacle. This was the case in 1571, with the celebrations that marked the victory of the Holy League over the Turks at Lepanto.[43] In a society which had assiduously cultivated the image of its special relationship with the Almighty, religious and devotional practices naturally formed an important element of the official arrangements. Two days after news of the victory had arrived, High Mass was sung in San Marco in the presence of the doge and signoria festally dressed for the occasion. This was accompanied by music, described by Rocco Benedetti as 'concerti divinissimi' in which the two organs of the basilica played together with voices and instruments, an unambiguous reference to the tradition of music for *cori spezzati*. Mass was followed by a procession around the square in which all the clergy of the city participated and the basilica's prized processional cross was carried by the doge, a clear sign of gratitude for Divine benevolence.[44] This was the first event in a cycle of religious occasions which included the official Requiem Mass for the Venetian dead, sung in San Marco in the presence of the doge and senate, at which the public orator, Giovanni Battista Rasario, delivered a Latin address in praise of all those who had fought for the glory of God and the 'universal liberty of the Christian Republic'.[45]

The passage from official rituals to public celebration was accompanied by a change from strictly liturgical ceremonies to popular modes which incorporated different orders of visual and musical experience. The Germans, for example, decorated

---

[41] For these documents see G. Musatti, *Storia della promissione ducale* (Padua, 1888).

[42] Sansovino, *Venetia città nobilissima*, p. 471.

[43] E. H. Gombrich, 'Celebrations in Venice of the Holy League and of the Victory of Lepanto', in *Studies in Renaissance and Baroque Art Presented to Anthony Blunt on his Sixtieth Birthday* (London, 1967), pp. 62–8; I. Fenlon, 'Lepanto: the Arts of Celebration in Renaissance Venice', *Proceedings of the British Academy* 63 (1987), pp. 210–36.

[44] Benedetti, *Ragguaglio delle allegrezze fatte in Venetia per la felice vittoria* (Venice, 1571), fol. [A4]-[A4]v.

[45] Benedetti, *Ragguaglio*, fol. B [1]; ASV, Collegio Ceremoniale I, fols. 40–41. For the text of the address see G. B. Rasario, *De Victoria Christianorum ad Echinadas oratio* (Venice, 1571).

their Fondaco with tapestries and then for three successive nights mounted firework displays accompanied by music; while the illuminated courtyard echoed to the raucous sound of drums, fifes and trumpets, more decorous ensembles played in pergolas.[46] Following this example, different parts of the community competed to produce the most impressive celebrations. Another three-day affair, this time organised by the drapers' guild, was concentrated in the area around the Rialto bridge and in the square in front of the church of San Giacomo di Rialto. Here too different kinds of music were played ranging from the 'celestial harmony' of sedate ensembles to the din of drums, piffari and the inevitable 'trombe squarciate'; the latter, according to one account, were intended to evoke the sounds of battle.[47] This sense of catering for different if overlapping audiences also extended to the visual. Alongside arms and other enemy trophies captured in battle, shops displayed works by Giovanni Bellini, Giorgione, Raphael, Pordenone, Sebastiano del Piombo, Titian and Bassano among others.[48]

The Rialto area, while substantially devoted to trade, also functioned as a secondary area of government; a number of state offices were located there, and two of the churches close to the market came under the *ius patronatus* of the doge and were the subjects of dogal *andate*.[49] One, San Giacomo, had come under the doge's jurisdiction as a result of a direct appeal by Andrea Gritti to Clement VII; its subsequent incorporation into Gritti's *renovatio* lent authority to the piazza in front of the church, in part derived from its own long history as the oldest church in Venice, and in part from its proximity to the Colonna del Bando from which official decrees were made.[50] During the celebrations organised around the Rialto bridge by the drapers' guild, each day began with a High Mass, 'con musiche rari', celebrated on temporary staging in front of the church. Later in the day clergy, singers and members of the guild walked in procession accompanied by drums, piffari and 'trombe squarciate', and in the evening sung Vespers were held.[51] There could hardly be a more explicit demonstration of the unity of commerce and religion in the affairs of the perfect Christian republic.

At dusk the area took on an almost magical appearance. To illuminate the scene candles were placed on the bridge and along the sides of the square, on balustrades and in windows, on the benches in front of the shops and under the porticoes. Circulating among the crowds, masked revellers strummed lutes and sang. From under the arcades other music could be heard, played so well, said Benedetti, that it was possible to believe that one had been listening to the Muses.[52] Elsewhere in the crowded lanes around the bridge, groups put on classical 'triumphs' in imitation of Scipio Africano or the Roman emperors. The example of the drapers was followed by the jewellers and goldsmiths and then by the Tuscan merchants and other trade guilds.[53]

The main unofficial celebration of the victory at Lepanto took place on Carnival Sunday, 1572, with a *mascherata*. According to the undated and crudely printed pamphlet which provides all that is known about the event,[54] 340 people took part, including a

[46] Benedetti, *Ragguaglio*, fol. [B2]–[B2]v; BNM MS It VII. 519 (8438), fol. 333v; MS It VII. 5, p. 31 and MS It VII. 73 (8265), fol. 395v.   [47] BNM MS It VII. 73 (8265), fol. 396r–v.

[48] Benedetti, *Ragguaglio*, fol. [B2]v.   [49] Sansovino, *Venetia città nobilissima*, pp. 186–7, 362–4.

[50] D. Calabi and P. Morachiello, *Rialto: le fabbriche e il Ponte 1514–1591* (Turin, 1987), and the same authors' 'Rialto, 1514–1538: Gli anni della ricostruzione', in Tafuri (ed.), *'Renovatio urbis'*, pp. 291–334.

[51] BNM MS It VII. 73 (8265), fol. 396r–v; Benedetti, *Ragguaglio*, fol. [B3].

[52] Benedetti, *Ragguaglio*, fol. [B3]v.   [53] *Ibid.*, MCV 1897 (unfoliated).

[54] *Ordine et dechiaratione di tutta le mascherata fatta nella citta di Venetia la domenica di carnvale MDLXXI per le gloriosa vittoria contra Turchi* (Venice, 1572).

large number of musicians and many costumed as Turkish slaves. Eighty large torches were carried and thirteen triumphant displays were mounted. Elaborate music seems to have been a particular feature of the procession and, as the anonymous pamphleteer is keen to point out, some of the pieces performed had been specially composed for the occasion, presumably a reference to Andrea Gabrieli's involvement. Beginning from the church of the Madonna dell'Orto in the north of the city, this vast cavalcade gradually wound its way through the narrow streets and along the Merceria to St Mark's Square before moving on through the Campo Santo Stefano to finish at the church of San Samuele, close to the Grand Canal. Despite the superficial semblance of unity provided by the regular insertion of groups of Turkish prisoners, whose presence recalls classical Roman triumphs, the *mascherata* falls into two quite distinct segments. The first presents a simple political allegory celebrating the defeat of the Infidel; the second relies upon traditional Carnival themes. In common with the other public processions and the celebrations organised by the merchant communities, the Lepanto *mascherata* was both widely propagandistic and socially inclusive. Much of its effect was achieved by drawing upon a simple and traditional series of images accompanied by rousing and unsophisticated music. At the same time some of the more dignified elements operated on a different level; this is true for example of the initial group of five allegorical floats with which Gabrieli's music was associated.[55] With its rather obvious structural division into two thematically distinct parts, the *mascherata* of 1572 is a perfect example of the differentiated modes of celebration which are characteristic of Venetian public ritual. Like Carnival itself, the procession did not have a single meaning or purpose, but a variety of them.

At a more official level a decree from the Senate ordered that an annual *andata* be held from St Mark's Square to the church and convent of San Giustina, on whose feast day the battle had been fought. The *cappella marciana* walked in the procession, singing litanies and psalms along the route. At the church itself a solemn mass was celebrated with polyphony, by one of the canons of St Mark's, and the doge presented specially minted coins to the nuns. The procession then returned to the piazza where the *scuole* and all the clergy of the city passed in front of the doge, a symbolic action emphasising his personal authority over the ecclesiastical establishment.[56] It was through such means that the Venetians were reminded of the unity of church and state, placed under the patronage of St Mark and guided by the doge as his representative. As in other Venetian victory celebrations, the Santa Giustina *andata* provided the Republic with a double opportunity; to honour a saint and commemorate the dead and to strengthen social unity through communal displays of piety and patriotism.

The ceremonial city was revealed in quite different terms to distinguished visitors.[57] During the course of the sixteenth century, the formula for the reception of distinguished foreign dignitaries had become standardised, based around the central focus of a welcome by the doge at the confines of the lagoon, the main theatrical apparatus being the Bucintoro escorted by a flotilla of smaller craft. As in the case of Henry III's

---

[55] A. Gabrieli, *Madrigali et ricercari a quattro voci* (Venice, 1589); the identification of Gabrieli's music with the *mascherata* is made in A. Einstein, *The Italian Madrigal*, 3 vols. (Princeton, 1949), vol. II, pp. 523–5.

[56] Fenlon, 'Lepanto', pp. 226–7.

[57] P. F. Brown, 'Measured Friendship, Calculated Pomp: the Ceremonial Welcomes of the Venetian Republic', in B. Wisch and S. A. Munshower (eds.), *'All the World's a Stage . . .:' Art and Pageantry in the Renaissance and Baroque*, 2 vols. (Pennsylvania, 1990), vol. I, pp. 137–86.

entry in 1574, this ceremony had normally been preceded by a formal reception by a group of appointed senators as the visitor left one of the territories of the *terraferma*.[58] One commentator specifically remarks on the imposing vista of Venice seen by Henry from Marghera, a vision of a mythical city built upon the seas but safe from attacks by land or sea, a theatre of marvels waiting to be explored.[59] In this way the entry was symbolically choreographed so that the ceremonial route, the Venetian equivalent to an entry through the gates of a city, passed through a number of stages in which the city was gradually revealed. The first marked departure from the Veneto, while the second delineated the moment of arrival in the city proper, or rather at the outer edge of its territory. In this context San Niccolò del Lido and the area in front of it functioned as an extension of the Piazza San Marco and the basilica. For Henry III's visit this became literally true, since Andrea Palladio was commissioned to design two temporary structures on the island: a triumphal arch, through which the king, the doge and other dignitaries passed, and a loggia where a number of religious rituals took place. It was at San Niccolò that the principal functionaries of church and state, together with some of the main components of the Venetian ceremonial machine (including the *cappella marciana*), welcomed the visitor on to Venetian soil and so into the Venetian *civitas*. At the same time, this point of arrival provided the Republic with the opportunity to honour its distinguished guests while at the same time impressing observers with the virtues and power of the state through a spectacle of unusual beauty, theatrically enacted at the boundary of land and sea. From the Lido Henry made his triumphal entry into the city. It was at this moment that a dialogue madrigal to a Latin text was performed by the choir, though it must be doubted that any of the detail could be heard above the noise described by most commentators, as the air resounded to the sounds of trumpet calls, drums and church bells. In its overall structure, the scenography recalls the annual ritual of the *sensa*, when the doge symbolically married Venice to the Adriatic. In the following days the city, its political structure and its 'wonders' were gradually revealed through a calculated series of planned events which made use of the most significant focal points of Venetian public life, including the Rialto, the Arsenal, the basilica and the state rooms of the ducal palace.

Historians have often stressed the corporate nature of early modern Venice. While the patrician class gathered in their own family clans and did not marry outside their caste, the *cittadini* (citizen class) joined one of the six *scuole grandi*. For the rest of the population there were the two hundred or so *scuole piccole*, and the trade guilds. Cutting across these divisions, designated by class and occupation, was the topographical system of six *sestieri* and more than seventy parishes, both of which functioned as focal points of local identity. In the realm of civic and religious life, these interlocking structures provided a kaleidoscopic sequence of experiences from the ceremonial to the informal. In this context, Venetian identity was clearly not such a monochromatic or unified state of mind as official historiographers and the patrician proponents of the 'myth of Venice' would have liked posterity to believe. On the contrary, even with the community of Venetians living in this, the most cosmopolitan city in Europe, experiences of liturgy and

---

[58] For a general introduction to Henry III's entry see P. Nolhac and A Solerti, *Il viaggio in Italia di Enrico III re di Francia e le feste a Venezia, Ferrara, Mantova e Torino* (Turin, 1890); N. Ivanhoff, 'Henri III a Venise', *Gazette des Beaux-Arts* 80 (1972), pp. 313–30.

[59] P. Buccio, *Le coronationi di Polonia e di Francia del Christianiss. Rè Henrico III. Con le attioni et successi de' suoi viaggi . . .* (Padua, 1576), fol. 205; see also T. Porcacchi, *Le attioni d' Arrigo terzo re di Francia et quarto di Polonia descritte in dialogo* (Venice, 1574), fol. 20v.

ceremony varied greatly according to circumstance. Indeed, what is sometimes described as wholesale societal attachment to the ideals of the 'myth of Venice', that vision of the city as the perfect state expressed and re-enacted in spectacular ceremonial acts, may also have functioned as a way of asserting some measure of patrician control over the population of a city which certainly contained heretical and dissenting elements.[60] The devotional geography of Venice was critical to this process. In the years after the Council of Trent in particular, stability and continuity were achieved by the increased use of the city and its main spaces for the annual cycle of ceremonies and rituals, strengthened by the enhanced conception of Venice not only as the Perfect Republic but also as the City of God.

[60] For a detailed revisionist view of the 'myth of Venice', see J. Grubb, 'When Myths Lose Power: Four Decades of Venetian Historiography', *Journal of Modern History* 58 (1986), pp. 43–94.

CHAPTER FOUR

SECULAR MUSIC IN THE BURGH OF HADDINGTON, 1530–1640

JOHN J. MCGAVIN

Founded as a royal burgh in 1286, Haddington is situated about eighteen miles to the east of Edinburgh and suffered in times of war because of that proximity. During the period under review, it was culturally important first as the seat of various Catholic orders and then of the reformed Presbytery; it was located near to leading Catholic families like the Setons and had close ties with significant reformist intellectuals, such as its minister James Carmichael. It was, and had always been, the chief town of East Lothian. Despite this, it was a medium-sized, second-rank Scottish burgh, which dropped from fifth to thirteenth in the league of wealth based on burghal taxation.[1] It experienced a gradual decline in wealth relative to the capital city and it almost certainly had fewer than 4,000 inhabitants.[2] It benefited from a situation in the fertile arable plains of Lothian; had its own tidal harbour at Aberlady from which it traded with continental Europe, as far east as Danzig, and its own coal mine on the common land at nearby Gladsmuir. Its wool and cloth trade was significantly damaged by the English invasions of the mid-sixteenth century, and was replaced by trade in skins.[3] The urban community, whether figured civically or ecclesiastically, left a substantial body of records. The burgh records (1423–) detail the activities of the municipal administration. These are supplemented by Presbytery records (1587–) from the time when Haddington was one of the regional seats of the Kirk of Scotland, and by Haddington's own Kirk Session records (1629–).[4] These institutional witnesses are partial in both main senses of that word.

Record-keeping and the survival rate of the records were affected by floods and other disasters, including civil and national wars and religious enmity. Burgh and church institutions were also occasionally impelled to investigate failures of record-keeping caused by dilatoriness, age and other personal failings. The Haddington Presbytery decided to include in its books the main acts of the provincial assemblies: 'Becaus experience of times

---

[1] See P. G. B. McNeill and H. L. MacQueen (eds.), *Atlas of Scottish History to 1707* (Edinburgh, 1996), p. 318.

[2] See M. Lynch, M. Spearman and G. Stell (eds.), *The Scottish Medieval Town* (Edinburgh, 1988), p. 285 n. 82. In the 1540s, the reformer George Wishart claimed that Haddington had been able to muster audiences of two to three thousand for its religious 'clerk' plays, but this probably included visiting countryfolk, and may well have been an exaggeration. Establishing the total population of Scotland is a difficult task, but a realistic estimate for the start of the sixteenth century has been given as around 700,000. See I. D. Whyte, *Scotland Before the Industrial Revolution: an Economic and Social History c. 1050–c. 1750* (London, 1995), p. 113.

[3] McNeill and MacQueen (eds.), *Atlas of Scottish History*, p. 246.

[4] For further information on Haddington, and on its early drama, see respectively, W. F. Gray and J. H. Jamieson, *A Short History of Haddington*, facsimile reprint (Stevenage, 1986), and J. J. McGavin, 'Drama in Sixteenth-Century Haddington', *European Medieval Drama* 1 (1997), pp. 147–59.

past may teache us y*at* ye registers of the kirk may be lost, or come into ye hands of evill willers of ye discipline of the kirk'.[5] Sometimes the entries were made months after the decision to which they referred, sometimes they were contemporaneous. In one unhappy case a Presbyterian minister had his entire *Book of Discipline* eaten by rats during an out-break of plague, and some lost records may have gone the same way. Moreover, what the records choose to mention and, even more importantly, what they leave out reflects national, local, institutional and even personal preoccupations. Most frequently, an entry signals a moment when the civic or ecclesiastical authority felt that something had gone wrong or might go wrong, thought it expedient to deal with the problem and had the time and the power to do so. Hence, the absence after 1603 of explicit references to local musi-cians in cases of Sabbath-breaking need not imply that the kirk had successfully curtailed their popular activities. It may simply mean that the kirk was not in a position to do any-thing about them and that some ministers were not themselves strict sabbatarians, or had easier targets and more flagrant abuses to pursue during the years when James VI imposed episcopalian government on the Scottish church. A church record of 1630 complains of the 'gret abuse and prophana*t*ione of the sabboth . . . in respect of the co*nn*ivence and small penalties inposit vpon the prophaner*is* y*air*of in tyme bygane'.[6] This, and the permitted use of Monday as a day of holiday from the end of the sixteenth century, may have denied us many references to music because fewer infractions of Sabbath legislation seemed worthy of record. In such a context of partial witness and inference, it must be acknowledged that an incontestable account of secular music at Haddington is a forlorn hope.

To this one must add the mixed blessing of ambiguous terminology which both obscures records of secular music and consequently has ensured that it is included in studies of drama and ceremonial, such as those of the Records of Early English Drama project.[7] Medieval and early modern manuscripts rarely make it clear whether actors or musical performers are being referred to. This ambiguity affects both English terms such as 'players' and Latin ones like 'lusores' or 'histriones'. In later records, the ambiguity of 'play' can stretch to include cards, backgammon and dice, but when it is applied to activ-ity in an alehouse, one cannot always be sure that music, or even theatre, is excluded from its meaning. When it is used to refer to outdoor activity, then sports, theatrical plays, or dancing with music may be involved. The first probable reference to secular music in Haddington falls under this ambiguity: in 1530, James Biris was to be recompensed 'for his fee & playing to wille dowglace' when the latter was Abbot of Unreason (the organiser of the May revels and other burghal entertainment).[8] Even the word 'minstrel' is not as clear as could be wished, for it sometimes means simply 'servant'.[9] In 1612, in order to reduce expenses on ceremonial, the Haddington Burgh Council cancelled attendance at certain events by its officers 'and vther menstrall*is*' *except* those involved in playing.[10] The Council seems to have distinguished between *menstrallis* in the sense of town servants and those *menstrallis* who might serve the town by playing music. The entry implies that

[5] 23 October 1639, *Haddington Presbytery Records: Register 1639–48*, NAS, CH2/185/5, fol. 4r.
[6] 28 February 1630, *Haddington Kirk Session Minutes 1629–31*, NAS, CH2/799/1, fol. 311v. I am grateful to Dr Alison Rosie of the NAS for help with this entry.
[7] See S. MacLean, 'Drama and Ceremony in Early-Modern England: the R.E.E.D. Project', *Urban History Yearbook* (1989), pp. 38–48, and the seventeen volumes so far produced in the series.
[8] 30 November 1530, *Haddington Court Book 1530–55*, NAS, B30/9/2, fol. 6r.
[9] A. A. Young, 'Minstrels and Minstrelsy: Household Retainers or Instrumentalists?' *Records of Early English Drama Newsletter* 20:1 (1995), pp. 11–17.
[10] 28 August 1612, *Haddington Council Book 1603–16*, NAS, B30/13/3, fol. 96r.

the musicians, whose presence was to continue, were like other town officers. If so, they would have been functioning like the waits so frequently found in English towns.[11] But this is the only such record of wait-like activity in Haddington. There is no evidence that the town called on official, let alone liveried, waits on occasions such as visits by gentry, by the prince regent in 1573 or by the king in 1617 or prestigious gatherings like the Convention of the Burghs of the realm or an Ayre Court. It is virtually certain that Haddington, like other towns in Britain, did entertain its royal visitors with music, but its musicians appear to be absent from the records of provision and formal reimbursement. Instead, Haddington's burghal records include payments for torches, coal, candles, spices, wine, shortbread or sweets, or for the loan of a tapestry hanging in the court room, or expenses for banqueting visiting churchmen. The only other hint that the town might have had waits is even more ambiguous than the 1612 entry. In 1553 we find a 'Iohne Wait menstraill' owed money by a burgess.[12] There is no way of knowing if 'Wait' is just a variant spelling of the name Watt or a surname which, despite this late date, implies profession. As we have seen, the fact that he is referred to as a *menstraill* does not increase or decrease the chance that he was indeed a town wait.

I believe that Haddington did not have a group of official waits, though it may have made informal use of a pool of local minstrels on ceremonial occasions. There is none of the contractual material one might expect in civic court or account books if there were salaried waits; nor are there instructions for waits to be present on special occasions.[13] Admittedly, the celebratory events which occurred annually on 5 August and 5 November during the reign of James VI, often referred to as the 'king's nights', do not usually attract much detailed comment in the records, so there could have been a lot of festive music-making of an officially sponsored kind which was just not mentioned because it was traditional, untroubled, paid on an informal basis and so on.[14] For example, it is surely a safe assumption that the craft guilds' Corpus Christi pageants, recorded intermittently in the Haddington Court Book in the 1530s and early 1540s, found some place for music even if no extant records mention it. One does not know if these pageants were processional tableaux, plays or, as is likely, both; there are no texts and nothing remains to suggest the rich musical heritage recently explored in the English mystery plays.[15] However, mention of the pageants seems to be triggered specifically by problems with organisation, dates of performance, craft reluctance and disputes about precedence (which were found throughout Scotland and England). It may well be, therefore, that a whole *tranche* of popular music-making is unrepresented because it posed no problem to the burgh authorities, its payment being organised at the craft level. The case (previously referred to) in which James Biris sought his fee from William Douglas did appear in the records because, as Abbot of Unreason, Douglas was a civic appointee, and was funded from the burgess entry fines. It is, therefore, probably an accident of institutional sponsorship that we hear of music in the one case and not the other.

[11] *s.v.* 'wait' in the volumes of Records of Early English Drama (Toronto and London, 1979–).

[12] 30 April 1553, *Haddington Court Book 1530–55*, NAS, B30/9/2, fol. 291v.

[13] See R.E.E.D. volumes, *passim*, and D. Mills, 'Music and Musicians in Chester: a Summary Account', *Medieval English Theatre* 17 (1997 for 1995), pp. 58–75, and P. Greenfield, 'Using Dramatic Records: History, Theory, Southampton's Musicians', *ibid.*, pp. 76–95.

[14] For the August and November celebrations see D. Cressy, *Bonfires and Bells: National Memory and the Protestant Calendar in Elizabethan and Stuart England* (London, 1989), pp. 57, 141–55.

[15] R. Rastall, *The Heaven Singing: Music in Early English Religious Drama*, 2 vols. (Cambridge, 1996), vol. I.

Also missing from Haddington records is the association of music with that perennially popular Scottish activity of 'guising', i.e. dressing-up in disguise at festivals such as May and Yule. Elsewhere in Scotland, particularly in Elgin records, for example, the association of guising, dancing, carolling and music is made clear.[16] In Haddington, one has to infer the performance of music from references to the other activities, but it is not an unfair inference since the point of guising depended on the guisers being noticed and the presence of trumpet, pipes, drums ensured this, in addition to those chamber instruments which could supply music for any subsequent dancing. It is highly unlikely that a parish Yule guising which Haddington Presbytery investigated as late as 1640 was a silent affair.[17]

The Haddington records explicitly direct our attention to other forms of music. They concentrate not on theatrically related music but on private celebrations, and even more on outdoor piping (which could imply a range of woodwind instruments) and drumming. For the purposes of this chapter one should allow that civic drumming in its various functions constitutes a form of secular music, rather than just ritual noise, although it certainly did not have the cachet of piping. In the records of town and Presbytery, pipers seem to be called pipers by virtue of their skill (whatever other trade they might have); drummers are called drummers by virtue of their employment as civic functionaries. Furthermore, though pipers could and did perform some of the same civic functions as the drummer, their performances were more widely sought after and their performing contexts could be less official. In Haddington, we find them piping the curfew hours of 8 p.m. and 4 a.m. but they also performed at marriages, baptisms and banquets. In 1645, the Presbytery prohibited 'all maner of Minstrelles' from such events in an attempt to stop people gathering at a time of plague.[18] Inevitably music-makers suffered when gatherings were curtailed for any reason. They were also in demand at dances on Sunday afternoons in streets and fields. In this last respect they were significant irritants to the Presbytery, who sought to make new acts against such profanation and collected the names of these pipers, who could move freely within the area, promising not to play after being caught in one parish but piping up again at another place shortly after. In an effort to focus their fire on individuals, which was their standard technique for getting rid of popular, widespread activities, in 1598 the Presbytery identified (for possible future prosecution) five pipers within their bounds (Patrick Scougall, John Cathie, James Ramsay, David Gibson and John MacCalyen). However, we know that this was not the total number and they must have known it too, for they were at the same time prosecuting a Robert Stewart, piper (also called a 'menstraller'), who is not mentioned in their list. They had tried to convict him for incestuous adultery, which he denied, and they finally prosecuted him for profanation of the Sabbath by playing the pipes in West Fenton. Their list then may have covered only the official or semi-official pipers in the area. It is possible that these musicians were also either suspected of performing at John Brownside's May play at Samuelston which had happened a couple of months earlier or that they were caught up in the sabbatarian drive which that play had provoked.[19]

The first name on the Presbytery's hit-list, however, was the tailor Patrick Scougall, none other than the Burgh of Haddington's official piper, in other words, the piper of the

[16] See entries for Elgin in A. J. Mill, *Mediæval Plays in Scotland*, reprint (London and New York, 1969), pp. 237–42.
[17] 5 February 1640, *Haddington Presbytery Records: Register 1639–48*, NAS, CH2/185/5, fol. 12v.
[18] 25 June 1645, *Haddington Presbytery Records: Register 1639–48*, NAS, CH2/185/5, fol. 139r.
[19] 10 May to 23 August 1598, *Haddington Presbytery Records: Minutes 1596–1608*, NAS, CH2/185/2, unfoliated.

town which was also the seat of the Presbytery. He had also been charged to mark the town's curfew in 1586, a position he held for three or four years, and the town authorities turned again to him for this task in 1622, describing him companionably as their 'comburges'. The intervening lengthy gap had been filled by a family of drummers, who had beaten the hours, and by Scougall's own son Richard, who predeceased him and who had also officiated as town piper.[20] By 1622, civic fashion had changed and Scougall was re-employed to beat rather than pipe the curfew. By 1630, this elderly musician was receiving charitable donations from the Kirk Session of Haddington. However, back in Scougall's heyday, the kirk had been less accommodating to him. In 1599, the Presbytery threatened him with excommunication if he played on a Sunday afternoon again. He was not the only piper causing them trouble, but he was the one whom they named and chased up time and again over a ten-year period from initial summonses in 1589 (which he failed to answer) through summonses which he answered and which led to him promising not to play on Sundays, up to the final threat. Why was this? The answer reflects the significance of the present volume for the history of late medieval and early modern towns.

The history of urban institutions cannot be written without close attention to the music that was played in and around them and it can be written more easily if music-making is closely studied. One only needs to consider how heterogeneous music is as a social phenomenon to appreciate this. Music can be popular or governmental in origin, spontaneous or organised; it can accompany leisure or constitute an educational discipline in itself; it can be produced by one person or a group; it is flexible, ubiquitous, and closely related to the social context in which it appears: it can match or change the prevailing mood; it carries resonances which create a quasi-textual inflection upon events. Its practitioners themselves can have many different kinds of relation to society: some of them will have trades independent of music (as Scougall had), others will need high-level connections to permit their concentration on their art; others again will owe more to those who pay them than to society at large. Living in the age of the ghetto blaster and of instant music production through open car or house windows or by one's own children, one knows that music is neither insignificant nor neutral. Furthermore, the lives of those who inhabit towns are framed by conventional, rather than natural, time. This was certainly true of those who lived in early modern towns and their less easily controlled hinterland. That temporal framework marking hours of leisure, work or sleep, of festivity or mourning, can give added meaning, and even offensive significance, to music. Time and place, volume and style, ethnicity, age and institutional associations and so on, make music more or less acceptable. For example, Scottish parliamentary acts from 1449 deplored 'bards', associating them with itinerant, probably clan-based, disorder. Local records from other burghs periodically (and especially in the second half of the sixteenth century) group 'singeris of vngodlie sangs pypers fydlers commoun menstralles' with other vagabonds, those who feign madness and those who stay up at night playing games of chance.[21] In 1580 the town of Dundee demanded that John MacGregor, fiddler, should desist and take up another trade, presumably because they did not want to establish the precedent whereby an incomer could set up in the town as an entertainer. The historian John Leslie, writing in the 1570s, reported that Governor Thomas Randolph had sought

[20] 23 November 1586, *Haddington Council Book 1581–1602*, NAS, B30/13/2, fol. 39r, and 26 July 1622, *Haddington Council Book 1616–24*, NAS, B30/13/4, fol. 50v.
[21] Several of these, including this from Edinburgh, are set out in Mill, *Mediæval Plays in Scotland*, pp. 294–8.

to establish order following the death of Robert the Bruce by executing all itinerants and sturdy beggars, but this was not enough for his courtiers:

> Sum requiret that quha [whoever] wan thair lyueng with the lute, harp, cyther, and sik sorte of musical instrumentis, suld be rekned with this number; the Gouernour denyes, and prudentlie to sik sorte of persounis grants pardoune, and priuilege to perseuir; because in the weiris [wars] thay war necessar, and nocht sindle [seldom] but verie oft to the commoditie [benefit] and vse of the peple.[22]

Whatever one might think about the military value of a lute, when Leslie was writing, the Scottish parliament felt that it had to be similarly discriminating, but this time in recognition of existing patterns of patronage rather than national defence. In 1574, it prohibited 'all menstrallis sangstaris and taill tellaris not avowit [acknowledged] in speciall seruice be sum of the lordis of parliament or greit barronis or be the heid burrowis and citeis for pair commoun menstrallis' [i.e., waits].[23] Music constitutes a focus, as language does, for tensions and for social contest. One can thus see bureaucratic manoeuvres and power-play by emerging interest groups through the attempted provision and control of music. It is the perfect index of politics, however marginal it might appear in comparison with the larger affairs of state.

Whatever Patrick Scougall's appeal for the people who heard him on Sunday afternoons and whatever pleasure or sense of responsibility he may have felt when playing, in the 1590s he was part of a much larger struggle in which the emerging Presbytery was attempting to control the authority of its rival, but closely related, institutions, the burgh and the local lairds. The last quarter of the sixteenth century and the start of the seventeenth saw a struggle for demarcation of roles, powers of regulation and quality control, and above all a battle for control of time.

This is the period in which the town clock was installed and regularly maintained, and the burgh records also show increasingly detailed contracts for the town piper or drummer who was to beat the curfew hours. At their most specific these contracts stipulate curfew times – 8 p.m. and 4 a.m. – the 1613 entry adds 'precisely' like the Speaking Clock, which the drummer essentially was. They also noted other occasions when the drummer would be required (such as musters, riding of bounds, etc.); where the drum should be beaten (through the whole quarters and streets of the town from gate to gate); how it should be beaten (without intermission); what the drummer should do if the weather was bad and therefore likely to damage the drum head (beat it under stairs); how he would be paid (in arrears so that any failures to beat the curfew could be fined before he got the money); the condition in which he should keep the drums (in good repair as they had been handed over to him); and the constituent parts of the drums to be so maintained (heads, rims and other necessaries).[24] This secular obsession was matched by the sabbatarianism of the Presbytery, who attempted to control time on a weekly and annual basis rather than daily, proscribing certain activities on Sunday mornings and afternoons

---

22 J. Leslie, *The Historie of Scotland*, ed. E. G. Cody and W. Murison and trans. James Dalrymple, Scottish Text Society, 2 vols. (Edinburgh, 1888–95), vol. II, p. 14.

23 T. Thomson and C. Innes (eds.), *The Acts of the Parliament of Scotland AD 1124 (-1707)*, 12 vols. (Edinburgh, 1814–75), vol. III, pp. 86–9.

24 For examples of these contracts, see 12 January 1591/2, *Haddington Council Book 1581–1602*, NAS, B30/13/2, fol. 72v, and 7 June 1605, *Haddington Council Book 1603–16*, NAS, B30/13/3, fol. 25r.

and also on those week days when there was an 'exercise', that is the exposition and discussion of scripture. They also aimed to control the festivities associated with Yule, Easter, May Day and so on. The ministers particularly ran up against music-makers on Sunday afternoons and the annual festivals. Then they fined those who piped and fiddled in streets and fields, or who served with music the people emerging from the traditional Sunday market at Tranent. They tried to stop musicians who played for couples dancing in the afternoon, even though the dancers might have had strong aristocratic connections. They acted against musicians playing at marriages, which were performed on Sunday until the Presbytery stopped them, or in private houses for Sunday evening banquets.[25]

Patrick Scougall was a prime target because he represented the burgh's interest. If the Presbytery could limit the piper of that town which was both the chief burgh of the area and also its ecclesiastical centre, they secured their own institutional power. We might think that it was a matter of sabbatarian principle, but it was actually complex power politics worked out in a context in which the kirk itself was poor but had past parliamentary acts on its side; the local gentry were often indifferent or hostile to it; the burgh had long-established traditions of its own; the ministers were not always too keen to preach on Sunday afternoons anyway and attendance at kirk could be thin (in neighbouring Tranent eighty to a hundred at best out of a potential population of 2,000, according to the minister).

The most complex aspect of the politics was, of course, that in a deep sense the kirk and the burgh were interdependent and had an eye on national trends, not just their local rivalries. They both felt a measure of local pride and responsibility; they were both anxious, according to their own lights, to preserve the reputation of their locality. Thus in the last analysis the kirk could threaten the burgh, as was done in the early 1580s, with removal of the seat of the Presbytery to the rival towns of Edinburgh and Dalkeith, an act which would have diminished the burgh's standing in the area. When the threat was made, the burgh magistrates quickly concluded that the town's interests were served by the Presbytery's presence and made solemn promises to comply with the principles of the General Assembly of the Kirk of Scotland, not least by stopping the very activities in which music customarily figured: 'superstitious Obseruatioun of festnall daiis callit of Yule pasche witsonday and the pasche of maj plaijs of robine hude litle Johne abitis of vnresoun setting furth of banefyris singing of carrellis within or about the kirk or ellis at certane seasonis of the Yeir'.[26]

Furthermore, there was one music-maker whose functions embraced both kirk and burgh: the master of the song school. Following the period of civil war at the end of Mary Queen of Scots's reign, parliament is found complaining that skill in music and singing 'is almaist decayit and sall schortly decay without timous remeid be prouidit'. That remedy was a royal request that 'the prouest baillies counsale and communitie of the maist speceall burrowis of this realme . . . erect and sett vp ane sang scuill with ane maister sufficient and able for instructioun of þe yowth in the said science of musik'.[27]

---

[25] Latterly the kirk appears to have been forced into allowing marriages (and hence music) on the Sabbath, which they had previously prohibited because of the riotous behaviour they inspired: session 6 of the General Assembly, convened 10 December 1602. A. Peterkin (ed.), *The Book of the Universall Kirk of Scotland* . . . (Edinburgh, 1839), p. 527.

[26] 4 December 1588 (recording a decision of 11 February 1583), *Haddington Presbytery Minutes 1587–96*, NAS, CH2/185/1, fol. 19r.   [27] 11 November 1579, *Acts of the Parliament of Scotland*, vol. III, p. 174.

In response to this act Haddington established its song or music school under John Buchan in 1583.[28] He was expected to teach whichever of the burgh's children were sent to him, for a fee paid by the burgh, and, interestingly, to hide no part of musical instruction from them. One of Buchan's successors seems also to have been called in to help support the burgh grammar school which was failing and experiencing competition.[29] But the master was also expected to be the kirk's precentor. He taught the children (probably of either sex) and the men of the burgh and countryside to sing and play on the 'virgina*lis* lute gutherne & sic<...> Instrument*is* q*uhair*voun he can play',[30] but he also took up the psalms in the kirk, acted as reader there if required, and combined the interests of burgh and kirk by teaching new psalms to the children in the grammar school and leading the singing of a psalm there nightly. By 1610, he was paid by the scholars themselves, receiving different fees depending on whether he taught them to sing, read and write or, at double that fee, to sing and play. If his pupils were from the countryside he could charge whatever rate he and they could agree. He was also to be paid by both the burgh and the Kirk Session and in 1622 this payment was understood to mean that he would teach burgh children for nothing. The burgh paid him at least double what it paid the town drummer and the Kirk Session added more than the equivalent of the drummer's fee.[31] Haddington music masters were usually appointed from outside the town and their removal expenses might be met (Patrick Dunbar from Ross, James Laurie from Montrose, and Robert Gray from Glasgow, for example). Their arrival thus provided an opportunity for defining institutional needs afresh. Such a master might also have options other than those provided locally: one had an eye on higher preferment, to the Chapel Royal; another was able to call on the interest of the King's Secretary Depute to get him a free burgess-ship in Haddington.[32] He might even resign, as their first music master, John Buchan, did apparently after building up debts in the face of tardy payment by the town. The music master was obviously considered a 'professional' in the sense that the town decided he must be paid in advance rather than in arrears, as with the town drummer, and that that advance should not be regarded as a debt to be worked off. In appointing him in response to the act of parliament, the burgh had its eye not just on local traditions in education but on national prescription. He was expected to teach in a way that would permit Haddington to match other burghs in its provision of music, a national quality control thus arising out of burghal rivalry.

With so much control focused on the regulation of music, it should be no surprise that music also became the medium of emulation and even subversion. In a Haddington Council Book entry for 1599 we encounter William Swynton, a fiddler. As is usually the case, the motive for making the original record is quite different from our motives in reading it. The manuscript only mentions him because he was to carry the town ensign as a representative of the crafts of the town to the general muster. The burgh wished to record this because it was insisting that the craftsmen, merchants, and other commoners should take it in turns to carry the banner, so as to eschew 'controversy'. In Haddington, as in many other late medieval and early modern towns, public display was

[28] 17 June 1583, *Haddington Council Book 1581–1602*, NAS, B30/13/2, fol. 12r–v.

[29] 26 December 1606 and 27 March 1607, *Haddington Council Book 1603–16*, NAS, B30/13/3, fols. 39r and 40r–v.

[30] Although I have not yet studied Haddington wills, I have yet to come across a musical instrument in the lists of inheritance goods held in trust for minors; these lists are intermittently recorded in the burgh records.

[31] For an example of such a contract see 30 December 1610, *Haddington Council Book 1603–16*, NAS, B30/13/3, fols. 76v–77r.   [32] 26 January 1624, *Haddington Council Book 1616–24*, NAS, B30/13/4, fol. 61v.

a focus for group rivalry. However the phrasal inflections of the record may suggest something more interesting. In this case, the entry reads that because Patrick Brown carried the ensign the last time, the provost and council have ordered 'w*illi*am swy*n*ton fidler for ye craft*is* to beir it this day'.[33] Is the fiddler William Swynton carrying the ensign for the crafts this day or is William Swynton, fiddler for the crafts, carrying the ensign this day? The latter seems more likely. Fiddling was not itself a recognised craft in Haddington, so to mention *en passant* that Swynton was a fiddler could only be because he was well known for it. Also, why did the scribe not write that the council ordered 'william swynton fidler to bear it this day for the crafts'? That would have been the more natural word-order if the emphasis was on the rotation of the job to the crafts. The phrasing supports the idea that Swynton was 'fiddler for the crafts'. Admittedly, nowhere else in the records do we encounter the notion that the Haddington crafts as a body appointed a fiddler, but equally, no mention was made of music at the craft pageants, and there must surely have been some.

This entry may well be an important witness to the tight articulation of music-making with group identity at an institutional level below that of the burgh authorities and separate from the purchasing power which allied musicians with the great houses. It would reflect the known ceremonial and organisational integrity of the guilds, and reminds us of the unrecorded layers of society, of their celebrations and entertainments. It also serves to show the ceremonial position of the music-maker. William Swynton, whether he was just a fiddler or a guild appointee, was *carrying* the ensign. He was not, one presumes, also fiddling, unless he belongs to that startlingly acrobatic group uncovered by David George in Lancashire – the 'tumbling fiddlers'.[34] He was the obvious figurehead for the crafts as a whole because his skill as a fiddler cut across individual rivalries of trade, but also because, through him, the crafts could emulate the ceremonial of the burgh's provost, baillies and council. These magistrates had their town drummer, as we have seen. They were prepared to get his clothes out of pawn, dress his son up in a new white doublet, blue breeks, shanks and new shoes so that he could beat the smaller of the town's two official drums, known as swasches; they would mend these drums, even when the drummer failed to meet his contractual obligation to do so within his own fee and so on. They did this to ensure that the town was well represented, in contexts where civic rights and identity were paramount, by someone who was known to be their civic appointee. The Muster of men and of the town's armour was one such occasion, so the burgh's drummer was to be present. In William Swynton, and their other fiddlers, the crafts may have had their own musical figurehead, and though he was, on this occasion, musically silent, he was ceremonially prominent, and an implicit reminder of the crafts' own hierarchy and internal organisation to all of the society's other constituent institutions which existed in a strangely competitive harmony.

Apart from instances of downright disobedience shown through music, as when in 1589 the young men, accompanied by their minstrels, took to the streets of Haddington in what the Presbytery thought was a revival of the traditions of misrule, we find music used as a weapon against institutional pressures.[35] Minstrels showed a remarkable capacity to be seduced to the cause of unrighteousness or disorder, regardless of whether offence was to be given to the kirk or the burgh. In 1597, Isobel Levington,

---

[33] 25 June 1599, *Haddington Council Book 1581–1602*, NAS, B30/13/2, fol. 116v.
[34] D. George (ed.), *Lancashire*, Records of Early English Drama (Toronto and London, 1992), p. 204.
[35] 30 April 1589, *Haddington Presbytery Minutes 1587–96*, NAS, CH2/185/1, fol. 25v.

daughter of the dowager Lady Saltcoats, was summoned for adultery with William Cockburn of Stirling. Not only did she not attend the Presbytery but her sister tore up the summons, called the minister, James Gibson, a 'briber' and refused to attend as well. The girls' mother took them into her protection and encouraged them in this. At this point, George Levington, brother of the Laird of Saltcoats, with two of his pals, decided to strike a blow for the family. Together with a minstrel, Patrick Fairbairn, they went round to Gibson's house at midnight when he was lying sick in bed (he claimed), thrust up the bedroom window and played a whistle and drum through it. The manuscript is damaged but it is clear that this 'suddayne & vnlukit for noyse' caused Gibson great perturbation.[36] The affront offered to Gibson was an aristocratic version of the rough music used for social condemnation. (The earliest example of this is documented from 1390, at the royal palace in Scone, Perthshire, and also on that occasion at a bedroom window.[37]) The effect of this, however, was substantially to shift the balance of power from the family to the kirk by giving the Presbytery an obvious and proved fault instead of the adultery which they still had to prove. The Levington women attended the Presbytery court the next week and had to show penitence.

A more remarkable instance of music used as subversion occurred in a wholly civic and secular context in 1610. John Wilkie, one of the town's notaries public, was imprisoned in the tolbooth for offering 'proude & Iniurious word*is*' to the provost and resisting demands that he withdraw them. Mindful of the fact that, while he was forbidden to escape, there was no law preventing others from joining him in prison, he invited in a group of his friends who sat up

> dri*n*kand & playand And gestand in Richert skowgall y*air* co*mm*oun pyper & swascher w*ith* ye swasch & his pype as also Iohne grahame pyper playand all y*at* ny*ch*t in ye tolbuth & vpoun ye wall heid y*air*of w*ith* y*air* pypeis & ye swasch schouting crying & makein p*ro*clamatioun vpoun ye walheid of ye tolbuith & vsing sindrie Insolenceis & co*n*tumeleis In co*n*tempt of ye mag*istr*atis q*uh*a had wairdit him In hie and manifest co*n*te*m*pt of o*ur* souerane lorde lawis & auctis & of ye said*is* mag*istr*atis & toun.[38]

This was not just a casual piece of drunken hooliganism. The town's normal authority and practice had been specifically parodied. One of the visitors of Wilkie (whose own hand is present in some of the burgh records) was Richard Scougall, son of Patrick, and by now the town's own piper and drummer. The use of the pronoun 'their' in 'y*air* co*mm*oun pyper & swascher' betrays the sense of outrage, that an appointee of the magistrates was acting against them. In addition Richard was using the instruments he employed for the town's business and specifically those he used to mark the very curfew which he was breaking. In addition, the pipe and drum would normally accompany proclamations by the burghal authority; here they accompanied subversive proclamations by Wilkie and the others. This breach of authority was happening at the tolbooth, the centre of the burgh's authority, and the place where its power to punish was customarily made manifest by the exhibition of malefactors at the main window. Now it had become a place

---

[36] 13 April 1597, *Haddington Presbytery Minutes 1596–1608*, NAS, CH2/185/2, unfoliated.

[37] See J. J. McGavin, 'Robert III's "Rough Music": Charivari and Diplomacy in a Medieval Scottish Court', *The Scottish Historical Review* 74:2 (1995), pp. 144–58. For a study of this form of folk justice, see M. Ingrams. 'Ridings, Rough Music and the Reform of Popular Culture', *Past and Present* 105 (1984), pp. 79–113.

[38] 26 September 1610, *Haddington Council Book 1603–16*, NAS, B30/13/3, fol. 72r–v.

where contempt for authority was manifested and institutional music parodied. If you want to stand the world on its head, there is no implement more effective than that of music.

Wilkie the notary was not exactly a beacon of civic rectitude. He was probably the same man who appears in records of 1630 for renting out a house to two unruly beggars, and then in a strange reprise of the 1610 case, also defends himself for drinking with a certain Catherine Kirkton in the tolbooth at the time of afternoon sermon by claiming that he had been locked in by the officer, Andrew Bain.[39] The next year, Andrew Bain himself was in trouble for drinking in his house at the time of morning sermon in the company of John Liddell, piper.[40] Liddell, in his turn, was married to Margaret Scougall, who was almost certainly related to Scougall *père et fils*.[41] What emerges from this is that local musicians, whose families might then (as now) intermarry, formed part of a burgh group which included civic functionaries operating below the level of the council and below the professional status of music master, and who both served authority and broke its rules, usually by their recreation. The livelihood of these families was not always secure; it depended on their retaining their good health, performing their duties well and on the efficiency of the treasurer who had to pay them. At the same time, if they fell on hard times, they might well figure among those citizens whom the burgh thought it right to support.

Richard Scougall was kept on as the town's piper. When, in 1613, he was replaced by Nicoll Brown, the drummer whom he had himself replaced in 1608, it was because he had ceased to be reliable in marking the hours, despite warning. Richard's inadequacy may well have been the result of illness, and he may have died shortly after, for his wife received £3 support from the burgh. Why was he not fired and replaced by Brown after the outrageous behaviour on the tolbooth? If he was friends with a notary, he obviously belonged to a slightly higher social group than the Browns. As a piper he had a higher-level skill than Brown and was more adaptable since he could play the drums as well. When the weather was bad he did not need to go under stair-heads with a drum; he could just play the great pipe instead. In addition to the family tradition in the post, Richard's father had an independent trade as a tailor and was not poor. We find him able to lend quite a sizeable sum and he appears in the main group of taxpayers in the burgh. Richard himself was not a craftsman but a burgess 'for the spyce and wine', in other words, a merchant burgess. Also, the records suggest that the authorities were more concerned, during a time of fairly significant disturbance in the town, to prevent the like happening again rather than to create long-standing enmity. They enacted laws to ensure that prisoners were only allowed visits from people bringing their food and they made a point of saying that Wilkie would be punished as a first offender. Somehow the musicians, both Scougall and the other piper, escaped formal attention in the records.

The history of secular music at Haddington in the late sixteenth and early seventeenth centuries is a matter of inference and controlled speculation. One senses a world of pipes, drums, whistles, fiddles, lutes and other parlour instruments, singing and dancing. Records of debt show that the town even had the odd trumpeter, though when Haddington briefly tried to establish town plays in the mid-1570s one of their largest expenses was for bringing in a trumpeter and drummers from Edinburgh, thus

[39] 18 April 1630 and 8 July 1630, *Haddington Kirk Session Minutes 1629–31*, NAS, CH2/799/1, fols. 309v and 307r, respectively. [40] *Ibid.*, 27 March 1631, fol. 300r.
[41] 29 April 1628, *Haddington Court Book 1628–32*, NAS, B30/10/12, fol. 9r.

indicating either that they did not have the former, and had insufficient of the latter, or that the trumpeters and drummers they had in the town were insufficiently skilled in the demands that plays might make of them and so more sophisticated players had to be brought in. Haddington's music lay at the heart of institutional contention in a fast-changing society. Its musicians were sought after for pleasure and by those who would control pleasure. They were employed in acts of rebellion which were sometimes born of a knowledge that the tide of events was flowing with their opponents, yet were sometimes tolerated because even the opponents were not sure which way the tide was flowing. Sometimes the contesting institutions which used them actually shared a common interest, knew that they did so and were only fencing for immediate advantage. In the midst of all this change, like members of the governing authorities and the Presbyterian ministers who intermittently tormented music-makers, the musicians formed their own little dynasties, Scougall succeeding Scougall, Brown training up younger Browns, one music- master, Patrick Dunbar, being succeeded by his son James. These silent histories unfold beneath the larger historical forces which a study of urban music does so much to point up.

CHAPTER FIVE

CIVIC SUBSIDY AND MUSICIANS IN SOUTHERN FRANCE DURING THE FOURTEENTH AND FIFTEENTH CENTURIES: A COMPARISON OF MONTPELLIER, TOULOUSE AND AVIGNON

GRETCHEN PETERS

The marked increase in the appearance of musicians on city payrolls in the mid-fourteenth century is now well documented for much of Europe.[1] Scholars have shown that trumpeters appeared on city payrolls by the beginning of the fourteenth century and that the civic wind band appeared in a few German cities between 1350 and 1370 and then throughout Germany, the Low Countries and Italy by the late fourteenth century. In contrast, the civic subsidy of music, and urban musical practices in general, in French cities during the fourteenth and fifteenth centuries have yet to be established, despite France's prominent role in the development of secular music during medieval times.[2] Recent research in the rich medieval holdings of the archives of south-central France, including municipal account books, contracts, ceremonial books, chronicles and tax records, as well as private notarial contracts, have yielded significant insights into a region as of yet largely unexplored. An examination of the size, function and composition of civic ensembles maintained by three of the principal cities in the region – Montpellier, Toulouse and Avignon – will reveal that the civic patronage of music in large southern French cities was at least comparable to and often rivalled that of other major European cities. In addition, a comparison of the history of these cities, focusing particularly on the extent to which

I would like to thank Keith Polk for reading an earlier version of this chapter and generously offering valuable and detailed suggestions.

[1] For the Low Countries see E. van der Straeten, *Les ménestrels aux Pays-Bas du XIIIe au XVIIIe siècle* (Bruxelles, 1878; reprint, Geneva, 1972); K. Polk, 'Wind Bands of Medieval Flemish Cities', *Brass and Woodwind Quarterly* 1 (1968), pp. 93–113; Polk, 'Municipal Wind Music in Flanders in the Late Middle Ages', *Brass and Woodwind Quarterly* 2 (1969), pp. 1–15; R. Strohm, *Music in Late Medieval Bruges* (Oxford, 1985). For Germany see K. Polk, *German Instrumental Music of the Late Middle Ages* (Cambridge, 1992). For Italy see L. Lockwood, *Music in Renaissance Ferrara, 1400–1505* (Cambridge, MA, 1984); F. d'Accone, *The Civic Muse: Music and Musicians in Siena during the Middle Ages and the Renaissance* (Chicago, 1997). For Spain see K. Kreitner, 'Music and Civic Ceremony in Late Fifteenth Century Barcelona', Ph.D. thesis, Duke University (1990).

[2] A few exceptional studies for southern France exist: L. Barthélemy, *Notice historique sur l'industrie des ménétriers* (Marseille, 1886); P. Pansier, 'Les débuts du théâtre à Avignon à la fin du XVe siècle', *Annales d'Avignon et du Comtat-Venaissin* 6 (1919), pp. 5–52; see also L. Charles-Dominque, *Les ménétriers français sous l'ancien régime* (Toulouse, 1994). For a brief description of music in the urban setting of Avignon see A. Tomasello, *Music and Ritual at Papal Avignon, 1309–1403* (Ann Arbor, 1983).

they were subject to external authority, suggests that the nature of civic sponsorship of music was related to the degree of autonomy possessed by their ruling elite.

Montpellier's location less than ten kilometres from the Mediterranean Sea (to which it is connected by a small river), as well as its position on principal trade routes, contributed to its development into a major commercial centre by the thirteenth century. The wealthy citizens of Montpellier successfully revolted against the ruling feudal family in 1203 and shortly thereafter a town government, consisting of twelve representatives from the wealthiest professions – including bankers, importers of spices and cloth merchants – became the primary ruling body. The town government made use of an official building, known as the 'consulate' (*consolat*), located in the central commercial district; it was acquired by 1205, a century earlier than most municipal authorities throughout France and northern Spain usually acquired them. At this same time, Montpellier became part of the Kingdom of Aragon and the non-residence of the Aragonese rulers over the next century furthered the growth of a powerful and autonomous town government.[3]

Notre Dame-des-Tables, which received its name from the surrounding commercial booths or tables, was one of the oldest churches in the city and was the centre of many important rituals. The local population, as well as numerous pilgrims, visited the church to venerate a wooden statue of the Virgin, which was thought to perform miracles and to serve as the protector of the city. The church, which was located next to the consulate, was the site for frequent ceremonies of the city council involving civic minstrels. In addition, city trumpeters sounded their music twice a day from its high bell-tower. The University of Montpellier, established in the early thirteenth century, competed with prestigious Italian universities and became particularly well known for its school of medicine. According to Kathryn Reyerson, there were few towns outside Italy that were as economically important or politically independent as Montpellier.[4] At its peak in the first half of the fourteenth century, Montpellier has been estimated to have had a population of between 30,000 and 40,000 people, which would have made it the largest city in the region and placed it among the leading cities in Europe (see Illustration 5.1).[5]

Like many other European cities, Montpellier reached its economic and demographic peak in the early fourteenth century. Throughout the later fourteenth and during the early fifteenth centuries it encountered bad harvests, natural disasters, epidemics and plundering by armies involved in the Hundred Years' War. As a result, Montpellier's population had decreased to between 15,000 and 17,000 by 1404 and 13,700 or less by 1470. Contributing to Montpellier's economic problems, a year after the Black Death ravaged the city in 1348 James III of Majorca sold the community and its nearby port town of Lattes to the King of France and the settlement became subject to heavy royal taxation. Under the King of France, who sought greater centralisation, royal representatives obtained control over communal affairs from the civic council and, by 1393, the original twelve-member government was reduced to six. According to Jean Baumel, by the final decade of the fourteenth century the 'glorious days' of the city council had ended and

---

[3] A. Ross Lewis, 'The Development of Town Government in Twelfth-Century Montpellier', *Speculum* 22 (1947), pp. 51–67.

[4] K. Reyerson, *Business, Banking and Finance in Medieval Montpellier*, Studies and Texts 75 (Toronto, 1985), pp. 6–7.

[5] J. Russell, 'L'Evolution démographique de Montpellier au Moyen Age', *Annales du Midi* 74 (1962), p. 352.

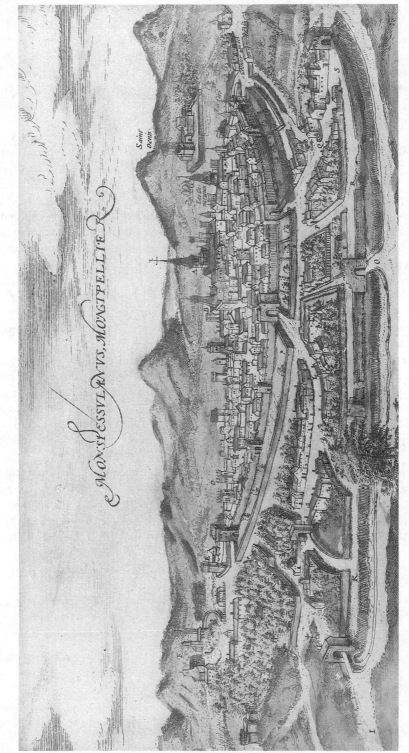

5.1 Map of Montpellier; G. Bruin, S. Novellanus, F. Hogenburgius, *Civitates orbis terrarum Liber primus* (Cologne, 1582), plate 8.

after two centuries of independent town government the members of the council became administrators who followed orders from royal sovereigns and bailiffs.[6]

The wealth and power attained by Montpellier and its ruling elite during the mid-fourteenth century are reflected in the unusually extensive civic subsidy of music used to accompany the city council in ceremonies. An official wind band was well established by the mid-fourteenth century in Montpellier and was thus one of the earliest official civic ensembles in Europe, coinciding with the appearance of civic wind bands in Germany.[7] The earliest extant account book of Montpellier, which dates from 1357/8, includes regular payments to five minstrels, consistently identified as 'our five minstrels' or 'the five minstrels of the consulate', to accompany the city council in fifteen processions.[8] This regular employment of five minstrels is all the more striking in comparison to civic wind bands throughout much of Europe during the second half of the fourteenth century which typically only had two or three members. Despite heavy financial obligations and other problems burdening the citizens of Montpellier during the mid-fourteenth century, money continued to be allocated for all five civic minstrels. In the next extant city account book from 1370/1, 'the five minstrels of the consulate' were hired for twenty-six processions; in the only other extant account book from this century, dating from a year later, five musicians were again employed in this capacity for thirty-one processions.[9] According to a city statute of 1375, the minstrels were to wear the official livery of the city, on which was embroidered the coat of arms, 'when the members of the council go in a procession or in other consular activities . . .' (*en autres fachs conssolars*), making their association with the city and the city council explicit.[10]

The instruments played by these five minstrels are never explicitly mentioned in the city account books; indeed, references to specific instruments other than the trumpet in all archival records from the region are rare. An unusually detailed entry in the city accounts from 1357, however, does document the purchase of new banners for two trumpets and two 'cornamusa'.[11] The latter term is usually interpreted as meaning a bagpipe or more generally a reed instrument. It appears that a player of the nakers (a pair of small kettledrums) was also included in the civic minstrel ensemble. Registers from the second half of the fourteenth century record the officers of the different professional guilds, including that of the minstrels' guild. In the 1350s three of the civic minstrels that performed this duty are identified as a 'cornamuzayre', a 'trompayre' and a 'nacharayre'.[12]

The documentary evidence suggests that one large, mixed ensemble was formed, rather than two smaller ensembles of a trumpet duo and a reed duo. For example, in the account books, these minstrels are always identified as one group ('our five minstrels'); all five are invariably hired for civic events for which each received identical remuneration and livery.[13] In addition, a city chronicle places the minstrels in the same location in civic celebrations, whether the event was a large royal reception or a smaller religious procession. For a religious procession in 1364 for the feasts of St German and St Remy, for example, the chronicle identifies all of the participants and places the minstrels

---

[6] J. Baumel, *Histoire d'une seigneurie du Midi de la France*, 3 vols. (Montpellier, 1971), vol. III, p. 145.

[7] Polk, *German Instrumental Music*, p. 110.   [8] AMMo, Inventory 9, no. 845, fols. 103v–104r, 111v.

[9] AMMo, Inventory 9, no. 846, fol. 52v; no. 847, fol. 25r–v.

[10] F. Pégat, T. Eugène and Desmazes (ed.), *Le Petit Thalamus de Montpellier* (Montpellier, 1840), p. 169.

[11] AMMo, Inventory 9, no. 845, fol. 84v.

[12] AMMo, Inventory 6, 'Regestre des senhors consoulz et curials de la villa de Montpelier', fol. 6r, 11v. For further descriptions of the various instruments mentioned in this essay see *Grove*.

[13] AMMo, Inventory 9, no. 847, fol. 28v.

directly in front of the baldachin of the city council.[14] Likewise, for the arrival of the Queen of Navarre in 1372, the chronicle meticulously describes how 'three old and three new members of the council met her with sixteen other important men of the city and sixty cavalrymen entering at Béziers and the minstrels of the council had led and they were all dressed in red livery . . .'[15]

The chronicle entries and the account books from the 1350s to 1370s indicate that Montpellier subsidised a mixed ensemble of reeds, trumpets and drums. Such combinations had been widespread in the urban centres of Europe in the twelfth and thirteenth centuries, largely as a result of Middle Eastern influence. Recent scholarship has suggested that by the 1350s their popularity waned and two distinct ensembles of reeds and trumpets were preferred for occasions sponsored by civic authorities. The former usually contained two or three members and performed music for processions, dances, banquets and concerts; the latter usually sounded fanfares at civic ceremonies of the highest solemnity.[16] Yet the documented example from Montpellier indicates that mixed ensembles with reeds, trumpets and percussion may have been maintained in some centres for longer than has been thought. In the light of this, the speculation concerning the make-up of civic ensembles elsewhere in Europe in the later fourteenth century could require modification.[17]

Although Montpellier appears to have maintained older medieval traditions later into the fourteenth century, by the early fifteenth century the size and composition of its civic ensemble was comparable to most other major European centres. The ensemble was reduced to two or three minstrels in the early 1400s and by 1431 and throughout the rest of the century, the personnel remained constant at four. This reduction in personnel could indicate a preference for three-part instrumental ensembles prominent throughout Europe at this time. It might also reflect economic and political changes in Montpellier; with its continued decreasing population and shortage of funds which occurred at the beginning of the fifteenth century, the city may have been unable to maintain the ensemble at that time. In addition, the reduction in minstrels corresponds to the decline in the size and power of the city council.

Evidence for the instrumental make-up of the group is sparse, but the little documentation that does exist indicates that the musicians formed a wind band and performed on different shawms and perhaps a slide-trumpet. For example, a private contract dating from 1429 documents two civic minstrels selling 'a bombard with a key and a shawm made in Bruges' (a well-known centre for instrument-making at this time) to two local 'superior wood workers'.[18] In 1469, a relative of a civic minstrel sold a number of wind instruments to pay for taxes, including three shawms with their case, a

---

[14] *Petit Thalamus*, pp. 366–7. The Petit Thalamus was compiled during the thirteenth to the sixteenth centuries and consists of distinct sections, including a chronicle of local events.   [15] *Petit Thalamus*, p. 389.

[16] The reed ensembles with usually two or three members remained separate from the trumpets until the early fifteenth century, when a slide-trumpet was introduced, and the trumpet ensembles expanded throughout the fifteenth century. K. Polk, 'The Invention of the Slide Principle and the Earliest Trombone or, The Birth of a Notion', in S. Carter (ed.), *Brass Scholarship: Proceedings of the International Brass Symposium, Amherst, 1995* (New York, 1997), p. 20.

[17] Trumpeters and reed players were also hired by charitable organisations in Montpellier and Marseilles during the mid-fourteenth century, raising the possibility of other such ensembles in this region. In 1367, the masons of Montpellier bought new pennons for two 'tubis' and two 'cornamusis' and in Marseilles in 1351, two 'cornamuzas', two 'tronbadors' and a 'naquarar' were hired by a charitable organisation to perform in a procession; AMMo, BB 10, fols. 4v–5r; ADB, Archives hospitalières de Marseilles, II H/E 7, p. 42.   [18] ADH, II E 95/547, fol. 291r–v.

bombard, and two 'charaminas'.[19] Shawms were the main instruments in this ensemble into the late fifteenth century, as the city made frequent payments to 'the loud minstrels' (*los autz menestries*) who played 'their shawms' (*suas calamillas*).[20] Shawms were double-reed instruments that first appeared in manuscript illustrations in the late thirteenth century, became widespread in Europe by the mid-fourteenth century and were the core instrument in civic wind bands by the fifteenth century. As was typical elsewhere in Europe, the percussion was no longer included in the wind band in Montpellier in the fifteenth century, even though the 'tambourin', a long cylindrical tabor often coupled with a pipe, was extremely popular in civic celebrations in southern France during this time.[21]

At the beginning of the fifteenth century, the city council of Montpellier sought foreign talent for its wind band, perhaps for the latest instrumental innovation in shawm bands, the slide-trumpet. In 1403, a citizen of Tournai, Petrus de Medie Camporum, who was identified as a 'menestrer', was offered a tax exemption on his personal estate for five years for settling in Montpellier and later became a member of the civic wind band. Slide-trumpeters from Tournai were particularly sought after at this time, as is evidenced by the city of Lille hiring many 'menestrels de trompette' from Tournai during the first decade of the fifteenth century.[22] Further suggestion that Petrus might well have been a slide-trumpeter in the civic wind band, or at least that a slide-trumpeter was included in this ensemble, is to be found in a contract from 1411 in which Petrus, the minstrel from Tournai, and his two minstrel colleagues promise to make their craft of both 'pifandi' (referring to shawm playing) and 'sonandi' (sounding the trumpet).[23]

This minstrel from Tournai appears to have been among only a small minority of minstrels in Montpellier who came from outside this region in southern France. It has long been known that the late medieval instrumental world was international in character and that, by the beginning of the fifteenth century, instrumentalists from the Low Countries and particularly Germany were prominent elsewhere in Europe. Yet it is striking that, of the approximately 125 musicians identified in civic records and private notarial contracts from Montpellier between 1350 and 1450, only a small percentage appears to have been foreigners.[24] Apparently, the members of the city council preferred to employ native musicians to represent themselves and their city in celebrations and only exceptionally employed foreigners, perhaps when the demands of a new instrument made this necessary.

The wind band, with its official livery and banners, performed directly in front of the city council through the streets of Montpellier in civic celebrations throughout the second half of the fourteenth and fifteenth centuries. These celebrations included special

---

[19] AMMo, Inventory 9, no. 853, 2nd vol. (CC 853, 2nd vol.), fols. 60r, 76v, 83r.

[20] AMMo, Inventory 8, no. 560 (CC 560), fol. 82r, 1480.

[21] During the last quarter of the fifteenth century, pipe-and-tabor players were so prominent in Montpellier that they made a separate donation to the city's charitable concerns, along with the trumpeters and the 'loud minstrels' of the city council. In 1496, a year in which the contributions of musicians were itemised, the donation of the 'taborins' was the largest among these three groups of musicians.

[22] Lille, Archives de la Ville, no. 16138, fol. 68v, 'item [pour] envoye a tournay pour avoir deux menstrels de trompette pour ses gages . . .', 1401; no. 16145, fol. 55v, 'deux manestrels [*sic*] dele trompette venus dele dit ville de tournay', 1403. I am grateful to Keith Polk for these references. Unfortunately, the city records of Tournai have been destroyed, making it impossible to identify Petrus.   [23] AMMo, BB 40, no folio number.

[24] For a complete list of these musicians see G. Peters, 'Secular Urban Musical Culture in Provence and Languedoc During the Late Middle Ages', Ph.D. thesis, University of Illinois at Urbana-Champaign (1994), Appendix One.

civic events, such as the annual 'day of charity' when bread was donated by professional organisations to the poor, a 'general procession for rain' in August of 1357 and a procession in 1371 when a new bell was mounted in the bell-tower of Notre Dame-des-Tables.[25] Most commonly, however, the wind band performed in processions for visiting nobility and for religious holidays, such as Christmas, Pentecost and 'the celebration of the miracles of Notre Dame-des-Tables'. In a typical procession on a religious holiday, the members of the city council would meet at the consulate and then process to and from a religious service at the nearby Notre Dame-des-Tables, with torches, a baldachin and their minstrels performing directly in front of them.

Some of the religious celebrations were more elaborate and involved the minstrels performing during services in the chapel of the consulate or Notre Dame-des-Tables. For the annual consecration of the chapel of the consulate, for instance, the minstrels performed in a procession within the Mass celebration itself, as well as in a lengthy procession through the streets of Montpellier. A description of the Mass appears in the *Ceremonial of the Council*, a set of detailed accounts of annual rituals and ceremonies of the city council. According to its author,

> When the next day comes, all the members of the council and other officers in the chapter of the Miracles of Notre Dame come to the consulate to hear a solemn Mass 'qui se chant en note solempnellement'. And there are good singers. One of the priests of St Fermin sings the Mass. In the said Mass a pretty procession is made in which the members of the council carry their baldachin. The minstrels in their livery go playing before the relics which are under the said baldachin. The sacristan of St Fermin, who is the Canon of Maguelone, is in the procession, and carries in his hands the head of St Cleophas. Each of the members of the council, the workers, the council of the sea, syndics and all other officers and servants of the council ought and are obligated to follow the said procession. And each carries a white candle of wax on which are painted the arms of the consulate.[26]

Following the Mass, the participants left the consulate, walked through Notre Dame-des-Tables, proceeded along a specified route through the streets of Montpellier and returned back to the consulate where the minstrels were paid.

The regular presence of the civic minstrels in religious celebrations is highlighted by the one procession in which they were expressly excluded: the annual procession honouring St Louis of Anjou celebrated on 25 August. This celebration was of unusual importance and solemnity in the region, as Louis (brother of Robert of Anjou, King of Naples) had been buried in Marseilles in 1297 after having died while in captivity in Spain.[27] According to the *Ceremonial of the Council*, 'On August 25 is the celebration of Saint Louis. On this day there is a procession in which one part of the council goes to the church of St Foy and the other part goes in the procession to Notre Dame du Chastel. Nobody is to carry a baldachin or a torch, and the minstrels are not to go.'[28]

A city chronicle provides frequent descriptions of processions honouring visiting nobility in which the civic minstrels of Montpellier also assumed a prominent role. On 9 January 1367, for example, the civic minstrels participated in a procession in honour

[25] AMMo, Inventory 9, no. 845, fol. 103v, and no. 847, fol. 25r–v.
[26] AMMo, 'Ceremonial' (BB 196), fols. 34v–35r.   [27] He was canonised in 1317.
[28] AMMo, 'Ceremonial' (BB 196), fol. 29r–v.

of Pope Urban V. This pope had particular associations with the area, for he had been born in Lozère, had received his doctorate in canon law at the university in Montpellier and made significant contributions to the welfare of the city on several occasions.[29] In this enthusiastic reception for the pope, as in other processions honouring important visitors, the minstrels served as official representatives of the city, displaying the civic livery and banners, both adorned with the coat of arms of the city. On this occasion, as was customary, the civic minstrels were among a small party that travelled on horseback to a nearby town to welcome the visiting party, while more people joined the procession as it approached Montpellier.[30] The city chronicle also describes numerous receptions involving civic minstrels for the Duchess of Anjou, the King and Queen of Navarre, the King and Queen of France and the Count of Foix, among others.

The civic minstrels of Montpellier were paid per service in the fourteenth century, but by the fifteenth century they received annual salaries and contracts. The annual wages of the civic minstrels were significantly lower than those of many other civic employees and must have constituted only a portion of their total annual income. In 1412, for instance, when a minstrel's annual wage was about 7 li, the city council offered its notary 100 li, its treasurer 60 li, and its squires 24 li each. The minstrels did, however, earn more than the individuals who were employed by the city council to repair the roads.[31] In addition to their wages, the minstrels received expensive livery and tips, often in the form of drinks. Although the minstrels received relatively low levels of remuneration, at least employment offered by the city was usually stable and permanent. In the mid-fifteenth century, for example, three of the four civic minstrels retained their positions for at least twenty years.[32]

The city of Montpellier did not limit its subsidy of instrumentalists to the civic wind band, but increasingly through the second half of the fourteenth and fifteenth centuries trumpeters were hired to perform ceremonial functions. In Montpellier, like in many other cities in Europe, trumpeters were regularly employed 'to sound the watch' from a central bell-tower. The musical skills and duties of the instrumentalists serving in this capacity varied throughout Europe. In southern Germany these officers were merely guards, probably with little musical ability, who were equipped only with signal horns. In the Low Countries, however, skilled musicians were employed who were capable of performing polyphonic chansons.[33] In Montpellier, by at least the late fourteenth century, the duties of the two guards placed on the central tower of Notre Dame-des-Tables included trumpeting in the morning and in the evening, as well as serving as guard and striking the hours. Skilled musicians were already among these tower-trumpeters at this time, such as Raymundus Salamon, who was named in numerous city records as a minstrel and was also hired by the city to perform in processions.[34] In 1410 a large clock was commissioned for the bell-tower, which was intended to replace the sounding of the hours by the guards; this was because – according to the city council – the guards received 'high wages' and demonstrated 'great negligence because they did not pull the hours'. In a contract a few years earlier, one of the tower-trumpeters was required to make a special promise not 'to entertain others, nor teach trumpeters, nor make a trumpet' while on duty, perhaps reflecting the behaviour that provoked the council's irritation and led to the construction of the town clock.[35] By 1434, the clock had finally replaced the tower-

---

[29] *Petit Thalamus*, p. 373.   [30] *Ibid.*, p. 389.   [31] *Ibid.*, pp. 179–81.
[32] Jacominus Mutonis (1419–50), Petrus de Mala (1431–50) and Jaufredus Julian alias Verdellet (1432–55).
[33] Polk, 'Wind Bands', p. 99; Polk, 'Instrumental Music', p. 162.   [34] AMMo, Inventory 9, no. 847, fol. 28v.

trumpeters in this capacity and a new obligation to play the trumpet for official entrances had been added to their duties. In the contract of that year two trumpeters promised to serve the customary duties of sounding the watch and serving as a night guard, but in addition 'also approaching with you [the city council] during entrances and exits of magnates trumpeting'.[36] During the next decade their obligation to guard the bell-tower was omitted altogether, leaving only their trumpet-playing duties of sounding the watch and performing in official entrances. Additional trumpeters were also hired for special occasions, as periodically throughout the fifteenth century payments were made to trumpet ensembles with four or five members and in 1502 eight trumpeters received livery. In addition, throughout this period the city council hired a crier who sounded the trumpet.

In summary, it appears that despite the political, economic and demographic decline of Montpellier throughout the fourteenth and early fifteenth centuries, certain established civic traditions were maintained and a still relatively strong civic government felt that, even during a period of limited funds, it was a priority to continue to regularly employ a strikingly large body of civic musicians. Indeed, the civic wind band of five members, already well established by 1357, the two tower-trumpeters, the official crier, as well as the additional trumpeters for special occasions were all a direct reflection of the prosperity and independence that Montpellier had enjoyed during the previous two centuries. Whether performing directly in front of the city council in processions, 'sounding the watch' from the bell-tower of Notre Dame-des-Tables, or making official pronouncements throughout the city and region these musicians – all in their official livery – served as an important tool in sustaining the image of power and wealth that the city and its ruling elite had enjoyed in days gone by.

Toulouse, further to the west in the foothills of the Pyrenees and on the banks of the Garonne River, was the other principal city in medieval southern France. While Toulouse was technically under the control of the Counts of Toulouse until 1271 when it was handed over to the French crown, by the late twelfth century the city had already gained its independence from nobility. By 1208, the city was in effect governed by the city council, with its twenty-four members, and an official meeting place for the city council (*maison comunal*) was constructed.[37] By the mid-fourteenth century, Toulouse had an estimated population of around 35,000 and was comparable in size to Montpellier. Like Montpellier, however, owing to the onslaught of the plague, floods, famine and the Hundred Years' War, Toulouse's population declined in the first decade of the fifteenth century; the city still maintained approximately 21,000 citizens and was thus significantly larger than Montpellier at that time. The city council in Toulouse in the fifteenth century, like that in Montpellier, was reduced significantly in size and lost its power as the officers of the King of France encroached on duties that once had been in its domain.

Over thirty account books of the treasurer of the city and numerous individual receipts dating from between 1330 and 1500 reveal that, as in Montpellier, both trumpeters and other wind players were on the city's payroll and played a conspicuous role in ceremonial life. The earliest evidence concerns trumpeters, a pattern typical for this region. By 1330, regular payments for the salary, livery and pennons of two 'trompayres' appear in the city account books. They were provided with silver instruments (*las trompas del argent*), which continued to be a major expense throughout the fifteenth century.[38] The

---

[35] AMMo, BB 36, fol. 55r, '... recolligere aliquos fayditos nec tubicinatores docere seu ibi trompam facere ...'
[36] AMMo, BB 49, fol. 11r.   [37] P. Wolff, *Les Toulousains dans l'Histoire* (Toulouse, 1984), p. 22.

trumpet duo, with their elaborate instruments and pennons, accompanied messengers to nearby cities and were a prominent part of events honouring visiting nobility. For instance, they performed on horseback during a reception for dignitaries from Perpignan in 1342, and they also played at an event that marked the visit of the Count of Clarmont in 1403.[39] In contrast to Montpellier, trumpeters did not perform the duty of standing guard and 'sounding the watch' from a central bell-tower; instead a separate 'gayca', who appears only to have rung the bells, was employed. In addition, throughout this period, a separate public crier, identified as a 'cornayre', signalled announcements in Toulouse with a simpler horn.

By at least 1383, the city council of Toulouse also employed a wind ensemble of instrumentalists other than trumpeters to perform in important ceremonies and celebrations. Isolated payments to an unidentified group of musicians appear in the accounts from 1372 and by 1383 the musicians formed an official civic wind band with a constant number of personnel who received annual pensions and livery.[40] From this point and throughout the fifteenth century the accounts indicate that there were two or three members in the group – a slightly smaller group than the ensemble maintained in Montpellier. The instruments they played on are not described and they are referred to only as 'menestries'. In a payment record from 1443, however, the three minstrels were identified as 'charaminayres', indicating that they formed a three-member shawm ensemble common at this time.[41]

As in Montpellier, the civic wind band in Toulouse played a prominent role on occasions involving the city council. For example, in an event marking the election of the members of the city council in 1398, both the trumpeters and wind band accompanied these municipal officers and other important members of the community in a procession to Saint-Sernin. This Romanesque basilica was built on the north boundary of Toulouse to shelter pilgrims on their way to Santiago de Compostela and housed the relics of Bishop Saturnin who was martyred in AD 250.[42] The minstrels were also involved in religious services at the consulate, as they were in Montpellier. Throughout the fifteenth century, account books contain annual payments to the civic musicians on 13 December. This was the feast of St Lucia and was the day the members of the city council entered office. In 1439, for example, the first entry in the expenses for the celebration of St Lucia was for the 'singers who say the Mass of the holy spirit at the consulate'. The second entry is for 'the minstrels who are five in number for the playing that was made in the said Mass on the said day'.[43] The composition of this five-person ensemble is revealed in later entries, which refer to both the 'trompetas' and 'haut menestries', a term commonly used at this time to refer to the minstrels of a wind band.[44]

The wages of these minstrels and trumpeters were comparable to those of the civic musicians in Montpellier and also must have constituted only a portion of their annual income. They both received 6 li 10 s in the second half of the fourteenth century and by

[38] AMT, CC 1843, p. 116; p. 126, 1330–1.   [39] AMT, CC 1846, fol. 45v; CC 2323, no. 7.
[40] AMT, CC 2284, p. 22, 1372; CC 1850, fol. 7v, 1383; CC 1850, fol. 35r, 1384.   [41] AMT, CC 2322, 1443.
[42] E. Roschach, *Inventaire des Archives communales antérieures à 1790, Série AA, Numeros 1–60* (Toulouse, 1981), p. 481.
[43] AMT, CC 2322, 1439, '. . . pagat lo jorn de Santa Lucia als chantres que disen la messa del sant esperit ha la mayzo communal' and 'als menestries que son en nombre sinc per la sonazo que fen en la dita messa lo dit jorn'.
[44] AMT, CC 2332, no. 20, 1450. During the late Middle Ages 'loud' (*haut*) minstrels were those who played instruments such as the trumpet or shawm, and 'soft' (*bas*) minstrels played instruments such as harp, lute and portative organ.

the second half of the fifteenth century they were receiving only 4 li.[45] Reflecting the importance of the visual image of these civic musicians, the livery they wore cost almost twice as much as their annual pension and even the pennons that were attached to their instruments cost approximately the same as their pension. That these were desirable positions to have, however, is clearly indicated by the fact that minstrels and trumpeters commonly held them for up to thirty years. In addition, the position often remained within a family from generation to generation; between 1416 and 1465 for instance, four members of the Gautier family successively held posts in the civic wind band.

Toulouse and Montpellier were the two largest cities in late medieval southern France and both had a long history of a powerful and independent city council. For important civic events, particularly those involving the city council, both centres employed a wind band and a pair of trumpeters during the second half of the fourteenth century. Despite the cities' demographic decline and reduction in consular power during the second half of the fourteenth and the fifteenth centuries, these musicians, with their expensive livery, pennons and instruments, remained on the payroll, reflecting their importance in urban ceremonial life.

The medieval history of Avignon, located further to the east in Provence at the confluence of the Rhône and Durance rivers, is dominated by the overpowering influence of the papal residency. Like Montpellier and Toulouse, early in the twelfth century the city of Avignon was granted a city government by one of its co-seigneurs, the Count of Forcalquier. Communal control of the city, however, only existed until the mid-thirteenth century when Count Charles I of Anjou installed a vicar to preside over its municipal administration. With the arrival of the papal court in 1309, Avignon effectively came under the control of the pope, though it was not until 1348 that the city was actually sold to Pope Clement VI by Joanna I of Provence. The presence of the papacy transformed Avignon into the principal market and commercial centre in the lower Rhône valley. The large entourage that followed the pope, including those attached to his court as well as those who sought newly created professional opportunities, resulted in an increase in population from only 5,000 or 6,000 in the early fourteenth century to between 25,000 and 45,000 by its peak during the years 1345 to 1347.[46] Like Montpellier and Toulouse, the population of Avignon decreased after the mid fourteenth century, a decline that was compounded by the pope's departure in the early fifteenth century. The population of Avignon was approximately 30,000 in 1370 and only around 18,000 one hundred years later. In the fifteenth century, a city council made up of wealthy citizens once again controlled the politics and economy of the city, even though papal legates were appointed.

The civic support of music in Avignon for festivities and ceremonies was more limited than in Montpellier or Toulouse and no official wind band appears to have existed until at least the mid-fifteenth century. While extant municipal accounts are sparse in the second half of the fourteenth century, it is evident that payments to musicians were for isolated occasions only. The documents reveal that an unspecified number and type of minstrels were hired on just a few occasions, including the arrival of Clement VII in the city and the departure of the King of Sicily; an agreement of peace between the kings of Spain and Portugal; and annual festal celebrations on Rogation Day and Ascension Day.[47]

---

[45] AMT, CC 1854, fol. 81r, 1391.
[46] B. Guillemain, *La cour pontificale d'Avignon (1309–1376): Etude d'une société* (Paris, 1962), p. 558.

This apparently limited civic support, however, would have been offset by the pope's frequent gifts to the minstrels in the entourage of the royal visitors. Although the popes did not maintain their own minstrels, by supporting visiting players they did in a sense fulfil the traditional role of the city in patronising music on such occasions.

A more regular pattern of civic employment of musicians is evident in a series of individual vouchers from the accounts of the general treasurer of the city throughout the second half of the fifteenth century, a period after the papal departure when the city council had begun to gain more autonomy. Musicians were hired for celebrations at important points in the liturgical year, such as Rogation Days and Carnival (*Caramentum*) which was celebrated right before the beginning of Lent. They were also hired for celebrations honouring the arrival of nobility and new legates. Participating in most of these celebrations were a pair of trumpeters and three or four minstrels who played wind instruments, particularly shawms (*chalamelis*) and pipes and tabors (*fistulis et taborinis*), which were particularly popular throughout southern France at this time.[48] For an annual banquet for the city council during Carnival, both an ensemble of loud instruments and an ensemble of soft instruments were hired. In 1475, for example, the city council made one payment to an ensemble of trumpets and different-sized kettle-drums and a second to 'the minstrels of stringed instruments, who are the harp, the lute, the rebec, the chaplechou', who are identified as those of the legate.[49] In 1481, a trumpet–kettledrum ensemble and four soft minstrels were again hired; that year the soft instruments were the pipe and tabor, the organ (most likely the small portative) a douçaine and again a 'chappe chault'.[50]

In addition, instrumentalists were hired either by the city or by the pope during the fourteenth century to perform from the central bell-tower of the episcopal palace which was later transformed into the papal palace. City statutes from the mid-thirteenth century document the custom of hiring a watchman 'to sound a horn' twice a day on the episcopal tower.[51] During the fourteenth century, it appears that the pope took responsibility for finding individuals to fill this position. During the 1360s and early 1370s, Pope Urban V hired two watchmen known as 'gaychatores' for the papal tower, of whom at least one was clearly identified as a trumpeter.[52] During the fifteenth century the city provided monthly stipends for both a 'trompete' and a 'mimus', or minstrel, in this position. The type of musical instrument that the 'mimus' played is not specified in the receipts, though one minstrel who sounded the watch from at least 1450 to 1463 was known as a player of the 'cornemuse' and another minstrel who served from at least 1473 to 1481 played the pipe and tabor in processions.

Even though the city accounts in the second half of the fifteenth century include regular payments to players of wind instruments and a trumpet duo and occasionally to players of soft instruments, clear indication of a salaried, liveried ensemble (like those maintained in Montpellier and Toulouse) is not evident for Avignon. The limited civic support of music in Avignon appears to be ultimately a result of the papal presence there. This created a highly mobile population that curtailed the development of civic practices and customs and, more specifically, the papal support offered to musicians of visiting

[47] AMA, CC 1019, fols. 236r, 325r, 426r, 722r–v; CC 36, no folio number. For a discussion of these events see Tomasello, *Music and Ritual*, pp. 38–40.   [48] AMA, CC 363, no. 180 and no. 192.

[49] 'Chaplechou' referred to bells or cymbals; AMA, CC 369, no. 201.   [50] AMA, CC 373, no. 127.

[51] R. de Maulde, 'Coutumes et règlements de la république d'Avignon au XIIIe siècle', *Nouvelle revue historique de droit français et étranger* 1 (1877), p. 565.   [52] Tomasello, *Music and Ritual*, pp. 21–5.

royalty might have replaced the obligation of the city to provide music on at least some of the important civic events. Perhaps most importantly, the lack of a strong and independent city council between the mid-thirteenth and the mid-fifteenth centuries limited the need for civic musicians.

From the evidence discussed above it is clear that civic-subsidised music was a prominent part of urban life in the larger cities of southern France during the fourteenth and fifteenth centuries. Musical practices in Montpellier – the early appearance of a civic wind band, the large number of musicians employed and the unusual nature of the ensemble of trumpets, reeds and percussion – were particularly striking and rivalled those of other major European cities in the second half of the fourteenth century. Furthermore, a comparison of Montpellier, Toulouse and Avignon suggests that in this area of southern France the extent to which city government was subject to external authority affected the degree and nature of its civic sponsorship of music. Montpellier and Toulouse, two cities whose councils had attained a high degree of independence relatively early in their history, employed an official civic wind band and a distinct trumpet duo to perform regularly at civic events. In contrast Avignon, a city which did not have autonomous power during much of this period, hired musicians on what appears to have been a more limited *ad hoc* basis.

CHAPTER SIX

MASSES, MORRIS AND METRICAL PSALMS: MUSIC IN THE ENGLISH PARISH, *c.* 1400–1600

BEAT KÜMIN

An ever-wider range of late medieval music has been studied in recent research. For a long time, cathedrals, courts and noble households, conventionally thought to be the most likely patrons of cultural activities, dominated accounts of the period. Metropolitan environments then received increasing attention, with extensive research conducted on a number of Renaissance cities.[1] Most recently, however, this emphasis on 'centres' has been complemented by a closer look at the geographical and cultural 'periphery'. Reinhard Strohm, for instance, pointed to the fact that 'the cultivation of chant and early polyphony in medieval Britain [looked] remarkably uncentralised', with 'a flexible network of musical practice' nurtured in both greater and lesser institutions – supporting what Roger Bowers has described as an atmosphere of comparatively extensive artistic freedom.[2] In a rather timely coincidence, parish churches started to attract renewed attention from religious and social historians. Growing interest in grass-roots attitudes towards Reformation change entailed closer scrutiny of the basic ecclesiastical unit in which English men and women conducted their public spiritual lives.[3] More recently, musicologists and parish historians have started to exchange their findings in a growing number of personal contacts, seminar series and interdisciplinary research projects. It seems a good time to take stock of all these endeavours.[4]

As units of research, parishes offer a number of advantages. A first attraction is the prospect of extensive geographical coverage, for by examining a network of roughly 9,000 local communities, one is literally looking at England as a whole. A second advantage consists in the now widely acknowledged vitality and variety of parochial life on the eve of the Reformation. From about 1350, churchwardens emerged as crucial local officials, devising sophisticated fundraising strategies for an ever-increasing range of

---

[1] See items listed in F. Kisby, 'Musical Culture in European Urban Societies to *c.* 1650: a Bibliographical Survey', *Royal Musical Association Research Chronicle*, forthcoming.

[2] R. Strohm, 'Centre and Periphery: Mainstream and Provincial Music', in T. Knighton and D. Fallows (eds.), *Companion to Medieval and Renaissance Music* (London, 1992), pp. 55–9; R. Bowers, 'Obligation, Agency, and *Laissez-faire*: the Promotion of Polyphonic Composition for the Church in Fifteenth-Century England', in I. Fenlon (ed.), *Music in Medieval and Early Modern Europe: Patronage, Sources and Texts* (Cambridge, 1981), pp. 1–15.

[3] A first survey of this work appeared in S. Wright (ed.), *Parish, Church and People: Local Studies in Lay Religion 1350–1700* (London, 1988).

[4] Members of the Music and History Departments at Royal Holloway College, University of London have been particularly active in this way.

religious and secular activities in their towns and villages.[5] Third, the basic ecclesiastical unit served as a kind of umbrella organisation for a plethora of individual and collective efforts within the church, most notably lights, anniversaries, guilds and chantries with countless personal, institutional or financial links to the main parish bodies. This is not to say that relations were always harmonious, but on the whole the impression is one of shared spiritual goals and pragmatic collaboration.[6]

What types of sources are available for our purpose? By far the most important records are churchwardens' accounts. Drawn up on a more or less annual basis, they provide unrivalled insight into the income and expenditure patterns of well over 200 parishes up and down the country. Inevitably, the sample is not fully representative, with more urban than rural communities, more parishes from the south than the north and much denser survival for the sixteenth than the fifteenth century. Still, it yields case studies for all types of contexts and offers as broad an insight into English local life as can reasonably be hoped for in this period.[7] Through investigations into this sort of material – supplemented by data derived from wills, inventories, visitations and various types of visual evidence – historians have come to appreciate just how much 'culture' took place in late medieval communities. In various forms and intensities, parishioners from Penzance to Carlisle rebuilt and embellished their churches, they commissioned wall paintings, vestments and rood screens on an unprecedented scale, they bought thousands of copies of devotional literature and they elaborated the festive calendar into an almost unbroken series of religious and secular celebrations.[8] The editors of the series Records of Early English Drama, for instance, keep supplying more and more evidence for the extensive scale of parish-based theatre, from simple elaborations of the liturgy to sophisticated productions of entire cycles of scriptural plays.[9]

This essay proposes to examine the historical context for musical provision in the English parish during the fifteenth and sixteenth centuries. In line with the topographical focus of this volume, it will concentrate on urban environments. The peculiarities of the latter, however, cannot be fully grasped without a comparative look beyond city walls. The identification of contrasting emphases in town and country, a somewhat neglected task, should result in a much sharper idea of what 'urban' parish music actually entailed. Developments will be studied very much from the perspective of the churchwardens and thus the local community as a whole, but other local sponsors such as individual benefactors or religious fraternities should not be forgotten. The essay opens with a survey of the plentiful evidence for late medieval music, then takes a brief look at Reformation

---

[5] See B. Kümin, *The Shaping of a Community: the Rise and Reformation of the English Parish c. 1400–1560* (Aldershot, 1996) and K. French, G. Gibbs and B. Kümin (eds.), *The Parish in English Life 1400–1600* (Manchester, 1997).

[6] G. Rosser, 'Communities of Parish and Guild in the Late Middle Ages', in Wright (ed.), *Parish, Church and People*, pp. 29–55; for musical activities of guilds see V. Bainbridge, *Gilds in the Medieval Countryside: Social and Religious Change in Cambridgeshire c. 1350–1558* (Woodbridge, 1996), esp. pp. 69–70.

[7] For a detailed list of sources see R. Hutton, *The Rise and Fall of Merry England: the Ritual Year 1400–1700* (Oxford, 1994), pp. 263–93; for methodical analysis see A. Foster, 'Churchwardens' Accounts of Early Modern England: Some Problems to be Noted, but Much to be Gained', in French, Gibbs and Kümin (eds.), *Parish in English Life*, pp. 74–93.

[8] R. Morris, *Churches in the Landscape* (London, 1989), p. 147; *SoA*, part I.

[9] A. Johnston and S. B. MacLean, 'Reformation and Resistance in Thames/Severn Parishes: the Dramatic Witness', in French, Gibbs and Kümin (eds.), *Parish in English Life*, p. 179; see also S. B. MacLean, 'Festive Liturgy and the Dramatic Connection: a Study of Thames Valley Parish Ceremonial', *Medieval and Renaissance Drama in England* 8 (1996), pp. 49–62, and the individual county volumes in the Records of Early English Drama series.

changes and concludes with some general observations on the preconditions and wider implications of parish music in the period.

So what does one find in parochial sources? Most fundamentally, perhaps, there were 'religious' as well as 'secular' occasions for parish music, although the two spheres cannot be neatly separated. Just as late medieval parishioners allocated communal resources to a piece of devotional art or the repair of a local bridge as and when the necessity arose, so they sponsored both pious and more worldly types of cultural activities. Religious music, however, is what one normally associates with an ecclesiastical institution, and our survey starts with this type of provision.

The ritual and ceremonial of the liturgy of the pre-Reformation Church was a great stimulus to musical production.[10] The solemnity and importance of parts of the canonical hours, processions, Masses and special intercessory services could all be enhanced by musical embellishment. The singers included local incumbents and parish clerks, at times supported by additional priests, choirmen and boy choristers, with congregations in the role of more or less attentive consumers. The words – if audible at all – were in Latin and instrumental accompaniment was provided by an organist, often seated in the rood loft separating chancel from nave, and sometimes other musicians.[11] The quality of performances thus depended on the available infrastructure and the importance of the occasion.[12]

Unadorned plainsong formed the backbone of the liturgy and was customary in all parish churches.[13] References to chant books appear in countless local records. In 1478 the rural Norfolk parish of Ranworth received an antiphoner produced by the monks of Langley Abbey near Loddon, which was subsequently 'customised' for its new community by the addition of services for the feast of St Helen, patron saint of the parish, and by annotations to the calendar concerning obits for the local gentry.[14] In certain parishes, polyphony would also have been performed. This added aural embellishment to the most important liturgical feasts and it was used, in addition to other forms of ceremonial, to distinguish the most significant parts of the ritual and the more important services of the day. Some of this was produced by singers who were familiar with the practice of *faburden*, a technique of improvisation whereby part-music was generated from a mid-voice plain chant using intervals of a third and sixth.[15] Other polyphonic works were written down in books of 'pricksong' which many parishes possessed. Descriptive entries in inventories frequently occurring in churchwardens' accounts indicate that it was the *Magnificat*, festal and votive Mass and antiphon that most often appeared in these sources[16] and a few surviving works offer glimpses of the music that was actually performed.[17] Preliminary research has

---

[10] *MMB*, pp. 109 ff., and R. H. Hoppin, *Medieval Music* (New York, 1978), pp. 143–214.

[11] W. Salmen, *Der Spielmann im Mittelalter* (Innsbruck, 1983), pp. 77–8, and illustration no. 93.

[12] Standard musicological surveys are N. Temperley, *The Music of the English Parish Church*, 2 vols. (Cambridge, 1979), esp. chapters 2 and 3, and *MMB*; for a historian's perspective see C. Marsh, *Popular Religion in Sixteenth-Century England: Holding their Peace* (London, 1998), pp. 33, 113.

[13] Canon law dictated which liturgical books were required: F. Kisby, 'Books in London Parish Churches, 1400–1603', *Proceedings of the 1999 Harlaxton Symposium*, Harlaxton Medieval Studies 11 (Stamford, 2001).

[14] *SoA*, pp. 418–19, and plates 132, 136; see also J. Deveson, 'The Ranworth Antiphoner: a Study of a MS and its Use in the Pre-Reformation English Liturgy', M.Mus. dissertation, University of Edinburgh (1994).

[15] *s.v.* 'faburden' in *Grove*, vol. VI; C. Story, 'GB-Lbl Harley MS 2942: Music in Context', M.Mus. dissertation, Royal Holloway College, University of London (1998).

[16] For a list of polyphony copied at St Margaret's Church Westminster in the early sixteenth century see F. Kisby, 'Music and Musicians of Early-Tudor Westminster', *Early Music* 23 (1995), p. 237.

[17] E.g. the *Magnificat* by Christopher Anthony from *c.* 1450; Temperley, *Music of the English Parish Church*, vol. II, pp. 3, 21–5.

shown that, of the 174 'lost' books of polyphony known to have been present in England before 1500, over thirty were kept, not in cathedrals or abbeys but in nineteen parish churches, many of them in urban communities *outside* the big cities and some in smaller villages.[18] We are reminded that many of these churches might have had 'no provision' for the actual performance of polyphony,[19] but the *potential* for sophisticated musical provision outside the big centres should not be underestimated. At Ashburton, for instance, a market-town-cum-manor parish in Devon with some 700 souls, accounts from the 1490s record numerous images and altars, a substantial number of obits, the names of many guilds and the presence of extra clergy, so it is not surprising to find that the wardens paid for a copy of the 'Christus Resurgens in iij partis in prykyd song'.[20] About half of the other parochial books in this list are similarly documented, through purchases or repairs financed by the local community, which would make little sense if it had no use for them. Other evidence points in the same direction. The parish of Hemingbrough in Yorkshire certainly had the prerequisites for the performance of polyphonic music, for it played host to a choral staff of six vicars-choral and four clerks from the early fifteenth century.[21]

The crucial role of lay benefaction in the gradual elaboration of musical provision is now widely accepted. Late medieval testators almost invariably specified a range of good works and intercessory services to speed the passage of their souls through Purgatory. Prayers for the dead thus multiplied in a myriad of different forms, most prominently through the endowment of votive Masses, anniversaries and chantries, resulting in a great 'increase' in divine service and liturgical variety.[22] The range and quality of religious music in some churches has received detailed scholarly attention. St Mary at Hill in London, a prosperous city-centre parish with a host of side altars and a great deal of landed resources, is perhaps the best documented example. From the pioneering work of Hugh Baillie and more recent studies based on the rich parochial archives, we know a great deal about the careers, endowments and repertory of its musicians. The priests of seven perpetual chantries and more specialised singing clerks allowed the performance of polyphony on regular occasions and the church purchased a number of pricksong books in the early sixteenth century. Rewards were also offered to Chapel Royal singers (some of whom actually resided in the parish) for their services on important feasts and payments were made to the renowned musician John Northfolke for 'kepyng the quere and the Orgons' in the church. During the latter's six years of activity at St Mary's, choral provision increased and a school for boy choristers emerges in the records.[23] At All Saints, Bristol, to move to another well-researched community in England's foremost provincial city, parishioners enjoyed a similarly complex repertory.

---

18 A. Wathey, 'Lost Books of Polyphony in England: a List to 1500', *Royal Musical Association Research Chronicle* 21 (1988), pp. 1–19.

19 A. Wathey, 'The Production of Books of Liturgical Polyphony', in J. Griffiths and D. Pearsall (eds.), *Book Production and Publishing in Britain 1375–1475* (Cambridge, 1989), p. 148.

20 A. Hanham (ed.), *Ashburton Churchwardens' Accounts 1479–1580* (Torquay, 1970), 1492/4; for polyphony in many other local churches see Temperley, *Music of the English Parish Church*, vol. I, p. 8; and P. le Huray, *Music and the English Reformation 1549–1660* (Oxford, 1967), p. 13.

21 R. B. Dobson, *Durham Priory* (Cambridge, 1973), pp. 156–62.

22 C. Burgess, '"For the Increase of Divine Service": Chantries in the Parish in Late Medieval Bristol', *Journal of Ecclesiastical History* 36 (1985), pp. 46–65, and B. Haggh, 'The Meeting of Sacred Ritual and Secular Piety: Endowments for Music', in Knighton and Fallows (eds.), *Companion*, pp. 60–8.

23 H. Baillie, 'London Churches: their Music and Musicians 1485–1560', Ph.D. thesis, University of Cambridge (1957), and his 'A London Church in Early-Tudor Times', *Music and Letters* 36 (1955), pp. 55–64; R. Lloyd, 'Music at the Parish Church of St Mary at Hill, London', *Early Music* 25 (1997), pp. 221–6.

Among the many local clergymen was a 'priest to sing in perpetuity at the Lady Altar in the said church' financed by an endowment of Sir John Gyllarde and Richard Haddon, there were seats for children taking part in the choir, extra singers were engaged for specific feasts such as Palm Sunday, clerks received rewards for singing the 'passion' in the rood loft and organ players were paid on a quarterly basis. In the late fifteenth century, chant books were bequeathed to the church by clergy formerly in employment there and chantry priests sometimes donated books of pricksong.[24]

In addition, All Saints attracted a great number of bequests for the celebration of obits or anniversaries. In return for substantial sums of revenue, the churchwardens organised rounds of prayers and requiem Masses, paid for extra clergy to attend the services, and distributed alms to the poor. The sources are rarely very explicit about the kind of musical provision, but given the sums involved it was clearly impressive, involving in at least one case the solemn singing of *Placebo* and *Dirige* with nine lessons as well as a Requiem Mass, all – as is specified explicitly – 'by note'. In the last pre-Reformation years, the wardens parted with a handsome £3 13s 6d per year to keep all their obits, some 10 per cent of their total expenditure.[25] Across the road, St Ewen's in Bristol spent a comparable 9 per cent (7–8s) of its annual expenses on obits and a further 4 per cent on other items augmenting its ceremonial life in the early sixteenth century.[26] But while the metropolitan communities of London and Bristol supported particularly elaborate – or perhaps just particularly well-documented – musical provision, they were by no means unique. If major endowments were wanting, parishioners reached into their own pockets. At the Hertfordshire market town of Bishop's Stortford at the end of the fifteenth century, for instance, a John Cosyn received regular payments for 'pleyyng at the organs' at Easter, Pentecost, Corpus Christi, Michaelmas, All Hallows, Christmas and a dozen other occasions throughout the year. The churchwardens also financed 'syngyng candles' for use in the choir, the repair of a 'processional' and the making of a new 'booke of prikkyd songge'.[27] Whatever the technical standard, musical investments reached striking levels even in rural communities. Yatton in Somerset spent £17 (a sum well in excess of the annual income of most parochial incumbents) on a new organ in 1527, which the parish commissioned and transported from the workshop of a craftsman in nearby Bristol. In the same year, the organ player received 2s 5d for his services.[28]

---

[24] The evidence for this parish derives mainly from its elaborate Church Book: P/AS/ChW/1, Bristol Record Office, now edited in C. Burgess (ed.), *The Pre-Reformation Records of All Saints', Bristol: Part I*, Bristol Record Society 46 (Bristol, 1995). The examples cited can be found in *ibid.*, pp. 8–11, and in Churchwardens' accounts of All Saints, 1453/4, 1461/2, 1472/3, and 1479/80: Bristol Record Office, P/AS/ChW/3. See also F. Harrison, 'The Repertory of an English Parish in the Early Sixteenth Century', in J. Robijns (ed.), *Renaissance-Muziek 1400–1600* (Louvain, 1969), pp. 143–7.

[25] C. Burgess, 'A Service for the Dead: the Form and Function of the Anniversary in Late Medieval Bristol', *Transactions of the Bristol and Gloucestershire Archaeological Society* 105 (1987), pp. 183–211; Kümin, *Shaping of a Community*, appendix 3. For musical provision at obits see also the essay by Lee-De Amici in this volume and R. Lloyd, 'Chantries and Music in Late Medieval London', Ph.D. dissertation, University of London (2000).

[26] Kümin, *Shaping of a Community*, appendix 3, and B. Masters and E. Ralph (eds.), *The Church Book of St Ewen's, Bristol 1454–1584* (Bristol, 1967), *passim*.

[27] S. Doree (ed.), *The Early Churchwardens' Accounts of Bishop's Stortford* (Hitchin, 1994), 1483/4, 1489/90, 1492/3.

[28] Churchwardens' accounts of Yatton, 1527/8: Somerset Record Office, Taunton, D/P/yat/4/1/2. Less than a quarter of English benefices had an income of £15 or more on the eve of the Reformation: C. Harper-Bill, *The Pre-Reformation Church in England 1400–1530* (London, 1989), pp. 44–5.

The placing of musicians in their social environment is now an important feature of musicological work. Tudor London has attracted most detailed attention, with extensive biographical information available for hundreds of individuals.[29] The organ builders of the Howe dynasty, for instance, are known to have worked for nearly all parishes in the capital and a number of churches elsewhere. By 1571, they owned one of the earliest full-time organ practices in the country and received regular maintenance payments from numerous churchwardens in the city. The case of John Mayhew, meanwhile, illustrates how laypeople helped out with musical services in this period. A clothworker by trade, Mayhew also earned a wage as a conduct at St Benet Gracechurch in the mid-sixteenth century and received some extra money 'to syng the suffrages in the mornyng' on Wednesdays and Fridays.[30] The growth of post-mortem endowments in the wealthier neighbourhoods also offered employment opportunities for the most distinguished names of the period. For example, the well-known composer Nicholas Ludford, who was verger-cum-organist in the royal college of St Stephen's Westminster, had a long association with the nearby parish church of St Margaret from around 1520. Ludford owned tenements in various areas of the town and – from 1525 – part of a pew in the parish church, where he was twice married and where he was buried in 1557. The relationship, however, went beyond mere physical presence and the administration of sacraments, for Ludford joined a guild, supported a number of traditional religious activities and even served as churchwarden from 1522 to 1524. St Margaret's maintained a choir competent in polyphony, which Ludford provided with one of its many 'pryke songe' books in 1533. It is conceivable that some of his works – and those of other composers associated with the church – were commissioned by parish bodies, even though Ludford does not seem to have had an active part in the music-making itself. The singing children, for instance, were taught by a John Moore, who in 1529 received 5s 4d for the 'prykyng of ix kyries ix alleluyas viij sequence vj anthems a masse of iiij parts for men and a exultant for children'.[31] It is also clear that the choirs of the Chapel Royal, the College of St Stephen's, Cardinal Wolsey's household and Westminster Abbey's Lady Chapel repeatedly performed at this 'focal point of the town's musical life' in the early Tudor period. Quite a large number of Chapel Royal members had extensive social contacts with parishioners of St Margaret's and no fewer than nine were buried in the body of its church.[32]

The presence of outstanding musicians, however, was not restricted to the metropolis. Robert Wilkinson, another distinguished representative of his profession, served as parish clerk at Eton, while many of his most renowned colleagues maintained associations with provincial churches as rectors or vicars, even though they were not often resident.[33] John Taverner, one of the most prominent and prolific composers of the early sixteenth century, started off as a humble lay clerk at the collegiate church of Tattershall in rural Lincolnshire in the early 1520s and sang in the same capacity at the parish church

---

[29] See Andrew Wathey's editorial to the thematic issue 'Music In and Around Tudor London', *Early Music* 25 (1997), pp. 180–2.

[30] Information on some 400 individual musicians appears in H. Baillie, 'Some Biographical Notes on English Church Musicians, Chiefly Working in London 1485–1560', *Royal Musical Association Research Chronicle* 2 (1962), pp. 18–57, esp. p. 40 (Howe) and p. 45 (Mayhew).

[31] D. Skinner, '"At the Mynde of Nycholas Ludford": New Light on Ludford from the Churchwardens' Accounts of St Margaret's, Westminster', *Early Music* 22 (1994), pp. 393–410, esp. pp. 393, 397, 399.

[32] Kisby, 'Music and Musicians', pp. 234, 225–8.

[33] J. and E. Roche, *A Dictionary of Early Music* (London, 1981), pp. 205 (Wilkinson), 58 (Thomas Damett, Rector of Stockton in Wiltshire in the early fifteenth century), 177 (Richard Smert, Vicar of Plymtree near Exeter, 1428–74).

of St Botolph, Boston, in the late 1530s. At the latter, a church boasting a cathedral-size choir of some thirty men supported by a local guild, he also acted as instructor to the choristers, before progressing to a number of important secular offices in the town.[34]

Apart from 'sacred' liturgical music, parishes supported the 'secular' type of entertainments nostalgically associated with 'Merry England'.[35] Even the most cursory look at churchwardens' accounts reveals evidence of social activities, organised out of a mixture of neighbourly conviviality and fundraising necessity. Apart from the dedication day and the feast of the church's patron saint, the most spectacular season of celebrations ran from Easter to Midsummer and focused on festivals such as Hocktide (the second Monday and Tuesday after Easter), May Day (1 May), Whitsun (fiftieth day after Easter) and Corpus Christi (the Thursday following the first Sunday after Whitsun). Profits were normally boosted by a range of special attractions, provided in an idiosyncratic mixture reflecting local custom and the requirements of the respective feast day. Major ingredients included the staging of plays (with religious as well as farcical elements),[36] the hiring of minstrels and 'fools', the equipment of morris dancers, the appointment of mock lords and ladies, the holding of processions,[37] the appearance of Robin Hood, or the organisation of summer games.[38] Women took an active part in proceedings, particularly in the West Country with its dense network of maidens' guilds. Recent surveys of their role emphasise the significant financial contributions made by public singing and dancing, the playful capturing of members of the opposite sex and many forms of unpaid labour recorded in churchwardens' accounts and other local records.[39] A parallel development was the construction of communal 'church houses', which provided a venue and facilities for social gatherings.[40]

Many individual case studies could be cited to illustrate the range of activities. The early sixteenth-century church book from the borough of Kingston-upon-Thames is perhaps the richest source for details concerning morris dancing and summer drama.[41] When the village of Boxford in Suffolk staged a major play in 1535, the parish hired various actors 'which cam owt of strange placys'. These were sent on a tour of neighbouring areas, and the investment returned a profit in excess of £19 for repairs to the church fabric. Some of the income came from 'drynkers in the bo[o]th', who presumably proposed a toast to the cultural patronage of the Boxford wardens.[42] Apart from playing host to touring companies, inter-parochial exchange was also promoted by the hire of expensive costumes and equipment by those who could not afford to buy such props themselves.[43] The main source of revenue was invariably the sale of ale, brewed locally at

---

[34] *s.v.* 'John Taverner', in *Grove*, vol. XVIII, pp. 598–602; Roche, *Dictionary of Early Music*, p. 184.

[35] Hutton, *The Rise and Fall of Merry England*.

[36] For the contents of plays and the props and costumes used see the 'Croxton Play of the Sacrament', discussed in *SoA*, pp. 106–8; Hanham (ed.), *Ashburton, passim*, and J. Wasson (ed.), *Devon*, Records of Early English Drama (Toronto, 1986), pp. 17–30.   [37] M. Rubin, *Corpus Christi* (Cambridge, 1991).

[38] For details of these celebrations see Hutton, *The Rise and Fall of Merry England*, pp. 1–68.

[39] S. B. MacLean, 'Hocktide: a Reassessment of a Popular Pre-Reformation Festival', in M. Twycross (ed.), *Festive Drama* (Woodbridge, 1996), pp. 233–41; K. French, 'To Free Them from Binding: Women in the Late Medieval English Parish', *Journal of Interdisciplinary History* 27 (1997), pp. 387–412, and her 'Maidens' Lights and Wives' Stores: Women's Parish Guilds in Late Medieval England', *Sixteenth Century Journal* 29 (1998), pp. 399–425.   [40] P. Cowley, *The Church Houses* (London, 1970).

[41] M. Heaney, 'Kingston to Kenilworth: Early Plebeian Morris', *Folklore* 100 (1989), pp. 88–104, and S. B. MacLean, 'King Games and Robin Hood: Play and Profit at Kingston-upon-Thames', *Research Opportunities in Renaissance Drama* 29 (1986–7), pp. 85–93.

[42] P. Northeast (ed.), *Boxford Churchwardens' Accounts 1530–61* (Woodbridge, 1982), pp. xiii and 19.

[43] A. Johnston, 'Parish Entertainments in Berkshire', in J. A. Raftis (ed.), *Pathways to Medieval Peasants* (Toronto, 1981), pp. 335–8; Heaney, 'Morris', p. 96.

moderate cost by the wardens themselves or by territorial and organisational subgroups of the parish. At Yatton, on average 84 per cent of fresh income in the last pre-Reformation years derived from the sale of ale, with just under 7 per cent of total expenditure absorbed by the costs of brewing and organising. The highest recorded income of over £18 occurs in 1533, the highest expenditure of nearly £4 for events in 1545. This may have been an extreme case, but church ales and other social events played an important part in many other parish budgets. In a sample of ten urban and rural communities from all over England, they accounted for about 20 per cent of the aggregate pre-Reformation income.[44]

Music was an indispensable component of popular entertainment, be it the performance of more 'serious' mystery plays or 'merrier' May Day celebrations, where 'a piper or fiddler to play for community dancing was probably the commonest form of entertainer'.[45] Evidence for the latter is abundant: St Ewen's, Bristol, gathered nearly 14s from a dancing day in 1464, parishioners of Great St Mary's, Cambridge, regularly danced on their church's dedication feast, the villagers of early Tudor Dunmow in Essex raised money from a dancing tour of twenty-three neighbouring settlements, and further examples could be cited from the boroughs of Plymouth, Southwark and Salisbury from at least the fifteenth century. In the Wiltshire county town, all three parishes held dancing events on different days during Whitsun week and there can be little doubt that such occasions were 'widely familiar to the English population'.[46] Minstrels appear regularly in the Yatton accounts from the 1520s, normally in association with one of the church ales.[47] Only rarely do we get more detailed insights into the type of musical entertainment offered on such occasions. One example is a fragmentary song-text from an Elizabethan treble part-book, which provides an apparently realistic description of the various folk customs performed on the feast of St Cuthbert in Durham. It alludes to 'disguising, piping and dancing', to the staging of a Robin Hood play where 'every man his horn did blow' and also to revels of the young women of the town. This latter passage, as John Milsom has argued, is the original context of the famous poem 'The Maidens Came'. The exact date and meaning of the song as a whole are now difficult to determine, but there are grounds to suspect that it is an early sixteenth-century composition, perhaps referring to some sort of competition between various parishes of the city.[48]

Most of the evidence for secular musical entertainment derives from rural and smaller market-town environments, but similar events could also take place in larger city parishes: Bristol has been mentioned and royal minstrels are known to have found employment as well as a social 'home' in at least fifteen parishes in the City of London during the Tudor era. St Olave Hart Street, All Hallows Barking and Holy Trinity Minories, all in the eastern part, had the densest clustering of royal instrumentalists, while their city colleagues settled above all in St Giles Cripplegate, St Stephen Coleman Street, St Michael Bassishaw, St Botolph Aldgate, St Dunstan Stepney and St James Garlickhithe.

---

[44] Churchwardens' accounts of Yatton, 1540–6: Somerset Record Office, Taunton, D/P/yat/4/1/2–3; Kümin, *Shaping of a Community*, appendix four.

[45] Heaney, 'Morris', p. 89 (quote); Hutton, *The Rise and Fall of Merry England*, p. 29.

[46] Masters and Ralph (eds.), *Church Book of St Ewen's*, 1464/5; all other examples cited from A. Douglas, '"Owre Thanssynge Day": Parish Dance and Procession in Salisbury', *Folk Music Journal* 6 (1994), pp. 600–16 (quote); cf. also Heaney, 'Morris', p. 88.

[47] Churchwardens' accounts of Yatton, 1528–47: Somerset Record Office, Taunton, D/P/yat/4/1/2–3.

[48] J. Milsom, 'Cries of Durham', *Early Music* 17 (1989), pp. 147–60.

Just as members of the Chapel Royal acted as parish officials at Westminster, so did royal minstrels in the City of London.[49]

The Reformation, or rather the multitude of heterogeneous and at times contradictory influences which shaped the process in England from Henry VIII's break with Rome in 1534 well into the Elizabethan age of the late sixteenth century, had an inevitable impact on the picture that has just been drawn.[50] Given the radical reformers' hostility to music, the abolition of the Sarum chants and the emergence of a new theology opposed to the efficacy of prayers for the dead and the spiritual benefits of good works, the rationale behind much of late medieval parish music looked doomed. Revisionist Reformation scholarship thus emphasises dramatic consequences in liturgical practice, the loss of trained musicians through the dissolution of chantries in 1547 and the 'silencing of all but a handful of choirs'. Secular celebrations, too, came under sustained Puritan attacks and suffered an irreversible decline.[51] As with every historical turning point, however, there were continuities as well as changes and notable gains as well as spectacular losses.

For a start, the reorientation of popular beliefs required time and ceremonial customs did not disappear overnight. A smaller number of calendar days continued to be marked by musical performances, albeit in honour of the Queen (Accession Day) rather than particular saints,[52] and while Merry England had passed its heyday, mimetic, musical and dance customs all proved remarkably resilient.[53] In the long run, however, public attention turned to new genres and fashions. Godly songs and anti-Catholic ballads helped the first generation of English reformers to widen the appeal of Protestant doctrines. As early as 1543, the Henrician 'Act for the Advancement of True Religion' identified rhymes and songs as dangerous weapons to pervert the people.[54] Thanks to the availability of cheap print, millions of copies of ballads on all imaginable topics circulated towards the end of the sixteenth century, but this genre was associated more with streets, fairs and alehouses than parish communities.[55] Musical entertainment clearly continued to appeal to a large part of the population. Thousands of ballad-sellers, city waits and minstrels managed to earn a living in early modern England.[56]

Music did not disappear from parish churches either. Until the death of Henry VIII in 1547, there were few actual changes made to the liturgy. The publication of Thomas Cranmer's English Litany in 1544 marked a first step in the promotion of vernacular elements in public worship. Two editions of it were published with monophonic notation, which presented syllabic settings of the Sarum chants preserved in the old service books.

[49] F. Kisby, 'Royal Minstrels in the City and Suburbs of Early Tudor London: Professional Activities and Private Interests', *Early Music* 25 (1997), pp. 199–219; W. Ingram, 'Minstrels in Elizabethan London: Who Were They, What Did They Do?', *English Literary Renaissance* 14 (1984), pp. 30–1.

[50] Various aspects of the urban Reformation are examined in P. Collinson and J. Craig (eds.), *The Reformation in English Towns 1500–1640* (Basingstoke, 1998).

[51] Detailed accounts of the Reformation impact on English parishes in *SoA*, esp. p. 465, and R. Whiting, *The Blind Devotion of the People: Popular Religion and the English Reformation* (Cambridge, 1989); for the attack on ceremonial customs see Hutton, *The Rise and Fall of Merry England*, pp. 69–152; for the disappearance of intercessory institutions P. Cunich, 'The Dissolution of the Chantries', in Collinson and Craig (eds.), *Reformation in English Towns*, pp. 159–74.   [52] Marsh, *Popular Religion*, p. 103.

[53] Johnston and MacLean, 'Reformation and Resistance', *passim*; Douglas, 'Parish Dance', 605.

[54] P. Collinson, 'Popular and Unpopular Religion', in his *The Religion of Protestants: The Church in English Society 1559–1625* (Oxford, 1982), p. 237; A. Luders *et al.* (eds.), *Statutes of the Realm: From Original Records*, 11 vols. (London, 1810–28), vol. III, 34–35 Henry VIII, c. 1.

[55] T. Watt, *Cheap Print and Popular Piety 1550–1640* (Cambridge, 1991), p. 11.

[56] W. L. Woodfill, *Musicians in English Society from Elizabeth to Charles I* (Princeton, 1953), pp. 242–3.

Its use would thus have effected little immediate change in musical ceremonial.[57] Given that this was not a prescribed text though, and owing to loss of records, the full extent of its usage is unclear. In London, however, almost 70 per cent of parishes for which records survive purchased this book.[58] As the *First Book of Common Prayer* introduced under Edward VI gave few unambiguous clues as to which items of the new Protestant services could be sung, in 1550 John Merbecke published *The Booke of Common Praier Noted*.[59] Like the English Litany, this was not an officially prescribed book and there is little evidence of parishes buying it, even in the capital.[60] After a temporary reversal to the old ways under Mary, the Elizabethan injunctions of 1559 brought the return to Protestantism and a relatively tolerant attitude with regard to music:

> for the comforting of such that delight in music, it may be permitted that in the beginning, or in the end of common prayers, either at morning or evening, there may be sung an Hymn, or such like song, to the praise of Almighty God . . . having respect that the sentence of the Hymn may be understood and perceived . . .[61]

One of the most distinctive innovations of Elizabethan worship – influenced by practices in continental and Marian exile churches – was the fact that parishioners became active performers themselves, for they now had the opportunity, at least in the earlier part of the reign, to sing metrical psalms.[62] Instrumental accompaniment by an organist and direction from skilled parish clerks may have been at a premium, but congregational singing of psalms provided 'a gateway to musical knowledge' for a very broad section of the English population. The printer John Day's *Whole Booke of Psalmes*, with monophonic tunes for the metrical texts, was first published in 1562 and reached nearly 500 editions over the next 125 years.[63]

Regular choral provision, meanwhile, was reduced to a few dozen churches, with some London parishes, such as St Dunstan in the West, St Mary at Hill, St Mary Woolnoth and St Stephen Walbrook, and some in the conservative West Country, such as the boroughs of Barnstaple and Launceston, offering occasional choral services.[64] Alan Smith has gone to great lengths to argue that the impact of the Reformation was not quite as devastating as might be thought. His register of parish church musicians during the Elizabethan reign contains detailed information for no fewer than 222 individuals and 81 different churches.[65] At St Laurence in Ludlow (Shropshire), to mention

[57] R. A. Leaver, *Goostly Psalms and Spirituall Songes: English and Dutch Metrical Psalms from Coverdale to Utenhove 1535–1566* (Oxford, 1991), p. 112.   [58] Kisby, 'Books in London Parish Churches'.

[59] Le Huray, *Music and the Reformation*, pp. 4, 22; transcripts of the works mentioned in this paragraph in Temperley, *Music of the English Parish Church*, vol. II, pp. 3–4, 25–30.

[60] Kisby, 'Books in London Parish Churches'. Even so, Judith Maltby describes it as 'a highly successful version of the Book of Common Prayer for singing': *Prayer Book and People in Elizabethan and Stuart England* (Cambridge, 1998), p. 41 n. 41.

[61] W. H. Frere and W. P. M. Kennedy (eds.), *Visitation Articles and Injunctions of the Period of the Reformation*, 3 vols. (London, 1908–10), vol. III, p. 8.

[62] Collinson, 'Popular and Unpopular Religion', p. 237; Marsh, *Popular Religion*, pp. 36–9.

[63] Woodfill, *Musicians in English Society*, pp. 156–7; Temperley, *Music of the English Parish Church*, vol. I, pp. 53–4 (John Day). One probable example for a parish purchase of Day's work is the reference to 8s spent for '4 books in print' at Ludlow in 1569: A. Smith, 'Elizabethan Church Music at Ludlow', *Music and Letters* 49 (1968), p. 112. A long tradition of using the organ 'to accompany the singing of the psalms' is asserted in a petition from St Wulfram's parish in the Lincolnshire borough of Grantham in 1641: Maltby, *Prayer Book*, p. 3 n. 7.   [64] Le Huray, *Music and the Reformation*, pp. 13–17.

[65] A. Smith, 'Parish Church Musicians in England in the Reign of Elizabeth I 1558–1603: an Annotated Register', *Royal Musical Association Research Chronicle* 4 (1964), pp. 42–93.

the most striking example, the town corporation supported a musical establishment 'similar to that of a cathedral', consisting of a master of choristers, an organist, six men and six choir-boys. The churchwardens' accounts provide detailed evidence of the compilation of music manuscripts (the last such reference being to '5 books of pricksong' in 1579), the buying of psalters and the upkeep of two organs. An agreement of 1581 between the Bishop of Hereford and the church on the form of service to be conducted on special occasions stipulated that 'the psalmes as well before the chapters as after shalbe songe in plaine songe in the quier' and the anthems 'in pricksonge', with the 'organs to be used betwine the psalmes or with the psalmes and with the Antheme or hymme', whilst the 'dailie service all the rest of the wick shalbe sayd and songe in plaine song'. There are also references to Latin motets, but even Ludlow was not immune to the general decline of non-congregational church music over the course of Elizabeth's reign, with hardly any additions to the repertory appearing in its records in the late sixteenth century.[66] Lack of endowments and inflationary pressures rather than Puritan attacks were the main reasons for the gradual contraction of this sort of provision in the country as a whole.[67]

In conclusion, it could be argued that the parish introduced 'the people' to new trends in musical provision. Unusually for the period, cultural activities were controlled by churchwardens and local communities rather than social elites or clerical bodies. In contrast to cathedrals, colleges and monasteries, the parish promoted secular as well as religious music and unlike municipal patronage, initiatives reached out into the country at large. Audiences were neither representatives of a tiny minority (as in courtly or noble households) nor exclusive in terms of gender or profession (as in some guilds). Parishes could thus be seen as the most 'democratic' and socially comprehensive patrons of music in this period.

There were three main reasons for the flourishing of parish culture on the eve of the Reformation. First, the vigour of traditional piety, above all the endowment of services for the dead. Second, the elaboration of 'secular' ceremonial customs through popular drama, summer games, morris dancing and a whole range of other events. Third, the contemporaneous 'rise' of lay parish institutions, which provided local initiatives with essential administrative and financial backing. There was, furthermore, no yawning cultural gap between town and country. Polyphonic works were bought by rural churchwardens and city parishioners staged many a dancing day. Still, the financial and clerical resources associated with obits, chantries and choirs were more likely to exist in wealthier metropolitan environments, where churchwardens administered a greater number of testamentary bequests, while celebratory fundraising tended to be more common in rural communities, whose financial regimes relied predominantly on contributions by the 'living'. As a rule of thumb, music drained the coffers of parishes in larger cities, through the costly presence of numerous singers and instrumentalists, while music augmented the funds of rural churchwardens, through its capacity to attract people to the seasonal festivals of the Church.[68]

---

[66] Smith, 'Elizabethan Church Music at Ludlow', pp. 110, 111 (quotes), and 113 (agreement of 1581); the appendix lists the contents of the church's fragmentary music manuscripts from 1570 to 1660 (individual part-books containing works by William Byrd, John Sheppard, Robert Stone, Thomas Tallis and a number of local composers: *ibid.*, pp. 116–21).   [67] Temperley, *Music of the English Parish Church*, vol. I, pp. 45–6.

[68] C. Burgess and B. Kümin, 'Penitential Bequests and Parish Regimes in Late Medieval England', *Journal of Ecclesiastical History* 44 (1993), pp. 610–30, and K. French, 'Parochial Fund-raising in Late Medieval Somerset', in French, Gibbs and Kümin (eds.), *Parish in English Life*, pp. 115–32.

The Reformation brought enormous losses in terms of intercessory endowments and qualified performers, but its overall effect was not so much a complete breakdown of parochial music as a notable shift of emphasis. Within the churches, parishioners moved from being patrons and consumers to performers of music. After the disappearance of a whole army of chantry and fraternity priests, organists and clerks were the only surviving specialists. Outside the church building, parishes played a proportionally smaller part in the cultural life of the nation. Their traditional plays and seasonal customs were in decline, while new fashions needed neither churchwardens nor communal resources to gain public support. It was a new cultural era, and parishes moved with the time.

CHAPTER SEVEN

THE ROLE OF RELIGIOUS GUILDS IN THE CULTIVATION OF RITUAL POLYPHONY IN ENGLAND: THE CASE OF LOUTH, 1450–1550

MAGNUS WILLIAMSON

In recent years there has been an upsurge of scholarly interest in the life of the medieval parish, its ritual patterns, the spiritual concerns of its inhabitants and the impact wrought upon the fabric of 'traditional religion' by doctrinal and political change.[1] Although much of this attention has been focused upon chantries and religious guilds, the central agents of voluntary lay religion, comparatively little attention has been paid to their role in promoting music within the church, either by historians or musicologists.[2] It is the role of these institutions, primarily the guilds, in the cultivation of ritual polyphony in the parish church which will be examined in this essay, with particular emphasis on the parish of St James, Louth. The surviving archival sources give an unusually clear picture of musical practice in Louth, a provincial town in which the religious guilds played a central role in realising the devotional aspirations of its inhabitants, in augmenting the churchwardens' resources of money and manpower and in enabling the wider community to enrich their worship in emulation of the greater ecclesiastical foundations.

Religious guilds varied greatly in size and wealth and most played little role in the cultivation of liturgical polyphony. The Lady Guild at St Botolph, Boston, enjoyed an annual income of between £495 and £1,364 and, through this wealth, was able to maintain a large Lady chapel choir of chaplains, lay clerks and choristers;[3] the guild of the Holy Trinity, Sleaford, was typical of the numerous guilds of only modest wealth and pretensions, which maintained no permanent staff of their own, but which held an annual Corpus Christi feast, celebrated members' obits and provided equipment for an annual

---

[1] See, for instance, *SoA*; B. Kümin, *The Shaping of a Community: the Rise and Reformation of the English Parish c. 1400–1560* (Aldershot, 1996); R. Hutton, *The Rise and Fall of Merry England: the Ritual Year 1400–1700* (Oxford, 1994); P. Collinson and J. Craig (eds.), *The Reformation in English Towns 1500–1640* (Basingstoke, 1998); S. Wright (ed.), *Parish, Church and People: Local Studies in Lay Religion 1350–1700* (London, 1988).

[2] See V. Bainbridge, *Gilds in the Medieval Countryside: Social and Religious Change in Cambridgeshire c. 1350–1558* (Woodbridge, 1996), on guilds in Cambridgeshire; G. Rosser, 'Going to the Fraternity Feast: Commensality and Social Relations in Late Medieval England', *Journal of British Studies* 33 (1994), pp. 430–46; C. Burgess has written extensively and authoritatively on the role of chantries within Bristol, particularly in the church of All Saints (for instance, '"For the Increase of Divine Service": Chantries in the Parish in Late Medieval Bristol', *Journal of Ecclesiastical History* 36 (1985), pp. 46–65). For recent studies of the musical role of guilds, see D. Mateer and E. New, '*In Nomine Jesu*: Robert Fayrfax and the Fraternity of the Holy Name in St Paul's Cathedral', *Music and Letters* 81:4 (2000), 507–19, and F. Kisby, 'Music and Musicians of Early-Tudor Westminster', *Early Music* 23 (1995), pp. 223–40.

[3] A compotus book for this guild survives for the years 1514–25: BL, MS Egerton 2886; the income in 1521/2, for instance, was £1,364 13s 4½d (MS Egerton 2886, fol. 203v).

play (in this case on Ascension Day).[4] Most guilds were unable to maintain singers and clergy of their own, only hiring minstrels for the fraternity feast. Religious guilds fulfilled a number of core needs: social, in the holding of annual fraternity gatherings on the patronal feast and in almsgiving; ritual, in the maintenance of obits and anniversaries for deceased guild members; and devotional, in furthering the cult of saints.[5] Religious guilds, even the most meagre, afforded laymen and laywomen involvement in, and thereby influence over, the spiritual and social direction of their community.[6]

The numerous religious guilds, or confraternities, of Louth were typical in their varied wealth, constitutions and functions. The context from which these guilds stemmed was provincial, semi-urban and moderately affluent, rather than spectacularly wealthy. Louth is a small market town in the Wolds of Lincolnshire: its population in 1524/5 has been estimated at just under 1,000.[7] The town is surrounded by rich agricultural land and its economy prospered in the later Middle Ages, benefiting from the export and processing of wool and the importation of wine. Among its more prominent citizens were merchants of the staple of Calais, whose trading connections extended through and beyond London to the Low Countries. Much of the wealth accruing from trade was channelled into the chief church of the town, St James's, where a substantial rebuilding programme culminated in 1515 with the completion of the splendid spire which remains the town's chief topographical feature. In addition to St James's, three other ecclesiastical foundations existed in medieval Louth: the chapel of St Mary, the chapel of St John and Louth Park Abbey, a Cistercian house dissolved in 1536.[8] The archival records of pre-Reformation Louth are unusually comprehensive, comprising an almost complete sequence of churchwardens' accounts for St James's (starting in 1500), as well as the account books for the town's two most prominent guilds.[9] The churchwardens' accounts on their own give only a partial picture of the devotional life of St James's. For example, in the returns for the 1526 clerical subsidy, twelve clergy were listed in Louth, including the vicar and the prebendary.[10] Most of these priests, although serving in St James's, were either chantry priests or guild chaplains, their stipends being paid, not by the churchwardens, but by the corporate institutions that hired them.

Between 1389 and 1546, at least nine religious guilds were extant in Louth, although some of these, for instance the guild of the Twelve Apostles, were probably extinct by the mid-fifteenth century.[11] Most of these guilds were attached to St James's church. The two principal guilds in St James's, the Lady Guild and the Trinity Guild, were the largest in Louth. Although the Lady Guild was formally established by letters patent

---

[4] BL, Add. MS 28533 (compotus book, 1477–1545), fol. 1v (1477).
[5] For numerous examples of guild ordinances, see T. Smith (ed.), *English Gilds: the Original Ordinances of More Than One Hundred Early English Gilds*, Early English Text Society, original series, 40 (London, 1870).
[6] See J. J. Scarisbrick, *The Reformation and the English People* (Oxford, 1984), pp. 19–39, for an overview of the functions and history of religious guilds in pre-Reformation England.
[7] A. Dyer, *Decline and Growth in English Towns, 1400–1640*, Studies in Economic and Social History (Basingstoke, 1991), p. 74.
[8] *LOCR*, p. 152; D. Knowles and R. N. Hancock, *Medieval Religious Houses, England and Wales*, 2nd edn (London, 1971), pp. 121–2.
[9] For the churchwardens' accounts, which were copied annually on or around Pentecost, see CWA 1, CWA 2, CWA 3. Transcripts of these, made in 1870, are in the John Rylands University Library, Deansgate, Manchester, English MSS 229–231. For the guild accounts see LG and TG.
[10] H. Salter (ed.), *A Subsidy Collected in the Diocese of Lincoln in 1526*, Oxford Historical Society 63 (Oxford and London, 1909), p. 12. This number included the Rector (Robert Shorton), a Prebendary of Lincoln Cathedral, who was not normally resident in Louth.   [11] See Appendix 1.

in 1447, it superseded an earlier guild founded in St James's church under the name of its older dedication to St Herefrith of Louth.[12] Similarly, the Trinity Guild, which was incorporated in 1450, probably superseded a fourteenth-century institution of the same name at St Mary's chapel.[13] The incorporation and re-endowment of the two principal guilds and the institution of a dynamic vicar, John Sudbury, in the mid-1440s coincided with the rebuilding of the church on a grand scale. Sudbury was among those who petitioned Henry VI for a licence to endow the Trinity Guild in 1450 and, although he was not listed among the (re-)founders of the Lady Guild, he helped to negotiate a licence to acquire further lands for that guild in 1454.[14]

There was clearly a desire to reinvigorate the religious guilds at a time when the parish church was undergoing fundamental – and costly – reconstruction in the mid-fifteenth century. This was animated in part by the vicar, but also by prominent laity: Ralph Caylstrope, who had been dean of the ailing Trinity Guild at St Mary's chapel in 1422/3, was among the signatories of the petition to re-endow the Lady Guild at St James's in 1447;[15] John Louthe, one of the signatories on behalf of the Lady Guild in 1447, subsequently founded a perpetual chantry in the Trinity chapel, which he had built at St James's.[16] Further endowments continued to be acquired by (and for) the guilds later in the fifteenth century. In 1476, for instance, license was given for 218 acres of land, a dovecote, four cottages and five messuages to be alienated to the Guild of the Blessed Virgin Mary (i.e. the Lady Guild), the petition having been presented by John Sudbury (vicar), John Enderby (one of the guild chaplains) and William Roughton (chaplain of John Louth's chantry);[17] the previous year, licences had been issued simultaneously to both of the principal guilds to acquire lands for rental.[18] Aided by the most prominent layfolk, the clergy took a leading role in consolidating the endowments of the town's religious guilds; as a result of this process, the incomes of the churchwardens' two principal guilds combined amounted to between £80 and £100 per year. Although each of the guilds was constitutionally autonomous, the accumulation of property and endowments was evidently a co-ordinated process: a similar pattern of co-operation between each of the guilds, and between both the guilds and the churchwardens, was manifested in the way that these endowments were put to use.

The Lady Guild and the Trinity Guild were constitutionally very similar. Both guilds were headed by an alderman elected annually and assisted by deans; both guilds included men and women among their members, who were entitled to wear a corporate uniform, and who held congregations, processions and obits; both guilds derived income not only through annual subscriptions and bequests but, as has been noted, through rental income;

---

12. *CPR Henry VI*, 6 vols. (London, 1909), vol. V, p. 81: letters patent issued 25 January 1447 (new style); according to the 1389 chancery return, the Guild of the Blessed Virgin Mary in St Herefrid's was founded in 1329 (*LOCR*, p. 160). The earliest surviving reference to the church's dedication to St James occurred in 1235 (R. N. Benton, *Louth in Early Days* (Cheddar, 1985), p. 48).

13. *CPR Henry VI*, vol. V, p. 405: letters patent issued 7 October 1450; *LOCR*, p. 167. A compotus roll of the guild of the Holy Trinity in St Mary's chapel survives for the year 1422–3 (LA, MS Goulding 4/A/1/2/1).

14. *CPR Henry VI*, vol. VI, p. 145: letters patent dated 16 January 1454 (new style). This licence, and another dated simultaneously, provided for the acquisition of over 205 acres of land, as well as sixty cottages and three shops.

15. *CPR Henry VI*, vol V, p. 81. LA, MS Goulding 4/A/1/2/1: the annual income of this guild in 1422/3 was £8 2s 6d.

16. *CPR Edward IV, 1461–1467* (London, 1897), p. 449: letters patent granted 20 February 1466 (new style).

17. *CPR Edward IV and Henry VI, 1467–1477* (London, 1900), p. 595.

18. *CPR Edward IV and Henry VI*, p. 528: letters patent were issued simultaneously to each guild on 26 May 1475.

both guilds maintained small bedehouses; and both guilds supported chaplains who sang separate liturgical cycles in the guild chapels in St James's. Greater emphasis was attached to the *Opus Dei* in the Lady Guild (which retained three chaplains) than in the Trinity Guild (one of whose two chaplains acted as the schoolmaster): the stated aim of the 'Trinitye beid house' was simply poor-relief, whereas the six bedesmen supported by the Lady Guild were expected to sing for their supper.[19] This divergence of roles most probably stemmed from the guilds' simultaneous refoundation, their different emphases deliberately intended to complement each other. Each of the guilds, including the smaller ones, served a different ritual function. St George's Guild, for instance, paid for the purchase and upkeep of a statue of St George on horseback and for lights before this image;[20] the guilds of Corpus Christi and the Twelve Apostles celebrated their annual congregations with a pageant on the feast of Corpus Christi, the float (or 'hearse') being carried by members of the Apostles' Guild;[21] and each of the guilds administered the obits and anniversaries of its own members. But behind this apparent autonomy there was much cooperation. The Lady Guild maintained the town's guildhall in which both they and other guilds held their fraternity feasts;[22] the Lady Guild also owned the clergy house abutting the church, rooms which were rented by clergy belonging to other guilds as well as the Lady Guild.[23] The Lady Guild joined other guilds in the great Corpus Christi procession, at which the guild banner was carried; this banner was also carried at the feast of the Ascension and, after 1495, the Assumption (the guild's annual gathering taking place on the Monday following).[24] The Lady Guild loaned funds to the guild of St George when it was unable to pay the salary of its chaplain.[25] When Thomas Beverlay, a mercer and member of a large local family, made arrangements for his obit to be celebrated by the Trinity Guild on 20 January each year, he ensured that chaplains from other guilds and chantries would attend as well as his own guild brethren.[26] This *de facto* collaboration between the guilds, the churchwardens and other institutions attached to St James was put on a permanent footing in 1516, when the muniments of these various bodies were all deposited in the rood loft in St James's (in a chest donated by the Lady Guild).[27]

[19] C. W. Foster and A. Hamilton Thompson, 'The Chantry Certificates for Lincoln and Lincolnshire, Returned in 1548 under the Act of Parliament of 1 Edward VI', *Associated Architectural Societies' Reports and Papers* 36/ii (1921), pp. 278–80 (§§44–45): the Blessed Virgin Mary Guild supported six paupers in 'Our Ladies Beidhouse', so that 'divers lay clerici cantatores, called "singingmen" should be sustained' (p. 280).

[20] *LOCR*, p. 175; in 1534, the churchwardens paid 46s 8d for 'guyldyng saynct George' (CWA 2, fol. 26v).

[21] *LOCR*, p. 159.

[22] In 1488, for instance, the Lady Guild paid for repairs to the benches in the guildhall (LG, fol. 121r, under *In reparacione ad aulam Gilde*).

[23] For instance, in 1502/3, only two of the four chaplains renting rooms in this house, John Gyrdyke and John White, were employed by the Lady Guild (LG, fol. 293, under *Per ecclesiam*). Richard Parkhouse, who was subsequently one of the Trinity Guild's two chaplains (1492–1505), rented a room in one of the Lady Guild's houses in Westgate in 1475/6, moving to the Lady Guild's clergy house in 1479 (LG, fol. 18r, under *Westgate*: 'Recepta Ricardo Parkhows ∧ capellano ∧ altera camera superior ibidem [no sum]'; fol. 53v, under *Per ecclesiam*). A Thomas Parkhouse was Dean of the Lady Guild in 1475/6 (LG, fol. 18r).   [24] LG, fol. 191r.

[25] LG, fol. 303r (1502/3): 'Md. that Thomas ffitzwilliam knyght then beyng Olderman of this gild toke fourth of the hooch [common chest] of oure ladie to pay Saynt george prest with assent of the breder of this gilde as it peers afor dyvers yers Wich some the brederhed shall pay agayn, xxvjs viijd'.

[26] TG, fol. 89 (1502/3); doles were to be issued, among others, to 'master wecare' (i.e. the vicar), to chaplains of the Lady Guild, the Trinity Guild, 'Corpus Christi preest', 'Saynt peter preest', 'Saynt george preest', the 'Chauntrey preest', the 'kepare of the organs' and 'two oder temporall men kepyng the qwere syngyng'.

[27] CWA 1, p. 182. Books deposited in this chest included two compotus books of the Trinity Guild, three of the Lady Guild, one book of churchwardens' accounts (plus a bag of silver), 'ij bokys of acomtt of oure lady light callid antyme light', one account book each of 'Sepulcure light' and 'lampe light', two account books of 'wever light', and a 'hole regenall of Corpus Christi play'.

The same degree of collaboration between the town's religious institutions is evident in their cultivation of music within the parish church. Boys were educated at the Trinity Guild's grammar school and at a song school; the six singer-bedesmen were supported by the Lady Guild, supplementing the two or three lay clerks retained by the churchwardens. In addition to the prebendary and the vicar, ten priests were employed by the various guilds. At least some of these chaplains were competent musicians: William Prince, one of the chantry priests (probably employed by the Lady Guild), copied a five-part *Salve regina* in 1513;[28] Robert Beverley, a chaplain in the Trinity Guild at its dissolution, had been a singingman before his ordination.[29] The primary role of the Trinity Guild's school was to instruct the youth of the town and surrounding countryside 'in good manners and polite letters' according to the 1546 chantry survey.[30] Edward VI refounded the school in 1551 because it was an established destination for those seeking an education.[31] The song school was maintained by the churchwardens, who paid for repairs in the 1530s, and also by the Lady Guild;[32] after the dissolution of the guilds, the song school was funded from the income of a charity established by bequest in 1523 by Thomas Taylor, draper.[33] It is not clear how many of the boys educated at either of these schools were trained polyphonists. Similarly, not all of the six bedesmen in the Lady Guild's almshouse were necessarily trained polyphonists. Until 1502 the Lady Guild paid a regular salary only to the choirmaster, whereas ten shillings were distributed annually by the Lady Guild as a lump sum to the men and boys, whose number is unspecified, who sang at Lady Mass.[34] Some suggestion of the size of the choir, however, can be found in the churchwardens' accounts, which record the purchase of belts for eight men and six boys in 1506/7.[35]

A choir of this size was well matched to the polyphonic repertory current in the early sixteenth century and regular payments were made for the copying of polyphony.[36] The Lady Guild paid 3s 3d in 1500 for songs bought from 'the synger of walsyngham' and 8d for an 'antym callid *Nomen ihesu*'.[37] But primary responsibility for funding new music rested with the churchwardens, who also had charge for its safekeeping;[38] the copying of polyphony was undertaken by the lay clerks employed by the churchwardens and the guild chaplains, except on two occasions.[39] This repertory

---

[28] CWA 1, p. 148.

[29] CWA 2, fol. 23r. G. A. J. Hodgett (ed.), *The State of the Ex-Religious and Former Chantry Priests in the Diocese of Lincoln 1547–1574*, Lincoln Record Society 53 (Hereford, 1959), p. 103; Foster and Thompson, 'The Chantry Certificates', p. 278. [30] Foster and Thompson, 'The Chantry Certificates', p. 278.

[31] *CPR Edward VI, 1550–1553*, 6 vols. (London, 1924–9), vol. IV, p. 119: charter, 21 September 1551. This charter restored many of the guild lands confiscated earlier in Edward's reign, re-establishing the grammar school and the guilds' bedehouses, reconstituting the administrative functions of the guilds in a new civic corporation, and confirming three fairs and a weekly market. See also *VCH Lincs*, pp. 460–3.

[32] CWA 2, fol. 33v (1535/6), fol. 42v (1537/8); LG, fol. 277r (1500/1), under *Reparaciones per ecclesiam*.

[33] *VCH Lincs*, p. 463.

[34] LG, fol. 176v (1492/3), under *Cellaria capellanorum cum stipendiis ffamulorum gilde*, for instance.

[35] CWA 1, p. 92.

[36] Payments were made for copying in 1499/1500, 1500/1, 1501/2, 1502/3, 1504/5, 1506/7, 1509/10, 1510/11, 1512/13, 1513/14, 1515/16, 1518/19, 1519/20, 1520/1, 1522/3, 1531/2, 1532/3, 1533/4, 1534/5, 1535/6, 1541/2 and 1553/4 (LG, fol. 259r; CWA 1, pp. 8–9, 28, 44, 72, 92, 124, 131, 148, 161, 180, 199, 203, 208–9, 219; CWA 2, fols. 18r, 22v, 26r–v, 30r, 34c, 56v, 106r). For a complete transcript, see M. Williamson (ed.), 'Lost Sources of Liturgical Polyphony in England, 1500–1550' (forthcoming).

[37] LG, fol. 259r, under *Reparacio in ecclesia*.

[38] CWA 1, p. 111 (1508/9): 'Item paid the said Robert [Clarke] makyng a coffer for pryke song books be the dore side in houre lady qwere, a stoule makyng in the rood lofte, makyng a croos for candyls of tenebre ewyns, and for settyng upe the Flemych organs in the rode lofte be .iv. dais, xxd'.

[39] In 1499/1500 (see above) and in 1510/11, when 16d was paid to 'Willm Prince prest for songs prekyng at Yorke' (CWA 1, p. 163).

included sequences for Lady Mass (1500/1 and 1515/16), items of the Mass Ordinary (1500/1, 1501/2, 1504/5, 1506/7 and 1532/3), votive antiphons (1512/13, 1513/14, 1532/3 and 1533/4), and a setting of the St Matthew Passion for Palm Sunday (1513/14). The copying of 'a sqwar apon the .viij. tunes' in 1535/6 indicates that poly-phonic *Magnificat* settings, either composed or improvised, were sung at the Office of Vespers.[40] Two items of note include the anthem *Nomen ihesu*, and *Argentum et aurum* (copied in 1502/3) which was probably a setting of the psalm antiphon at Lauds on the feast of St Peter and St Paul (29 June).[41] These are early instances of, on the one hand, a Jesus antiphon, commemorating the new feast of the Name of Jesus, and, on the other, of a polyphonic ritual (as opposed to votive) antiphon.[42] Nevertheless, it was the votive antiphon, sung each evening beside the crowned image of Our Lady, together with polyphony for the Mass, which formed the choir's staple repertory.[43] The central place which the *Salve* ceremony enjoyed among both the clergy and the townsfolk is indi-cated by the existence of a separate fund, the 'antyme light', which paid for lights at this ritual, as well as an 'antym bell' which summoned townsfolk each evening from the streets and the fields.[44]

Major capital expenditure necessitated by building works put a considerable strain on the community's resources and could not be financed by the churchwardens alone. The construction of the spire between 1500 and 1516, marking the structural and sym-bolic climax of the fifteenth-century reconstruction of St James's, was assisted with financial help from the guilds as bankers or pawnbrokers: the churchwardens borrowed money (over £44 in all), not only from the two principal guilds, but also from the much poorer Guild of St Peter.[45] The loan made by the Peter Guild, £6 12s, is unlikely to have been raised from either its annual cash income of five shillings or its meagre capital (it had no lands): the likeliest source of the loan was therefore a subscription of its members. The new spire was a symbol of civic prosperity and piety and its completion was recorded with pride in the churchwardens' accounts:

> And the wethercoke was sett upon the broche of holy rode ewyn. And haloyde with many prests ther present and all the rongyng and also much pepull and all to the plesure of god. Amen.[46]

This is not an isolated instance in which the financial resources of the community were mobilised by the churchwardens and the guild aldermen; other large-scale acquisitions were funded in similar ways, their successful completion leaving similarly enthusiastic traces in the generally prosaic written records. Among these acquisitions were two organs bought for St James's.

In 1531, a large new organ was built for the church by William Betton, the King's Organbuilder, funded jointly by the Lady Guild and a benefactor, Richard Taylor, a

---

[40] On squares, *s.v.* 'Square', *Grove*, vol. XVIII, pp. 29–30, and H. Baillie, 'Squares', *Acta Musicologica* 32 (1960), pp. 178ff.   [41] See W. H. Frere (ed.), *Antiphonale Sarisburiense* (London, 1901–24), pl. 447.
[42] See R. W. Pfaff, *New Liturgical Feasts in Later Medieval England*, Oxford Historical Monographs (Oxford, 1970).
[43] CWA 2, fol. 84r (1548/9?), under *Receates*: 'Item rec. of Anne balif wydow for our Ladyes Crown, iiij li'.
[44] CWA 1, p. 168; see Appendix 1. A similar 'salve bell' was rung at All Saints', Bristol, at least as early as 1472/3 (C. Burgess (ed.), *The Pre-Reformation Records of All Saints', Bristol: Part I*, Bristol Record Society 46 (Bristol, 1995), p. 112).
[45] CWA 1, pp. 47 (memorandum of debts, 1502/3), p. 85 (ditto, 1505/6). The final cost of the spire was reck-oned in 1515 to have been £288 3s (CWA 1, p. 183); LG, fol. 291v (memorandum of £10 loan by the Lady Guild for 'the beldyng of the broch', 1501).   [46] CWA 1, p. 181.

member of a local family and rector of St Mary's, Feltwell (Norfolk).[47] Its purchase was recorded in a long memorandum in the churchwardens' accounts:

> Memorandum that the honest men of this towne of Lowthe desyryng to have a good payr of organs to the lawde, prayse and honor of god and the hole holy company of heffen, made an assemble together for this said purpose . . . at whiche tyme Mr Richard Taylour . . . heryng of the good devoute mynde and vertuouse intent of the said townes men . . . offerd to cawse them to have a payre made of a cunnyng man in Lyn . . . for which beneficiall acte I praye Jhesus acqwyte and rewarde hym in his kyngdom of heven. Amen for charite.[48]

This new organ, which cost £22, was set up on the north side of the chancel on the eve of St Barnabas (10 June) 1531. It either replaced or supplemented an older instrument, the 'gret organs', which was standing in St James's when the churchwardens' accounts commenced in 1500 (and which had probably been there since before 1478).[49] Another, slightly smaller, organ had been imported from Flanders by a local merchant in 1501 and placed in the rood loft in 1508/9;[50] the purchase was facilitated by a short-term loan of £3 from the Trinity Guild.[51] In the purchase of both organs, in 1501 and in 1531, the guilds played a central facilitating role as donors or lenders, reflecting a corporate desire to enrich parochial (and hence civic) worship through the purchase and use of organs. These were projects which engaged the individual, as well as the collective, imagination: in 1531 a native of Louth gave a substantial benefaction, although he now lived elsewhere; the costs incurred in 1501 were defrayed by a generous donation from the estate of the deceased vicar and by a small donation by an artisan of apparently modest means.[52] This consensus between clergy and laity, and between corporate and individual activism, manifested itself on other occasions. Richard Curson, for instance, was one of the leading figures in the town during the middle of the sixteenth century: he was alderman of the Trinity Guild in 1545; in 1536 he provided the wages of one of the singingmen when the churchwardens were unable to take a collection and in 1552 he paid 4s to the players at the Corpus Christi pageant.[53] The provision of polyphonic music was itself an issue of civic piety and, like other adornments to the church's ritual and physical fabric, it was clearly seen to reflect well on the community's economic and spiritual health. In 1535/6 a surplice was made for 'strange syngyng men when they cum to sett in the qwere to the honour of God and the honeste of the towne' and in 1557 the organ player was given 6s 8d 'by the advise of the towne'.[54] What was good for the church was good for the town.

The enrichment of parochial worship through the cultivation of choral polyphony was therefore central to the community's configuration of its identity. This is perhaps not surprising, given that many of the clergy and singers employed at St James's were of local origin and had extensive personal ties with the community. John Cawod junior, who was choirmaster at Louth until his death in 1529, was the son of John Cawod

---

[47] On Taylor see A. B. Emden, *A Biographical Register of the University of Cambridge to 1500* (Cambridge, 1963), p. 578; on Betton see A. Ashbee, *Records of English Court Music*, 8 vols. (Aldershot, 1993), vol. VII, pp. 75, 100, 115, 118, 123, 133, 269–320, 378; vol. VIII, pp. 9–10.   [48] CWA 2, fol. 19v.

[49] CWA 1, p. 9 (1500/1); LG, fol. 32r.   [50] See above, note 38.   [51] CWA 1, p. 31.

[52] Three pounds were donated by the executors of Thomas Sudbury, vicar of Louth, who died in July 1504 (CWA 1, p. 59), and 6s 8d by the executors of William Bayos, a Smith.

[53] *LOCR*, p. 171; CWA 2, fol. 34v and fol. 10r; Curson served as churchwarden in 1538/9 (CWA 2, fol. 44).

[54] CWA 2, fol. 34r and fol. 126v.

senior, Dean of the Trinity Guild in 1496/7; a William Cawod, perhaps the son of John Cawod junior, audited the accounts of Louth Park Abbey and served as bailiff and auditor for other religious houses in Lincolnshire.[55] John Cawod junior was employed jointly by the Lady Guild and by the churchwardens between 1475/6 and his death in 1529, acting not only as singer, organist and choir trainer, but also as scribe for both the churchwardens and the two principal guilds; a memorandum of 4 June 1478 in the Lady Guild's account book, setting out Cawod's responsibilities as choir trainer, is an early example of a parish musician's contract.[56] Cawod was unusual in that he derived his salary (and free accommodation) as a church musician and scribe. William Man sang in the choir and was master of the song school.[57] Thomas Foster and his son, William, were landed yeomen and Arthur Gray a merchant, as well as singers at St James's.[58] Robert Beverley, briefly a lay clerk in 1534, chaplain of the Trinity Guild in 1548 (when he was aged forty) and a parish chaplain in the 1550s, was a member of a large local family of mercers which included Thomas Beverlay (Dean of the Lady Guild, 1480/1), Robert (*d.* 1519), William (priest in 1514, *d.* 1521), Richard (Dean of the Lady Guild, 1513/14, and one of vicar Thomas Sudbury's executors, 1505) and his wife Dorothy (*d.* 1539/40), Hugh (churchwarden, 1522/3 and 1534/5, *d.* 1544/5), John (a chaplain who died in 1509/10), another John and Betrys his daughter, Jenet, Issabel and another Thomas Beverlay.[59] A William Beverley, who was a chorister in the Lady Guild choir at St Botolph Boston, was probably a member of this family.[60] With this one exception – an understandable exception, given the wealth and prestige of the Boston guild and given the close trading links between Louth and Boston – the Beverlay family and their parish church were spiritually and materially interdependent: what one Beverlay gave (in rents, in guild subscriptions, or in the offertory) another received as fees or clergy stipend. This is an extreme, but not untypical, instance of the intricate interweaving of

---

55 LA, MS Goulding Papers 5/10/15 ('John Cawod, and the First Volume of the Louth Churchwardens' Accounts': paper delivered by R. W. Goulding before the Louth Naturalists', Antiquarian and Literary Society, 22 May 1911), fols. 4r–6r; LA, Court Paper 92/6/1/F (compotus, Louth Park Abbey, undated), under J. Caley (ed.), *Annuitates and feoda*; *Valor Ecclesiasticus temp. Henr. VIII auctoritate regia institutus*, 6 vols. (London, 1810–34), vol. IV pp. 43 (Tattershall College), 51–2 (Legbourne Priory), 82 (Bardney Abbey). A William Cawod of Boston, Merchant of the Staple of Calais, may have been the same man as William Cawod of Louth who made numerous bequests to guilds in Boston on his death in 1478 (D. S. Josephson, *John Taverner: Tudor Composer*, Studies in Musicology 5 (Ann Arbor, 1979), p. 238, note 39). William Cawod was paid his last quarter-salary by the churchwardens in 1529/30 and served as churchwarden in 1521/2 and 1536/7 (CWA 1, p. 212; CWA 2, fol. 11r, under *Expences for reparacion*; fol. 36r (1536/7)).

56 LG, fol. 24r (1475/6), under *Soluciones stipendiorum*, and fol. 32r (memorandum, 4 June 1478): Cawod's duties included attendance at Lady Mass, the evening *Salve* ceremony and other hours of the day, to sing and to play the organ, for which he was paid 33s 4d per year and given rent-free accommodation in the Lady Guild's clergy house next to St James's; LA, MS Goulding Papers 5/10/15, fol. 9a.

57 *LPFD*, xii/1, §70. A William Man was steward of the choristers' house at Lincoln Cathedral from September 1567 (J. Harley, *William Byrd: Gentleman of the Chapel Royal* (Aldershot, 1997), p. 37, note 33). A William Mann (probably not of Louth) was listed as a lay clerk at Tattershall College, south Lincolnshire, in 1558/9 (*Report on the Manuscripts of Lord De L'Isle and Dudley Preserved at Penshurst Place*, Historical Manuscripts Commission 77/i (London, 1925), p. 202).

58 London, Public Record Office, C 1/1428/45–8; *LPFD*, xi, §828; *CPR Edward VI*, vol. IV, pp. 119–120 (foundation charter of Louth Corporation, 21 September 1551).

59 See above, p. 86. Like Gray and the Fosters, Robert Beverlay had independent means, by way of lands worth 40s per year (Hodgett (ed.), *The State of the Ex-Religious*, p. 103); CWA 2, fol. 95r (1551/2), under *Receates*; fol. 106r (1553/4); LG, fols. 67r, 99v; CWA 1, pp. 9, 72–3, 117, 121, 161, 163, 180, 196, 209, 212, 217, 219; CWA 2, fol. 28r (1534/5); fol. 48v (1539/40); fol. 67v (1544/5).

60 BL, MS Egerton 2886, fols. 235r and 238v (1522/3), under *Exhibiciones choristarum* and *Expense necessarie*; fol. 262v (1523/4), under *Exhibiciones Choriste cum emendacionis vestiment' et alia*; fol. 296 (1524/5), under *Regarda data diversis personis*.

lay and ordained, and of townsfolk, religious guilds and clergy, that appears to have been a defining hallmark of pre-Reformation Louth.

The townsfolk of Louth invested heavily in the spiritual and physical fabric of their church during the century preceding the Reformation. One of the central elements of this investment was the provision of music, singers and organs to augment divine worship at St James's. When the financial, institutional, theological and ritual strands which made up this fabric began to be unpicked in the 1530s, the reaction was spontaneous. The Lincolnshire rebellion began at Louth on 1 October 1536, collapsing less than a fortnight later under the threat of armed suppression. In hindsight, the Lincolnshire rebellion served as a curtain-raiser to the more widespread (and threatening) Pilgrimage of Grace, but it encapsulates the grievances which gave rise to the wider uprising: the dissolution of the monasteries (Louth Park Abbey was dissolved less than a month before the disturbances began); taxation (the rising was sparked in part by the imminent arrival of Henry VIII's commissioners of subsidy); distrust of royal policies and their effects on religious practice (rumours of impending church closures and royal confiscations of church plate had spread following a visitation held at Louth by the Bishop of Lincoln's commissary); liturgical change (the Ten Articles, published on 11 August, abolished numerous feasts including that of St Herefrith, the local saint, on 21 August); and heresy (a book by John Frith, probably his tract against transubstantiation, was burned in the market place).[61]

Among those implicated in the rebellion were singers and clergy from St James's: Thomas Kendall, the vicar, who was subsequently executed; Arthur Gray, a singer, who threw Frith's book into the flames; William Man, the song school master; Thomas Foster, a singer who fanned rumours that church plate would soon be confiscated and processions abolished; William Dycheham, Thomas Lincoln and Thomas More, all of whom were guild and chantry chaplains; and Richard Curson, Dean of the Trinity Guild.[62] But, while the local clergy may have provided much of the leadership, the large number of people taking part in the rebellion (between 10,000 and 20,000 or more according to reports hastily despatched to London) suggests that the rebellion, and the causes which the rebels espoused, enjoyed popular support.

In the aftermath of the rebellion, pardons were issued to most of the rebels and in 1537 the bells were rung in celebration of Prince Edward's birth.[63] The religious changes which Edward's accession heralded ten years later, however, were to confirm the rebels' worst suspicions when the guilds and chantries were dissolved in 1548 and the *Book of Common Prayer* was introduced the following year.[64] Latin liturgical and devotional polyphony came under attack from two directions simultaneously with the abolition of the Catholic liturgy, the Mass and the cult of the Virgin Mary and with the removal of the guilds' role as employers of chaplains and singingmen. In 1551 the guilds were reconstituted and re-endowed as the town's corporation, with responsibility for the grammar schools and poorhouses, but not for the cultivation of liturgical and devotional

---

[61] *SoA*, pp. 394–7; *LPFD*, xi, §§531, 533–4, 552–3, 556, 559, 563, 568–9, 576, 598, 600, 670, 827–43, 852, 967–75, 1062, 1224; *LPFD*, xii/1, §§19, 69–70, 192, 201, 380, 392, 481, 581, 590, 639, 734.

[62] See above, pp. 88–9.   [63] CWA 2, fol. 42r.

[64] Given that Latin votive antiphons were replaced with English anthems at Lincoln Cathedral, St James's mother church, in April 1548, it is likely that Marian antiphons were discontinued at Louth, as well, in advance of the Act of Uniformity (see Peter le Huray, *Music and the Reformation in England 1549–1660* (London, 1967), pp. 8–9). The effect of Edwardine reforms on parish churches is discussed in N. Temperley, *The Music of the English Parish Church*, 2 vols. (Cambridge, 1979), vol. II, pp. 13–19.

polyphony in St James's;[65] with the departure of William Man in 1560, the choristers' song school came to an end, to be replaced by the 'petie scole', an elementary school set up by the corporation in 1553.[66]

This said, however, a number of guild chaplains and clerks remained in Louth during the 1550s, having been assigned pensions at the time of the dissolution;[67] the continued presence also of boy choristers at St James's, at least until the mid-1560s, is suggested by the journeys made to Louth by William Byrd when he recruited choristers for the choir at Lincoln Cathedral.[68] Psalters and song books were bought to service the new Anglican liturgy: nine English psalters were bought by the churchwardens in 1549/50 and nine 'song bookes' in 1553/4.[69] Organ music continued to be played, albeit less frequently: although the Lady Chapel organ was dismantled in 1552/3, minor repairs continued to be made to the remaining organ and 10d was paid annually to an organ blower, his fee returning to its pre-1549 level of 40d after Mary Tudor's accession (and the temporary restoration of Catholic liturgy) in 1553.[70] The purchase of multiple copies of psalters and song books, the shoe-string maintenance of the organ and the continuing presence in Louth of boy choristers and of those who had once been chantry priests, guild chaplains or singingmen cumulatively suggest that the choir did not vanish at a stroke in 1549. But the liturgical and social role of music within the church and community had fundamentally changed, and as each of the one-time chaplains and clerks died, the choir-stalls gradually emptied and memories of the old religion, its sights and its sounds which had once enriched the life of the town, faded away.

APPENDIX 1: GUILDS, CHANTRIES AND LIGHTS

All guilds and chantries were based at St James's Church, except those (marked 'SM') which were based at St Mary's Church.

1 **Lady Guild in St James's**
- letters patent 25 January 1447 (new style)
- three chaplains and six bedesmen ('so that divers singingmen should be retained') who sang Lady Mass and *Salve regina* each evening before image of the Blessed Virgin Mary
- landed endowments, annual income £44 6s 5d
  (*CPR Henry VI*, vol. V, p. 81, *LOCR*, pp.168–9; Foster and Thompson, 'The Chantry Certificates', pp. 279–80)

2 **Lady Guild in St Herefrid's**
- incorporated 1329 (although in existence prior to 1317)
- one chaplain: sang daily Requiem Mass and *Salve regina* at twilight before the image of the Blessed Virgin Mary

---

[65] *VCH Lincs*, pp. 461–3. [66] *VCH Lincs*, p. 463.
[67] Hodgett (ed.), *The State of the Ex-Religious*, pp. 21, 57, 102–4, 112.
[68] Harley, *William Byrd*, p. 35: Byrd visited Louth in 1562/3 and 1564/5. [69] CWA 2, fols. 86r, 106r.
[70] CWA 2, fols. 86r, 97v, 100v, 102r, 105v, 106v, 110v. During the Marian restoration, the same man (William East, a weaver and one-time chaplain of the Lady Guild) was paid for blowing the organ (CWA 2, fols. 106v, 125r); only in 1557, following the death of Arthur Gray (once a singingman in the Lady Guild), was a separate payment made to an organ player (CWA 2, fol. 126v), suggesting that Gray had previously acted as unpaid organist.

- funded seven lights
- lands and tenements: forerunner to **Lady Guild in St James's**
  (*LOCR*, pp. 160–2; *VCH Lincs*, p. 460)

3 Trinity Guild in St James's
- letters patent 7 October 1450
- one chaplain and one schoolmaster plus six bedesmen
- lands and tenements, annual income £19 17s 5d
  (*CPR Henry VI*, vol. V, pp. 405–6; Foster and Thompson, 'The Chantry Certificates',
  pp. 278–9)

4 Trinity Guild at St Mary's (SM)
- founded in 1376
- one chaplain
- funded tapers on Sundays and double feasts
- poor: amalgamated with **Chantry of Thomas of Louth** by 1400: probably superseded
  by **Trinity Guild in St James's**
  (*LOCR*, p. 167; compotus roll, 1422/3, LA MS Goulding 4/A/1/2/1)

5 Guild of the Twelve Apostles
- founded 1361
- one chaplain
- held annual procession on Corpus Christi day
- no land: probably defunct by 1450
  (*LOCR*, pp. 159–60)

6 Guild of St Swithun (SM)
- lights
- held procession on the eve of St Swithun
- no endowments
  (*LOCR*, p. 160)

7 Corpus Christi Guild
- founded 1326
- congregated on Corpus Christi day
- no endowments
  (*LOCR*, p. 160)

8 Guild of St Peter
- one chaplain
- no endowments
  (*LOCR*, p. 175)

9 Guild of St George
- lights and image of St George
- no endowments
  (*LOCR*, p. 175)

10 **Chantry of Thomas of Louth**
- episcopal charter 3 April 1317
- one chaplain: said Requiem Mass daily and sang in quire on feast days
- land endowments
  (*LOCR*, pp. 163–5)

11 **Chantry of John Louthe**
- letters patent 20 February 1466 (new style)
- one chaplain
- lands (twelve marks or £8 rental income *per annum*)
  (*CPR Edward IV*, p. 449; *LOCR*, p. 173)

12 **Oure Lady Light** (or **Antyme Light**)
  (CWA 1, p. 182)

13 **Sepulcure Light**
  (CWA 1, p. 182)

14 **Lampe Light**
- a Eucharistic guild
  (CWA 1, p. 182; *SoA*, p. 331)

15 **Wever Light**
  (CWA 1, p. 182)

CHAPTER EIGHT

ACADEMIC COLLEGES IN THE OXFORD COMMUNITY, 1400–1560[1]

BETH ANNE LEE-DE AMICI

By the end of the fifteenth century, the University of Oxford had blossomed from a collection of small schools into a thriving community supporting hundreds of scholars who lived in the academic halls and colleges. The colleges (of which there were about fifteen in the late medieval period) were largely self-contained foundations situated within the university, of which college fellows and scholars also were members. Because several of the colleges maintained their own chapels and chapel choirs, these foundations have long engaged the special attention of music historians. Authors such as Frank Ll. Harrison and Roger Bowers have presented much vital information about the college choirs, discussing the structures of the choral establishments, the lives and activities of their personnel and their performance and production of sacred music.[2]

However, certain aspects of the history of religious and musical practice in the colleges remain unexplored. Musicologists have preferred to concentrate on the chapel choirs as discrete groups within the colleges, treating the colleges themselves as individual corporations with little connection either to the university at large or to Oxford as an urban community. But the collegiate foundations that employed skilled singers and composers were not cut off from relations either with the university or with the Oxford citizenry.[3] Evidence survives on many levels that the academic colleges used sacred liturgy as a means by which to interact with fellow members of the university, scholars from sister colleges and with the Oxford townsfolk. As a result, sacred rite – and, by extension, sacred music – operated as a means by which the colleges could sustain an active role in both the university and the town.

Religious obligations beyond the usual round of Masses and Offices fell to college members according to both college and university statutes. Ceremonies particular to a college were performed in the college chapel by the fellows, scholars and their chapel servants, but college fellows together with scholars from throughout the academic

---

[1] Extracts from college archives are reproduced here by the kind permission of the Warden and Fellows of All Souls College, Oxford; the Warden and Fellows of Merton College, Oxford; the Warden and Fellows of New College, Oxford; and the President and Fellows of Magdalen College, Oxford.

[2] *MMB*, esp. pp. 30–6, 157–68; R. Bowers, 'Choral Institutions Within the English Church: their Constitution and Development 1340–1500', Ph.D. thesis, University of East Anglia (1975), esp. pp. 4012 ff.

[3] For discussions outside the musicological literature of interactions between the university and the town, see C. I. Hammer, 'Oxford Town and Oxford University', in *The History of the University of Oxford*, vol. III, *The Collegiate University*, ed. James McConica (Oxford, 1986), pp. 69–116, and C. I. Hammer, 'The Town–Gown Confraternity of St Thomas the Martyr in Oxford', *Mediaeval Studies* 36 (1977), pp. 466–76.

community also celebrated rites incumbent upon them as individual members of the university. Such rites were held in the University Church of St Mary the Virgin, which served a local parish as well as the university as a corporate body. For example, university statutes mandated yearly processions for the welfare of the king and queen and other benefactors on the feast of St Edmund the Confessor, as well as a Mass and procession on the feast of St Frideswide, the town's patron saint.[4] Furthermore, certain members of the university (usually graduates in the faculty of arts) also were bound by statute to attend the funerals of their peers, which might be held variously at St Mary's or another parish church, or in a college chapel.[5]

In addition to fulfilling the university's statutory demands, members of the colleges also maintained informal arrangements among themselves, evidenced by their practices of giving each other small gifts of money called 'oblations' on patronal feast days. They also extended invitations to other members of the university and to Oxford citizens in general to attend services in their chapels through the employment of 'bellmen', who were paid to go through the town announcing upcoming memorials. Of these two practices, only one – the public advertisement of commemorative rites – has been addressed by scholars, primarily for centres such as Bristol and London.[6] Neither the employment of bellmen nor the practice of giving oblations among the colleges have yet been investigated for either the university or Oxford town before the Reformation, or from a musicological standpoint.

Because these kinds of exchanges affect our understanding of the conduct of religious services in the academic colleges, in many ways they affect how we perceive both their musical practices and the wider functions of college ceremony and music. The act of opening the college chapels, normally not accessible except to college members and their hired ministers, calls into question some of the distinctions commonly made between 'public' and 'private' liturgy with respect to commemorative rites and the status of the colleges as ostensibly 'private' foundations. Moreover, the expanded audience presumably generated through advertising and by members of one college attending services at another in order to present an offering at Mass may have been the means by which practice at one foundation could affect that of another. Finally and, perhaps, most importantly, permitting outsiders to attend chapel services allowed the colleges to employ these ceremonies and their music as elements in a system of temporal and spiritual exchange. Within this system, they could reaffirm ties to one another as members of the university and maintain an active presence in the town at large through the elaborate performance of sacred ritual.

In order to explore these issues, I will first demonstrate connections among selected colleges as manifested by their practice of giving oblations on feast days and then show how the members of these foundations used other ceremonies to maintain their status within the interlocking communities of both the university and the town. To this end, I will draw upon documentary evidence taken from the archives of the university and of four Oxford colleges: Merton, New College, All Souls and Magdalen.

Throughout the accounts of these four Oxford colleges are entries noting regular payments of oblations (*oblaciones*) to each other and to an additional college or two on

---

[4] S. Gibson (ed.), *Statuta Antiqua Universitatis Oxoniensis* (Oxford, 1931), p. 62.   [5] *Ibid.*, 59–60.
[6] C. Burgess, 'A Service for the Dead: the Form and Function of the Anniversary in Late Medieval Bristol', *Transactions of the Bristol and Gloucestershire Archaeological Society* 105 (1987), esp. pp. 189–90; C. Gittings, *Death, Burial and the Individual in Early Modern England* (London, 1984), pp. 134–5.

Table 8.1 *Summary of inter-collegiate oblations 1400–1548*

Receivers and associated feast	Givers			
	Merton	New College	All Souls	Magdalen
Merton (John the Baptist, 24 June)	—	1461–1545	1449–1547	1482–1547
Balliol (Katherine, 25 November)	1400–1540	1454–1538	1447–1537	1494–1544
Exeter (Thomas Becket, 29 December)	1400–1543	1454–1537	—	1494–1537
Durham (Cuthbert, 20 March)	1417–1539	—	—	—
New College (Annunciation, 25 March)	1400–1546	—	1449–1547	1482–1548
All Souls (All Souls, 2 November)	1445–1544	1454–1547	—	1481–1544
Magdalen (Mary Magdalen, 22 July)	1484–1547	1484–1548	1480–1546	—
University Church (Assumption, 15 August)	1400–1546	—	—	—

their patronal feast days (see Table 8.1).[7] Not every medieval college participated in this rota: neither Queen's nor Lincoln College, for example, ever appear in the oblation-lists of Merton or the three Wykehamist foundations.[8]

The tradition of giving oblations on a foundation's patronal feast was an old one at the university. Merton was making contributions to the University Church, Exeter, Balliol and New College by 1400, and to Durham College by 1417.[9] Table 8.1 summarises the beginning and ending dates for inter-collegiate oblations between 1400 and 1548.[10] All Souls had the fewest obligations, paying oblations to Balliol, New College, Merton and Magdalen. Magdalen had a similar schedule, also paying to All Souls and Exeter. New College's list was the same as Magdalen's, reciprocating with a gift to that college on its feast day. Merton had the largest number of payments, by the sixteenth century sending money to the University Church and Durham College in addition to Balliol, Exeter and the three Wykehamist colleges.

[7] An example of such an entry is 'de xiid pro oblacione in Collegio Ballioli die Katerine', ASCA c.276, 1448/9. This formula, with slight variations, is applied fairly consistently in the records of all four colleges. I am grateful to Dr Roger Bowers and Dr Eamon Duffy for their help on the subject of oblations.

[8] The Wykehamist colleges include New College, All Souls and Magdalen. The statutes of the latter two are based in large part on those for New College, founded by William of Wykeham.

[9] MerCA 3726, *B1* 1400 (University Church); 3727, *B1 c.* 1400 (Balliol); 3728, *B2* 1400 (Exeter and New College); 3742, *B3* 1417 (Durham). It is possible that the practice predates the turn of the fifteenth century, but I did not examine any account rolls dating before 1399.

[10] Information in the table has been extracted from MerCA 3724, *B2* 1399/1400 to 3898, *B1* 1548 (accounts for 1482/3 to 1493/4 in *Dom. Acc.*); NCA 7413, 1454/5 to 7513, 1547/8; ASCA c.276, 1447/8 to c.282, 1546/7; and MagCA *Lib. comp. 1*, 1481/2 to *Lib. comp. 5*, 1547/8.

Thirty years had passed since Magdalen's foundation (by William of Waynflete) before it began receiving gifts regularly from Merton, but this is not entirely surprising. Magdalen's fellows and scholars did not inhabit the college buildings or start using the chapel there until *c.* 1480: the initiation of gifts to Waynflete's foundation is therefore roughly coincident with occupation of the then newly constructed college.[11] New College, although founded at the end of the fourteenth century, appears not to have signed on to this charitable rota until Thomas Chaundler became warden in 1454. In this year, the first payments to All Souls, Exeter and Balliol appear in the New College accounts; Merton appeared on the list somewhat later, by 1461.[12] All Souls' fellows also took a little time to join in, beginning their giving *c.* 1448.[13] The loss of the early accounts for Magdalen College makes it impossible to determine exactly when that foundation began presenting such gifts, but by 1481/2 they were paying oblations to New College, Merton and All Souls, adding Balliol and Exeter in 1494.[14]

The purpose of these gifts, which rarely exceeded 14d, and the means by which they were conveyed to the colleges in question are, to a certain extent, matters for speculation. No formal indentures survive wherein the colleges pledge oblations to one another, making it difficult to determine both the intentions behind the presents and what criteria a college used in deciding which other foundations ought to receive an oblation from them. Further, from time to time the colleges chose to pay oblations to some, but not all, of the colleges on their lists.[15] Despite these obstacles, the evidence that does survive may be marshalled towards a provisional explanation for the practice.

Of primary importance is whether the oblations were religious in nature, as opposed to a simple expression of goodwill and solidarity among the colleges. If the latter were the case, payments demonstrate merely the esteem in which the colleges held one another, an important point but not necessarily pertinent to a study of their musical and ceremonial practices. However, if the former were the case, and the offerings were given in the course of the Mass as a sacred gift, the custom has implications for our understanding of the degree to which outsiders participated in college chapel services, ceremonies which on a patronal feast day would have been performed with the greatest solemnity and, therefore, with music.

The language of the payment records is in itself suggestive. The word used consistently throughout each college's accounts is 'oblation' (*oblacio*), not 'reward' (*regardis*) or 'consideration' (*consideracio*). Although *oblacio* could be used in the general sense of 'payment', it is never employed that way in any of the accounts. Besides the entries for patronal festivals, the only other uses of the term are in connection with offerings received on the greater feasts, or else received or paid for funerals.[16] More telling than the vocabulary used for these payments, however, is the history of the practice through the middle of the sixteenth century. If these gifts had not been closely associated with religious observance,

---

[11] *Dom. Acc.*, pp. 56–7. H. E. Salter and M. D. Lobel (eds.), *The Victoria History of the County of Oxford*, vol. III, *The University of Oxford* (London, 1954), p. 204. [12] NCA 7413, 1454/5; NCA 7713, 1460/1.

[13] ASCA c.276, 1447/8 (Balliol); 1448/9 (New College and Merton).

[14] MagCA *Lib. comp. 1*, 1481/2; *Lib. comp. 2*, 1494/5.

[15] For example, Magdalen gave to Exeter, New College, Merton and All Souls, but not to Balliol, in 1509/10. MagCA *Lib. comp. 3*, 1509/10.

[16] See, for example, the payment record in MerCA 3735, *B1* 1409, 'Item in oblacionibus sociorum in die funeracione magistri Ricardi Albary, ixd'. The receipt rolls at New College contain a section devoted to oblations, which record amounts received on many feasts, including the patronal feast day. See, for example, NCA 7363, 1406/7.

it is reasonable to expect that they would not have been much affected by the changes in the English church from the mid-1530s onward. This was not the case, however.

The colleges gave up making these offerings at differing rates, but payments for oblations cease to be recorded at every college after 1547, the year in which Edward VI gained the throne and the reformers put in motion policies more stringent than those initiated under Henry VIII.[17] Even so, this is not to say that Henry's reforms had had no effect: at New College and Magdalen, payments to Exeter College on the feast of St Thomas Becket are lacking after 1538, the year in which the saint's feast was struck off the English calendar and his cult outlawed.[18] Merton College, by contrast, apparently ignored Becket's ouster, continuing to present money to Exeter until 1543.[19] Defiance of Reformation policies could not, however, preserve Merton's relationship with Durham College, a monastic foundation. Records of payments to Durham stop after 1539, the year in which Henry VIII dissolved the greater monasteries. Durham College, which had been supported by Durham Abbey, ceased to exist shortly thereafter.[20]

Equally important are the records (or lack thereof) in the accounts after 1547. Throughout the reign of Edward VI, no entries for oblations were made in the accounts of any of the colleges. But after Mary's accession in 1554 and the reinstatement of the Catholic faith in England, the colleges revived their round of offerings to sister foundations and started anew recording payments for oblations.[21] Soon after Elizabeth took the throne, these payments ceased yet again. The imposition of the Act of Uniformity in 1559 sounded the death-knell for the custom and the colleges gradually abandoned the practice entirely. An examination of surviving accounts rolls dating from *c.* 1560 to *c.* 1569 failed to turn up even one payment *in oblacione* on a patronal feast at any of the colleges under consideration.[22]

It is the evidence of the accounts after 1547 and the termination of payments to Exeter after 1538 that most strongly suggest a religious basis for the presentation of monetary gifts among the colleges on their patronal feasts. If the practice had had no religious basis, there would have been little reason for the colleges to have stopped making offerings in this fashion during Edward's reign (or at least stopped recording that they were doing so, when they so consistently documented the practice earlier), only to resume giving after the reinstitution of Catholic observance under Mary. That the colleges ceased making oblations entirely after the Act of Uniformity abolished the Mass as a form of worship in England is a further indication of the sacred nature of these feast day gifts.

It is most likely, therefore, that college oblations were Mass-pennies, offerings presented to the priest by the congregation. At the time of the Offertory, worshippers

[17] The last records of oblations before *c.* 1550 are in MerCA 3891, *B1* 1545; NCA 7513, 1547–8; ASCA c.282, 1546/7; and MagCA *Lib. comp. 5*, 1544/5.

[18] The last payments to Exeter are in NCA 7495, 1537/8 and MagCA *Lib. comp. 4*, 1537/8.

[19] MerCA 3886, *B2* 1543. Merton seems to have been defiant of Reformation legislation in other regards as well. See, for example, the subwarden's account for 1546/7 noting receipts in connection with a celebration of veneration of the cross on Good Friday, a practice the reformers tried to abolish. MerCA 4043, *SA* 1546/7. *SoA*, pp. 443–4.

[20] Salter and Lobel (eds.), *University of Oxford*, p. 239. MerCA 3867, *B3* 1538/9 records the last payment to Durham.

[21] Payments for oblations during the reign of Philip and Mary begin in MerCA 3911, *B2* 1554; NCA 7523, 1554/5; ASCA c.283, 1554/5; and MagCA *Lib. comp. 6*, 1554/5.

[22] Payments for oblations during the reign of Elizabeth cease after MerCA 3297, *B1* 1561; NCA 7533, 1559/60; ASCA c.283, 1559/60; and MagCA *Lib. comp. 7*, 1560/1.

brought their oblations to the celebrant in a public fashion and handed the offerings to him directly on the chancel step.[23] Assuming that the oblations recorded in the college accounts were indeed Mass-pennies presented in this fashion, it seems reasonable to assume that at least one representative of the college making the gift would have attended Mass (most likely High Mass) at the foundation celebrating its patronal feast day.

The custom of making oblations at these ceremonies thus reveals a possible avenue for transmission of traditions of religious music and practice from one foundation to another. Fellows from one college could observe how another foundation conducted a festal Mass and bring home new ideas for celebrating services in their own chapels, possibly including the suggestion that their choir obtain copies of any written polyphony performed at the foundation they visited.

Fellow members of the university were not the only strangers to whom colleges opened their chapel doors, nor were the colleges alone in making public certain of their liturgies. On some occasions, Oxford citizens also were formally invited to participate both in college chapel services and in rites performed by the university as a corporate body. These ceremonies were announced throughout the town by 'bellmen', who gave notice of the time and place of the services (most commonly exequies and Masses of Requiem, services collectively known as an 'obit').[24] To this end, the bellman served warning to Oxford clergy (whose job it was to pray for the living and the dead), to the poor (who might be assisted through receiving a dole) and to any other interested members of the urban community to assemble at the church for the event.[25]

Frequently, charters founding observances at the colleges and university have contractual stipulations providing for bellmen to announce the rites in perpetuity. The contract that established Thomas Ingledew's scholarship and obit at Magdalen in the late fifteenth century contains an example of terms requiring the employment of a bellman:

> Also, the bellman is to be paid four pence annually for his labour in publicly proclaiming for John Bowke and myself . . . on the day of the said exequies, according to the Oxford custom.[26]

It is possible that texts in some medieval university documents represent the actual content of some of these announcements, which apparently were made in the precincts of the church of St Mary the Virgin. One such text reminds the chancellor and graduate scholars of an upcoming obit for Humphrey, Duke of Gloucester, which all graduates were bound to attend.[27]

The texts of the university proclamations and indentures like the one founding Ingledew's obit confirm salient aspects of the bellman's office. In Ingledew's contract, the

---

[23] *SoA*, p. 125.   [24] The Latin terms for this officer include *campanarius, preco, vociforator* or *preconizator*.
[25] *SoA*, p. 359.
[26] 'Item, communi campanario, more Oxoniensi solito pro magistro Joanne Bowyke et me . . . publice proclamanti, in die dictarum exequiarum, annuatim deliberatur quatuor denarii pro labore suo'; E. A. Bond (ed.), *Statutes of the Colleges of Oxford; with Royal Patents of Foundation, Injunctions of Visitors, and Catalogue of Documents Relating to the University, Preserved in the Public Record Office*, 3 vols. (Oxford, 1853), vol. II, p. 82.
[27] 'Honorande Domine Cancellar[i]e, Domini Doctoris, & Magistri singuli. Placet Reverentijs vestris interesse Missæ crastino die in hoc Templo celebrandæ, post pulsationem magnæ campanæ, pro animabus illustrissimi principis Humfridi, quondam Ducis Gloucestresis, et Alinoræ, consortis suæ. Cui Missæ et exequijs tenentur omnes graduati interesse ad quodlibet verbum, præstita Universitati.' C. E. Doble, D. W. Rannie, H. E. Salter (eds.), *Remarks and Collections of Thomas Hearne*, vol. VI, Oxford Historical Society Publications 43 (Oxford, 1902), p. 274.

language 'by the usual Oxford custom' indicates that the practice was considered a normal part of the conduct of obits in that town. The text of the university's announcements, probably representative of what any bellman might be expected to say on such occasions, told the scholars when the obit was to be held, who was obliged to attend and for which intention the service was being performed.[28]

The university as a corporate body made use of these criers in order to publicise the many anniversaries, like Duke Humphrey's, which its members were bound by statute to attend.[29] Announcements were necessary not only because such observances fell outside the familiar liturgical calendar but also because their dates were not absolutely fixed. On several occasions the register of Congregation (the university's governing body) records their decision to postpone anniversaries in order to accommodate feasts with precedence over the commemorations.[30]

A few university proctors' accounts from the latter half of the fifteenth century have survived, recording some payments to the bellmen.[31] Announcements were aimed at members of the university, although participation by Oxford townsfolk cannot be ruled out entirely because the services were held in the church of St Mary the Virgin, which served its own parish in addition to the university, as mentioned above. Entries in university accounts dating from 1472 and 1474 indicate that at least a few people did bother to attend: at the Duke of Gloucester's obits in those years, brawls broke out, and Oriel College, to which control of the parish belonged, received payment for quelling them.[32]

Statutes and contracts likewise obligated members of most Oxford colleges to perform commemorative rites for their founder and other benefactors. However, not all of these events were announced. Each college had its own practice, informed by the priorities of the foundation and the legal constraints of contracts made with benefactors. In contrast to the Wykehamist colleges, Merton seems not to have hired bellmen to make announcements, except very rarely.[33]

By far the most important anniversary was that of the founder. As the primary benefactor and person to whom a college owed its very existence, colleges deemed commemoration of the founder one of their most solemn duties, not least because most founders went to some trouble to ensure the perpetuation of their memories through rules laid down in the college statutes. Records of announcements for William of Wykeham's obit start in the New College account for 1406/7.[34] At All Souls, payments to the bellmen do not begin until the decade after Henry Chichele's death in 1443: the first notices appear in 1453/4.[35] And at Magdalen, the account for 1486/7 preserves the first

---

[28] A text in the statutes for Richard Sherborne's benefaction to Chichester Cathedral describing the bellman's proclamation for his obit is very similar to the university's announcement for Duke Humphrey. NCA 9432, fol. 5r.

[29] See, for example, Gibson (ed.), *Statuta Antiqua*, p. 155 (Edward III's obit; Humphrey de Charlton's obit), and pp. 209–10 (obits for Henry IV and others).

[30] W. A. Pantin and W. T. Mitchell (eds.), *The Register of Congregation 1448–1463*, Oxford Historical Society Publications, n.s. 22 (Oxford, 1972), for example pp. 103, 108.

[31] Several of these payments were for announcing the Duke of Gloucester's obit, for which the text of the notice survives, discussed above. H. E. Salter (ed.), *Mediæval Archives of the University of Oxford*, vol. II, Publications of the Oxford Historical Society 73 (Oxford, 1919), for example pp. 299, 303.

[32] Salter (ed.), *Mediæval Archives*, vol. II, p. 308. Unfortunately, no further information about the cause of the disturbances or who was involved seems to have survived.

[33] The sole example is in MerCA 4018, *SA* 1504/5, recording payment to a bellman for announcing Thomas Lee's obit. Lee's benefaction contract requested that the college hire a bellman. MerCA 804.

[34] NCA 7365, 1406/7. Wykeham died in 1404. The roll for 1406/7 is the next surviving roll after 1404.

[35] ASCA c.276, 1453/4.

record of William of Waynflete's obit, closely following the bishop's death in August 1486.[36]

Bellmen announced the obits of important benefactors on occasion, most frequently in fulfilment of demands made in the benefaction charter. Magdalen regularly paid bellmen to proclaim the anniversaries of two such individuals, Thomas Ingledew, mentioned above, and William Preston.[37] At All Souls, James Goldwell, former Fellow and Bishop of Norwich, received this benefit as well, according to the terms of his contract with the college.[38]

In the accounts of the three Wykehamist colleges are found much less frequent payments for announcements of single obits, which were probably held close to the time of death and burial of the person for whom the rites were being performed. Most often, these individuals were current or past members of the college deemed to merit a more solemn observance. For example, New College in 1449/50 paid for the announcement of two obits for Robert Thurbarn.[39] Thurbarn was a New College man who had held positions of importance at the college and at the university, and from 1413 until his death he was warden of New College's sister foundation at Winchester.[40] As a person of status, Thurbarn was considered worthy of a more extended observance of his obit, probably consisting of one ceremony on or near his burial-day and a trental Mass a month later.

Payments for public notices for commemorative rites disappear from all the college accounts after 1548, probably as a result of the implementation of Reformation policies under Edward VI. However, the practice of announcing funerals of members of the university apparently either continued without being recorded in college accounts or else was revived some time later and persisted well into the seventeenth century.[41]

Anniversaries and funerals were not the only ceremonies for which the bellmen were paid. In 1444, Archbishop Stafford granted indulgences for anyone saying *Pater Noster* and *Ave Maria* for the souls of the faithful departed in All Souls College chapel on the feast of Relics and the commemoration of All Souls.[42] Payments to proclaimers for the indulgence begin in the account for 1456/7 and appear more or less regularly until *c.* 1525, when the college seems to have ceased to advertise it.[43] While the bull makes no direct mention of when during the day these prayers were to be said, it is not inconceivable that those wishing to receive the indulgence might choose to say them at Mass or Office in the college chapel.

---

[36] MagCA *Lib. comp. 1*, 1486/7. Magdalen's accounting cycle began and ended variously on 29 September or 11 November. The first obit announcement, therefore, occurred in August 1487. The college observed Waynflete's obit in 1486, but it was not announced. MagCA *Lib. comp. 1*, 1485/6.

[37] *Statutes of the Colleges of Oxford*, vol. II, pp. 81–4 (Ingledew's composition); payments for a bellman for Ingledew begin in MagCA *Lib. comp. 1*, 1481/2. Payments for announcing Preston's obit begin in MagCA *Lib. comp. 2*, 1491/2, although his contract did not explicitly demand that the college hire a bellman. *Statutes of the Colleges of Oxford*, vol. II, pp. 100–3.

[38] Oxford, All Souls College, MS 1, fols. 45v–46v. ASCA c.279, 1502/3 records the first payment to a bellman for Goldwell's obit.   [39] NCA 7411, 1449/50.

[40] Before giving up his fellowship in 1413, Thurbarn served as bursar and subwarden at New College at various times between 1394 and 1412. He was senior proctor of the university in 1399. A. B. Emden (ed.), *A Biographical Register of the University of Oxford to A.D. 1500*, 3 vols. (Oxford, 1957–9), vol. III, pp. 1871–2.

[41] Apparently, the practice continued as late as 1661, although the Parliamentary Visitors had banned it in 1647 or 1648. Gittings, *Death, Burial and the Individual*, pp. 134–5.

[42] Oxford, All Souls College, MS Foundation Charters no. 12.

[43] ASCA c.277, 1456/7. Accounts after ASCA c.280, 1525/6 most commonly enter payments to the bellmen as lump sums that appear not to include the indulgences.

Admittedly, the old adage about leading horses to water applies to any attempt to interpret the evidence regarding proclamations for these ceremonies. Surviving documents suggest strongly that the colleges and university issued invitations to the general public, but it is much more difficult to determine whether citizens and scholars took advantage of these offers, especially when doles were not distributed. However, it seems unlikely that the announcements would have gone entirely unheeded, especially when the situation is viewed in the context of medieval attitudes toward ceremonies of this kind and the system of temporal and spiritual exchange they generated.

An active role for the living existed within the medieval understanding of the soul's path to the afterlife via purgatory. Although they could no longer assist their deceased friend or kin corporally, the living could speed the dead to heaven by their prayers, especially the prayers of the Mass.[44] In a society that understood acts of mercy on earth to be a means of gaining one's eternal reward in heaven, prayer for the dead became a system of exchange between those still on earth and those having died.[45] Prayer for the dead helped their souls get to heaven and it conferred benefits on the living by allowing them to perform a work of mercy for the dead, which in turn created a favourable balance for the living in God's ledger.

Similarly, the dead could continue to help the living, especially the poor, by making provision for doles to be given on the occasion of their commemorations. Doles were a common item in late medieval wills, stipulating the amount of money, bread, cloth, or other items to be given to each poor person attending the service.[46] All Souls College distributed a dole on the founder's obit from the early sixteenth century onward with servings of bread and beer, and Magdalen performed corporal acts of mercy on certain obit-days as well.[47]

The practice of advertising liturgy, therefore, highlights an important function of sacred music in medieval English culture. In pre-Reformation Oxford, sacred ceremony – and, consequently, sacred music – functioned as a medium of exchange among the colleges and, presumably, other members of the university and Oxford citizens. The colleges provided opportunities for citizens and scholars to perform works of mercy and helped the poor with gifts of food, drink or money, thus confirming their membership in a wider community. In exchange, citizens and scholars assisted those performing the ceremonies by adding their prayers and may have left behind small offerings of money in the college chapel.

As we have seen, colleges and other foundations employed bellmen presumably expecting people from outside their immediate community to join them in prayer on important days in their calendars. That they did so therefore calls into question the tendency to characterise nearly all commemorative observances as 'private', at least for some of the more important anniversaries held throughout Oxford during the course of the year.[48] The same applies, to a certain extent, to patronal feast days within the circle of col-

---

[44] Performance of prayers or Masses for the dead dates as far back as the third century AD and had become a well-established custom by the thirteenth century. K. L. Wood-Legh, *Perpetual Chantries in Britain* (Cambridge, 1995), pp. 2–5; P. Binski, *Medieval Death: Ritual and Representation* (London, 1996), pp. 24–8.

[45] See *SoA*, pp. 357–62, for a discussion of English customs and beliefs surrounding the connections between works of mercy and the salvation of souls.   [46] *SoA*, p. 360.

[47] See, for example, ASCA c.281, 1531/2. The benefaction charter made by Charles, Bishop of Hereford, provided for an augmentation of the college's dole on the day of the founder's obit. Oxford, All Souls College, MS 1, fol. 95r–v. Ingledew's composition with Magdalen College required distribution of 7d to the poor on certain feasts throughout the year, for example. *Statutes of the Colleges of Oxford*, vol. II, p. 82.

[48] See, for example, Binski, *Medieval Death*, pp. 32–3; and B. Haggh, 'Foundations or Institutions? On Bringing the Middle Ages into the History of Medieval Music', *Acta Musicologica* 68 (1996), pp. 89–92. Recently,

leges participating in the annual round of offerings and the indulgence-days at All Souls, since college chapels were ostensibly 'private' foundations meant for their members and chapel ministers only. Nevertheless, some feast days and anniversaries clearly were seen as public ceremonies, insofar as attendance and, possibly, a degree of participation in these rites may not have been restricted to those who lived in the college holding the service.[49]

An engagement with the historical evidence for the customs of giving oblations and of advertising certain religious rites demands consideration of the implications these traditions have for the writing of music history, not only for the academic colleges but also for the town and university of Oxford and for other foundations and urban centres in England before the Reformation. On days as important as the feast of the college's patron saint or the anniversary of the founder, at which all the fellows, scholars and chapel ministers were expected to be present by statute, music must have played a key role.[50] At least some of the liturgies for the day – especially High Mass on a patronal feast – could have been celebrated polyphonically in acknowledgement of the solemnity of the occasion.[51]

Of course it is not possible to recover from extant documents what listeners thought or felt about the music they heard and the ceremony they saw. But we do know of at least one instance in which the situation at one college affected decisions made at another: Merton College in the late 1480s commissioned a new rood screen and organ fashioned after those at Magdalen. The contract between Merton and the carpenters for the rood screen specifically requested that the new screen be of the same design as the one at Magdalen, but with better doors.[52] William Wotton, the organ builder hired by Merton in 1488, had constructed a new organ at Magdalen College in the same year. Merton College demanded that Wotton make their instrument similar to Magdalen's, as well.[53]

Previous authors have offered no explanation for Merton's emulation of Waynflete's college. However, tracing traditional practices such as the advertisement of obits and the presentation of oblations allows us to reconstruct the sequence of events that may have influenced decisions made by the college's fellows and scholars and precipitated the new construction at Merton. In July of 1484, Merton began to offer oblations to Magdalen College on the occasion of Magdalen's patronal festival, as mentioned above. Wotton began work on a new organ at Magdalen in 1486/7, the same year in which that college began advertising the obit of their founder, who had died in August of 1486.[54] Coincidentally, on

---

however, other scholars have argued for the integration of chantry foundations and their cantarists into the life of the parish as a whole, and for the participation of the laity in mortuary rituals. C. Burgess, 'Chantries in Fifteenth-Century Bristol', Ph.D. thesis, University of Oxford (1981), esp. pp. 143ff; *SoA*, pp. 220–1, 368–70.

[49] Duffy has documented instances of lay participation in memorial rites, especially the prayers comprising the Office for the Dead. *SoA*, pp. 220–1. See also note 47, above.

[50] For example, the fellows and scholars at New College and All Souls were obliged by statute to perform services with music on the patronal day. Queen's Commisioners, 'All Souls College' and 'New College' in *Statues of the Colleges of Oxford*, vol. I, New College, p. 69 and All Souls, p. 47 (each set of statues paginated individually).

[51] All four of the colleges under consideration did maintain choirs capable of singing written or improvised polyphony, but it is almost impossible to link surviving repertory specifically to the celebrations under consideration here. *MMB*, pp. 30–6 and 157–68, describes the chapel choirs at New College, Magdalen and All Souls. See also my dissertation, '*Ad Sustentacionem Fidei Christiani*: Sacred Music and Ceremony in Medieval Oxford', Ph.D. thesis, University of Pennsylvania (1999), for detailed histories of the chapels at All Souls and Merton.   [52] *MMB*, p. 167.   [53] *Ibid.*, pp. 167–8.   [54] *Ibid.*, p. 167.

the very day on which Waynflete breathed his last, Merton hired workmen to create a new rood screen, modelled on the one at Magdalen.[55] Wotton received the final payment for his work on the organ at Magdalen in 1487/8 and in March 1488 Merton engaged him to construct an instrument for their chapel.[56] Emulation of Magdalen's musical establishment may have extended to Merton's decision to create the post of *precentor* in June 1489, in an attempt to enhance the quality of the choir there.[57]

It is not possible to determine which particular religious service at Magdalen was the catalyst for Merton College's decision to purchase a new organ like Magdalen's or hire a *precentor*. After all, Waynflete's was not the only requiem advertised by Magdalen; evidence of opportunities for Merton's fellows to have attended chapel services at Magdalen as early as 1481/2 does survive.[58] However, in conjunction with the arrival of an energetic new warden at Merton in 1482, the timing of the events surrounding that college's purchase of a new organ and rood screen is suggestive.

The warden and fellows at Merton knew what the organ and rood screen at Magdalen were like and they knew who Magdalen had hired to make the organ, at least. Wotton's craftsmanship was sufficiently good for Merton College to want to hire him to make an instrument of similar or better quality in their chapel and a favourable impression of Magdalen's chapel establishment after having observed it in action could have influenced Merton's decision to employ someone to direct their own choir. Tracing the history of Merton's festal-day gifts and Magdalen's advertisement of obits therefore furnishes a discrete set of opportunities for Merton's fellows to have observed the conduct of ceremonies at Magdalen, which then can be applied as evidence in a history of the chapel improvements at Merton. It is possible that further research might uncover additional connections of this kind among other colleges and, perhaps, the parishes and monasteries of medieval Oxford.

Clearly, the traditions that have been examined here have implications beyond the situation in the Oxford colleges. Such seemingly minor practices as the giving of oblations or the advertisement of obits, which at first glance appear unrelated to musical practice, provide music historians with a specific, documentable series of events and interactions (as opposed to vague notions of geographical proximity) on which to ground arguments about lines of exchange, influence, or the transmission of music among different foundations.[59]

In medieval Oxford, a college choir was more than just an element in a college's ritual observance – it assisted with more than just the beautification of college liturgy and provided more than an outlet for the talents of composers and singers. As participants in such important liturgies as the anniversary of a founder or the Masses and Offices for the feast or saint from which the college took its very name, the choirs in fact made tangible contributions to the affirmation of their colleges' status as members of the university and residents in the town. And, as the example of Merton's activities in the late 1480s attests, it is reasonable to assert that outsiders attending another foundation's services brought ideas back home with them, the advertised liturgies thus becoming an avenue for the transmission of music and other elements of religious observance.

---

[55] The contract is dated 11 August 1486. H. E. Salter (ed.), *Registrum Annalium Collegii Mertonensis 1483–1521*, Oxford Historical Society Publications 76 (Oxford, 1923), p. 521.   [56] *MMB*, p. 167.   [57] *Ibid*, p. 167.

[58] See note 37.

[59] See also Haggh, 'Foundations or Institutions?' pp. 98–9, for a discussion of similar potential results from application of her suggested methodology for investigating networks of foundations.

But we cannot discover such situations by attending exclusively to the archival evidence appearing to relate directly to choirs or musical matters, narrowly defined. Ancillary traditions such as the employment of bellmen or the giving of oblations, heretofore unstudied by musicologists, in fact formed vital parts of the fabric of religious – and, therefore, musical – practice in Oxford and, almost certainly, other urban centres throughout medieval England. Only through an awareness of all the processes that contributed to the realisation of sacred ritual and its music can we more fully understand the place of pre-Reformation choirs and music within their proper historical and cultural contexts.

CHAPTER NINE

MUSIC AND COURT IN CHARLES V'S VALLADOLID, 1517–1539

SOTERRAÑA AGUIRRE RINCÓN

As a member of one of the principal sovereign dynasties of early modern Europe, Charles V, Holy Roman Emperor, was both ruler of The Netherlands and heir to the Habsburg dominions in Austria and southern Germany. He also inherited the Spanish kingdoms of Castile and Aragon upon the death in 1516 of his grandfather Ferdinand II the Catholic. Charles had been brought up with his own Flemish household in Brussels and on 18 November 1517 he arrived in Valladolid where his first triumphal entry into Spain took place, and it was there that he acceded to the throne and became Charles I, King of Castile, in February 1518.[1]

Charles left the town in May 1518 in order to be crowned King of Aragon. Subsequently, he used Valladolid as one of the main bases of his operations in his Spanish kingdoms. In the following twenty years, until the death of his wife Isabella of Portugal in 1539, he returned there with his peripatetic Flemish court many times: from August 1522 to August 1523; during the summer of 1524; from February to August 1527; for twenty-two days in the months of June and July 1534; from January to April 1537 and also for a few days in December, the month of August and the greater part of September of 1538.[2] Every time the monarch returned a large number of festivities were organised in his honour, many of which included musical performances.

Although music must have played a prominent role in the history of Valladolid under Charles's rule, little has been written on its function in and impact on this important urban centre.[3] By examining the music performed in certain events that occurred around the time of the festivities organised during two of the most important periods of Charles's residence – the enthronement in 1518 and the royal baptism in 1527 – this essay will make some preliminary observations and highlight areas for future research. It will attempt, moreover, to demonstrate that the repeated presence of the court in Valladolid modified the uses to which music was put by its citizens.

---

[1] In addition to his Flemish household, Charles also shared a Castilian one with his mother Joanna; L. Robledo Estaire, 'La música en la corte madrileña de los Austrias. Antecedentes: las casas reales hasta 1556', *Revista de Musicología* 10:3 (1987), pp. 753–96.

[2] Dates taken from the 'Journal de voyages de Charles-Quint' written by Jean de Vandenesse, administrator of the king. Reproduced in M. Garchard (ed.), *Collection des voyages des souverains des Pays-Bas*, 4 vols. (Brussels, 1876–82), vol. II, pp. 53–464.

[3] For preliminary work see M. A. Virgili, 'Música y Corte en el Valladolid de los Austrias', unpublished paper presented at the conference 'Poder, Mecenazgo e Instituciones en la Música Mediterránea. 1400–1700' (Ávila, 18–20 April 1997).

Located in the fertile valley of the river Duero, Valladolid had a population about the size of the city of Bruges[4] and it ranked below the other great Castilian cities of the period such as Burgos, Segovia, Toledo or Seville. According to an anonymous sixteenth-century author, Valladolid was characterised by the dynamism of its population and its capacity for production and commercialisation.[5] This writer indirectly identified some of the social groups most actively involved in the promotion of culture in the town as the educated civic oligarchy known as *caballeros* or gentlemen, the merchants and the craftsmen. The clergy – whose presence was taken for granted – was not mentioned. Only a few noble families resided in the town at the beginning of the century, but they remained largely outside the urban system.[6]

The topography of the town reflected its social composition (see Illustration 9.1). Its most important space was the Plaza del Mercado; the university and the Palacio de la Chancillería were also prominent features of the townscape. Of the religious institutions, the most important was the collegiate church of Santa María, San Benito (the chief monastery of the Spanish Benedictine order) and the Dominican monastery of San Pablo with its church and the recently constructed college annexe of San Gregorio. Next to these last buildings was the house of the Marqués of Astorga that became the property of the Count of Ribadavia, and it was here that Charles resided and kept his court during his visits.

Whenever a king, heir to the throne or regent entered Valladolid for the first time or after a major event, *entradas* (triumphal entries) were organised in their honour. Between 1497 and 1513 this happened on five different occasions. The first was dedicated to Princess Margaret of Habsburg (future regent of The Netherlands) recently married to Prince John, heir to the Spanish crown; in 1502 and 1506 *entradas* were prepared for Charles's parents, Joanna the Mad and Philip I the Fair of Burgundy (first as prince and princess of Castile and then as king and queen); and in 1509 and 1513 some were staged for Ferdinand II (King of Aragon), as Regent of Castile, the latter in honour of his recent conquest of the kingdom of Navarre.[7] As the direct precursors of the *entrada* dedicated to Charles I in 1517, these earlier festivities are interesting. In all of them, the most outstanding celebration was linked to the entry ceremony when a procession through the town was made by the guest of honour; this customarily passed through the Plaza del Mercado.[8] On these occasions, decorated wooden arches were built and it seems that costumed figures commonly acted out stories, usually with music, for which there was an established tradition in Valladolid.[9] These representations, organised by the town guilds, were called *entremeses*.[10] However, certain changes were introduced into the entries for Ferdinand the Catholic. Fortunately, *relaciones* or printed accounts of the two *entradas*

---

[4] Thus it was described by Antonio Lalaing, Chamberlain of Philip the Fair, in 'Voyage de Philippe le Beau en Espagne, en 1501', in Gachard, *Collection des voyages*, vol. II, p. 168.

[5] Biblioteca del Real Monasterio de El Escorial, Códice M-I-16, fol. 47; A. Rucquoi, *Valladolid en la Edad Media. El Mundo Abreviado (1367–1474)*, 2 vols. (Valladolid, 1987), vol. II, pp. 485–6.

[6] On this subject see Rucquoi, *Valladolid*, vol. II.

[7] T. Knighton and C. Morte García, 'Ferdinand of Aragon's Entry into Valladolid in 1513: the Triumph of a Christian King', *Early Music History* 18 (1999), pp. 119–63.

[8] The *entradas* also involved other festivities such as bullfights, *juegos de cañas*, banquets etc.

[9] AMV, *Libro de Acuerdos* (1497–1500), fol. 187v [June 1498].

[10] As far as I have been able to establish, in Castile staged *entremeses* that formed part of processions were usually organised by religious confraternities or lay guilds, which collaborated with the town council or the relevant religious institutions. The thematic content of these *entremeses* was linked to the particular set of beliefs and interests of the townspeople.

9.1 View of Valladolid; G. Bruin, S. Novellanus, F. Hogenburgius, *Civitates orbis terrarum Liber primus* (Cologne, 1582), plate 3.

for Ferdinand have survived, and both were written by Luis de Soto, a member of the musical chapel attached to the peripatetic household of Ferdinand (dissolved at his death in 1516).[11] He was a native of Valladolid and he was the programme-organiser and author of the narrated and sung texts and, as a professional musician, may well have composed at least some of the polyphonic items performed at both receptions.[12] De Soto devised four *triumphos* (triumphal arches) for the first *entrada*, dedicated to Fortune, the Virtues, Fame and Time; and two for the second *entrada* – one dedicated to Victory, the other to the Catholic Church. When the king arrived at these events, a short representation was performed in which music played a special role. The staged event consisted of a series of monologues recited by allegorical characters followed by the singing of a villancico, the characteristic vernacular form. Exceptionally, in the triumph to Victory of 1513 which commemorated the conquest of Navarre, 'some well-composed songs' were performed on 'seven ministriles altos [wind band], four sackbuts and three cheremias [shawms]'.[13] In both events, eulogies to Ferdinand were presented which portrayed the king as a 'Great Sovereign', ranking alongside Roman emperors, biblical kings and distinguished Castilian monarchs.[14]

The instrumental and vocal music performed in both *entradas* was not printed in these *relaciones* and does not appear to have been preserved in any other sources. However, it is likely that the villancicos were written, as Knighton and Morte point out, in the musical idiom characteristic of other propagandist songs of the time.[15] A simple, largely homophonic and clearly phrased style can also be seen, in my opinion, in many other works of the period that were not necessarily propagandist in tone but rather dramatic or, in the wider sense, representational.[16] In fact, it is not by chance that the poet, composer and above all playwright Juan del Encina (1469–1529) was one of the most important contributors to this style. Since both aspects – the propagandist and the theatrical – would have been found in these villancicos, it could be said that they would have adopted these compositional traits, as represented by the repertory of the musical collections known as cancioneros.[17] It has been suggested that although 'medieval' traits persisted in both receptions, certain innovative features demonstrate the emergence in Spain of the classically inspired *entrada*.[18] The

[11] L. de Soto, *Este es el recebimiento que se fizo al rey don fernando en valladolid* ([Seville, 1509]), in A. Gómez Moreno, *El Teatro Medieval Castellano en su marco románico* (Madrid, 1991), pp. 151–8; and *El recebimiento que le hizo al muy alto . . . rey don Fernando . . . en la villa de Valladolid* ([Valladolid, 1513]), El Jardín de la Memoria 1 (Madrid, 1982). [12] Soto, *Este es el recebimiento*, p. 151.

[13] Soto, *El recebimiento*, fol. 1v (unfoliated). Note the significance of the link between wind instruments and the theme of Victory, and the fact that they performed songs ('canciones') and not villancicos. These could perhaps have been Franco-Flemish chansons of the kind included in later Spanish manuscript collections of music for wind band.

[14] Both entries are part of a series, which began with the 1506 reception of Ferdinand the Catholic in Naples and continued in Valencia (1507), Seville (1508) and Valladolid. All these emanated from the royal court with the aim of enhancing the prestige of the Aragonese king.

[15] Knighton and Morte García, 'Ferdinand of Aragon's Entry', pp. 151–2.

[16] The relationship that can be seen between such works and the simple style as described here has not been studied hitherto. Reinhard Strohm points out (*The Rise of European Music, 1380–1500* (Cambridge, 1993), p. 580) that a similar connection can be made with regard to Italian song *c.* 1500 which would provide further evidence of the close relationship between the Castilian and Italian song repertories. See S. Aguirre Rincón, 'Teatro, música y humanismo en la España del Renacimiento: el repertorio de los cancioneros y la "teatralización"', unpublished paper presented at the Universidad Complutense, Madrid, October 1988.

[17] For example, Madrid 1335 (olim Madrid 5-I-20), Madrid, Biblioteca del Palacio Real: H. Angles and J. Romeu Figueras (eds.), *La música en la corte de los Reyes Católicos. Cancionero Musical de Palacio (siglos XV y XVI)*, Monumentos de la Música Española V, X, XIV (Barcelona, 1947–65).

fact that Soto's *relaciones* used the term *triumpho* rather than *entremes* is evidence of this, as is the laudatory style of the scenes dedicated to the monarch.[19]

Relatively little documentation concerning the events which occurred during the first entrance of Charles into Valladolid on 18 November 1517 has survived. It seems likely that the occasion was organised with some haste, because Burgos was the town originally selected for the honour. An account by Laurent Vital, the *garderobes* of Franco-Flemish origin in Charles's household, however, provides some details of the day.[20] In his narrative, Vital distinguished between the reception organised by the inhabitants of Valladolid and the royal procession which traversed the town and which was organised by the monarch's Flemish household. With respect to the first, Vital stated that:

> Now, that the town and its inhabitants were present at this entry is not surprising, since they were not used to such events. In any case, there were, in the openings and entrances of the streets, in five or six places where the king was to pass, wooden arches lightly built and decorated with figures who represented stories with explanations in writing in Castilian; but as I did not understand it and had no one to tell me what it meant, I took no notice of them.[21]

Even though this urban reception may not have displayed the luxury and pomp of the Flemish cities which must have served as Vital's point of comparison,[22] it would be inaccurate to say that the inhabitants of Valladolid were not accustomed to organising them; it was simply that other urban traditions predominated. Owing to political circumstances, it is unlikely that it was merely a paean of praise to the monarch like those in the aforementioned *entradas* dedicated to Ferdinand II. In an attempt to defend their civil liberties, the citizens of Valladolid had risen up against the restrictive policies of their former regent, Cardinal Cisneros, in 1516–17.[23] By the time of the *entrada* in November, this revolt had been interrupted in the hope that the king would fulfil his promise to meet their demands. The town council was directly involved in the rebellion and also in the organisation of the *entrada*. For example, it contracted the 'minstrels, drummers and trumpeters which the Duke of Bejar sent . . . for the reception of the king . . .' The *Libros de Acuerdos* of the town council also indicate that, among other things, property belonging to the council had to be sold in order to finance the reception.[24] Furthermore, as the town guilds and the prior of the collegiate church of Santa María had been involved in the revolt they were probably involved in the organisation of the 1517 reception, as had been the case with other royal receptions promoted by the civic authorities.[25]

Given this evidence, it is very likely that the 'figures who represented stories with written explanations in Castilian' described by Vital followed in the tradition of the

---

[18] Gómez Moreno, *El Teatro Medieval*, pp. 93–4.

[19] Roy Strong considers this emphasis to be one of the traits that distinguishes Humanist entries from Medieval ones, which were more concerned with exalting the town than the monarch; *Arte y poder: Fiestas del Renacimiento, 1450–1650* (Madrid, 1988), p. 60.

[20] The main accounts are from L. Vital ('Premier Voyage de Charles Quint en Espagne') and Jean Vandenesse ('Journal de voyages de Charles-Quint'), both in Gachard, *Collection des voyages*, vol. III, pp. 1–303; vol. II, pp. 53–464. See also F. Prudencio de Sandoval, *Historia de la vida y hechos del Emperador Carlos V, 2 pars. (Valladolid, 1604 y 1605)* (Madrid, 1956), vol. I, pp. 122–34.

[21] Vital, 'Premier Voyage', p. 154.

[22] Charles had been received in the cities of Ghent, Brussels, Louvain, Antwerp and Bruges shortly before this entry.   [23] Sandoval, *Historia de la vida*, vol. I, pp. 89–93, 106–7.

[24] AMV, *Libro de Acuerdos*, 4 (1517–1520), fols. 396v (20 July 1517) and 429r (18 November 1517).

[25] On the participation of the prior see AMV, *Libro de Acuerdos*, 1 (1497–1500), [28 July 1497].

entremeses. However, these stagings also surely incorporated some of the new elements of the receptions for Ferdinand the Catholic, especially if the devising of them was once again the responsibility of Luis de Soto. His experience in the programming of the two previous royal entries in Castile would surely have been drawn on by the promoters. Moreover, it is highly likely that he was then in Valladolid; Soto's former patron, Ferdinand the Catholic, had died in 1516 and it is possible that he remained in his native town seeking an ecclesiastical benefice at Santa María, since some years later he held the prestigious position of canon. Other indirect evidence exists to support this hypothesis and show that Soto was often closely associated with royal *entradas.* When, ten years later, the authorities of Valladolid were preparing the reception for Charles's wife Isabella, they decided 'to give to canon Soto the sum of ten thousand *maravedis* to pay the expenses . . . [incurred] . . . in organising and providing the personnel for this reception'.[26] If Soto devised the 1517 *entrada,* it is probable that the representations incorporated music, including polyphony, and it is also possible that the musicians of the collegiate church of Santa María, to which he was attached, were involved in its performance.[27]

The kind of music that was definitely performed at this *entrada* was, as usual, that of trumpets and drums and other minstrels. As we saw, the town council had contracted the musicians of the Duke of Béjar to accompany a procession of citizens welcoming the monarch. Perhaps these musicians, or some of them, also took part in the stagings on the triumphal arches. In addition, owing to the importance which the *entrada* of 1517 held for Charles V, the largest group of instrumentalists was that which formed part of the royal procession which accompanied the king through the streets of Valladolid. Trumpets and drums processed behind Charles's army and among the nobles of Castile, Burgundy and Aragon. Amongst the musicians were twelve trumpeters of the king's Flemish household, which accompanied him everywhere, and others carrying 'kettle drums, on horseback, who belonged to [Charles's brother] Ferdinand, and other important noblemen'.[28] It is also likely that the trumpeters of the Castilian royal household formed part of the procession since Charles had made contact with them at Tordesillas, where a few days prior to his entry into Valladolid he had visited his mother, Queen Joanna I the Mad, with whom he would, until her death, share the Castilian throne.[29] Similarly, Charles had come across the six trumpeters and four drummers of the Aragonese household of Ferdinand when on 24 October 1517 he was welcomed into Aguilar de Campóo.[30] Moreover, there is documentary evidence for their presence in Valladolid a few days later.

It was the royal procession, rather than the civic reception, that was used as the vehicle for the political expression of the monarch. Its magnificence, fully complemented by the large musical group, could not fail to impress the inhabitants of the town. Yet the way in which Charles (soon to be crowned king) and the townspeople (anxious

---

[26] AMV, *Libro de Acuerdos,* 5 (1527–1531), fols. 10r, 290r [23 January 1527]; Knighton and Morte García ('Ferdinand of Aragon's Entry', p. 138) have found new evidence to confirm this.

[27] Little is currently known about the musical life of Valladolid, but documents preserved at the Archivo General de Simancas and the Archivo Histórico Provincial de Valladolid, show that the collegiate church was the only religious institution at that time to have a properly funded musical chapel.

[28] Vital, 'Premier Voyage', p. 153. The Count of Benavente, the Admiral of Castile, the Duke of Alba or the Constable of Castile may have been among the nobility present.

[29] The Castilian household, inherited from Isabella I of Castile, remained in Spain and served Queen Joanna and eventually her son Charles when in Spain. On music at this court see H. Anglés, *La música en la Corte de Carlos V. «Libro de Cifra Nueva para tecla, harpa y vihuela» de Luys Venegas de Henestrosa,* Monumentos de la Música Española II (Barcelona, 1984), pp. 5–9.   [30] Vital, 'Premier Voyage', p. 126.

to maintain their liberties) both used the trumpets and drums to their own ends, albeit not to the same extent, reflects a duality of interest and resources.

Ceremonial music continued to be heard in Valladolid during the seven months of this first royal visit. For example, when the Castilian nobles, such as the Duke of Béjar, the Marqués of Aguilar and the Duke of Nájera came to the town with 'great pomp and triumph' they were accompanied by trumpets and drums.[31] This music was also performed at the many entertainments such as jousts, tournaments and *juegos de cañas* which were organised in Valladolid for the enjoyment of the monarch and the nobility. These took place chiefly in the Plaza del Mercado, as well as in and around the Plaza de San Pablo where Charles's residence was to be found. Here the royal household made a constant show of its wealth, paying for most of the spectacles and indulging in conspicuous consumption.

These various entertainments extolled the monarch as Lord and Master of his Knights and created fame and renown for other participants; also, the music that accompanied them considerably enhanced their aural and visual impact. Charles certainly performed his role as Lord and Master of the Knights when, at the climax of the celebrations during his first visit, on 16 February 1518 (a few days after his enthronement) he entered the lists as a participant in the jousting. According to the chronicler Vital certain instrumentalists announced the royal arrival at the contest:

> xxx drummers on horseback, each with two huge kettledrums, one on each side, which made an enormous resounding noise . . . lx other drummers as well as lx Castilian, Neapolitan and Aragonese trumpeters making such a loud noise that one could not even have heard God unleashing a thunderclap . . . xii trumpeters of the King, playing loudly and vigorously with fine skill . . . x German drummers on foot, and six German fife-players playing with great zest . . .[32]

Also, the victors of the contests were granted the privilege of being accompanied by the musicians back to their quarters and to places where a celebratory banquet was to be held; because of this accompanying noise, the whole town was made aware of their triumph.

Charles's presence in Valladolid encouraged many other nobles and gentlemen to reside there, who also participated in the many tournaments. The ceremonial needs of this elite social group meant that their appearances were often accompanied by their trumpets, drummers and other instrumentalists; thus, Valladolid experienced an increase in the number of instrumentalists present in the town during this period. For example in the Grand Joust on 16 February there were 'twenty drummers . . . making a great noise, followed by twenty-eight Spanish trumpeters and then the king's twelve trumpeters', dressed all in the distinctive livery of their masters. In this way, all these aristocratic activities and their associated pageantry had an impact on the musical life of the town. The music which accompanied them – 'visual' in that it sought to draw attention to individuals – now principally defined the 'soundscape' of Valladolid during this period.

Ceremonial fanfares were also performed at the coronation of Charles which, after long negotiations, took place on 7 February 1518 in the monastery church of San Pablo. Protocol required that the service began with a 'very solemn Mass', which may have involved polyphony. The identity of the group who sang on this occasion is at present

---

[31] *Ibid.*, pp. 156–7.   [32] *Ibid.*, pp. 211–12, 194–222.

unknown. It is quite likely that they were members of the chapel of the Flemish household which accompanied Charles during his stay in Spain, for several reasons. First, only a very few chaplain singers and an organist were available from the monastery of San Pablo; also, a series of confrontations between the canons of Santa María and members of the royal household made the participation of the musicians of the collegiate church impossible,[33] while the choir of the royal Castilian chapel had already been dispersed. Moreover, the service was conducted by Cardinal Tortosa (a native of Utrecht), former tutor to King Charles who later became Pope Hadrian VI (1522–23). Since he was chosen for this event despite the presence of several Spanish archbishops, it is highly likely that the Flemish chapel participated, just as was the case in Barcelona for the funeral of the Emperor Maximilian.[34]

Nor would this have been the first time that the Flemish chapel performed in Valladolid; Philip the Fair was accompanied by his chapel musicians when he visited the town in 1502 and 1506. In 1517–18 there were twenty-eight members of the Flemish chapel, including the two souffleurs dorghes Franskin du Breuc and Bauduwin, and the organist Henry Bredemers.[35] Unfortunately no documentary evidence survives as to which Mass or motet might have been performed, but these works would have been selected with great care, and may have been specially composed for the occasion. After the ceremony of enthronement, the *Te Deum* was sung as usual and was immediately followed by 'the trumpets and drummers of the king . . .'[36]

Musicians employed in Charles's Flemish household also took part in the banquets, soirées (*saraos*) and other celebrations held at the royal residence in Valladolid, although little information describing the events has survived. Rare evidence of one banquet at which the monarch and members of his household were present, hosted by the president of the Valladolid Chancellery, is, however, provided by Laurent Vital. This was held a few days before the king left the town. According to Vital, 'while the king feasted, the harmony and sweet resonance, as much from the various instruments as from the fine voices and sweet chords which they sang and played, made it seem like paradise . . .'[37] Vital gives no clues as to the identity of the singers on this occasion. It is possible that the Chancellor specially contracted musicians for this event to increase the resources of the musical chapel he probably already had in his service.[38]

Following this first visit of the royal household to Valladolid in 1517–18, a series of events occurred which had a significant impact on the aspirations and outlook of the town's inhabitants. This was the uprising and subsequent failure of the *Comunidades* (1520–21). Rebel bourgeoisie and craftsmen of the Castilian towns who were keen to protect their industries joined forces with members of the urban oligarchies to fight for the independence of their cities.[39] Opposing them, on the side of the king, were those

---

[33] *Ibid.*, p. 180.

[34] E. Ros-Fábregas, 'Music and Ceremony During Charles V's Visit to Barcelona', *Early Music* 23:3 (1995), pp. 374–92.

[35] Gachard (ed.), *Voyages des Souverains*, vol. II, pp. 502–3; Ros-Fábregas, 'Music and Ceremony', pp. 381, 388–9.   [36] Sandoval, *Historia de la vida*, vol. I, p. 127.   [37] Vital, 'Premier Voyage', p. 254.

[38] In general, little is known about the musical patronage of noble citizens in Spain and future research will no doubt yield interesting results. It is quite likely, in my opinion, that the dispersal of the forty singers of the Aragonese royal chapel in 1516 resulted in a boost to the resources of noble musical chapels.

[39] See, amongst others, S. Haliczer, *Los Comuneros de Castilla: la forja de una revolución (1475–1521)* (Valladolid, 1987). This relative independence of the cities had been guaranteed by the previous Castilian monarchs, who sought through them to curb the power of the nobility. But in the reign of Charles they would lose this power when it was assumed by the king in the process of consolidating the absolute monarchy.

nobles and members of the merchant class who had used their profits to acquire territorial estates. Valladolid sided with the rebel cause, although owing to the power of the monarchy and its supporters this was ultimately lost and the town fell definitively into the power of the king and his administration.

The social transformations precipitated by this shift in the balance of power occurred more comprehensively and more immediately in Valladolid than in other Castilian urban centres, because it was one of the main Spanish residences of the king. This brought about an influx of nobles as permanent or seasonal residents, who built palaces of their own in order to take advantage of the patronage to be gained from residing in proximity to the sovereign. They were also able to view and participate in the numerous *fiestas* which occurred whenever the king visited the town. These nobles, and their retinues, now the courtiers of the king, had an impact on the cultural profile of Valladolid for, in order to emulate the conspicuous consumption of the monarch, they too hosted their own banquets and dances which required musical entertainments. By this time then, Valladolid ceased to be an inward-looking town dominated by a local oligarchy who set cultural and social norms. Instead, it had become inhabited by socially and culturally self-aware individuals who were acquainted with contemporary artistic innovations, including those in music.

These changes in the social composition of the population had become consolidated by the time of another extended visit Charles I made to Valladolid in 1527, a sojourn which was marked by the birth of a prince, the future Philip II. Two documentary sources, one written by a Castilian chronicler, the other compiled by an anonymous French author, describe the event.[40] The first describes the instruments and decorations used for the events; the author of the second, clearly connected with the organisers of the festivities, records the musical texts sung. After the birth on 21 May had been made public, the king, accompanied by prelates, nobles and the town council as well as his court, went to the church of San Pablo where 'those of his chapel sang *Te Deum laudamus*'. The chapel mentioned here was the Flemish royal chapel, although no documents have yet been found indicating which singers were members of the chapel on this particular occasion. A list from 1525 has, however, survived, and mentions fifteen singers, twelve boy choristers, an organist (Florens Nepotis) and organ-blower.[41] As Charles stayed in Spain between 1525 and 1527 the chapel membership is unlikely to have changed much between those two dates, although it is known that Nepotis returned to his native Netherlands. Among those who remained were Nicolas Gombert (*c.* 1495–*c.* 1560) and the future music master of the chapel Nicolas Payen (a chorister in 1525).

The baptism took place on 5 June and was entirely organised by the royal household. In every detail it was planned so as to glorify the emperor, royal family and the new heir through symbolism loaded with references to Imperial Rome and the Christian world, all in the service of the ideology of the state. The place of baptism (the church of

---

[40] The first source, though written during the event, was copied by Fray Juan de Osnaya in 1544 and formed part of a manuscript entitled *Relación de la guerra del Almirante de Francia contra el Emperador Carlos V*, published in G. de Arriaga, *Historia del Colegio de San Gregorio de Valladolid*, ed. M. M. Hoyos (Valladolid, 1928), pp. 487–94; the French source is entitled *Nativite et baptesme de Don Philippe Prince de Espaigne*, published in J. M. March, *Niñez y Juventud de Felipe II. Documentos inéditos sobre su educación civil, literaria y religiosa y su iniciación al gobierno (1527–1547)*, 2 vols. (Madrid, 1941–2), vol. I, pp. 28–40. See also Sandoval, *Historia de la vida*, vol. II, pp. 246–50.

[41] E. Vander Straeten, *La Musique aux Pays-Bas avant le XIXe siècle*, 8 vols. (Bruxelles, 1867–88; revised by E. Lowinsky, New York, 1969), vol. VII, p. 303.

San Pablo) was less than 100 metres from the prince's birthplace (the house where the court usually resided when in Valladolid). A corridor, covered by wooden arches, was constructed between the two places and along this, five platforms decorated in the classical style were erected, upon which dramatic scenes with music were performed. In the first of these, four angels, represented by 'four Flemish boys', sung *Dicite in magni dum spes altera mundi*, a polyphonic motet composed by Gombert.[42] The text is a typical humanist allegory in which the prince as a descendant of God-Caesar and of the Virgin-Empress, represents the hope of the great universe.[43]

In the second tableau, with texts from Isaiah 9 and Matthew 3, seven boys representing in turn the heavenly bodies – the Sun, Venus, Mercury, the Moon, Saturn, Jupiter and Mars – appeared, singing verses in praise of the prince. In this case the performance was probably monodic, since each character was represented by only one actor-musician. The choice of theme, and the content and vocabulary of the sung texts that are included in the French account, make quite clear the connection with the classical world, but above all they highlight the importance of the political metaphor: for example, Venus refers to Jupiter and *Phoebus* (the epithet of Apollo, god of prophecy and of music, but also a warlike god), and so on.

The third and fourth tableaux, although dedicated to the customary four moral and three theological virtues, were presented in the same way as the 'planets' in the second tableau. The Castilian account describes 'four angels [choristers] and Our Lady, all singing "verses" in the third tableau, and a harp and portable organs were played'. Although this author suggests that five characters were singing in the third tableau, the French manuscript, which states that 'there were four moral virtues singing the following verses' is more accurate in this respect. Voices and polyphonic instruments were probably combined in the four pieces sung by 'angels'. Instruments such as harp and organ often symbolised celestial harmony in iconographic sources of the period, and thus it is not surprising that they featured in dramatic presentations dedicated to the moral virtues.

It is quite possible that the harp and the organs were also played by musicians of the king's Flemish household and that one of these represented the figure of 'Our Lady'.[44] The absence of Florens Nepotis, organist of the Flemish chapel (mentioned above), makes it likely that this task fell to Isabella's keyboard player, Antonio de Cabezón, who was a great favourite of Charles V.[45] The organs actually used may have been the two which Charles had commissioned from Wolf Reichard, which arrived in Spain in 1524.[46]

Like the third tableau, the fourth also featured 'boys dressed as angels singing, and the minstrels of the Emperor playing' and it is therefore likely that they gave a performance similar to the one which had occurred in the earlier scene. And in the fifth tableau, under a palio, there was a representation of the 'Baptism of Jesus Christ by John the Baptist'; this would certainly have been a representative scene with statues.

---

[42] Nicolas Gombert, *Cantiones Sacrae*, ed. J. Schmidt-Görg, Opera Omnia 5 (American Institute of Musicology, 1961), pp. 15–22.

[43] I would like to thank Cristina Rosa Cubo, University of Valladolid, for her help with these texts.

[44] There were a number of other musicians in Charles's household besides those in the chapel, such as his chamber harpist, or harpist of the pages.

[45] After her marriage to Charles in 1526, Isabella maintained her own separate household. In 1527 it already included a considerable number of singers of polyphony as well as Cabezón; Anglés, *La música en la Corte de Carlos V*, pp. 28–30.   [46] Anglés, *La música en la Corte de Carlos V*, p. 18.

The French source reveals that, after the prince's baptism, 'the singers of the emperor's chapel then began to sing *Te Deum laudamus*. And then the high trumpeters, shawms and various other instruments in the church began to play', as had happened ten years earlier at the king's accession to the throne. At that moment, the bells in the town began to peal and the prince was taken back to the palace 'in the same order in which they had come, except that all the instruments played. In the evening, fireworks, dancing, mumming and other entertainments were held in the street'; these were undoubtedly organised by the town.

The underlying themes of the texts sung during these baptism tableaux suggest that they were composed by a single individual. This author, as well as referring back to the Classics, gathers together well-known essentially hyperbolic formulae to construct a hymn to glorify the arrival of the 'son of Caesar' into the world. It is clear that the author was concerned with the political propaganda of imperial ideology which found its expressive apotheosis in Charles's coronation as Holy Roman Emperor in 1530. It also reminds us of the *Carmen Saeculares* which Horace composed in 17 BC on the orders of Augustus to demonstrate the latter's divine origin; he conjures up a new era which would start with the celebration of secular games, in which twenty-seven young men and twenty-seven maidens sang a hymn of thanks for the new age of peace.

Of the pieces performed during the baptism tableaux, only the first (from the first scene), Gombert's *Dicite in magni*, was published together with its music in his *Musica Qvatvor Vocum (Vulgo motecta) . . . Liber Primus* of 1539.[47] Stylistically, this motet is comparable to other compositions produced by Gombert in the 1530s and 1540s. The continuous imitative counterpoint that structures the poetic text ends in a strictly homophonic style, which underlines the joy felt at the arrival of the new prince. Its clef system (C3, C3, C4, F3) denotes a tessitura too low to have been sung by 'four Flemish boys [choristers]'. Nevertheless, the narrow range of the entire composition lends itself to the possibility of being transposed to higher registers (either an octave, or, perhaps more appropriately, a fifth) above the given pitch, which could be more easily sung by boys.

This was not the only work by Gombert which was performed during the festive events dedicated to Charles V and other members of the royal family, but it was apparently the first and it represents an early example of the composer's work, and it presages his future role as 'master of the choristers' in the chapel of Charles's Flemish household. This, together with the other motets performed at the prince's baptism, shows the importance which music customarily had at political events organised in honour of Charles V.

As for the rest of the festivities which took place during the visit of 1527 – banquets, *saraos* (soirees), jousts and bullfights etc. – one fundamental difference distinguished them from those which occurred during the visit of 1517–18: the participation of the civic oligarchy. After the failure of the *Comunidades* of 1520–21, these formerly powerful citizens of Valladolid endeavoured to recover their lost sense of power by becoming true Renaissance courtiers, converting themselves into cultivated men, able to serve inside the apparatus of royal government or in the new openings that this brought to the town. These new 'aristocratic' aspirations were satirised in the *Coplas del Segundo Provincial*, which circulated in the town at that time.[48] This change was evident in 1527, and would have more impact in the years that followed.

---

[47] Gombert, *Cantiones Sacrae*, p. i. The motet was reprinted in Venice by Antonio Gardano in 1551.

[48] B. Bennassar, *Valladolid en el Siglo de Oro. Una ciudad de Castilla y su entorno agrario en el siglo XVI*, 2nd edn (Valladolid, 1989), p. 490.

Music was integral to this type of social change. From the1530s, inventories and accounts indicate that instruments such as the vihuela on which polyphony could be performed were owned by urban professionals such as lawyers, governors, bankers and also noblemen. For example, in the 1540 will of Juan Bravo, a doctor, household goods including books such as 'La natura de Aristóteles' and 'Las moradas de Séneca' were listed, as well as 'a vihuela and a *discante* or guitar'.[49] Such was the popularity of the vihuela (the Spanish court instrument *par excellence*) in Valladolid that by 1536 the *violero* (vihuela-maker) Pedro Amatia was already established in the town.[50] Moreover, two Valladolid citizens, Francisco de los Cobos (*Comendador mayor* and private secretary to the king) and Diego Hernández de Córdoba, were respectively responsible for the patronage and publication of the second book of music for vihuela published in Spain, and the first in Castile, Luys de Narváez's *Los seys libros del Delphin de musica de cifras para tañer vihuela* of 1538. Among his own compositions Narváez included his intabulations of works by other Spanish and Flemish composers.[51] Narváez, who worked in the service of both Francisco de los Cobos and Prince Philip, lived in Valladolid for many years and made his fame there as a musical performer. The presence of Flemish works – six by Josquin, two by Gombert and one by Jean Richafort – in this Spanish source is not surprising given that Narváez probably had opportunities to witness the performance of Flemish works associated with the many festivities organised in honour of the king, including the music by Gombert performed at the 1527 baptism. Narváez also included his arrangement of Josquin's *Mille regretz* giving it the title of the *canción del Emperador*. That Josquin was fairly well known in Valladolid at that time is also evidenced by a complimentary reference to him in the *Ingeniosa comparación entre lo antíguo y lo presente*, a work by Cristobal de Villalón, Professor of Logic at the University of Valladolid.[52] Polyphonic music became an established part of the cultural life of this 'enlightened' group.

In conclusion, it is clear from the evidence presented above that the frequent presence of Charles V's court, as well as changing Valladolid into one of the principal Castilian urban settlements, was the catalyst for the metamorphosis of the cultural life of the town. The transformation extended the consumption of polyphonic works from a court elite to other members of the Valladolid citizenry amongst whom the *vihuela* achieved particular popularity. Furthermore, Valladolid during this time became a magnet for musicians, instrumentalists as well as singers, who took advantage of the increased professional opportunities to be found in this newly revitalised urban cultural life, which at the same time created the ideal environment for the exchange of musical ideas.

---

[49] Archivo Histórico Provincial de Valladolid, Leg. 40, fol. 580r.
[50] A. Rojo Vega, *El Siglo de Oro: Inventario de una época* (Salamanca, 1996), p. 430.
[51] Luys de Narváez, *Los seys libros del Delphin de musica de cifras para tañer vihuela*, ed. E. Pujol, Consejo Superior de Investigaciones Cientificas, 2nd edn (Barcelona, 1971), with an introductory study.
[52] Cristobal de Villalón, *Ingeniosa comparación entre lo antíguo y lo presente* (Valladolid, 1539), Bibliófilos Españoles, XXII (Madrid, 1898), fol. cijr.

CHAPTER TEN

CHANGE AND CONTINUITY IN THE REFORMATION PERIOD: CHURCH MUSIC IN NORTH GERMAN TOWNS, 1500–1600

JOACHIM KREMER

Sixteenth-century historians are largely agreed that the German Reformation marked a turning point in ecclesiastical, political, cultural, social and juridical terms.[1] However, the Reformation was not a sudden event. When Luther posted his *Ninety-Five Theses* in 1517 on the castle church in Wittenberg, the term 'reformatio' was already in vogue, used largely in humanist criticism of the church. Early efforts had been made to secure a 'reformatio' of the church, for example, in the so-called Golden Bull issued by Emperor Charles IV in 1356 and in the reforming councils of Pisa (1409), Constance (1414–17) and Basel (1431–49). Also, from the late fifteenth century, numerous juridical decrees were promulgated, such as the *Neue Nürnberger Reformation* of 1479–84, the oldest printed German municipal body of law.[2] Thus reforming concerns were turned into weapons of power politics directed against the Emperor and the Empire. This development, against a social background articulated in the revolts of peasants and some cities in south and central Germany (the so-called Peasants' War in 1524–5) together with the transition from efforts at reform into denominational separation, turned the Reformation into an intricate network of interests which cannot be explained purely in confessional or liturgical terms.[3] The history of the concept of the Reformation also indicates that its defining elements betray chronological discontinuities. In other words, the word 'reformation' was not self-evidently confessional in significance.

In the same way, for the music history of the mostly Protestant towns of north Germany the Reformation is rightly regarded as an important turning point. This can be seen in the reorganisation of the church service, liturgy, ecclesiastical offices, charitable work, the revision of the education system through the foundation of Latin schools (*Lateinschulen*, *Gelehrtenschulen*) and the publication of hymnbooks. This was achieved on the basis of the introduction, in rapid succession, of local *Kirchenordnungen*, for example by the cities of Hamburg (1529), Lübeck (1531), Göttingen (1531), Lüneburg (1531) and Bremen (1534), and by territories such as Pomerania (1535), the duchy of Mecklenburg (1540) and the province of Hadeln (1542). In addition, a tendency may be noted towards standardisation and inter-regional co-operation in reform. In northern Germany this tendency may be traced in the development of the *Kirchenordnungen*: many of those promulgated before 1544 derive from that of Brunswick (1528), which was

---

[1] J. Weiss, 'Reformation', in A. Erler and E. Kaufmann (eds.), *Handwörterbuch zur deutschen Rechtsgeschichte*, 5 vols. (Berlin, 1971–98), vol. IV, col. 459.   [2] *Ibid.*, col. 460.   [3] *WA IV*, vol. V, pp. 220–1.

one of the earliest written by Johannes Bugenhagen (1485–1558).[4] Moreover, emissaries from the cities of Lübeck, Bremen, Hamburg, Rostock, Stralsund and Lüneburg met in Hamburg on 15 April 1535 to discuss Reformed doctrine and liturgy. The outcome of these efforts to standardise Lutheran liturgy and doctrine (in other words, to create a 'concordia ceremoniarum'), was the so-called *Hamburg Articles* of 1535.[5]

Similarly, the legislation for school visitations in Saxony (the *Unterricht der Visitatoren in Sachsen*, 1528) by the Reformer Philipp Melanchthon (1497–1560), Luther's main collaborator, established a 'highly influential norm' (in the words of Klaus-Wolfgang Niemöller) for regulating schools. Many *Schulordnungen* in Lower Saxony drew on the work of the Reformers Johannes Bugenhagen and Urbanus Rhegius and thus show parallels in their content.[6] The 1529 *Kirchenordnung* of Hamburg expressly referred to Melanchthon in its regulations concerning the school that was to be set up: 'Therefore, the form shall be adopted for the other classes, and exercises shall be conducted, according to the rules outlined by *Magister* Philip Melanchthon in his *Visitatie der pastoren tho Sassen*.'[7]

These structural and institutional changes were conducted in conformity with a view of music typical of Luther, three of whose writings in particular represented decisive guidelines for reforming the liturgy.[8] Moreover, Luther gave the spoken word a central place, as the most important means of grace. Consequently, the sermon increasingly became the focus of the liturgy. In the same way, the priest was no longer the agent of transubstantiation and the Sacrifice of the Mass, but became a proclaimer of the Word, a 'preacher' in the true sense. This is reflected also in the basic features of Luther's conception of music, which was coloured above all by theology.[9] Music was considered a neutral element, an 'adiaphoron', and only in combination with theology did it achieve its status in the liturgy: it was to be a form of divine praise, 'enfolded' (*eingewickelt und verschlossen*) within theology.[10] For this reason, liturgical music was a partner to the sermon in the service of proclamation, since 'the Word of God desires to be preached and sung'.[11] Music did not merely engender joy, but could also be efficacious in countering Satan, the 'spirit of melancholy' (*geist der traurigkeit*). Liturgical music simultaneously represented divine praise, confession of faith and proclamation and thus served the Gospel; its basis, like that of the sermon, combined 'cantio' (song) with 'contio' (speech), in subordination to the Word of God and not to canonic rule.[12] Luther explicitly spelt out this opposition between Gospel and Law and the possibility of the Gospel being preached through music 'as is seen in Josquin': 'Was lex ist, gett nicht von stad; was euangelium ist, das gett von stadt. Sic Deus praedicavit euangelium etiam per musicam, ut

---

[4] H. Hettwer, *Herkunft und Zusammenhang der Schulordnungen* (Mainz, 1965).

[5] E. Sehling *et al.* (eds.), *Die evangelischen Kirchenordnungen des 16. Jahrhunderts*, 15 vols. (Leipzig, 1902–77), vol. V, p. 482. For the text of the *Hamburg Articles*, see pp. 540–3.

[6] Sehling, *Die evangelischen Kirchenordnungen*, vol. V, p. 495.

[7] K. W. Niemöller, *Untersuchungen zu Musikpflege und Musikunterricht an den deutschen Lateinschulen vom ausgehenden Mittelalter bis um 1600*, Kölner Beiträge zur Musikforschung, ed. K. G. Fellerer, 54 (Regensburg, 1969), p. 618.

[8] M. Luther, *Von ordenung gottis diensts ynn der gemeyne* (1523); *Formula missae et communionis pro ecclesia Wittenbergensi* (1523); *Deudsche Messe und ordnung Gottis diensts* (1526).

[9] For Luther's own view of music, see O. Söhngen, 'Luthers Bedeutung für die Geschichte der Musik', *Musik und Kirche* 53 (1983), pp. 225–33.

[10] J. Walter, preface of *Lob und Preis der löblichen Kunst Musica* (Wittenberg, 1538); quoted from A. Strube (ed.), *Spielleute Gottes: Ein Buch vom deutschen Kantor* (Berlin, 1935), p. 23.   [11] *WA II*, vol. XVII, p. 120.

[12] On the relationship between sermon and music, see C. Bunners, *Kirchenmusik und Seelenmusik: Studien zur Frömmigkeit und Musik im Luthertum des 17. Jahrhunderts*, Veröffentlichungen der Evangelischen Gesellschaft für Liturgieforschung, ed. O. Söhngen, 14 (Göttingen, 1966), pp. 53, 54.

videtur in Iosquin.' Accordingly, music was 'not bound and approvable by rule',[13] and could aspire to become the 'living voice of the Gospel' (*viva vox evangelii*).[14] Within this distinctively theological comprehension of sacred music the congregation assumed an active role. If 'the Word of God or song should abide among the peoples',[15] song would lead the congregation to an understanding of the Word of God.

The implementation of these Reformation conceptions of music was tied decisively to basic structural constraints. They can be found within the sphere of the institutions, of their financing and also of the ordering of the liturgy and the understanding of the offices held by church musicians. Supported by the respective interests of the towns, these aspects contributed to the melting pot of the cultures of the cities, and the rich musical culture of the north German cities of Danzig, Königsberg, Rostock, Lübeck and Hamburg in the seventeenth century is a sign of the long-term efficacy of those sixteenth-century structural innovations. Yet, even in terms of music history, the Reformation in north German cities can be characterised only to a limited extent by geographical and chronological unity. Rather, there was an overlapping of progressive and reactionary elements and we find, just as in the history of the conception of 'reformation' itself, successive and simultaneous discontinuities. This means not only that certain areas and cities were late to subscribe to the Reformation, but also that premature and transitional stages of reformation existed and that some pre-Reformation institutions survived even after the imposition of the Reformation. Since the concept of reformation, in its prefix, already suggests such chronological complications, the dichotomy between 'change' and 'continuity' in the title of this chapter describes only the extremes of a broad spectrum of processes and phenomena that varied according to region.

CHRONOLOGICAL DISCONTINUITIES IN THE IMPLEMENTATION OF THE REFORMATION

Even though the Reformation was imposed and new institutions were founded energetically and ubiquitously, obstacles to progress existed side by side with new developments. In the large cities of Lübeck and Hamburg, the Reformation was swiftly and comprehensively imposed and the founding of central Latin schools (*Lateinschulen*) soon followed (e.g. in Hamburg in 1529). In many smaller cities such as Kiel or Wismar, however, secondary schools and cantorships (the office of the church musician) were not founded until around 1560; in Buxtehude, according to its *Schulordnung*, in 1552; in Wismar in 1576 and in Jever in East Friesland in 1574; in the smaller Holstein cities of Itzehoe, Meldorf and Husum, from the 1580s onwards; and in the Holstein city of Plön a secondary school was not founded until 1705.[16] Until then, pre-Reformation structures continued to exist and the 'rector', as *regens chori*, led the church music.[17] On the other hand,

---

[13] *Tischreden* no. 1258, in *WA II*, vol. II, p. 11.

[14] O. Söhngen, 'Theologische Grundlagen der Kirchenmusik', in K. F. Müller and W. Blankenburg (eds.), *Leiturgia: Handbuch des evangelischen Gottesdienstes*, 5 vols. (Kassel, 1954–70), vol. IV, p. 79. See also *Tischreden* no. 2545b in *WA II*, vol. II, p. 518.

[15] Luther, in a letter to Georg Spalatin *c.* 1523 (*WA I*, vol. XXXV, p. 73).

[16] Niemöller, *Untersuchungen zu Musikpflege*, pp. 66 and 187, and J. Kremer, *Das norddeutsche Kantorat im 18. Jahrhundert: Untersuchungen am Beispiel Hamburgs*, Kieler Schriften zur Musikwissenschaft, ed. Fr. Krummacher and H. W. Schwab, 43 (Kassel, 1995), p. 75.

[17] Even after the establishment of a cantorship in many towns around 1550 the rector retained an overseeing function, whereas musical and pedagogical duties were shared between rector and cantor.

some towns had already founded cantorships at municipal schools before the Reformation.[18] In the rich mercantile cities of Lübeck and Hamburg, city parish schools had already been founded in the thirteenth century (Lübeck in 1262 and Hamburg in 1281). Similarly, in Helmstedt (1407), Brunswick (1415–20), Hanover (1441) and Schöningen (1499) the establishment of cantorships was linked with the founding of city parish schools. In historical terms, the civic school cantorship represents a precursor of the Lutheran cantorship, rather than the German cathedral cantorship.[19] The rapid imposition of the Reformation, completed by 1535 in towns of Lower Saxony such as Lüneburg, Celle, Hanover, Brunswick, Goslar, Göttingen and Minden, thus coincided with a preliminary stage in the history of schools and cantorships which enhanced the efficiency of Reformation music education. A phenomenon characteristic of Lower Saxony, namely, the production of numerous didactic treatises for teaching music, may owe its origin to this local coincidence.

On the other hand, cathedrals and monastery churches were very often late to adhere to the Reformation. Even in the economic centre, Hamburg, the imposition of the Reformation was completed only in 1564 and in Ratzeburg only in 1566. Thus these cathedral chapters retained their special constitutional and juridical position as independent enclaves; in Hamburg, Bremen, Schwerin, Schleswig, Magdeburg and Güstrow they formed separate ecclesiastical territories, or, after their transformation into duchies after the Thirty Years' War, autonomous aristocratic principalities. But they lost their former central position in the cities and the standard of the cathedral schools and music in Hamburg and Lübeck, for instance, dropped sharply. This was owing to the fact that city schools no longer had the customary obligation of surrendering talented singers from among their pupils to the central church and school of the town, namely the cathedral. The confirmation of the central position of the cathedral schools in the musical life of the cities had been a basic requirement, and was contractually recognised when the parish schools were founded in the central Middle Ages. A contract to this effect had been agreed between the council and the cathedral chapter in Lübeck in 1262, laying down the obligation to transfer boys to the cathedral school;[20] and also in Hamburg it was agreed in 1337 that pupils competent in elaborate song (*ad maiorem cantum*) at the church school of St Nicholas (founded in 1281) were to be transferred to the cathedral school in that city.[21] Owing to the Reformation, this support in terms of finance and personnel was transferred to the newly founded municipal Latin schools, which now became the central musical institutions. At the beginning of the eighteenth century the headmaster of the Hamburg Latin school, the Johanneum, complained about the decline of the former practice of transferring choirboys from parish schools to his school.[22]

It was not only structural considerations, such as the size, economic power or demographic structure of cities, that influenced the differences in date outlined above at which the Reformation was imposed, but also regional considerations. Indeed a retarded version of the process can sometimes be noticed for complete regions. This is true of the

---

[18] Niemöller, *Untersuchungen zu Musikpflege*, pp. 145–8, 181.

[19] These cathedral cantorships had become mere sinecures as early as the tenth century, and the musical duties were mostly fulfilled by a 'succentor'; cf. M. Schuler, 'Zur Geschichte des Kantors im Mittelalter', in C. Dahlhaus *et al.*, *Bericht über den internationalen musikwissenschaftlichen Kongreß Leipzig 1966* (Kassel, 1970) p. 171, and Niemöller, *Untersuchungen zu Musikpflege*, p. 181.

[20] Niemöller, *Untersuchungen zu Musikpflege*, p. 181.

[21] E. Meyer, *Geschichte des Hamburgischen Schul- und Unterrichtswesens im Mittelalter* (Hamburg, 1843), p. 132.   [22] Kremer, *Das norddeutsche Kantorat*, p. 183.

whole of Mecklenburg, owing to a development that had already taken place before the Reformation: here, unlike the municipal cantorships mentioned above, there is hardly any evidence of the existence of 'succentores' or 'cantores'.[23] Thus, in contrast to the cities of Lübeck, Hamburg, Helmstedt, Brunswick or Hanover, Mecklenburg lacked the institutional structure which defined the preliminary stage described above. Moreover, in Mecklenburg the Reformation was imposed only hesitantly. In Sternberg, the priest sought to resign in 1541 on account of the lack of support he was receiving for church music, since the 'schoolmaster [was] still a notorious Papist';[24] the background for incidents such as this was certainly the fact that the Reformation was not conducted here by an effective government, but was based on a compromise regime between a Protestant, Duke Heinrich V of Schwerin (*d.* 1552) and a Catholic, Duke Albrecht I of Güstrow (*d.* 1547). In Mecklenburg, cantorships were established only in the late sixteenth century, the high efficiency in musical training typical of Lower Saxony was absent and musical treatises were not prescribed during the Reformation century, nor are they likely to have been written or published.[25]

SACRED MUSIC IN TERMS OF THE REDEFINED RELATIONSHIP BETWEEN STATE AND CHURCH

Martin Luther's doctrine of the Two Kingdoms, named the 'Zwei-Reiche-Lehre' by twentieth-century scholars, not only constituted a juridical theology, but also redefined the relationship between state and church. Luther's fundamental division between secular and sacred (the 'Kingdom of the World' and the 'Kingdom of God') found a counterpart in his doctrine of the Two Regiments, one serving piety and the other peace, and also in his doctrine of the Three Estates, the *status oeconomicus*, *status politicus* and *status ecclesiasticus*. Following this doctrine, primacy is not granted to any of these, not even the *status ecclesiasticus*, but the existence of each is justified through its divine vocation. Thus, even secular aspects of music which do not serve an immediate religious purpose are still recognised as legitimate.

A second Lutheran category also decisively furthered music, namely, the installation of the territorial lord as the 'summus episcopus'. Although the new *Kirchenordnungen*, such as that of Brunswick (1528), which served as an exemplar to north and middle Germany, were concerned less with creating a new denomination than with reforming abuses, the obligation placed on the lord to pay attention to religious practice laid the foundation for the conception of territorial ecclesiastical government (*landesherrliches Kirchenregiment*). By the end of the Peasants' War at the latest, the Reformation was being implemented by territorial lords and this activity was linked decisively with their role as 'summus episcopus'. With the Peace of Augsburg (1555), the right of territorial governments to decide between confessions was generally accepted. Since a city government, in its capacity as 'summus episcopus', also had the highest authority for deciding the outcome of ecclesiastical cases, official positions in church music also differed from those in the pre-Reformation tradition. Like the liturgy and the priesthood, such positions were subjected to desacralisation by the Reformation; they changed from clerical offices, with sacramental ordination, to offices that were integrated in city schools and civic social structures. The former central role of monasteries and cathedral schools as venues for the education of

---

[23] Niemöller, *Untersuchungen zu Musikpflege*, p. 66. [24] *Ibid.*, p. 67. [25] *Ibid.*, p. 80.

clerics as church singers was now transferred to city Latin schools, their teachers and pupils.

Even the office of cantor was now dependent on these schools. Accordingly, cantors were no longer clerics, but teachers of music and scholarship. The schools were no longer supported by the church, but by city governments. Thus the setting up of Latin schools and the establishment of cantorships and choirs represented indispensable structural conditions for the cultivation of Protestant church music.

As a consequence of the imposition of the Reformation, direct power struggles sometimes developed between the city governments and reform-minded citizens and these were also important for sacred music. Events in Lübeck and Hamburg may be taken as symptomatic. Here liturgical music became a vehicle for protest and propaganda when Luther's hymn *Ach Gott vom Himmel sieh darein* (1524) was sung in Lübeck in 1529; previously, with the expulsion of Protestant preachers and the prohibition of the singing of hymns in the vernacular, the city council had suppressed all Reformation tendencies. In this situation the hymn, particularly in its text, amounted to a 'general settling of accounts with the old ecclesiastical system': since it articulated the complaints of the 'poor' against the suppression of the new doctrine, it assisted in the establishment of a distinctive Protestant identity in Lübeck.[26]

At the church of St Nicholas in Hamburg, liturgical music was performed for the first time by laymen at Christmas 1526. The necessity for this had arisen because the Catholic priests of St Nicholas had refused to attend services, on account of attacks by the Protestant preacher Johannes Ziegenhagen, and had thus prevented the services from being conducted. However, the liturgical music was performed by the schoolmaster of the St Nicholas church school, with his assistants and pupils. Thus this confrontation resulted in the performance of liturgical music by laypeople. Later, Ziegenhagen forbade the vicars even to participate in the liturgy, a development which further consolidated the new position occupied by sacred music in the church school. Above all, the events at Hamburg point to the striving of the Reformation movement to free the performance of music from the influence of the clergy, an aim that was realised in the task of the Latin schools to perform monophonic and polyphonic sacred music.[27]

CIVIC CHOIRS AND MUSIC EDUCATION

The new organisational structures of civic church music can be traced also in their system of finance. The system of ecclesiastical livings which, coupled with numerous endowments of altars and Masses, had provided for church music, was hardly reconcilable with the new doctrine. In its place, schools and cantorships were now paid for by the city finance authorities. This method of financing them was firmly grounded, for example, in the *Kirchenordnung* of Hamburg of 1529, in that the fees to be paid are precisely specified there.[28] Substantial local variations in this pattern are to be expected, however, despite the inter-regional influence of the Reformer Bugenhagen: above all, the evidence

[26] W.-D. Hauschild, 'Der Kirchengesang in der Reformationszeit', in A. Edler and H. W. Schwab (eds.), *Studien zur Musikgeschichte der Hansestadt Lübeck*, Kieler Schriften zur Musikwissenschaft 31 (Kassel and New York, 1989), p. 35. The first stanza of the text refers to the poor who were 'abandoned' and the third stanza clearly formulates the rejection of the old juridical system and places it in opposition to the interests of the citizens.

[27] H. Leichsenring, *Hamburgische Kirchenmusik im Reformationszeitalter*, ed. J. T. Kite-Powell, Hamburger Beiträge zur Musikwissenschaft, 20 (Hamburg, 1982), p. 14.

[28] The level of remuneration did not, of course, remain permanently at the level prescribed by Bugenhagen.

of the sources is uncertain, since the account books for those years do not survive, even for the north German metropolis of Hamburg. The sparse indications so far published concerning the financing of cantors and choirs in north Germany yield a heterogeneous picture.[29] They show that even endowments and new foundations continued to be made, as for example in Königsberg and Leipzig. In the Hanse cities of Lübeck and Hamburg, however, little or no provision of this kind had been made for cantors or choirs. At the cathedrals, the pre-Reformation system of livings continued even after the Reformation had been implemented there: Johann Mattheson was still complaining in 1740 of the inadequacy of this method of remuneration.[30] His protests show not only that cathedrals retained the system of finance, but also that the level of payments lay far below that of civic institutions, because the cathedrals had lost their central position. The decreasing significance of cathedral music in the seventeenth and eighteenth centuries is also to be ascribed to this development, in the context of rising inflation, and an increase in the cultivation of music outside churches.[31]

Not only did the new *Kirchenordnungen* promote sacred music in institutional terms, but they also explicitly required the cultivation of music as one of the duties of secondary schools. According to the Hamburg *Kirchenordnung* (written in Low German):

> At noon the cantor is to teach singing to all the older and younger children, not merely according to custom, but, in time, artistically, and not only chant [*den langen sanck*] but also polyphony [*in figurativis*]. The four teachers [*de veer pedagogi*] whose duty it is to sing in church are to assist him occasionally as necessary in the school. He is also to be assisted by the schoolmasters [*scholegesellen*], with the exception of the headmaster, when he desires to celebrate a festival with his choir in the churches, so that the children shall be given good and cheerful training.[32]

This indicates that there was no formally articulated office of *cantor choralis* in north Germany as was usual in central Germany, but that the other secondary school teachers (*de veer pedagogi*) were also involved in music education and practice. They assisted the cantor in teaching and also collaborated as singers in the choir (*cantorie*). This picture of the vocation of a schoolmaster at a Latin school, combining didactic and musical activities, characterised the image of a Reformation teacher generally. However, it characterised not only the vocation of the schoolmaster, but conversely also that of the cantor: the latter certainly had its centre of gravity in music, but also included the teaching of philological and religious topics. The professional specialisation usual among teachers today, whose exclusivity is a feature only of modern times, was absent at that period: it developed only in the eighteenth century and also affected the office of the cantor which (owing to the increase in activity in the field of composition) was transformed into a specifically musical post like that of a *Kapellmeister*.

Above all, however, a further advance is associated with the prescription of both chant and mensural polyphony in the Hamburg *Kirchenordnung*. Before the Reformation, polyphony was restricted to only a few German cathedrals and collegiate churches. Although there are references to polyphonic performances of Masses in Hamburg's city

---

[29] Kremer, *Das norddeutsche Kantorat*, pp. 187–96. [30] *Ibid.*, p. 101.
[31] At present there are no comparative studies on the history of the cathedral chapters and their cultivation of music in the eighteenth century. [32] Sehling, *Die evangelischen Kirchenordnungen*, vol. V, p. 495.

Table 10.1 *Books of musical instruction by north German cantors and schoolmasters*

Author	Occupation and place of work	Title	Place and date of origin/ publication
Auctor Lampadius	Cantor (Lüneburg)	*Compendium musices*	Bern 1537
Heinrich Faber	Rector (Naumburg)	*Compendiolum musicae*	Brunswick 1548 (more than 30 editions)
Johann Zanger	Cantor/Rector (Brunswick)	*Practicae musicae praecepta*	Leipzig 1554
Lucas Lossius	Conrector (Lüneburg)	*Erotemata musicae*	Nürnberg 1562
Nicolaus Roggius	Cantor (Brunswick)	*Musicae practicae sive artis canendi elementa*	Nürnberg 1566
Christoph Praetorius	Cantor (Lüneburg)	*Erotemata musicae*	Wittenberg 1574
Andreas Crappius	Cantor (Hanover)	*Musicae artis elementa*	Helmstedt 1599
Johann Magirus	Subconrector/Cantor (Hanover), Pastor (Brunswick)	*Artis musicae . . . libri duo*	Frankfurt 1596
Otto Siegfried Harnisch	Cantor (Helmstedt, Wolfenbüttel, Göttingen)	*Idea musicae* *Artis musicae delineatio*	Frankfurt 1601 Frankfurt 1608

churches, the surviving pre-Reformation repertory is exclusively monophonic.[33] Similarly, there is very little evidence for polyphonic liturgical music in Lübeck before the Reformation. According to the 'Oratio de Luca Lossio', a speech delivered by Lucas Bacmeister in Rostock in 1585, polyphony was introduced at Lüneburg in 1516.[34] Polyphonic performance also occurred only at a late date at Lübeck (1486), Göttingen (1491) and Hanover (1504); in his speech, Bacmeister suggests that this was generally characteristic of north Germany: 'At that time, there was little or no polyphony [*figuralis Musica*] in these parts, but only plainsong or Gregorian chant, as they call it, although it began to be cultivated somewhat earlier in the courts of kings and princes, brought first from Italy or from England, as some say, and taken thence into Belgium.'[35] In view of this estimation, the explicit prescription of polyphony through the *Kirchenordnungen* represented a strong stimulus to polyphonic liturgical music.

In Lower Saxony, above all, the training of choirs was provided for by the work of the Reformers in music education, since a series of didactic works was written and published here soon after the introduction of the Reformation. These works include the titles listed in Table 10.1. They are directly related to the concerns of the Reformers in music education, as is illustrated in the treatise of Auctor Lampadius. In its characterisation of Josquin's compositions as worthy of imitation, this draws directly on Luther's opinions to the same effect. Moreover, the authors Heinrich Faber and Christoph Praetorius were pupils of Melanchthon and promoted his conceptions both of general and musical education.

[33] Leichsenring, *Hamburgische Kirchenmusik*, pp. 5, 10–13.
[34] H. Walter, *Musikgeschichte der Stadt Lüneburg vom Ende des 16. Jahrhunderts bis zum Anfang des 18. Jahrhunderts* (Tutzing, 1967), p. 18.   [35] *Ibid.*

THE MUSICAL REPERTORY AFTER THE INTRODUCTION OF
THE REFORMATION

Even though the Hamburg *Kirchenordnung* had called for polyphonic music (*in figurativis*), a discontinuity can be discerned in the sacred repertory, namely in the survival of pre-Reformation provisions. In their discussion of the history of the cantors and music education, Klaus Wolfgang Niemöller and Dieter Krickeberg have emphasised that, as a result of the humanist orientation of education in northern and eastern Germany, the survival of Latin was favoured and the establishment of a German-language Protestant repertory was retarded. Thus the situation in north Germany was clearly different from that in central Germany, where a predominantly vernacular hymnal was available as early as 1524 in the *Geystliches gesangk Buchleyn* of Johann Walter (1496–1570), the friend of Luther and Melanchthon.

In fact, the recommendation in many *Kirchenordnungen* to retain the old repertory, the old textbooks and the cultivation of Latin, corresponds with the favouring of Latin texts in such hymnals as the *Psalmodia, hoc est, Cantica sacra veteris ecclesiae selecta*, published in 1553 by Lucas Lossius (1508–82, *corrector* at Lüneburg), and the *Cantica sacra* (1588) of Franz Eler (after 1500–90, teacher at the Hamburg Johanneum).[36] The problem of the language of the liturgy was acute at Rostock, where the local Reformer, Joachim Slüter, demanded the abolition of all Latin hymns. In 1531 this caused a dispute with the other preachers in the city, which was settled by the Reformers Rhegius and Bugenhagen: it was agreed that Latin hymns could be retained for subsidiary services 'for the sake of the pupils'.[37] This ruling remained in force over the following decades and in conformity with the *Kirchenordnung* of 1552 the choirs in the cities of Mecklenburg were obliged to sing prodominantly in Latin. Lossius's *Psalmodia* was accordingly 'bought by many churches, including Latin schools'.[38]

Moreover, this development was not local or specific to Rostock. Rather, it tended in the direction of the *Hamburg Articles*, which sought, besides liturgical standardisation, the retention of Latin for the sake of the school pupils.[39] The Hamburg *Kirchenordnung* also repeatedly prescribed the singing of Latin texts and required classical literature to be taught and traditional textbooks to be used, such as the familiar grammar by Donatus. This allegiance to humanist tradition underlies the comprehensive cultivation of Latin as the educational language of Protestant Latin schools, in an orientation that scarcely changed until the eighteenth century.

The late discontinuation of Latin as the language of the liturgy in north Germany around 1700[40] follows the tendency of the Brunswick *Kirchenordnung*, which often provided a model for others and in which goals in the realm of education and church music were outlined in humanist terms.[41] With this survival in north German liturgical music, Latin proved extremely resilient, since a central concern of the Reformation was the introduction 'in opposition to the Church of Rome' of vernacular liturgy and consequently also of vernacular texts and hymns.[42] Luther's translation of the scriptures, his

---

[36] Niemöller, *Untersuchungen zu Musikpflege*, p. 150. This attitude is reflected also in the high regard given to Gregorian melodies in Lower Saxony, and the strong representation of older compositions by Lassus, De La Rue, Josquin, Obrecht, Ockeghem and Gombert. [37] Niemöller, *Untersuchungen zu Musikpflege*, p. 74.

[38] *Ibid.*, pp. 75–6. [39] Sehling, *Die evangelischen Kirchenordnungen*, vol. V, p. 541.

[40] On Walter and on Franz Eler's *Cantica sacra*, see J. Mattheson, *Grundlage einer Ehrenpforte* (Hamburg, 1740; reprint, Kassel, 1969), p. 325. [41] Niemöller, *Untersuchungen zu Musikpflege*, p. 150.

[42] Bunners, *Kirchenmusik und Seelenmusik*, p. 64.

German Bible, served this purpose in the same way as did the collection and diffusion of many hymns. In this development the *Bapstsche Gesangbuch* of 1545 was exemplary, because its repertory was adopted in many other hymnals, including Eler's *Cantica sacra*, which was widely diffused in northern Germany, and the equally well-known *Psalmodia* of Lossius, both mentioned above.[43] However, these hymnals did not succeed in establishing vernacular liturgical music as obligatory, since they continued to transmit the pre-Reformation repertory as well as Reformed hymns. Both collections remained in use for a long time, Lossius's *Psalmodia* until well into the seventeenth century and Eler's *Cantica sacra* certainly until the publication of the Hamburg *Gesangbuch* in 1700. On account of this strong adherence to tradition, the composition of vernacular hymns and the translation and replacement of the Latin portions of these books remained problematic in the seventeenth century. In Hamburg, Joachim Gerstenbüttel (1647–1721), the cantor at the Johanneum, addressed this problem soon after his appointment in 1675 in numerous letters to the council and clergy of the city. The problem was only resolved in 1700 with the publication of the Hamburg *Gesangbuch*.[44] In Lüneburg there were similar efforts to promote vernacular hymns: at the instigation of the superintendent there, Petrus Rehbinder, the list provided in the *Usitatus Ordo Cantionum in Ecclesia Lunaeburgensi* predominantly suggests German metrical psalms for the Temporale.[45] Even though these innovations were adopted at the church of St John in late 1649, the churches of St Nicholas and St Lambert continued to use hymns with Latin texts. After the death of the cantor at St John in Lüneburg, Michael Jacobi (1618–63), his successor Friedrich Funcke (1642–94) filed a petition on 9 July 1670 which stimulated another rejoinder from Rehbinder: the diverging opinions of Funcke and Rehbinder – the cantor favouring polyphony and Rehbinder congregational singing – gave rise to sharp conflicts. These incidents do not merely demonstrate how the bitterness of debates concerning the repertory of liturgical hymns deepened in the second half of the seventeenth century, however, but they also show the persistence of the pre-Reformation repertory and of Latin as the language of the liturgy. Both of these were underpinned, not least, in the so-called *Hamburg Articles* (1535), which 'agreed to the preservation of pre-Reformation traditions' in relation to sacred music and endorsed the use of Latin.[46]

The cultivation of pre-Reformation polyphony was legitimised by Luther's recommendation of Josquin's works as compositions worthy of imitation. However, the full supraregional effect of these comments can be seen only through the study of inventories and library catalogues, which provide a picture of the repertory performed in the sixteenth century.[47] A catalogue of music from the church of St John at Lüneburg (the *Designatio Librorum Cantionum pro schola Lüneburgensi ad D. Joannis*, 1607) contains the international repertory of vocal music of the period between 1570 and 1590.[48] Although it does not list any of Josquin's works, it provides evidence for an important aspect of the musical repertory of the Reformation century. The church possessed the works of some local composers, such as Johannes Chustrovius, sacristan at the church of

[43] W. Merten, 'Die Psalmodia des Lucas Lossius: Ein Beitrag zur reformatorischen Musikgeschichte in Niedersachsen (Lüneburg)', Ph.D. thesis, University of Göttingen (1951), and F. Onkelbach, *Lucas Lossius und seine Musiklehre*, Kölner Beiträge zur Musikforschung, ed. K. G. Fellerer, 18 (Regensburg, 1960).

[44] J. Kremer, *Joachim Gerstenbüttel (1647–1721) im Spannungsfeld von Oper und Kirche: Ein Beitrag zur Musikgeschichte Hamburgs*, Musik der frühen Neuzeit. Studien und Quellen zur Musikgeschichte des 16. – 18. Jahrhunderts, 1 (Hamburg, 1997), pp. 134–59.

[45] Walter, *Musikgeschichte der Stadt Lüneburg*, pp. 103–9. [46] *Ibid.*, p. 541.

[47] Niemöller, *Untersuchungen zu Musikpflege*, p. 169. [48] Walter, *Musikgeschichte der Stadt Lüneburg*, p. 38.

St Nicholas at Lüneburg, who published motet collections in 1589 and 1603; Andreas Crappius, cantor at Hanover; and Euricius Dedekind, formerly cantor at Lüneburg. Above all, however, it was the works of internationally famous composers such as Crecquillon, Regnart, Rore, Vincenzo Ruffo, Lassus and de Wert that were performed. These latter were musicians who, to a great extent, served Catholic patrons: Crecquillon, a canon at Termonde and Béthune, worked as a member of the Imperial Chapel, Regnart was a member of the Imperial Choir at Vienna, and Rore was a singer at St Mark's in Venice. The Lüneburg inventory thus reflects a state of affairs in which no specifically Protestant musical repertory yet existed, soon after the juridical and institutional imposition of the Reformation and in which, moreover, no taint was attached to works by those termed 'Papists' at the time in Germany. The example of Vincenzo Ruffo is particularly instructive: he was, among other things, 'maestro di cappella' at the cathedrals of Verona and Milan. Under the direct influence of the Archbishop of Milan, Charles Borromeo, who worked for the Counter-Reformation, Ruffo's musical style changed abruptly after 1563, along lines laid down by the Council of Trent. A *Magnificat* of his, extant at Lüneburg, dates from this phase of his output and must have been taken from the collection *Li Magnificat brevi et aierosi . . . con tutti li falsi bordoni* (Venice, 1578).[49]

Thus Protestants continued to set Latin texts to music; but on the other hand Catholic composers also set Protestant texts.[50] In the sixteenth century there was no sharp denominational borderline between the Catholic and Protestant repertories. Only after the concept of 'reformatio' had progressively lost its significance as a 'renewal' (*renovatio*), and only after the often vague and imprecise provisions of the *Kirchenordnungen* had become more rigid did a progressively stronger denominational self-consciousness develop.[51]

An analogous picture is offered by sacred music in Hamburg in the sixteenth century, both for the monophonic and the polyphonic repertories. Strangely enough, the foundation of the cantorship and the introduction of polyphony after the Reformation are barely attested in the sources, although in institutional terms the conditions were favourable for these, since a city church school had been founded in the thirteenth century, a *Kirchenordnung* had been prepared at an early date and a secondary school associated with it had been set up. The uncertainty in the sources extends to the musical repertory as well as to the office of cantor:[52] evidence of polyphony dates only from a relatively late date (1566), that of the *Opus musicum excellens et novum, continens sacras selectissimasque Quatuor, Quinque, Sex et Octo vocum cantiones*, written by Jacob Praetorius the elder, organist of the church of St James.[53] Moreover, it was dedicated to the two dukes of Mecklenburg, Johann Albrecht and Ulrich, and was intended for liturgical use in Rostock.

Only towards the end of the sixteenth century does evidence of the buying of music, or of the sending of compositions to Hamburg, increase in quantity. In 1594 the *Opus musicum* by Jacobus Gallus was bought; in 1597 Nicolaus Langius, Kapellmeister at Brunswick, received payment from the church of St James for a *Magnificat* and other

[49] *s.v.* 'Vincenzo Ruffo', in *Grove*, vol. XVI, pp. 320–1; Walter, *Musikgeschichte der Stadt Lüneburg*, p. 284.

[50] H. M. Brown, *Music in the Renaissance* (Englewood Cliffs, 1978), p. 275.

[51] The heightened denominational self-awareness that developed after Luther's death also coincided with the rise of biographies of Luther; E. Wolgast, 'Biographie als Autoritätsstiftung: Die ersten evangelischen Lutherbiographien', in W. Berschin (ed.), *Biographie zwischen Renaissance und Barock: Zwölf Studien* (Heidelberg, 1993), pp. 41–71.   [52] Leichsenring, *Hamburgische Kirchenmusik*, pp. 128–9.

[53] The six surviving volumes are preserved in Rostock University Library (shelfmark Mus. Saec. XVI, 49, 1–6).

works; Valentin Haussmann and Johannes Polonus each provided one composition for St James, in 1600 and 1602 respectively; and in 1601 settings by Theodoricus Sommerau were dedicated to the four city parishes. Already in 1597 Johannes Wendius had published the two parts of his three-voice collection of *Newer Teutscher Geistlicher Lieder* in Hamburg and had dedicated them to the town's dignitaries.[54]

Thus the cultivation of the international polyphonic repertory is not as well documented at Hamburg as at Lüneburg. However, Praetorius's *Opus musicum* provides numerous clues: its city of origin was Hamburg and Praetorius, the copyist, was employed at the church of St James; its dedication and purpose points to Rostock. Therefore, it permits conclusions not only about the repertory performed at Rostock, but also about that performed at Hamburg.[55] This collection, which originally comprised eight volumes, contains only two compositions that definitely originated in Hamburg: *Te Deum* settings by Praetorius and Paul Russmann, organist at St Peter's. Both are based on the pre-Reformation *Te Deum* melody which had been printed in Franz Eler's *Cantica sacra* (Hamburg, 1588). Above all, however, it is music by supraregional, well-known composers that recurs here: the *Te Deum* settings include two by Josquin and one by Leonhard Schröter, the twenty-five Masses in Part II include two by Josquin (*Missa Pange lingua* and *De Beata Virgine*), two by Crecquillon (*D'amours me plaint* and *Kein in der Welt so schön*) and three ascribed to Jacquet of Mantua (*Si bona suscepimus*, *In die tribulatione* and *La fede non debet esse corrotta*). A further anonymous Mass (*Missa super quem dicunt homines*) was apparently also part of the repertory of the papal chapel. There are also works by Gombert, Susato, Senfl and Adam Rener. However, Johann Walter, a composer who was significant for creating a Protestant repertory, is also represented in Part IV, if only by psalm and hymn settings with Latin texts. Moreover, some of the works in this collection occurred in Reformation hymnals such as the *Vespertina Precum Offici* (published by Rhau at Wittenberg in 1540), the *Liber I Sacrorum Hymnorum* (Rhau, Wittenberg, 1542) or the *Wittenbergisch Deudsch Geistliches Gesangbüchlein* of 1551.[56] Thus in exemplary fashion, Praetorius's *Opus*, which presumably reflects the sixteenth-century repertory both of Hamburg and Rostock, demonstrates the heterogeneous nature of the polyphonic liturgical repertory. In this, the heterogeneity that appears in the Lüneburg *Designatio Librorum Cantionum pro schola Lüneburgensi* occurs, in terms of the language of the settings, the provenance and the denominational affiliation of the composers.[57]

THE PROGRESSIVE INNOVATIONS OF THE REFORMATION

The foundation of city Latin schools in the humanistic tradition and the integration into them of the office of cantor created a profession whose representatives were no longer clerics. The increased value attached to secular life – and also luxury – by Luther's teaching of the Two Regiments permitted the music of cities and churches to represent a wider range of interests. This allowed the enlargement of *a cappella* choirs into 'mixed'

[54] Leichsenring, *Hamburgische Kirchenmusik*, pp. 142–4.
[55] For a detailed description of the *Opus musicum* see Leichsenring, *Hamburgische Kirchenmusik*, pp. 132–41.
[56] Leichsenring, *Hamburgische Kirchenmusik*, pp. 139–41.
[57] On the polyphonic repertory in Lübeck and performances of the works of Josquin and De La Rue see U. Haensel, 'Die Musik der Reformationszeit', in A. Edler and H. W. Schwab (eds.), *Studien zur Musikgeschichte der Hansestadt Lübeck*, Kieler Schriften zur Musikwissenschaft, ed. Fr. Krummacher and H. W. Schwab, 31 (Kassel, 1989), p. 27.

vocal/instrumental ensembles, in turn permitting city music to compete with court ensembles.[58] This development is evident in the *Schulordnung* of the Hamburg Johanneum (1556), which rated a 'gude Sengerie' a 'particular adornment', and in the increasing inclusion of instrumental musicians in church music from about 1560 in Hamburg and about 1539 in Lübeck.[59] The effective work of instrumentalists such as William Brade, Johann Schop and also of the organists Jacob Praetorius the elder and Hieronymus Praetorius at Hamburg, is based on this Lutheran conception of music. The diverse musical culture that arose in the seventeenth century is inconceivable without these fundamental changes in the previous century, namely, the fact that power in matters of ecclesiastical politics and sacred music was now vested in the cities and was therefore interwoven with municipal interests,[60] even if this consolidation had not taken place very rapidly in the field of the musical repertory in the sixteenth century.

Because of the denominationally determined homogeneity and the similarity of economic and social structures across the region of north Germany, this development can be traced especially clearly there. In his *North German Church Music in the Age of Buxtehude*, Geoffrey Webber also takes into account compositions from Danzig, Königsberg and Stockholm, towns that are today in Poland, Russia and Sweden.[61] He thus presents a concept of 'north Germany' that is coloured more by cultural history than geography or politics. But this extension to the Baltic region and Scandinavia is justified, not least by the introduction of Lutheranism to Denmark and Sweden in 1537 and 1544 respectively and by the German culture of the Baltic cities. The cultural influences, the dependence of the *Kirchenordnungen* on the Brunswick model and the mobility of musicians and of representatives of learning such as Melanchthon or Bugenhagen, also justify this broad understanding of the concept of 'north Germany', apart from geographical or political implications. For comparative regional research with particular emphasis on church music and institutional history, this broad 'north German' region therefore offers a highly favourable point of departure. However, many of the questions raised here concerning civic history, such as the politics of education, the history of cantors and choirs, the history of repertory and the financing of church music, have not been the subject of recent research. Thus the present discussion offers hypotheses and an outline of a possible project for future investigation, rather than a synopsis of research findings. Besides the structural differences between the cities listed here, Plön, Kiel, Wismar, Rostock, Lüneburg, Hamburg and Danzig, it is precisely the chronological proximity of the Reformation changes, the broad diffusion and the supraregional and unifying influence of the Reformers, Melanchthon and Bugenhagen, that offer an ideal platform for comparative studies. This comparative approach embraces a dimension of research into regional music history that has hitherto received too little attention.[62] And it can be expected to yield an increasingly precise description of the aspects presented in this chapter, of the chronological skewing of the implementation of the Reformation, of the institutional and administrative aspects of city choirs and of the survival of the pre-Reformation repertory after 1530.

[58] M. Ruhnke, *Beiträge zu einer Geschichte der deutschen Hofmusikkollegien im 16. Jahrhundert* (Berlin, 1963), pp. 271–5.

[59] Niemöller, *Untersuchungen zu Musikpflege*, p. 194; Kremer, *Das norddeutsche Kantorat*, p. 29; Hauschild, 'Der Kirchengesang in der Reformationszeit', p. 39.

[60] Thus the topic of 'patronage' is a centrally important one for the history of Protestant music as well as elsewhere.   [61] G. Webber, *North German Church Music in the Age of Buxtehude* (Oxford, 1996).

[62] H. Kaelble, *Der historische Vergleich: Eine Einführung zum 19. und 20. Jahrhundert* (Frankfurt and New York, 1999).

CHAPTER ELEVEN

CATHEDRAL MUSIC, CITY AND STATE: MUSIC IN REFORMATION AND POLITICAL CHANGE AT CHRIST CHURCH CATHEDRAL, DUBLIN

BARRA BOYDELL

During the medieval and early modern periods cathedrals played a central role in the lives of the cities of which they formed so prominent a feature. The medieval cathedral-priory of Holy Trinity, otherwise known as Christ Church, not only served as the spiritual centre of the city of Dublin (see Illustration 11.1), but also played an important civic and political role, a role whose nature was to change during the post-Reformation period when the strong links which had evolved between cathedral and city would be largely replaced by closer links with the government and state. The Protestant Reformation in Ireland was closely identified with English colonial rule[1] and during the late sixteenth and early seventeenth centuries Christ Church slowly became an arm of Protestant reform within an increasingly recusant city. By the mid-sixteenth century the lord deputy regularly attended services on Sundays and on other days of liturgical and state importance, Christ Church serving in effect as the Chapel Royal (this title was first formalised by Charles II in 1672). The cathedral's music, which had already reflected Christ Church's civic role in the later medieval period, was affected by, and on occasions played a role in, the advancement of English political and religious control.

Christ Church Cathedral was founded in c. 1028, and in 1163 the regular Arroasian canons of the Augustinian order were introduced by St Laurence O'Toole (Lorcán Ó Tuathail), Archbishop of Dublin. O'Toole's successor, John Comyn, erected a collegiate church dedicated to St Patrick outside the city walls, which was subsequently raised to cathedral status with the result that Dublin now had two cathedrals, one of which was monastic, the other secular.[2] St Patrick's Cathedral, however, never enjoyed the same degree of identification with the citizens of Dublin during the later medieval and early modern periods as did Christ Church. Great public occasions centred on Christ Church, situated as it was close to the Tholsel (city assembly rooms) and the Guildhall, the centres of municipal and commercial life, and it was the site of parliaments and great councils throughout the later medieval period, the prior being *ex officio* a member of the upper

---

I am grateful to Raymond Gillespie and to Colm Lennon for their critical reading of earlier versions of this paper, and to Roger Bowers for his comments on the later fifteenth-century choral foundation at Christ Church.

[1] See especially A. Ford, *The Protestant Reformation in Ireland, 1590–1639*, 2nd edn (Dublin, 1997).

[2] Both Dublin cathedrals became anglicised at the Reformation with the result that Dublin still has two cathedrals of the minority Anglican (Church of Ireland) religion. On the background to the existence of two cathedrals in Dublin see G. J. Hand, 'The Rivalry of the Cathedral Chapters in Medieval Dublin', in H. Clarke (ed.), *Medieval Dublin: the Living City* (Blackrock, 1990), pp. 100–11.

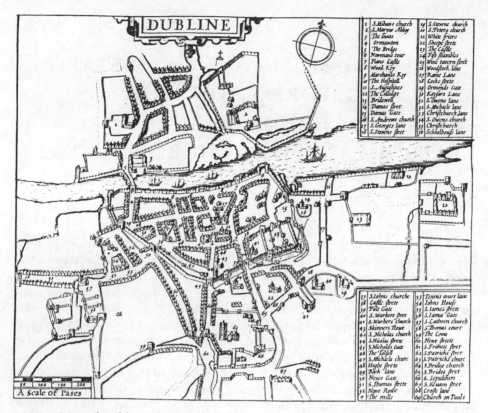

The map includes the title "DUBLINE" and numbered legend entries:

1 S.Mihans church	19 S.Stevens church
2 S.Maryes Abby	20 S.Peters church
3 The Inos	21 White friers
4 Ormanston	22 Sheepe strete
5 The Bridge	23 The Castle
6 Newmans tour	24 Fyssh shambles
7 Flans Castle	25 Wine tavern strete
8 Wood Key	26 Woodstock Line
9 Marchants Key	27 Rame Lane
10 The Hospitall	28 Cockes strete
11 S.Austines	29 Ormonds Gate
12 The Colledge	30 Kaysars Lane
13 Bridewell	31 S.Owens Lane
14 Damas strete	32 S.Michaels Lane
15 Damas Gate	33 Christchurch Lane
16 S.Andrews church	34 S.Owens church
17 S.Georges Lane	35 Christchurch
18 S.Stevens strete	36 Schoolhouse Lane

37 S.Johns churche	53 Tennis court lane
38 Castle strete	54 Johns House
39 Pole Gate	55 Lames strete
40 S.Werbers strete	56 Lames Gate
41 S.Werbers church	57 S.Cathren church
42 Skinners Rowe	58 S.Thomas court
43 S.Nicolas church	59 The Come
44 S.Nicolas strete	60 Newe strete
45 S.Nicholas Gate	61 S.Franses strete
46 The Tassell	62 S.Patricks strete
47 S.Michaels churc	63 S.Patricks churc
48 Haghe strete	64 S.Brides church
49 Back Lane	65 S.Brides strete
50 Newe Gate	66 S.Sepulchers
51 S.Thomas strete	67 S.Kevan strete
52 Nove Rowe	68 Crofs lane
+ The mills	69 Church on Pauls

A Scale of Paces

11.1   Map of Dublin; John Speed, *The Theatre of the Empire of Great Britaine*
(London, 1614), after page 141.

house of the Irish parliament. As the priory was the most substantial stone building outside Dublin Castle, the exchequer used it for the safe-keeping of money, as did citizens who stored chests there containing their valuables.[3] Solemn contracts were agreed and sealed in the cathedral, often over the relic of the *baculus Jhesu* (staff of Jesus), one of a number of relics which made Holy Trinity an important pilgrimage centre,[4] or at the tomb of Strongbow, leader of the Anglo-Norman conquest of Ireland in the twelfth century.

The book of obits of Holy Trinity, compiled in the late fifteenth and early sixteenth centuries largely from earlier sources, records the names of over 1,000 benefactors and others for whose souls the community prayed.[5] This reflected a system that was of mutual benefit to both cathedral and the civic community: while those remembered in the book of obits received spiritual benefits through the prayers said on their behalf, the cathedral benefited through grants and bequests of land, money and valuables, or other benefits.

---

[3] J. Mills (ed.), *Account Roll of the Priory of the Holy Trinity, Dublin 1337–1346*, reprint, introduced by J. Lydon and A. J. Fletcher (Dublin, 1996), pp. xiv–xv.

[4] On the *baculus Jhesu* see M. V. Ronan, 'St Patrick's Staff and Christ Church', in Clarke (ed.), *Living City*, pp. 123–31.

[5] TCD, MS 576; edition in R. Refaussé and C. Lennon (eds.), *The Registers of Christ Church Cathedral, Dublin* (Dublin, 1998), pp. 37–86.

By the fourteenth century Holy Trinity had become the most richly endowed of all the religious houses in Ireland,[6] and during the troubled period in the mid-fourteenth century when the native Irish living in the nearby Dublin and Wicklow mountains posed a constant threat, the priory contributed to the defence of the city and its environs where so much of its property lay.[7] Many of those commemorated in the book of obits were members of the cathedral confraternity, three-quarters of the names being those of lay people constituting 'a roll-call of civic and gentry families who were prominent in the Dublin area particularly in the later fifteenth and earlier sixteenth centuries'.[8] The mayors of Dublin were regularly enrolled in the book of obits and the swearing-in ceremony of the new mayor also took place in the cathedral. A number of highly placed officials in the central government administration were also remembered in the book of obits. A further link between cathedral and city was the presence in the south aisle of the nave of the guild chapel of the Trinity (or Merchant's) Guild, the senior and most powerful guild in the city.[9]

The close links between Christ Church and both the city of Dublin and the offices of state are reflected in and had a significant impact on the provision and development of music in the late medieval cathedral-priory and the uses to which the choir was put in the post-Reformation period. Little is known about the practice of music at Christ Church before the late fifteenth century. Documentary references to music are lacking[10] and, with the exception of brief plainchant antiphons to some of the psalms in the 'Christ Church psalter'[11] and a small number of manuscripts with plainchant which may possibly have originated in the cathedral, no music (least of all polyphonic) survives from the medieval cathedral.[12] The existence of a number of medieval dramas associated directly or indirectly with Christ Church demonstrates the Augustinian canons' interest in the moral and religious education of the citizens of Dublin. A later fourteenth-century morality play, the 'Pride of Life', was copied into an account roll of the priory.[13] Although no music is associated with this play (except for an unspecific stage direction for one character to sing), a liturgical play of the same period, the *Visitatio Sepulcri*, survives in two processionals with music which came from the church of St John the Evangelist, only yards from the cathedral and whose cure was the responsibility of the canons of Christ Church.[14] It is very possible that they came originally from the cathedral.[15] Drama, in at least one case with associated music, was thus performed under the aegis of the canons

---

[6] Mills (ed.), *Account Roll*, pp. ix–x.

[7] Founded as a Viking trading centre in the ninth century and subsequently the seat of Anglo-Norman rule in Ireland, Dublin remained essentially a foreign, English-speaking city within a Gaelic-speaking country. On the early history of Dublin see H. Clarke (ed.), *Medieval Dublin: the Making of a Metropolis* (Dublin, 1990).   [8] Refaussé (ed.), *Registers*, p. 21.

[9] For more information on the Trinity Guild see M. Clark and R. Refaussé (eds.), *Directory of the Historic Dublin Guilds* (Dublin, 1993), pp. 23–5.

[10] The only exceptions are payments in the account roll of 1338 to the justices' trumpeters in the refectory and also to a harper when the prior entertained the visiting justices, Mills (ed.), *Account Roll*, p. 19.

[11] Oxford, Bodleian Library, MS Rawlinson G. 185.

[12] In addition to the processional containing the *Visitatio Sepulcri* play cited below (note 14), an antiphonal copied *c.* 1435 (TCD, MS 79) may also have originated from Christ Church. For a fuller discussion of music in Christ Church during the Middle Ages see B. Boydell, 'Music in the Medieval Cathedral-Priory', in K. Milne (ed.), *Christ Church Cathedral, Dublin: a History* (Dublin, 2000) pp. 142–8.

[13] Text in Mills (ed.), *Account Roll*, pp. 126–42.

[14] Dublin, Marsh's Library, MS Z.4.2.20; Oxford, Bodleian Library, MS Rawlinson liturg. D.4; see M. Egan-Buffet and A. J. Fletcher, 'The Dublin *Visitatio Sepulcri* play', *Proceedings of the Royal Irish Academy* 90C, no. 7 (1990), pp. 159–241.   [15] A. J. Fletcher in Mills (ed.), *Account Roll*, p. xxxii.

of Holy Trinity for the education and benefit of the citizens of Dublin. As late as the mid-sixteenth century on the eve of the Reformation the canons of Holy Trinity were still actively involved in the performance of liturgical dramas: in 1542 payments were made for 'singing the passion' and 'playing the Resurrection',[16] while in 1528 the prior had co-operated with the priors of two other Dublin monasteries to produce plays on the Passion and on the deaths of the Apostles.[17]

In Dublin boy choristers are first recorded in 1431 at St Patrick's Cathedral when a college of six minor canons and six choristers was instituted.[18] It was nearly fifty years before boys were added to the choir of Christ Church: in 1480 Thomas Bennet, son of a former mayor, granted an endowment for four boy choristers.[19] Significantly, while the choir at the secular cathedral of St Patrick's was established by the church authorities through the archbishop, at Christ Church the endowment came from a private citizen. Thomas Bennet endowed certain of his rents to find and maintain four *paraphonistis* 'or four boys trained step by step in the science of music'.[20] They were to sing daily both in the high choir of the cathedral and at the Mass of the Blessed Virgin in the lady chapel with plainsong and 'set song' or 'pricksong' (i.e. composed polyphony) and for other unspecified services with the expressed intention that the singing of more complex polyphony should be developed in the cathedral.[21] While Bennet's concern was primarily spiritual – honouring the Holy Trinity and the Blessed Virgin and providing for the salvation of his and his family's souls – the grant also refers to the boys' serving 'as it behoves such *paraphonistae* to serve cathedral churches of this type and to sing as custom demands for the honour of God'.[22] He also appreciated how the musical elaboration of the cathedral's liturgy to bring it into line with contemporary practice would add prestige to the city of which he was a prominent citizen.

Five years later in a further endowment John Estrete, Gentleman and Sergeant-at-law, provided for a Mass to be said in the chapel of St Laurence O'Toole and for the choir to sing, every Thursday, 'be note a masse with playn song and sett song, yf it may be, and yf no, att the lest gode and tretable playn song'.[23] In order for the choirboys to be trained, as specified in the 1480 grant, they must have had a teacher since that time. There is no evidence that there was an alms school attached to Christ Church from which the boys might have been recruited for the choir and their music master must have been paid since then on some informal basis. This was addressed in 1493 when Prior David Wynchester presented a charter providing for the stipend of a music master to teach the four singing boys and for their food, clothing and accommodation, the money for this provision to come from offerings to the *baculus Jhesu* and from other specified sources.[24] The duties of the choir master included teaching the boys 'plainchant, polyphony, descant, and counter'[25] for the daily Mass of the Blessed Virgin and the Mass and antiphon of Jesus on Fridays in Lent, as well as at other unspecified services. While this provision came from

[16] Barra Boydell (ed.), *Music at Christ Church before 1800: Documents and Selected Anthems* (Dublin, 1999), p. 41.   [17] W. Harris, *History and Antiquities of the City of Dublin* (Dublin, 1766), p. 144.

[18] W. H. Grindle, *Irish Cathedral Music* (Belfast, 1989), pp. 7–8.   [19] Boydell (ed.), *Music*, pp. 29–31.

[20] 'quatuor Paraphonistas sive quatuor pueros successive scientia musicali eruditos'. The training of choristers in this period is described in J. Flynn, 'The Education of Choristers in England During the Sixteenth Century', in J. Morehen (ed.), *English Choral Practice, 1400–1650* (Cambridge, 1995), pp. 180–99.

[21] 'ut ipsi sic successive inveniendi in eisdem perfectius erudiri possint, prout consuetum est et consonum nonullas partes missae in Choro.'

[22] 'et deserviendum prout talibus Paraphonistis hujusmodi Ecclesiis Cathedralibus incumbit deservire, et usualiter pro honore Dei habetur cantare.'   [23] Boydell (ed.), *Music*, pp. 32–3.   [24] *Ibid.*, pp. 34–7.

[25] 'planum cantum fractum cantum discantum et counter.'

the prior, it was establishing on more secure terms practices for which the initial impetus had come from citizens of Dublin.

In the absence of any surviving music from this period, neither the polyphonic repertory nor the standards that were achieved by the newly endowed choir with boy trebles are known. The fact that the cathedral was both a civic and a state centre suggests the ability, at least on occasions of special public importance, to provide more elaborate music suitable to the occasion. The most famous (if not bizarre) of these public occasions was the crowning of the ten-year-old Lambert Simnel, pretender to the English throne, in Christ Church on 24 May 1487,[26] an occasion on which the full panoply of regal magnificence, including music, must surely have been employed.

The profound changes which were to transform the church during the mid-sixteenth century affected Ireland as elsewhere, although the progress of the Reformation followed a different course to that in England. Most Irish religious houses were dissolved between 1536 and 1539, but when Christ Church was itself threatened with suppression in 1539 the mayor and aldermen, supported by the lord deputy and council, protested to the king's principal secretary of state that the cathedral, like St Paul's in London:

> standith in the middes of the said citie . . . hit is the verie station place, wher as the Kynges Graces honorable Parliamentes and Counsailles ar kepyn, all sermons ar made, and wher as the congregacions of the said citie, in processions and station daies, and at all other tymes necessarie, assemblith, and at all tymes of the birth of our mooste noble Princes and Princesses, and othir tymes of victorie and tryumphe, processions ar made, and 'Te Deum laudamus' customabilie is songe, to the laude and praise of God, and the honor of our said Princes and Princesses.[27]

As a result of this, dissolution was averted, statutes to convert the priory into a secular cathedral were drawn up in December 1539 and Christ Church was formally re-established as a new foundation cathedral in 1541.[28] The eight canons of the former priory who were not dignitaries became vicars choral, the three senior (dean's vicar, precentor's vicar and chancellor's vicar) being appointed prebendaries, and all being in holy orders. Exceptionally, all the vicars choral were made members of the chapter whether or not they were prebendaries.[29] From 1543 leases were made by the dean and chapter 'with the consent of the vicars choral' who in other cathedrals had no such rights. This unusual arrangement may have arisen because of the cathedral's position within the city's life and through the influence of prominent citizens: the surnames of the canons at the new foundation suggest that, with the exception of two Englishmen, they were members of well-established Dublin families with backgrounds in the law, land, trade or the church.[30] In addition to the eight vicars choral and the four boys, the statutes of the new foundation provided for three choral clerks: the organist and master of the boys, the sacrist who also assisted the singers at Mass and a third clerk who assisted the celebrant at Mass. One of the vicars choral was appointed succentor, whose duties included instructing the boys of

---

[26] F. X. Martin, *The Crowning of a King at Dublin, 24 May 1487* (Dublin, [1987]).

[27] *State Papers. King Henry the Eighth*, 11 vols. (London, 1830–52), vol. II, part iii, p. 545.

[28] Ironically it was the secular cathedral of St Patrick's which would be reduced to the status of a parish church in 1547, although it was subsequently restored as a cathedral in 1555.

[29] For the sections of the charter of the new foundation relating to music see Boydell (ed.), *Music*, pp. 37–41.

[30] R. Gillespie, 'The Coming of Reform 1500–1558', in Milne (ed.), *Christ Church Cathedral*, pp. 153–4.

the choir in singing; the chancellor's vicar was responsible for the correction of any mistakes in the Latin texts of the choir books and the organist and master of the boys was required to be trained 'both in playing the organ and in singing plainchant and polyphony, and likewise sufficiently in the art of descanting for the training of the boys'.[31]

The duties of the choir in 1539 represent substantially a continuation of those established in the 1480s: the organist and master of the boys, as well as the four minor vicars, were required to be present at the daily Lady Mass and High Mass, as well as on Thursdays when a Mass was to be celebrated 'with singing and choristers and other ministers' (*cum cantu et Choristis et aliis ministris*). Masses were to be celebrated with plainchant (*cum cantu plano*) three times a week for the state of the king at the principal altar and the Mass of the Name of Jesus was to be sung 'with solemn singing' (*cum solemni cantu*) every Friday. When Robert Heyward was appointed organist in 1546 he was to instruct the 'choristers and children' in 'pricksong and discant to four minims' (i.e. polyphonic improvisation over a plainchant melody) and to teach the choristers 'to play Our Lady's Mass, all instruments being found for them during the time of their child's voice', suggesting that (unspecified) instruments joined with the voices in polyphonic music and that unbroken boys' voices were not now used in the Lady Mass, a change from the late fifteenth-century practice. Heyward was also required 'to play the organ, to keep Our Lady's Mass and anthem daily, Jesus Mass every Friday, according to the custom of St Patrick's, and Matins when the organs play on the eight principal feasts, and major doubles', as well as 'to procure at the expense of the cathedral suitable songs'.[32]

With the dissolution of St Patrick's cathedral in 1547, Christ Church's role as the cathedral for the diocese of Dublin was assured. The cathedral benefited through the transfer of the plate, jewels, ornaments and organs from St Patrick's and through the enlargement of the choir by six priests and two singing boys. This was to be paid out of money received by the exchequer, in recognition of which the choir did homage and sang in the court of exchequer at the end of the law terms, a tradition which continued into the late nineteenth century.[33] Later in 1547 additional incomes were granted by the archbishop of Dublin for the maintenance of the vicars choral.[34] Following the restoration of St Patrick's as a cathedral in 1555 the enlarged choir at Christ Church was retained, at least for the immediate future. Christ Church was also allowed to hold on to the possessions, including organs, which it had received from St Patrick's in 1547.[35]

At least in the shorter term, the Reformation brought about no sudden or profound change in Ireland which was to some extent cushioned from the rapidly changing religious climate in England. A document dating from the reign of Queen Mary which relates to the order of service reflects the return to the Latin rite, but the only reference to music concerns the appointing of 'certain of basses and countertenors' for the daily Lady Mass.[36] Following the accession of Queen Elizabeth in November 1558 religious change took some time to make itself felt at Christ Church, the Mass still being celebrated at Easter 1559. But when the deputy, Lord Sussex, attended the cathedral on 26 August

---

[31] 'tam in pulsatione Organorum, quam in cantu plano et fracto, pariter et in sufficienti discantu, pro instructione puerorum.'

[32] Boydell (ed.), *Music*, p. 42; on instrumental teaching for choirboys in English cathedrals in the sixteenth century, see I. Payne, *The Provision and Practice of Sacred Music at Cambridge Colleges and Selected Cathedrals c. 1547–c. 1646* (New York and London, 1993), pp. 134ff., and Flynn, 'The Education of Choristers'.

[33] Boydell (ed.), *Music*, pp. 43, 246.   [34] *Ibid.*, p. 44.   [35] *Ibid.*, pp. 45–6, 246–7.   [36] *Ibid.*, pp. 44–5.

the litany was sung in English, probably within the context of the Mass as had been the practice in England in previous months.[37] The Irish parliament met at Christ Church in 1560 when the Acts of Supremacy and Uniformity were passed. The latter differed from its English counterpart as it allowed the use of Latin wherever priests 'had not the use or knowledge of the English tongue'; it also permitted much of the paraphernalia of medieval worship to be retained, including the wearing of traditional Mass vestments.[38] The rood loft and screen were still in place at Christ Church in 1565 and, although the rood itself and a painting of the passion had been removed, the structure of the liturgical year was still observed by a cycle of saints' days of varying importance. The gift of half a beef in 1565 by the (at least nominally) Protestant Mayor Richard Fyan to ring a knell for the soul of the Catholic chanter of the cathedral under Queen Mary further demonstrates the continuation of pre-Reformation rituals in the Protestant cathedral. The close links with the city were initially retained, Christ Church remaining in the earlier part of Elizabeth's reign as much a civic institution as a Protestant cathedral. Catholic and Protestant found common ground there, many Catholic citizens contributing to the rebuilding of the cathedral following the collapse of the nave in 1562.[39] However, the cathedral now began to fulfil the role of state church, a role not normal for cathedral churches. It was the place of worship of the lord deputy and ceremonies associated with his administration, including his swearing-in and the creation of knights, took place there. Also, the privy council usually met within the precincts where the Four Courts (the courts of the king's bench, exchequer, chancery and common pleas) would be located from 1608.[40] With the resurgence of Catholicism from the 1590s political and religious issues began to be more clearly defined and Christ Church was to evolve into an island of state-sponsored Protestantism within an increasingly recusant city.

The choir of Christ Church had sung for the lord deputy and 'present[ed] his honour with songs and new verse' in 1569 and 1570,[41] and in 1593 the dean and chapter had to accept as a vicar choral a singer recommended by the lord deputy despite the fact that the maximum number of vicars choral permitted by the foundation statutes had already been reached.[42] The lord deputy also maintained his own band of musicians who became actively involved alongside the choir in the cathedral's music on important feasts in the liturgical year and other state days. For example, in 1594 they played at Hallowe'en (Eve of All Saints) and on Christmas Eve; the following year they were present, apparently on the 'queen's day' (17 November, marking the accession of Elizabeth I), as well as performing with the vicars on Christmas Eve.[43] Musical links were also maintained with the city corporation which included a small group of committed Protestant aldermen.[44] Walter Kennedy, the cathedral organist, was admitted a freeman of Dublin in 1594 'with condicion that he shall attend with his boyes upponn the Mayor, and sing, on stacion dayes and other tymes, when he shalbe called uppon, during his lyfe'.[45]

---

[37] TCD, MS 591, fol. 20; BL, Add. MS 4813, fol. 65.

[38] H. A. Jefferies, 'The Irish Parliament of 1560: the Anglican Reforms Authorised', *Irish Historical Studies* 26 (1988), pp. 128–41.

[39] Raymond Gillespie (ed.), *The Proctor's Accounts of Peter Lewis, 1564–65* (Dublin, 1996), pp. 15–16, 39.

[40] The courts remained within the precincts of Christ Church until 1796 when they moved to the present Four Courts building north of the river Liffey.   [41] Boydell (ed.), *Music*, pp. 84–5.   [42] *Ibid.*, pp. 55–6.

[43] *Ibid.*, pp. 80–1. For the 'queen's day' see D. Cressy, *Bonfires and Bells: National Memory and the Protestant Calendar in Elizabethan and Stuart England* (Cambridge, 1989), pp. xi–xv.

[44] C. Lennon, *The Lords of Dublin in the Age of Reformation* (Dublin, 1989), pp. 135–8.

[45] Boydell (ed.), *Music*, p. 85.

The appointment as organist in 1596 of John Farmer may be linked to the growing role of Christ Church as a centre of state policy towards Ireland. When a vacancy arose for an organist following Kennedy's resignation in November 1595, John Farmer may have been selected not only on the strength of his reputation following his *Divers and Sundry Waies of Two Parts in One* (London, 1591) and his significant contributions to Thomas East's *The Whole Booke of Psalmes* (1592), but also in order to strengthen links with the established English Anglican music tradition. Under the leadership of Adam Loftus, Archbishop of Dublin and Lord Chancellor, the Church of Ireland was being actively anglicised from the 1590s through the appointment of English personnel.[46] This policy would not have been without repercussions: penalties for vicars choral arising from 'differences between nations' had already been cited in 1579.[47] Further evidence of Christ Church becoming more closely involved in the musical world of English cathedrals is provided by the appointment as a vicar choral and, it appears, as master of the choristers in May 1600 of John Fido. He may have been the man of the same name who supplied polyphonic music to various English cathedrals in the early seventeenth century and who was organist variously at Hereford and Worcester between 1591 and 1597 and subsequently a vicar choral at Wells in 1605.[48]

A new charter for Christ Church granted by King James I in 1604 provided the opportunity for a restructuring of the choir. The anomalous situation whereby the vicars choral had been members of the chapter since the new foundation but without there being any canonical prebendaries was reformed. The former vicars choral were transformed into three prebendaries and the six priests who had been added in 1547 were now established as vicars choral.[49] Thus, while the overall size of the choir remained as it had been in 1539, the vicars choral no longer held places in the chapter and the foundation was laid for the later employment of choirmen who would be primarily musicians rather than churchmen. It was some time however before the full complement of vicars would be filled. In 1607 the chapter noted that the sixth vicar's place 'hath long time been void', a situation which still applied when John Hoskins was appointed sixth vicar in 1609, the question of assigning rents and tithes to support this position remaining unresolved.[50] This may explain why the sixth vicar's place continued for some time to be treated as a position of inferior rank compared to the other five.[51]

The appointment as organist on 5 April 1609 of Thomas Bateson, the most distinguished musician to hold this position during the sixteenth and seventeenth centuries, provides further evidence of the growing anglicisation of Christ Church. Organist at Chester Cathedral before coming to Dublin, Bateson had already established his reputation as a composer through his first book of madrigals published in 1604. The importance placed by the dean and chapter on securing as organist a musician of the calibre of Thomas Bateson is seen in the fact that in no other case between the new foundation and the present day was the wording of the contract appointing an organist at Christ Church deemed worthy of being copied into the chapter acts.[52] In the dedication of his second book of madrigals (1618) to Lord Chichester, Lord Deputy between 1605 and 1616, Bateson states that 'it is not the least of your Honour's favours conferred upon me, to

[46] Ford, *Reformation*, pp. 32–5.   [47] Boydell (ed.), *Music*, pp. 53, 249.
[48] *Ibid.*, p. 58; W. Shaw, *The Succession of Organists of the Chapel Royal and the Cathedrals of England and Wales from c. 1538 . . .* (Oxford, 1991), pp. 134–5, 306; Payne, *Provision and Practice*, pp. 76–7.
[49] Sections relating to the choir in Boydell (ed.), *Music*, p. 85.   [50] *Ibid.*, p. 60; RCB, C6/1/8/1, p. 141.
[51] Boydell (ed.), *Music*, p. 148.   [52] *Ibid.*, pp. 60–3.

grace me with your Honourable service, and to call me to a more immediate dependency upon your Lordship', later referring to 'that relation I have to your Honour' and 'your Honour's favours unto me'. To what favours was Bateson referring? As organist at Christ Church Bateson was closely associated with Chichester and his reference to the favours granted him may well include his having been supported, possibly even selected, by Chichester in his appointment as organist. At the very least, as Brian Boydell has argued, the initiative for Bateson's being awarded in 1612 with what was the first music degree from the recently founded University of Dublin, Trinity College, may have come from Chichester.[53] At this period music degrees (awarded by Oxford and Cambridge and now by Trinity College, Dublin) were neither taught nor examined, but were awarded to musicians of proven ability or upon recommendation. It was usual to submit an exercise as evidence of one's skill in music. Bateson's only surviving sacred work, his anthem *Holy, Lord God Almighty* whose text is taken from the epistle for Trinity Sunday, was very likely written for the occasion of his conferring (which may have taken place in Christ Church), being scored unusually for seven voices and honouring as it does the Holy Trinity to which both Trinity College and Christ Church were dedicated.[54]

After the accession of Charles I in 1625 the vigorous growth of Counter-Reformation Catholicism which had taken place during the previous decades was seen by England as presenting a serious political threat which needed to be countered by more positive action. Following their defeat at the Battle of Kinsale in 1601 many of the Gaelic nobility had fled to France and Spain, and England feared the potential explosiveness of Irish–Spanish and Irish–French Catholic links: recusants began to be regarded as the main threat to the government.[55] When Lancelot Bulkeley, Archbishop of Dublin, carried out his visitation at Christ Church in April 1627 one of his greatest concerns was the propagation of Protestantism in the face of the potential Catholic threat. The regular celebration of holy communion was emphasised and what were seen as lax practices within the church were addressed. Archbishop Bulkeley's orders following his visitation required all vicars choral and stipendaries (the title by which choirmen who were not vicars were known at Christ Church) to take communion whenever it was held, precise orders were given as to when gowns and surplices were to be worn, the organist was to sing in the choir when not needed at the organ and discipline was to be enforced through fines deducted from their wages.[56] Discipline amongst the choir was further increased following the appointment as sub-dean in 1630 of John Atherton, an English cleric who had formerly been private chaplain to Adam Loftus, Lord Chancellor and Lord Justice (son of the former eponymous archbishop and chancellor). In July 1630 the whole choir was reminded of the 1627 orders, and the following month the organist (Randall Jewett, Bateson having died the previous March) was 'admonished not to walk in the body of the church in time of divine service, as also to teach daily the choristers their art of singing'.[57]

Lord Deputy Wentworth, sworn in at Christ Church in July 1633, set about the further reform of the Church of Ireland with the support of Archbishop Laud of Canterbury and the assistance of his close adviser John Bramhall, Treasurer of Christ

---

[53] Brian Boydell, 'Thomas Bateson and the Earliest Degrees in Music Awarded by the University of Dublin', *Hermathena* 146 (1989), pp. 53–60.

[54] Boydell (ed.), *Music*, pp. 187–93; on the dedication of the anthem, see Grindle, *Cathedral Music*, p. 164.

[55] M. McCurtain, *Tudor and Stuart Ireland* (Dublin, 1972), p. 132.   [56] Boydell (ed.), *Music*, p. 64.

[57] *Ibid.*, p. 65.

Church and subsequently Bishop of Derry. Arminian clerics from England were appointed, and Puritan and Presbyterian clergy removed.[58] The Arminian emphasis on elaborate worship, the 'beauty of holiness', made itself felt at Christ Church which was to be the flagship for a state-sponsored religious experiment which could not be allowed to fail. The building was repainted, the altar refurbished, new communion silver acquired, and there is clear evidence for the elaboration of the music during the 1630s. Already since Archbishop Bulkeley's reforms instruments had regularly accompanied the choir, William Bedell (later Bishop of Kilmore and Ardagh) being described when he was provost of Trinity College, Dublin between 1627 and 1629 by his contemporary biographer as being:

> much dissatisfied with the pompous service at Christ's church in Dublin, which was attended and celebrated with all manner of instrumental musicke, as organs, sackbutts, cornets, viols, &c, as if it had been at the dedication of Nebuchadnezar's golden image in the plain of Dura . . .[59]

Cornettists were paid in 1629/30, while in 1636/7 a 'place for the violin' was made and a 'Seate for the Sacke-but' in the following year.[60] In 1638 'two Sagbutts and two Cornetts' were paid for their regular attendance, 'the L[ord] Deputies Musicke' and 'the musicons' being mentioned in 1637/8 and 1638/9.[61] There is also evidence for the provision of new music: three service books were bought in 1629/30, four in 1632/3 when 'rul'd books' were also bought, boxes made in the choir for 'each vicarr to putt his bookes in' and one of the vicars was paid for his costs in collecting a 'sett of bookes for the quire'. A total of five service books including one for the organist were paid for in 1637/8 and the following year Peter Stringer, a member of the choir and possibly the same person who was organist and master of the choristers at Chester after 1660, bought 'certain anthems and services' for the cathedral.[62]

The choir at Christ Church became directly involved in the relationship between church, city and state when steps were taken to control the revenues of the religious Guild of St Anne. Wentworth's reforms included an active policy of reclaiming the revenues of the church, most particularly where these had remained in Catholic hands and attention turned to the chantries and religious guilds or confraternities which, despite the attempts of reformers, had remained undissolved in Ireland.[63] The guild of St Anne was one of a number of such lay confraternities which persisted under Protestant rule and its guild chapel was located in St Audoen's parish church. As a prebend of St Patrick's Cathedral, St Audoen's had no formal associations with Christ Church; however, it was proximate to the latter institution which subsequently became involved in attempts to control the revenues and activities of the guild.

The guild appointed chantry priests (also referred to as chaplains) until 1564. In the 1540s they were required to sing at all divine services; there were also two clerks who sang and read daily in the choir, one of whom played the organ at all services, principal feasts and holy days.[64] Links between the guild and the parish were close and continued

---

[58] Ford, *Reformation*, pp. 214–15.

[59] E. S. Stuckburgh (ed.), *Two Biographies of William Bedell, Bishop of Kilmore* (Cambridge, 1902), pp. 153–4.

[60] Boydell (ed.), *Music*, p. 83.   [61] *Ibid.*, pp. 70, 83–4.   [62] *Ibid.*, pp. 75, 83–4.

[63] Some of these organisations even survived into the nineteenth century; C. Lennon, 'The Survival of the Confraternities in Post-Reformation Dublin', *Confraternitas* 6 (1995), pp. 5–12.

[64] C. Lennon, 'The Chantries in the Irish Reformation: the Case of St Anne's Guild, Dublin, 1550–1630', in R. V. Comerford, M. Cullen, J. R. Hill and C. Lennon (eds.), *Religion, Conflict and Coexistence in Ireland: Essays Presented to Mgr Patrick J. Corish* (Dublin, 1990), pp. 6–25, esp. p. 14.

into the seventeenth century, but the guild concerned itself increasingly with social and charitable rather than spiritual concerns, stressing its role as an adjunct to the city council, its membership including a high proportion of the aldermen of the city. By the late sixteenth century the guild, which was manifestly recusant in its membership and sympathies, was becoming the object of scrutiny by the established church. As late as *c.* 1597 High Mass was celebrated at St Audoen's with (unspecified) musical accompaniment,[65] but a series of direct challenges to the guild from officials of church and state seeking to acquire the guild's revenues and to enforce conformity had begun in 1593/4.

By 1606 the positions of the guild's six chantry priests and two clerks had been transformed into six singing men and two choirboys who received regular salaries thereafter from the guild for singing in St Audoen's. These positions were filled by members of the choirs of both Christ Church and St Patrick's together with the organist of Christ Church.[66] In March 1609 the guild paid Thomas Bateson, who had just arrived from Chester to become organist at Christ Church, for 'making up' the organ and playing on Sundays and holy days.[67] Evidently, between the late 1590s and 1606 control of the guild had been largely assumed by the Protestant minority (control of the guild was to remain unresolved for some time to come). By 1606 the guild was thus supporting a fully fledged musical establishment at St Audoen's which was drawn from the members of the two cathedral choirs.[68] Such was the identity of the guild with the parish church that when the organ in St Audoen was repaired in 1624 it was paid for by and described as belonging to St Anne's Guild.[69]

Wentworth's interest in St Anne's Guild resulted from the discovery by Reverend Thomas Lowe, one of the vicars choral of both Christ Church and St Patrick's cathedrals,[70] of the rent book of St Anne's Guild which showed that a majority of its properties were leased to Catholics, in accordance with a papal bull of 1569 enjoining Catholic members of confraternities to lease properties to their co-religionists only.[71] Accordingly, Wentworth established a commission in 1635 which recommended in June 1638 that the guild's revenues be appropriated to enlarge the cathedral choir and enhance its music. The commission also proposed that the guild should meet in the cathedral ostensibly because Christ Church was a more appropriate location than St Audoen's; in reality this request was a bid to keep the guild under closer supervision.[72] Protestant control of the guild was effected by the admission to its membership of the Archbishop of Dublin, Bishop Bramhall of Derry, the Bishop of Waterford and Lismore, the vice-treasurer, the Lord Chief Justice, the deans of both Christ Church and St Patrick's cathedrals and other prominent members of church and state.[73] St Audoen's was to be compensated by an

---

[65] E. Hogan (ed.), *Ibernia Ignatiana* (Dublin, 1880), p. 41. I am grateful to Dr Colm Lennon for drawing this and other references relating to St Audoen's and the Guild of St Anne to my attention.

[66] Account book of St Anne's Guild, RIA, MS 12.D.1, fol. 29r.

[67] *Ibid.*, fol. 23v. This reference to Bateson (9 March 1608/9) predates the earliest reference to him at Christ Church.

[68] The annual salaries of organist, choirmen and choristers were respectively £10, £4 (£5 6s 8d for the choirman who had responsibility for the boys) and £5 6s 8d for the two choristers; *ibid.*, fols. 25v, 29, 32.

[69] *Ibid.*, fol. 33v.

[70] It was common for choirmen to be appointed as vicars to both Dublin cathedrals until the late nineteenth century.

[71] R. Ware, *The Hunting of the Romish Fox and the Quenching of Sectarian Fire-Brands . . .* (Dublin, 1683), pp. 120–8; Lennon, 'Chantries', p. 22.   [72] Boydell (ed.), *Music*, pp. 71–4.

[73] RIA, MS 12.D.1, fol. 41r; these new Protestant members were subsequently expelled in 1653 when the established church was in disarray after the Cromwellian settlement, Clark and Refaussé (eds.), *Directory*, p. 34.

increase in the salary of its organist (the cathedral organist Randall Jewett, as is confirmed in the guild's accounts of 1639/40[74]). The members of the cathedral choir were to receive an increase in salary and the vicars were increased from eight to ten with two boys also being added to the existing four. The provision for two cornetts and two sackbuts to accompany the choir provides further evidence for the use of instruments in Christ Church at this period. This enlarged choir was to attend on the two anniversaries of the guild (the feasts of St Anne and of the Purification) which would continue to be celebrated in St Audoen's church, when the dean and chapter would be present together with the lord deputy and council. Commenting that 'being very sensible of the disorder by the haveing of soe many Tenors and Such a Scarcitie of bases and Countertenors in the Quire of Christchurch', the commission recommended that the choir should include two tenors and four countertenors, i.e. that there should be up to four basses to make up the total of ten vicars. The deed providing for these changes was not enacted until September 1643,[75] but the guild accounts show an increase to at least ten 'singing men' between 1639 and 1640, all of whom were members of the choir of Christ Church and some of whom were specifically appointed according to the terms of Wentworth's order of 19 June 1638.[76] The singers' salaries were increased and the direct involvement of Christ Church is apparent in the petitioning by the dean for the payment of salaries due to the choir and to the 'sackboots and stipendaries to the guilde serving in Christchurch'.[77] A number of vicars were appointed at Christ Church under the terms of the certificate in 1638 and 1639.[78] This episode demonstrates the use of the cathedral choir as a tool in the religious and political struggles of the time. An enhanced choir with regular instrumental support provided compensation for the guild's having to move to the cathedral, but even on those occasions when the guild still met in St Audoen's its ceremonies were brought under the direct control of the established church and state.

As a monastic cathedral, the choir of Christ Church, Dublin had been enlarged by the addition of boy choristers as a result of an endowment which reflected its close links with the city. Surviving the threat of dissolution because of its intimate links with the city, the cathedral emerged in the later sixteenth and early seventeenth centuries with a choir which played an important role in state-sponsored Reformation policy. This role culminated in the central use of the choir in attempts by church and state to control the activities and revenues of the recusant Guild of St Anne.

---

[74] RIA, MS 12.D.1, fol. 72v. [75] Boydell (ed.), *Music*, pp. 86–8.
[76] RIA, MS 12.D.1, fols. 43v–51r, 72r–73r. [77] *Ibid.*, fols. 51r, 72r.
[78] Chapter acts, 19 June, 16 October 1638; 22 July 1639, RCB, C6/1/8/2, pp. 89, 98.

CHAPTER TWELVE

SINGERS AND SCRIBES IN THE SECULAR CHURCHES OF BRUSSELS

BARBARA HAGGH

Most urban Renaissance musicians known from archival sources served court and church: few musicians were paid directly from civic coffers. Although the duties and functions of these musicians, the titles of their offices and the ways of paying them were very similar throughout Europe, the place of polyphonic performance in their careers differed from church to church and city to city. In some cities, as in Cambrai, polyphonic singing was part of the daily routine; in others, as in Ghent, it remained an exceptional ornament for special occasions. A look at the musicians and music of some of the leading secular churches in Brussels (see Illustration 12.1), the city that was home to the Burgundian-Habsburg courts in the latter half of the fifteenth century, reveals who contributed to the well-known developments in the music of the early Renaissance. In turn, this casts some light on the development of polyphonic Mass Ordinaries, motets and instrumental settings. We address the musicians by their functions and titles, one by one, before drawing conclusions, not only about the changing place of polyphony in musicians' lives, but also about the influence of the urban environment upon it.[1]

Direction of polyphony and chant in the collegiate church of St Gudula and other parish churches in Brussels was assigned to musicians and clerics in different posts. The cantor and sometimes the *zangmeester* directed performances, the *hebdomadarii* were assigned by week to begin chants and administrative officers controlled the finances.[2] Only the *zangmeester*, the tenor and the leader of the *cotidianen* had charge over the singing of polyphony. The cantor of St Gudula led all chanted services and was usually present in person. He selected soloists for the antiphons and readers from among the canons, chaplains, vicars and 'mercenaries' (or hired priests). Only in the sixteenth century did the chapter provide a vicar who could replace the cantor should his duties conflict with those of his other benefices.[3]

This paper is dedicated to the memory of Lucyane Guedes, Simon Lim, Herbert Wentz and Janet Wheeler, four music students at the University of North Texas who died prematurely in January and February 2000.

[1] See also IIMLC and B. Haggh, 'Foundations or Institutions? On Bringing the Middle Ages into the History of Medieval Music', *Acta Musicologica* 68 (1996), pp. 87–128.

[2] See B. Haggh, 'Crispijne and Abertijne: Two Tenors at the Church of St Niklaas, Brussels', *Music and Letters* 76 (1995), pp. 325–44, and E. Jas, 'De koorboeken van de Pieterskerk te Leiden: Het zestiende-eeuwse muzikale erfgoed van een Hollands getijdencollege', Ph.D. thesis, University of Utrecht (1997). No extant evidence describes rehearsals (known in Cambrai: see C. Wright, 'Performance Practices at the Cathedral of Cambrai, 1475–1550', *Musical Quarterly* 64 (1978), p. 307).

[3] P. Lefèvre, 'Les constitutions du chapître de Sainte-Gudule à Bruxelles', *Bulletin de la Commission Royale d'Histoire* 105 (1940), p. 216; P. Lefèvre, *L'Organisation ecclésiastique de la ville de Bruxelles au Moyen Age* (Louvain, 1942).

12.1   Map of Brussels; G. Bruin, S. Novellanus, F. Hogenburgius, *Civitates orbis terrarum Liber primus*
(Cologne, 1582), plate 14.

The *zangmeester* directed the musical education of the choirboys, recruited singers and occasionally led a smaller choir. At St Gudula, his post was unrelated to that of the cantor. Although he was not usually a music scribe (the task of the tenor), at least one *zangmeester* at St Gudula (Johannes du Sart, *d.* 1485) was a composer.[4] In Brussels, *zang-meesters* received salaries for only a few months at a time. Indeed, *zangmeesters* and discant singers in north European churches, the latter often poorly paid stipendiary chaplains, belonged to a distinctly lower class than court musicians, who collected preb-endary benefices with ease.[5] No known *zangmeester* from the Low Countries ever held a canonicate at the same church.

Zangmeesters are documented only at St Gudula and at the two wealthiest parish churches in Brussels – that dedicated to St Nicholas (the Brussels guilds' church) and Our Lady of the Sands (the church of the nobility). In St Gudula the post (distinct from that of cantor), first appears in the early fifteenth century; in the latter two it appears only later in the fifteenth century after these churches had established choristerships, and this suggests that the *zangmeester* was recruited specifically to train the boy choristers. Master Joannes, the first *zangmeester* recorded at St Gudula, taught the *boninfanten* (choirboys) from 1402–7 until *c.* 1423/4;[6] his successor, Wouter, appears from 1426/7 to 1440/1.[7] Thereafter, the *zangmeesters* are documented continuously for the rest of the century, except from 1461 to 1470, in 1475/6 and from 1477 to 1483 (a period of great political and economic upheaval in the Low Countries).[8] *Zangmeesters* at St Nicholas belonged to the *cotidiane* foundation established in 1472: in the Fabric accounts of 1490/1, the term *zangmeester* appears only to designate the functions of Master Nicasius from Ghent and Master Aert Salass, *cotidiane* singers who had already been listed in 1485/6 and 1487/8, respectively.[9] One individual not described as *zangmeester*, who nevertheless taught choirboys along with the *zangmeester*, was Crispin vander Stappen, a singer of the *cotid-iane* of St Nicholas from 1485 to 1487.[10]

Little scholarly attention has previously been paid to the role of choirboys in secular churches. Choirboys can be traced back to the earliest times at Notre Dame of Paris, the first secular church to introduce polyphony as a standard embellishment for high feasts. In Notre Dame and in other secular churches, as in monasteries, boys were always assigned the melismatic chants that were later set to polyphony (the gradual, alleluia, *Benedicamus Domino* and responsory verses), but it is not known when boys

[4] On the *zangmeesters* of St Gudula, see J. vanden Bussche, 'Zangers en zangpraktijk aan de kapittelkerk van St Goedele te Brussel (ca. 1350–1555)', MA thesis, University of Louvain (1956); G. Huybens, 'Le personnel des maîtrises liturgiques à Bruxelles du XVe au XVIIIe siècle', *Belgisch tijdschrift voor muziekwetenschap/ Revue belge de musicologie* 25 (1971), pp. 16–45; R. Wangermée, *Les maîtres de chant des XVIIe et XVIIIe siècles à la collégiale des Saints-Michel-et-Gudule à Bruxelles* (Brussels, 1950), pp. 23–5. On Jean du Sart, see B. Haggh, 'Du Sart, Johannes', *The New Grove*, 7th edn (in press), and HMLC, pp. 582, 655. Another pos-sible composer-*zangmeester* at St Gudula was Jacobus van der Cammen (*d.* 1491), perhaps the composer of a work cited in D. Fallows (ed.), *The Songbook of Fridolin Sicher* (Peer, 1995), pp. 15, 17, 21, and pp. 24–5 of facsimile; HMLC, pp. 561, 566–7.

[5] On court musicians' benefices, see L. Lockwood, 'Strategies of Music Patronage in the Fifteenth Century: the *Cappella* of Ercole d'Este', in I. Fenlon (ed.), *Music in Medieval and Early Modern Europe* (Cambridge, 1981), pp. 227–48; C. Reynolds, 'Musical Careers, Ecclesiastical Benefices, and the Example of Johannes Brunet', *Journal of the American Musicological Society* 37 (1984), pp. 49–97.

[6] ASG 1373–1377 and ASG 1389, 1423/4, fol. 3r, and 1424/5, fol. 3r–v (HMLC p. 615, see 'Janne').

[7] ASG 1389.

[8] For other fifteenth-century *zangmeesters* of St Gudula see HMLC, pp. 578–9, 593, 595–6, 680, 688, 692.

[9] Haggh, 'Crispijne and Abertijne', pp. 327–9. This cannot be Nicasius Weyts from Bruges (*d.* before 1492), author of a theory treatise (R. Strohm, *Music in Late Medieval Bruges* (Oxford, 1985), p. 189).

[10] Haggh, 'Crispijne and Abertijne', p. 330.

began to sing polyphony. Existing studies of *maîtrises*, a term never used in the Middle Ages, rarely recognise that choristerships were established and organised as foundations.[11]

The first choristerships founded at St Gudula were the *boninfanten*, a foundation type known throughout Europe, especially in the thirteenth and fourteenth centuries.[12] The *boninfanten* of Brussels were founded by Petrus van Huffel, chaplain of St Gudula and city clerk, in his will of 31 August 1358, with the approval of Jan 'tSerclaes, canon of St Gudula and later bishop of Cambrai.[13] Later numbering twelve, though their number was not fixed in van Huffel's will, the boys, aged nine to eighteen, were to be recruited from amongst poor schoolboys in Brussels or Machelen (near Vilvoorde). Van Huffel's will ordered the boys to be instructed by a preceptor appointed by the masters of the Fabric of St Gudula and one alderman representing the wealthy patrician Clutinc family. All boys had to wear the same liveries and remain at St Gudula until they were eighteen.[14] On 10 October 1377, Jan 'tSerclaes added revenues to the then-failing foundation, donating his house, its furniture and its library to the boys, who would live there under a provisor and a teacher.[15] In 1437, Pope Eugenius IV granted permission for a portable altar for the house, at which three Masses would be celebrated each week by a priest selected by the chapter.[16] Jan 'tSerclaes's house later provided revenues for the second group of choirboys founded at St Gudula in 1466, the *choraelen*.

High expectations of the boys' musical competence were demonstrated in a chapter decision of 16 December 1447, which required that new *boninfanten* be able to sing, and should have attended at least six weeks of high school, unless the priest in charge of the choir could swear to the chapter that the boy was docile and had a good voice.[17] (Statutes of 1320 indicate that plainchant was part of the high school curriculum in Brussels as elsewhere in the Low Countries.)[18] In 1448, the *zangmeester* and rector of schools were appointed to live in the house of the boys and teach them the rudiments of grammar, law and Latin, using the writings of Donatus as a text; a 1483/4 inventory also indicates that dictionaries, grammar books and books of chant were also used.[19] In the later fifteenth century, the Brothers of the Common Life often delivered sermons to the

---

[11] C.f. H. De Ridder-Symoens, 'La sécularisation de l'enseignement aux anciens Pays-Bas au moyen âge et à la Renaissance', in E. Thoen and A. Verhulst (eds.), *Peasants and Townsmen in Medieval Europe: studia in honorem Adriaan Verhulst* (Ghent, 1995), pp. 721–37; M. Kintzinger, 'Scholaster und Schulmeister: Funktionsfelder der Wissensvermittlung im späten Mittelalter', in R. Schwinges (ed.), *Gelehrte im Reich: zur Sozial und Wirkungsgeschichte akademischer Eliten des 14. bis 16. Jahrhunderts* (Berlin, 1996), pp. 349–74.

[12] See L. Baratz, 'St Gudula's Children: the Boninfanten and Choraelen of the Collegiate Church of Brussels During the Ancien Régime', in *Archives et Bibliothèques de Belgique. Musicology and Archival Research: Colloquium Proceedings, Brussels 22–23 April 1993*, Archives et Bibliothèques de Belgique 46 (Brussels, 1994), pp. 214–305. For *boninfanten* in other European cities see E. Persoons, 'De Broeders van het Gemene Leven in Belgie', *Ons geestelijk erf* 43 (1969), pp. 3–30; L. Halkin, 'La maison des Bons Enfants de Liège', *Bulletin de l'Institut archéologique Liègeois* 64 (1940), p. 22.

[13] J. Paquet, 'La collaboration du clergé à l'administration des villes de Bruxelles et d'Anvers aux XIVe et XVe siècles', *Le Moyen Age* 56/iii–iv (1950), pp. 357–72; A. d'Hoop, *Inventaire générale des archives ecclésiastiques du Brabant*, 6 vols. (Brussels, 1905, 1914), vol. I, p. 62; Lefèvre, *L'Organisation ecclésiastique*, p. 220.

[14] A. Wauters, *Inventaires des cartulaires et d'autres registres faisant partie des archives anciennes de la Ville de Bruxelles*, 2 vols. (Brussels, 1894), vol. II, p. 487.

[15] See Brussels, Stadsarchief/Archives de la Ville 1345, fol. 29r; Lefèvre, *L'Organisation ecclésiastique*, p. 20; Halkin, 'La maison des Bons Enfants', p. 24; ASG 6395–8.

[16] ASG 5162, fols. 26v, 64r–v; ASG 6396, 6398, 6483.

[17] P. Lefèvre, 'Statuts capitulaires du chapître de St Gudule à Bruxelles durant le XIVe et le XVe siècle', *Bulletin de la Commission Royale d'Histoire* 99 (1935), pp. 206–7.   [18] See HMLC, pp. 149–53.

[19] ASG 6398, fols. 444v, 466r, 488v, and Lefèvre, 'Statuts capitulaires', pp. 206–7.

boninfanten.[20] The boys had clearly become an indispensable part of the choir by the end of the fifteenth century.

The second foundation for choirboys at St Gudula introduced the *choraelen*, who were not singers of polyphony at first, but poor schoolboys sought by the chapter to assist the *boninfanten*. Several lived with and were taught by the Brothers of the Common Life until 1462, when Johannes Jacquemijns, minor canon of St Gudula, bequeathed his house to the *choraelen* and provided for one of the Brothers to teach them.[21] The charter of foundation stipulated that the boys, aged ten to fourteen, were to be selected from students of the city's schools, were to be clever and studious, knowing Latin and Christian doctrine, able to read the seven penitential psalms, and having voices suitable for learning chant (*ad discendum cantum*). They had to have the clerical tonsure within six weeks of admission and were to serve in the choir on feast and ferial days. A tutor, one of the clerics of St Gudula, had overall responsibility for their moral and intellectual education; the *zangmeester*, who lived with them, and a minor canon serving as assistant, taught the boys the principles of music (possibly polyphony) and plainchant. The boys could not remain after they reached eighteen, and so a scholarship fund was established to enable superannuated *choraelen* to finish their studies.[22] Like the *boninfanten*, the *choraelen* sang as an independent ensemble, singing offertories at Requiem Masses or at services in side chapels. In 1487 they sang, possibly in discant, the daily Marian Masses founded by Canon Slabbaert in 1338 and 1345 at the altar of St Mary Magdalene.[23]

On 26 March 1498 Willelmus de Castro, minor canon of St Gudula, founded the schoolboys of the Crown of Thorns. De Castro asked Jacobus Aerts (his nephew and a priest) to care for the boys, numbering two at first, who would reside in De Castro's house after his death. If funds sufficed, a third schoolboy could be added, preferably one from the parish of St Gudula, and eventually all three would be entrusted to the minor canons. These boys, aged seven to eighteen, would be instructed in the moral way of life by a priest and attend school daily to learn grammar and *planum cantum gregorianum*. One boy would be a relative of the founder and another would be from the parish of Ghiseghem.[24] There is no documentary evidence for the presence of these boys in services at St Gudula, even though this seems likely.

Yet more children were taught by clerics at St Gudula, although there is no evidence that they sang in the church; specific foundations already provided boys for that purpose. In 1361/2, after the *boninfanten* were founded, the canons of St Gudula paid for the upkeep of a schoolchild.[25] A century later, the estate of Walter Lonijs, canon (*d.* 1489), paid a schoolmaster for teaching four poor children.[26] In 1500, the estate of Willem Coels, priest and chaplain of St Gudula, paid Jan van Halen, rector of the high schools, for having lodged and instructed eighteen children in his house.[27]

The parish church of St Nicholas also introduced *coralen* in 1490 or earlier; the three boys of this foundation were taught by the resident tenor, Crispin vander Stappen.[28]

---

[20] R. R. Post, *The Modern Devotion* (Leiden, 1968), p. 413.

[21] See P. Lefèvre, 'Documents relatifs aux Frères de la Vie Commune établis à Bruxelles au XVe et XVIe siècles', *Bulletin de la Commission Royale d'Histoire* 103 (1938), pp. 41–114, and HMLC, pp. 160–1.

[22] ASG 6397–6399; Lefèvre, 'Documents'; Post, *The Modern Devotion*, pp. 613–15; d'Hoop, *Inventaire*, vol. I, p. 62.   [23] ASG 9363 (Fabric accounts), and HMLC, p. 716.

[24] On the choirboys of the Crown of Thorns, see ASG 10294–10312 and ASG 897, *Liber censualis Jacobi Aerts*; also Brussels, Stadsarchief/Archives de la Ville, 2960 III.

[25] ASG 4962 (account of non-resident chaplains).   [26] ASG 268, fol. 426r.   [27] ASG 281, fol. 238r.

[28] ASG 11179, fol. 1r, and ARBH 21459, 1490/1, fol. 6r.

In 1492/3, Jan Mosselman, apparently a teacher and not a member of the *cotidiane*, took the four *coralen* of St Nicholas to sing for the aldermen of Brussels.[29] The choirboys at Our Lady of the Sands are only mentioned with regard to their receipt of a gift from the estate of Gherem Quas, a priest at that church.[30]

The training of choirboys was as important in Brussels as elsewhere. Some lived in the same house as their teachers and sang in the choir, following the injunctions of their respective foundations; others served as apprentices to individual clerics in poorly documented *ad hoc* arrangements. In any case, singers from Brussels were appreciated in other cities. Two singers at the court chapel of Albert of Bavaria in the Hague, Martinus Fabri (a composer) and Jan van Roost, came from Brabant, and singers from Brussels visited 'sHertogenbosch in the early fifteenth century. In 1470/1, two choirboys from Hal near Brussels were recruited at St Rombaut in Mechelen. Also, in 1523, Crispin vander Stappen, formerly of St Nicholas, left Cambrai Cathedral to go to Brabant to recruit singers.[31] Thus, in Brussels, the musical education of choirboys, as well as of adults, was emphasised and encouraged. Polyphony was taught to the *choraelen* at St Gudula and St Nicholas and, perhaps, elsewhere.

Many adult clerics were expected to sing plainchant during the Office and Mass in the choir: organists, bell-ringers (sextons) and polyphonists (who, after being introduced in the fifteenth century, were required to sing liturgical chant as well as polyphony). The canons, whose principal duty was to sing the Office and Mass as a chapter, also participated – at least in principle – in funerals, obits and processions. As a chapter, they regulated music and musicians through their powers to appoint vicars, chaplains and choirboys, and to prescribe ceremonies. Most canons were present at chapter meetings and for important ceremonial occasions, including high feasts and processions but, in practice, resident canons seldom sang ferial Offices and Masses, their places being taken by deputies. Only the minor canons of St Gudula were required to attend the Office, though they, too, could be absent for a legitimate reason.[32]

Most Brussels canons were well educated, enjoying the same status as the sons of wealthy merchants and nobles: fourteenth-century canons of St Gudula were often members of the patrician families of the city, the 'tSerclaes, Pipenpoy, Wesemael, Eggloy and Meldert.[33] With support from the chapter, they attended the University of Paris, the nearby University of Louvain (after its foundation in 1424), the University of Cologne or the papal Curia.[34] By June 1417, seven of the twelve senior canons of St Gudula had the title of *Magister* and by the second half of the fifteenth century, most canons were graduates.[35] In 1488, one canon of St Gudula, Walter Henrici, founded two scholarships for study at the College of the Falcon in Louvain.[36] Indeed, in 1458, Pope Calixtus III had described the city of Brussels as a place where many lettered men with degrees in Holy Scripture resided and where many sermons were given for the people in sumptuous buildings and edifices.[37]

Recipients of canonries at St Gudula included men from prominent local families and clerics serving in ducal households: Petrus de Leyda, chaplain of the duchess of

---

[29] Haggh, 'Crispijne and Abertijne', p. 330.   [30] ASG 279, fol. 112r.

[31] HMLC, pp. 196–8, and Haggh, 'Crispijne and Abertijne', p. 331.

[32] See Lefèvre, 'Les constitutions', pp. 245–6.   [33] See Lefèvre, *L'Organisation ecclésiastique*, p. 57.

[34] From 1469, the dean of St Gudula was one of three keepers of the privileges of the University of Louvain: E. Reusens, 'Décision de Paul II', *Analectes pour servir à l'histoire ecclésiastique de la Belgique* 29 (1901), pp. 34–8.   [35] Lefèvre, *L'Organisation ecclésiastique*, p. 58.   [36] ARBH 11754.

[37] E. de Moreau, *Histoire de l'église en Belgique*, 4 vols. (Brussels, 1949), vol. IV, p. 389; Vatican City, Archivio Segreto Vaticano, Reg. Vat. 462, fol. 161r.

Brabant (canon, 1357); Nicholas Pinckengy, chaplain at the court of Brabant and possibly the composer Pykini (canon, 1381); Johannes Plattelet, tenor of the Duke of Brabant (minor canon, 1407).[38] Conflict of interest was evidently a problem, for in 1376, the chapter of St Gudula decided that minor canons who also served the court of Brabant could not receive daily or obit distributions unless they found vicars to replace them in their absence.[39] Similarly, the dukes of Burgundy gave benefices in Brussels to singers, household chaplains and leading officers at the court. Although these included the best musicians living in Brussels, their canonicates were usually non-resident: only after their retirement from the service of the court did some become resident – and musically active – within the chapter.

Canons who made great changes at St Gudula with their foundations for music included Jan Bont, diplomat and counsellor to the Duke of Burgundy, who raised the ranks of ten feasts to duplex in 1450, permitting them to include polyphony, and founded discant Masses in the chapel of St Sebastian.[40] Incomes from the properties of Richard de Bellengues and Simon le Breton, composers, court chaplains and canons at St Gudula, were used to support the *boninfanten and choraelen*.[41] In his 1482 will, Philippe Siron, first chaplain of the dukes of Burgundy (1465–82), established the singing of *O salutaris hostia* by the canons of St Gudula during the Elevation at High Mass on major feasts; he also founded several Masses at his death.[42] Walter Henrici, choirboy at Cambrai Cathedral, later court chaplain, then canon and scholaster at St Gudula, founded several Masses, the chapel of the Annunciation and a new Marian feast, the *Recollectio festorum beate Marie virginis*, at St Gudula.[43]

Although the sextons' primary responsibility was to maintain vestments, reliquaries and clocks, to ring the church bells, to clean the church and to provide bread and wine for the Mass, they were sometimes ordered to sing chant if not otherwise occupied and to help with exceptional chores. In Brussels, sextons also wrote and repaired books and mended the organs. Throughout the Low Countries, the sextons were usually resident and their appointments were renewed annually.[44] The rules established in the 1460s for the sexton of the convent of St Denis in the forest of Soignes describe typical duties, which included ringing bells on high feast days and eight days preceding church fairs; and finding *bellemannen* (town criers) to announce fairs. At funerals, the sexton's pay depended on the status of the deceased.[45]

Mercenaries, the lowest-ranking clerics who were often priests without stable benefices, substituted for the chaplains. Like sextons, they sometimes participated in the chanting of the Office and Mass, but there is no evidence that sextons or mercenaries ever sang polyphony in Brussels. Nevertheless, one mercenary, Michel Lievens (*d.* 1495), at

[38] HMLC, p. 623; on the composer Pykini, see R. Sleiderink, 'Pykini's Parrot: Music at the Court of Brabant', in *Musicology and Archival Research* (see n. 12), pp. 358–91; Huybens, 'Le personnel des maîtrises', p. 40.

[39] Lefèvre, 'Statuts capitulaires', pp. 160–2.   [40] HMLC, pp. 553–4.

[41] ASG 1390, fol. 104r; HMLC, pp. 544–6, 559.

[42] HMLC, pp. 658–9, especially ASG 8163, fols. 398v–399v and 401v–402r, also ASG 1391, fol. 14r.

[43] See HMLC, pp. 605–7; M. Soenen, 'Un amateur de musique à Bruxelles à la fin du XVe siècle: Gautier Henri, chanoine et écolâtre de Sainte-Gudule', *Album Carlos Wyffels* (Brussels, 1987), pp. 423–36; B. Haggh, 'The Celebration of the "Recollectio Festorum Beatae Mariae Virginis", 1457–1987', in A. Pompilio *et al.* (eds.), *Trasmissione e recezione delle forme di cultura musicale: Atti del XIV Congresso della Società Internazionale di Musicologia*, 3 vols. (Turin, 1990), vol. III, pp. 559–71.

[44] See J. Laenen, *Kerkelijk en godsdienstig Brabant vanaf het begin der IVe tot in de XVIe eeuw of voorgeschiedenis van het Aartsbisdom Mechelen*, 5 vols. (Antwerp, 1935), vol. I, pp. 271–2.

[45] ARBH 7086, fol. 28r–v; see also HMLC, p. 821.

the parish church of Our Lady of the Chapel (Kapellekerk), had a considerable library containing sixty-three volumes, including sermons and treatises on scholasticism, medicine and even music.[46]

Vicars substituted for canons at St Gudula as early as the twelfth century, but knowledge of polyphony only became a requirement in 1446, when a statute stipulated that all vicars under the age of fifty had to learn to 'add discant'. Efforts would be made to replace those who did not have this skill.[47] Some vicars sang polyphony before 1446, however, since Michael Valx, vicar, was paid in 1440/1 for having sung discant for a 'long time'.[48] In 1465/6, payments were made 'to support the song introduced recently in the church', almost certainly the polyphony performed at Mass and Office by the vicars and chaplains, now required to know discant.[49] The vicars of St Gudula were often selected to serve as *hebdomadarii* in the second half of the fifteenth century: two vicars intoned from the end of each side of the choir and on Sundays they intoned in the middle of the choir, probably when polyphony was sung.[50]

From the thirteenth century, beneficed chaplains in Brussels's churches were entrusted with founded services held in the side chapels, the Offices and Masses in the nave and with the administration of property and money associated with their chaplaincies. Residentiary chaplains assigned by the collegiate churches to altars in dependent churches were also required to be present at the Offices and Masses of their home church.[51] Because St Gudula appointed to all chaplaincies in churches under its jurisdiction, it was common for chaplains to serve at altars in several churches simultaneously.[52] Some non-resident chaplains – among them, the Burgundian court composer, Antoine Busnois – held such chaplaincies in plurality.[53]

During the fifteenth century, the chaplains of St Gudula were required to learn to sing polyphony as part of efforts to increase the solemnity of ceremonies. The chapter of St Gudula solicited papal sanction which allowed them to stipulate that new chaplains be able to sing discant: the bull, issued on 12 April 1444, permitted the chapter to appoint ten such chaplains.[54] These chaplains, unlike the others, had to swear to reside personally, celebrate their chaplaincy Masses, be present and punctual at the Offices and at all other services held in quire at St Gudula, and sing plainchant or polyphony as required, unless their chapel duties interfered. If a chaplain did not do his duty another would be selected with adequate skill in music.[55] This legislation did not introduce the first singers of polyphony to St Gudula however: one Jan Fabri *de Condeit, discantatore* appears in accounts from 1411 to 1419, assigned to Masses in the Marian chapel.[56]

Little distinction appears to have been made between the status and duties of chaplains (sometimes called 'rectors of the chapels' in some documents) and vicars.[57] The collegiate churches of St Gudula in Brussels and St Peter in Anderlecht near Brussels both hired chaplains who sometimes acted as vicars. For example, Judocus Alsteen served as

[46] Lefèvre, *L'Organisation ecclésiastique*, p. 244.

[47] Transcribed in Lefèvre, 'Statuts capitulaires', pp. 203–5; also see Lefèvre, 'Les constitutions', p. 188.

[48] HMLC, pp. 680–1.   [49] ASG 9360, fol. 19r.   [50] Lefèvre, 'Les constitutions', pp. 181–2.

[51] See Lefèvre, *L'Organisation ecclésiastique*, pp. 99, 246–8; P. De Ridder, *Inventaris van het oud archief van de kapittelkerk van Sint-Michiel en Sint-Goedele te Brussel*, 3 vols. (Brussels, 1987–8), vol. I, pp. 392–500.

[52] See the accounts of the *villicus* of St Gudula.

[53] 'Busnoys and "Caron" in Documents from Brussels', in P. Higgins ed., *Antoine Busnoys: Method, Meaning and Context in Late Medieval Music* (Oxford, 1999), 295–315.

[54] ASG 197, fols. 162v–163r, and ASG 211, fols. 250v–252v.

[55] The oath of the chaplains is published in Lefèvre, 'Les constitutions', pp. 248–9.

[56] ASG 4988–4995 (1411–19), and HMLC, p. 588.   [57] AH 138, where they are called *rector capellanie*.

vicar at St Peter's and, simultaneously, as chaplain at St Gudula.[58] At St Gudula in 1440/1, Michael Zuetman, vicar, was assigned to celebrate the Mass for the dead *per annum cantandum*, a Mass usually assigned to a chaplain.[59] Many chaplains attended university and in 1440/1 for example several chaplains at St Gudula were at the recently established University of Louvain.[60] Nevertheless, chaplains were low in the clerical hierarchy until the end of the fifteenth century when they became a corporate entity at St Gudula, with their own administration and seal.[61]

In Brussels, the tenor led performances of polyphony and was therefore most often entrusted with copying polyphonic music and even teaching it. Tenors were present and named as such at many services requiring polyphony that were held in the nave and side chapels.[62] For example, in 1499/1500, Johannes, tenor of St Gudula, was paid for the evening *Salve regina* with prayers (the *lof*), for Masses of St Sebastian sung in discant in the side chapels, for three weekly Masses celebrated in the choir and for singing discant on specified feasts.[63] Some tenors were evidently well connected with leading members of the clergy in Brussels, for in 1495 the same tenor, Johannes, was nominated executor of the will of the dean of St Peter's collegiate church in Anderlecht.[64] That the tenor held a privileged place at the court of Burgundy as well is evident from later fifteenth-century records: tenors so designated advanced in rank more rapidly than the other chaplains.[65]

Tenors are identified only in the archives of St Gudula, St Nicholas and Our Lady of the Sands. In 1446, Michael Valx, vicar and tenor at St Gudula, was paid for having sung for a 'long time'.[66] Henricus, tenor of the same church, was paid on 9 February 1472 (new style) for celebrating his first Mass.[67] Two tenors are paid at St Gudula beginning in 1472/3;[68] two new tenors were hired on 14 February 1500.[69] St Nicholas had several tenors in its *cotidiane*[70] and a tenor at Our Lady of the Sands received a gift from the estate of Gherem Quas, chaplain and priest of St Gudula, in the 1470s.[71] Lay polyphonists usually served as vicars or chaplains, that is, amongst the lower clergy, but in the late fifteenth century lay singers without the tonsure also participated in worship. In 1472, the church of St Nicholas received papal dispensation to hire married singers if others could not be found.[72]

In Brussels and throughout the Low Countries, wealthy confraternities hired singers for the services held in their patronal side chapels. Confraternity singers usually held supplementary chaplaincies to augment their incomes and had therefore to be present at services in the main choir. The first confraternity singers known in Brussels were hired by the Marian confraternity of St Gudula by 1470, when the surviving confraternity accounts begin. These singers were paid jointly by the confraternity and church Fabric.[73] The joint management of confraternity singers at St Nicholas is outlined in an agreement of 24 February 1488 between the curate, the *kerkmeesters*, who managed the accounts, and the provosts of that church's Marian confraternity. The document ordered the provosts and the *kerkmeesters*, with the consent of parishioners, to elect chaplains

[58] HMLC, p. 537.   [59] ASG 1390, fol. 228r.   [60] ASG 1389 and other accounts of the *villicus*.

[61] Lefèvre, *L'Organisation ecclésiastique*, pp. 20, 52.

[62] J. Igoe, 'Performance Practices in the Polyphonic Mass of the Early Fifteenth Century', Ph.D. thesis, University of North Carolina at Chapel Hill (1971), pp. 75–90.   [63] HMLC, p. 617.   [64] *Ibid.*

[65] B. Haggh, 'The Status of the Musician at the Burgundian-Habsburg Courts', MA thesis, University of Illinois at Urbana-Champaign (1980).   [66] Transcribed in Lefèvre, 'Statuts capitulaires', pp. 203–4.

[67] ASG 1390, fol. 186r.   [68] ASG 1390, fol. 200r.   [69] ASG 9368, fol. 110r.

[70] Haggh, 'Crispijne and Abertijne'.   [71] ASG 279, fol. 112r.   [72] ARBH 21499, fol. 22r.

[73] ASG 8990 (accounts of Marian confraternity of St Gudula, 1466–72, 1473–80, 1482–4 and 1485–7).

skilled in polyphony to serve the confraternity in their new chapel and in the main church nave. Singers of St Nicholas not hired specifically for the Marian confraternity neverthe-less received distributions if they sang with the others in the Lady chapel.[74]

Supplementing the singers described above were itinerant performers, who left little trace of identity or past affiliation. Documents of 1460 and later from the collegiate church of St Peter in Anderlecht near Brussels cite *discanteerders* along with the vicars and chaplains, and at St Gudula, statutes mention fines given to vicars and *discantores*.[75] Such singers without a specific clerical office already appear in the accounts of the *villi-cus* of St Gudula of 1361, in which one Wouter was paid 'on behalf of the singers'.[76]

Singers from outside Brussels came individually and in choirs, often by invitation, and were reimbursed for their travels. At St Gudula in 1434/5 and 1437/8, a choir from Hal chanted on St Michael's Day and in 1443 on the feast of St Gudula.[77] In 1440, singers from Tournai with two preachers and Joannes Facuwez, canon of St Peter in Anderlecht, took part in the Corpus Christi ceremony;[78] and on 10 June 1471 unnamed *buytensang-ers* or singers 'from outside' received wine.[79] In addition, singers working in Brussels occasionally performed outside their home churches. In 1424, singers 'from Brussels', perhaps from St Gudula, sang High Mass at the collegiate church of St Peter in Anderlecht on the day of the first *kermes* (the fair held on the feast of the Dedication).[80] In 1470/1, singers from St Gudula were part of the procession in honour of St Guido, the patron saint of the church of St Peter. In 1486/7, the Brothers of the Common Life sang Lady Mass at the parish church of St John in Molenbeek and one of the Brothers was paid for participating again the following year.[81]

Local singers from churches favoured by the court sometimes performed at court. In 1469, singers, chaplains and choirboys of the church of Our Lady in Hal, whose Marian icon was venerated by Philip the Good, sang Mass for the duke;[82] singers from Our Lady of the Sands and choirboys from St Gudula and Our Lady of the Sands were paid for singing for the duke on St Nicholas Day in 1482 and 1486 respectively.[83] The dates, composition of the ensembles and what we know of music at the churches in ques-tion, suggest that these ensembles performed polyphony.

In Brussels, most service books were copied by minor clergy at the church at which the books were used;[84] books with polyphony were prepared only by musicians such as the tenor or organist and were generally for their personal use. Some service books, however, were commissioned from outside, especially the scriptoria of the Benedictine monasteries in the forest of Soignes, Groenendael, the Roodklooster and Zevenbronnen, or from scribes at the Charterhouse or the Victorines at Jericho. The Brothers of the Common Life often bound or printed books used by the choir of St Gudula or at the request of individual canons, and received commissions to write books from churches and convents throughout Brussels.[85]

---

[74] ARBH 21600.   [75] Lefèvre, 'Les constitutions', p. 191.   [76] ASG 4962, 1361/2.

[77] Huybens, 'Le personnel', p. 33.   [78] Vanden Bussche, 'Zangers', p. 92.

[79] ASG 1390, fol. 186r. Singers also came from Antwerp in 1475/6 and Aalst in 1498/9 (ASG 1390, fol. 244r; ASG 1392, fol. 21v).   [80] AH 64; HMLC, pp. 444–5.   [81] ARBH 25376, 1486/7, p. 62, 1487/8, p. 84.

[82] Brussels, Algemeen Rijksarchief/Archives du Royaume, Rekenkamer/Chambre des Comptes/Rekenkamer, 1924, fol. 223r–v.

[83] Lille, Archives départementales du Nord, B 2127, fol. 170r, and B 2135, no. 69489.

[84] For example, Wilhelmus Goetkint (*d.* 1485), chaplain and minor canon of St Gudula (HMLC, p. 597).

[85] See *Le Livre, l'estampe, l'édition en Brabant du XVe au XIXe siècle* (Gembloux, 1935); E. Persoons, 'Prieuré de Sept-Fontaines à Rhode-St-Genèse', *Monasticon belge* 4/iv (1970), pp. 1105–16 especially p. 1110; A. Derolez, 'A Late Medieval Reading List of the Priory of Zevenborren near Brussels', in R. De Smet,

Other service books were purchased or donated from the estates of deceased members of the clergy of St Gudula, often for specific foundations. Canon Walter Lonijs (*d.* 1489) donated a missal for the Mass held daily after Matins at the high altar.[86] Henricus de Mera, chaplain (*d.* 1492) gave missals to the chaplaincy of St Anne and St Cecilia.[87] In 1501, the *villicus* purchased chant books from the estate of Nicolas *zang-meester*.[88] Yet service books received by gift or purchase did not necessarily follow the use of St Gudula: in the early sixteenth century, a missal of the use of Liège was acquired for the altar of St Michael in St Gudula.[89]

Conscious efforts were made to use and preserve existing books until they were beyond repair and replacements were only obtained in cases of great need; new pages or gatherings were frequently inserted into older books (probably following changes in ritual) and new bindings made for older manuscripts. Great efforts were often made to recover books that were lost, pawned or confiscated. On 8 March 1469, St Gudula paid to retrieve a gradual which had been taken from the church by the Lombard bankers in Lier.[90]

Church accounts reveal little about the physical appearance of books, or the process of writing them, although payments for binding a manuscript always followed those for writing. Some scribes also decorated or bound books.[91] Sizes of manuscripts are rarely described, but books comprising five gatherings were written at St Gudula (1463/4 and 1474/5) and St Nicholas (1490/1) respectively. Table 12.1 lists payments made for the writing of service books with music at St Gudula and the parish churches of Brussels in the fifteenth century.[92]

The singing of polyphony was a specialised occupation in fifteenth-century Brussels and certain offices and foundations were directly responsible for it: the *zang-meester*, *choraelen* and *cotidiane* at St Gudula and St Nicholas, perhaps also at Our Lady of the Sands. Yet the musicus/cantor distinction still held and singers of polyphony in the local churches belonged to a lower social and clerical stratum. The social organisation of singers of chant and polyphony within the church did not differ, however. Characteristic of late medieval society were the many small groups of people organised by statute or rule and often praying for each other's souls. Within the church of St Gudula in Brussels, these were foundations such as the chapter, the vicars, the choirboys, or organised groups like the chaplains of the end of the fifteenth century; at the parish churches, we notice the *cotidiane* foundations and confraternities; and outside the church, we can cite craft and rhetoric guilds and archery societies. An individual's allegiance was primarily to these groups and only secondarily to the church, city or state, as is apparent from the numerous petty disputes between such groups of the clergy regarding payment and position in the choir or in processions, and the fidelity to each other of members of the same group as evident from their wills and obituaries – members relied on each other for earthly social support and heavenly salvation.

H. Melaerts, C. Saerens (eds.), *Studia varia Bruxellensia ad orbem graeco-latinum pertinentia*, 2 vols. (Leuven, 1990), vol. II, pp. 21–7; Alexandre Pinchart, 'Scribes et enlumineurs, comptes des chartreux de Notre Dame de Scheut, lez Bruxelles, relatifs à l'execution des manuscrits', *Messager des sciences historiques, des arts, et de la bibliographie de Belgique* ser. 6, 35 (1867), pp. 86–8; M. Soenen, 'Les manuscrits liturgiques de la Chartreuse de Scheut d'après une liste de 1551', *Archives, bibliothèques et musées de Belgique/Archief en bibliotheekwezen in België* 49/iii–iv (1978), pp. 488–503.   [86] ASG 276, fol. 148r.   [87] ASG 1392, fol. 79v.
[88] ASG 268, fols. 426r–432r.   [89] ASG 4999, fol. 21v.   [90] ASG 9361, 1468/9.
[91] See M. Laffitte, 'Le vocabulaire médiéval de la reliure d'après les anciens inventaires', in O. Weijers (ed.), *Vocabulaire du livre et de l'écriture au Moyen Age* (Turnhout, 1989), pp. 61–78.
[92] See HMLC, pp. 466–74; E. Schreurs (ed.), *Music Fragments and Manuscripts in the Low Countries* (Peer, 1997); E. Schreurs (ed.), *An Anthology of Music Fragments from the Low Countries* (Peer, 1995).

Table 12.1 *Music writing in Brussels, 1400–1500*

Year	Scribe	Description of work
written at St Gudula		
1412/13	Henricus de Aska	binding and repairing a missal of the chapel of St Gertrude (ASG 4989, accounts, non-resident chaplains)
1463/4	unnamed	copying Masses and other compositions into five quaterns (ASG 1390, accounts of villicus, fols. 223r, 244r)
1464/5	Dominus Cornelius	*librum cantualium* (ASG 1390, fols. 85v, 98r)
1468/9	Wolven	three Masses in the 'book of the canons' (ASG 1390, fol. 144r)
1474/5	Abertijne Malcourt	Masses and other music in five gatherings 1475/6 (ASG, 1390, fol. 223r)
1483/4	unnamed	three books for the *boninfanten* (processional responsories; responsories, verses and antiphons; Sunday Gospels, Epistles and hymns; ASG 6398, accounts of the *boninfanten* and *choraelen*, fols. 182v–183r)
1492/3	Claes Tayman	repairing the binding of an old breviary, antiphonal, two psalters and a *Venite* book (ASG 9364, Fabric accounts, fol. 121v)
written for St Gudula outside the church		
1466/7	Andrie, a Dominican	books written by the Dominicans (ASG 1390, fol. 110r)
1477	Brother Thomas, prior of Groenendael	service books delivered to the Fabric of St Gudula (ASG 10033, receipt in form of charter)
1499/1500	the *pater* of the Brothers of the Common Life	writing and notating the responsories for the feast of St Agnes (ASG 9368, fol. 114r)
written at St Nicholas		
1441/2	unnamed	writing the *Liber generationis* with the *sange* for Christmas Eve (ARB 21458, Fabric accounts, fol. 4r)[a]
1447/8	Lambrechte Biners	binding an antiphonal and adding new feasts (ARB 21458, fol. 3v)
1448/9	Mathijse van Orsmale	fixing the large antiphonals (ARB 21458, fol. 4r)
1460/1	Janne Meens, organist	writing tracts, hymns and sequences to be played on the organ at vigils (ARB 21459, fol. 3v)
1484/5	Anthoenise Block	ten quaterns of parchment with various lessons (ARB 21459, fol. 4r)

Table 12.1 (*cont.*)

Year	Scribe	Description of work
1490/1	unnamed	writing duplex feasts on parchment (ARB 21459, fol. 4v)
written for St Nicholas outside the church		
1480/81	Janne Everarts	book purchased from Groenendael with Venites, alleluias, responsories and verses (ARB 21459, fol. 4r)
1481/2	(written at Jericho)	three processionals (ARB 21459, fol. 5r)
1485–7	Abertijne Malcourt	copying thirty sexterns with motets and *Salve regina* settings with twenty-two Masses and motets for the choirboys of St Nicholas (ARB 21460, accounts of the daily distributions 1485/6; ARB 21459, Fabric accounts 1485/7)
written at the parish church of St John in Molenbeek		
1447/8	Aert	illuminating a missal (ARB 25375, Fabric accounts, p. 44)
1448/9	Brother Jan Marscalc	binding a missal (ARB 25375, p. 48)
1448/9	unnamed	repairing a missal (ARB 25375, p. 49)
1451/2	Janne Hoelbeke, organist	hired to perform compositions in a newly written organ book (ARB 25375, p. 71)
1466/7	unnamed	two antiphonals (ARB 25375, p. 621)
1486/7	anthoenise *den scriment*	copying quaterns and adding them to a manuscript (ARB 25376, p. 51)
written for the parish church of St John in Molenbeek outside the church		
1454/5	'den heer die tsinte Lijsbetten woent'	two processionals (ARB 25375, p. 129)

Note

[a] Polyphonic conclusions to the *Liber generationis* sung on Christmas Eve and Epiphany were written *c.* 1250 into a gospel book from Tongeren. See Schreurs (ed.), *An Anthology*, p. 7.

The urban environment did afford musicians and choirs opportunities for extra-curricular singing: the possibility of visiting other churches or the court from time to time or of performing at civic events. Increasingly sophisticated methods of book-keeping and of distributing duties efficiently led to better pay, greater stability and more opportunities. Consequently, singers of polyphony found more numerous residential posts in the sixteenth century, a phenomenon which led to better choirs and greater consumption of polyphony.[93] In the urban environment, music scribes such as Abertijne Malcourt profited by receiving commissions from more than one church. At the same time, increased communication between cities and countries contributed to musical competition, an international musical style and a corresponding notation which could be understood by all, the latter furthered by the development of printing.

Yet the example of Brussels presented here is unique, not representative. At nearby Ghent, the rise of polyphony only occurred in the sixteenth century, whereas Tournai, Bruges and Antwerp preceded and set the stage for Brussels in this respect. Further analyses of the lives and occupations of urban church musicians outside as well as inside the Low Countries will provide a more secure basis for evaluating the musical contributions of church musicians in Brussels in the fifteenth century.[94]

[93] B. Haggh, 'Itinerancy to Residency: Professional Careers and Performance Practices in 15th-Century Sacred Music', *Early Music* 17 (1989), pp. 359–66; and R. Wegman, 'From Maker to Composer: Improvisation and Musical Authorship in the Low Countries, 1450–1500', *Journal of the American Musicological Society* 49 (1996), pp. 409–79.

[94] I wish to thank Fiona Kisby, Rebecca Ringer and Magnus Williamson for their assistance with the preparation of this article.

CHAPTER THIRTEEN

MUSIC AND MOONLIGHTING: THE CATHEDRAL CHOIRMEN OF EARLY MODERN ENGLAND, 1558–1649

JAMES SAUNDERS

The necessity for cathedral choirmen to supplement their stipends by 'moonlighting' in other jobs was a much-lamented fact of life in sixteenth- and seventeenth-century England.[1] Campaigning in the time of Charles I for an improvement in stipends and conditions of employment, the anonymous author of one tract complained that 'the poore singingman that was brought up to have his living in the Churche by his facultye must least of all attend that, and folow some other indirect trade or worse imployment of baser condicion, and thereby neglect the dayly attendance of his service . . . or els himself, his wyfe and children must starve'.[2] In later years, Thomas Mace lamented the fact that it was only a dean and chapter's tolerance of choirmen working 'in the barbers trade, the shoemakers trade, the taylors trade, the smiths trade, and divers other . . . inferior trades' which kept them from starving.[3] Even the dean and chapter of Durham Cathedral tacitly admitted the inadequacy of what they paid, describing two 'poore laye singingmen' as 'sore charged . . . haveing nothing but their stipends'.[4]

The truth was that while the stipend a man earned by singing in a cathedral choir may have been important to him, it does not tell anything like the whole story of his working life. Taking work outside the choir, and often outside the cathedral, was crucial if a choirman was to maintain a reasonable standard of living. Indeed, for many, such 'moonlighting' was the only thing which kept them above the poverty line. It was only because early modern cathedral choirmen located themselves both socially and economically within the wider urban community that cathedrals could maintain choirs at all.

While this fact was widely recognised in the early modern period, it has received scant recognition from modern research. Understandably enough, virtually all investigations into the history of the choirs of the English cathedrals have been undertaken with

---

[1] The terminology used to describe the offices held by choirmen in the early modern period can occasionally be confusing. A layman who belonged to the choir of a new foundation cathedral (see note 10) is usually termed a 'lay clerk' (occasionally 'conduct'), while his equivalent in cathedrals of the old foundation was a 'lay vicar'. Ordained clergymen singing in a choir, meanwhile, are usually called 'minor canons' (or 'petty canons') in new foundation establishments and 'priest vicars' in the old foundations. St Paul's Cathedral, London, however, had minor canons and lay vicars, while St George's, Windsor and Hereford Cathedral gave the title 'minor canon' to their senior priest vicars. 'Singingman' and 'choirman' usually refer to laymen, but were sometimes used as all-inclusive terms. While in practice an author's meaning is almost always obvious, I have endeavoured to avoid careless or confusing usages.   [2] BL, MS Royal 18 B XIX, fol. 6v.

[3] T. Mace, *Musick's Monument; or, a Remembrancer of the Best Practical Musick, Both Divine and Civil, that has Ever Been Known to Have Been in the World* (London, 1676; reprinted Paris, 1958), p. 25.

[4] DCD Chapter Act Book 1578–83, entry for 26 June '1592' (*recte* 1582).

the primary purpose of better understanding the music they performed. As a result, it is very much from a musicological perspective that the choirmen have been viewed. Scholars have painted a richly detailed and hugely important picture of repertory and performance practices, but have rarely acknowledged the fact that this represents not so much a full portrait of most choirmen's lives as a finely painted detail. This short essay is intended to demonstrate that performing music was only one part of most choirmen's lives and that most of them had a number of other irons in the fire, using the cities of which they were citizens to make a living.

It is actually not difficult to show that choirmen did take employment outside the choirs. Understanding exactly what they did and how much they earned by it is, unfortunately, less simple. The written records necessary for such a project have frequently disappeared (if indeed they ever existed) and because employment, particularly among lay choirmen, may have been taken almost anywhere, it is difficult to know where to begin looking for such evidence as may have survived. Because of these difficulties, the picture which follows is, of necessity, impressionistically, rather than systematically drawn. The intention is to indicate how wide was the range of careers that a choirman might have followed and to suggest how significant they might have been in his working life. However, it must be recognised that evidence of the true extent of choir 'moonlighting' is never likely to be recovered.

Many choirmen were able to begin their quest for additional paid work within the cathedral itself. As large and paternalist employers, deans and chapters had various types of patronage at their disposal, some of which were deemed suitable for existing employees. William Grimball, lay clerk of Peterborough Cathedral, is recorded as receiving payments for a whole range of minor duties, including acting as deputy sacristan, scouring the drains, ringing the 'curfue bell', winding the clock, and washing the cathedral linen, earning himself £1 8s 10d on top of his lay clerk's stipend in 1597 and 1598. Robert Bate, lay clerk of the same cathedral, received payment of £1 in 1583 and £2 in 1584 for overseeing 'le Parcke woode, Dame Agnis wood, and Grimshawe woode'.[5] At Ely, Thomas Wiborough seems to have made himself indispensable. A lay clerk from 1584 to 1635, he also acted as deputy treasurer, taught 'the [grammar school] schollers on the vialls' and held the office of caterer of the common hall. Outside the cathedral, but still in its employ, he acted as bailiff for the dean and chapter's manor of Ely Porta, collected rents due from 'Mullicoath' (probably Mollicourt Priory, a cell of the pre-Reformation cathedral priory), received payments for his 'charges in going to Swaffam, for timber there' and was responsible for 'overseeing the workes'.[6] Lay clerk Robert Masham acted as rent collector for the dean and chapter of Durham '*infra lez Balies*' (i.e. within the parishes of North and South Bailey), earning himself 6s 8d in 1594/5. His colleague Robert Prentice (a minor canon) presided over the court of the officiality of the dean and chapter, in his capacity as surrogate for Prebendary Henry Dethick.[7] In Canterbury, minor canon John Shepherd was bold (if somewhat artless) in his attempts to squeeze money from his employers, petitioning the chapter in 1633:

---

[5] PCM 50, accounts 1597, 1598; accounts 1583, 1584.

[6] EDC 3/1/2, fols. 64v, 7v; 2/1/1, pp. 44, 132, 118; 3/1/2, fols. 22r, 68v.

[7] DCD Treasurer's Book 15 (1594/5); J. Barmby (ed.), *Memorials of St Giles's, Durham, Being Grassmen's Accounts and Other Parish Records with Documents Relating to the Hospitals of Kepier and St Mary Magdalene*, Surtees Society 95 (Durham, 1895), p. 123, note 1.

to let you understand what good I have done to the church since I came hether, and never had a peny recompence. First I made a cradell that have saved the church a great deale of money. Then I mended one of the pinnackells of Belhary steple, very like to fall downe. It was a very dangerous peece of worke: noe man wold take upon him to mend it till I devized a way to make it fast . . . I being then sackherst [sacrist], Dean Nevell had a letter sent him . . . that I was very neclygent to look to the decayed places of the church, and that there was a place it would take a hundred pound to mend, but it was not so, for I did mend it for fower nobles . . . Nowe for all this I desier you of your gentell curtessye to bestow £3 upon me, and I wilbe very thankfull to you for it, and pray for you as long as I lived [*sic*][8]

For those members of the cathedral choirs who were ordained clergymen (that is, the minor canons and priest-vicars), having the cure of souls in a parish church became an increasingly important source of income. Until 1547, many of the cathedrals' minor clergy had earned a useful income from the celebration of chantry Masses. With the abolition of the chantries in 1547, however, they began to turn more frequently to service in a parish, sometimes as rector or vicar, but most frequently as a curate. Archival evidence would suggest that the practice increased in popularity from about the late 1570s.[9] New Foundation cathedral[10] statutes allowed minor canons to hold a benefice in addition to their cathedral post without penalty, that they might be 'encouraged the more diligently to attend to their several employments' in the cathedral. So long as the second benefice was within twenty-four miles and they continued to perform their duties in the cathedral, they were absolved from any penalties under the laws against pluralism.[11]

Although the surviving evidence is somewhat patchy, it seems safe to suggest that a fairly high proportion of the total number of minor canons did gain posts in a parish. In the 1580s, seven minor canons of St Paul's Cathedral in London were 'knowne to bee double cur[ates]' and by 1598, all eight held additional livings.[12] In Ely between 1560 and 1640, at least twenty-eight minor canons held parish livings in addition to their cathedral stall.[13] Most served in one of Ely's two parish churches (Holy Trinity and St Mary's) or their dependent chapels of Stuntney and Chettisham. Both parishes were in the gift of the dean and chapter and it was evidently deliberate policy that minor canons should provide for the cure of souls there.

[8] C. E. Woodruff (ed.), 'Some Seventeenth-Century Letters and Petitions From the Muniments of the Dean and Chapter of Canterbury', *Archaeologia Cantiana* 43 (1930), pp. 133–4.

[9] For evidence of the trend in York, see C. Cross, 'Priests into Ministers: the Establishment of Protestant Practice in the City of York 1530–1630', in P. Newman Brooks (ed.), *Reformation Principle and Practice: Essays in Honour of Arthur Geoffrey Dickens* (London, 1980), pp. 213–14, 220–1.

[10] 'Cathedrals of the New Foundation' were those which had been monastic foundations until the Reformation. Following the dissolution of the monasteries by Henry VIII, they were re-founded as institutions governed by secular priests. 'Cathedrals of the Old Foundation' were those which had always been governed by a chapter of secular priests, and whose constitutions were therefore left unchanged.

[11] See, for example, the statutes of Peterborough Cathedral, in W. T. Mellows (ed.), *Peterborough Local Administration: The Foundation of Peterborough Cathedral A.D. 1541*, Northamptonshire Record Society 13 (Northampton, 1941; reprinted 1967), p. 112.

[12] WAM Muniment Book 15, fol. 80r; London, Guildhall Library, MS 25, 175, fols. 17v, 28v.

[13] This figure is derived by cross-referencing Ely's capitular and diocesan archives. Both collections are held in Cambridge University Library.

The practice of Ely Cathedral was not unusual. Where the patron of livings held by a choirman can be determined, it proves to have been the cathedral dean and chapter far more often than any other body or individual. Service in a parish was encouraged particularly actively in the 1620s and 1630s when interest in augmenting choir salaries increased. Archbishop Laud himself wrote to the dean and chapter of Norwich in 1634 urging it to give the minor canons first refusal of benefices in the chapter's gift. In the past, he recalled, it had been 'generally thought fitt . . . that such small benefices and cures within the citie or suburbs as are in the churches guifte, should, as they fell voyd, bee given to the petty canons respectively and to noe other'. This custom, he added, was 'usuall with other churches where the quire is as meane as yours, and it beinge great help to them'.[14] In a similar manner, when Winchester Cathedral's statutes underwent their Laudian revision, it became official policy that vacant benefices in the gift of the cathedral should be offered first to the prebendaries, and if they did not want them, to the minor canons. 'No benefices must be given to outside persons, unless in the judgement of the dean and chapter the minor canons should be unsuitable, or they should be unwilling to take them when offered.'[15] The chapter of Durham Cathedral certainly had plans for a similar policy, even if it was ultimately unable to put them into permanent effect. A chapter act of July 1636 ordered that 'all severall livinges in the guifte of the Deane & Chapter of Durham under the value of fortie pounds *per annum* . . . shalbe then proferred to the peticannones & other members of this Church before strangers', although the decree was 'repealed and annihilated' in 1639, for reasons not disclosed.[16]

In a few cathedrals, it was not only ordained choirmen who eked out their stipends by service in a parish. In Chichester, the stipend provided by many of the city's tiny parishes was apparently so low that at times no clergyman could be found to minister to them. This gave the opportunity for some of the cathedral's lay vicars to find employment as readers (*lectores*) – men who would read the Prayer Book services 'in poorer parishes destitute of incumbents' and in other places allowed by the ordinary.[17] Between 1571 and 1639, at least seven of the lay vicars served in this way and a greater number might well be identified if the coverage of the surviving evidence were greater. Certainly, by 1625, Valentine Austin and John Clifford wrote as if their appointment to a reader's post were more a right than a privilege. While admitting that they were 'not any of us in orders, but mere lay men', they asserted that 'by our statutes any of us to our knowledg[e] may serve a cure . . . as our predissessors have heretofore done'.[18]

If ecclesiastical employment was one obvious way of a choirman earning extra money, then exploiting his musical abilities was another. A few, presumably possessed of a reasonably high level of musical competence, therefore took private pupils. John Lilliat, whose career had taken him from being a chorister at Christ Church, Oxford, through service in the choirs of Wells Cathedral and Westminster Abbey, taught a young woman

[14] W. S. Simpson (ed.), *Registrum Statutorum et Consuetudinum Ecclesiae Cathedralis Sancti Pauli Londiniensis* (London, 1873), p. 420.

[15] A. W. Goodman and W. H. Hutton (eds.), *The Statutes Governing the Cathedral Church of Winchester given by King Charles I* (Oxford, 1925), pp. 18–19.

[16] DCD Chapter Act Book 1619–38, fol. 162v; Chapter Act Book 1639–61, fol. 5r.

[17] The quotation is from the 'Injunctions to be Confessed and Subscribed by Them That Shall be Admitted Readers' of 1561, reprinted in E. Cardwell (ed.), *Documentary Annals of the Reformed Church of England*, 2 vols. (Oxford, 1839), vol. I, pp. 268–9. Most of the city of Chichester was a peculiar jurisdiction and so the 'ordinary', in many cases, was the cathedral dean.   [18] WSRO, MS Ep I/20/10a.

named Dulcebell Porter to sing while he was a priest-vicar in Chichester.[19] Edmund Hooper, Master of the Choristers at Westminster Abbey and Gentleman of the Chapel Royal, acted for a time as private tutor to the daughters of Lady Knyvett, arranging dancing lessons, purchasing lutes for them and teaching them to play the virginal and sing, for which he received payment of ten pounds.[20] Martin Peerson, Master of the Choristers at St Paul's Cathedral, took pupils including the daughter of a prebendary of Southwell and the daughter of the procurator of the Court of Arches, teaching them to play the virginal.[21] On a less exalted level, Francis Standish, Precentor of Peterborough Cathedral just before the Civil War, was paid 26s 4d a year 'in consideration of the paynes which he tooke with the boye [Daniel Bull], in trayning up in musick, to make him fit for the service of the church and capable of a choristers place'. Standish had similarly trained two other boys.[22] In sixteenth-century Durham, 'Thomas Harrison, singing man, . . . did exercise the roome and place of keeping schoole, for bringing up of young children to be instructed in the catechisme & further made fit to go to the grammar schoole, & likewise to be taught there plaine song and to be entred in their prick song'.[23]

Other choirmen made money by performing music, rather than by teaching it. Eight lay clerks of Norwich ('ffydling & pyping knaves' in the opinion of one of their colleagues) doubled as city waits.[24] The mundum book from King's College, Cambridge for 1575/6 records a payment of 5s to '[Hugh] Hookes, le singing man of Elye, for his paynes in the commensment time'.[25] In Chester, expenses arising from a play mounted by one of the city's guilds included small payments to '2 clarkes of the menster', to the precentor 'to gett singers' and to Robert White, Master of the Choristers, 'for singinge'. In the early seventeenth century, St Oswald's parish church (which met in the north transept of the city's cathedral) spent 3s 4d 'uppon the synginge men of the queere going with the vicar & parishioners upon procession in cyttie & countrey'.[26] William Smith, a minor canon of Durham in the 1580s, added the skills of an organ builder to a talent for singing. While he had no formal apprenticeship in the trade, he claimed to have spent time 'markinge men of greater skill that haith bene here in tymes passed', so enabling him to spend a week 'in mendinge the sownd boord, the wynd stop, the springe, wyers, and in tuninge the pipes' of the cathedral's quire organ. 'They will', he announced proudly, 'much delight bothe the auditorie and the player, because they yeld the most principallest and imperiall sound of all the rest.' He received 30s for his labours.[27]

Not all jobs taken by choirmen were connected with the church or with music, however. So varied, in fact, were the additional sources of employment (particularly among lay choirmen), that even after time has taken its toll on the records, far too much evidence remains for it to be possible to provide anything like a full list here. The best educated (usually graduate) minor canons might hope for appointment as master or usher of one of the grammar schools attached to the cathedrals – although to be strictly

[19] See Lilliat's 'Ditie Upon the Death of Dulcebell Porter, my Scholler', reprinted in E. Doughtie (ed.), *Liber Lilliati – Elizabethan Verse and Song (Bodleian MS Rawlinson Poetry 148)* (London, 1985), pp. 104, 106.

[20] BL, MS Egerton 2713, fols. 448r, 455r.

[21] A. Jones, 'The Life and Works of Martin Peerson', M.Litt. thesis, 2 vols., Cambridge University (1957), vol. I, pp. 15, 27, 29.   [22] PCM 12, fols. 50r, 30r.

[23] Durham Cathedral Library, MS Hunter 13, no. 56. The quotation comes from a transcription (*c.* 1691) of a document no longer extant. Harrison was a lay clerk of the cathedral from 1558 until 1580 or 1581.

[24] D. Galloway (ed.), *Norwich 1540–1642*, Records of Early English Drama (Toronto, 1984), pp. 352, 69.

[25] A. H. Nalson (ed.), *Cambridge*, Records of Early English Drama, 2 vols. (Toronto, 1989), vol. I, p. 274.

[26] L. M. Clopper (ed.), *Chester*, Records of Early English Drama (Manchester, 1979), pp. 78, 66, 86, 226.

[27] DCD Miscellaneous Charter 3198.

accurate one should perhaps say that masters at the grammar schools might hope for the perk of a minor canonry and that the school was always the first call on their time, for not all minor canons were expected to sing, even though they were nominally part of the choir.[28] More likely is that the majority of less well-qualified minor canons may have taken private pupils. Teaching was certainly a common sideline for parish clergymen[29] and given the number of minor canons who also served in parishes, it seems probable that many of them would have taken the opportunity to earn a few extra shillings a week. While only a small proportion of minor canons were educated at university, almost all had attended grammar school and should have been capable of giving instruction in reading, writing and elementary Latin. Lay choirmen too may have supplemented their stipends in this way. In addition to Thomas Harrison, mentioned above, Jacob Hillary of Chichester was granted a licence to teach boys English, while Francis Gardiner of the same city was permitted to teach boys the three 'R's (*legendi, scribendi, et calculandi*).[30]

Small-holding and stock-rearing were also popular occupations for choirmen, most cathedral cities being no more than small islands of urban development in predominantly rural areas. Nicholas Cheseldine and Thurstan Murray, both minor canons of Peterborough Cathedral, were fined by the dean and chapter's manorial court for keeping pigs on the common fen without first having put rings through their snouts. Richard Foster, lay clerk then minor canon of the cathedral in the 1590s, was fined for allowing beasts and cattle onto the common fen and later for keeping a horse and cattle on Brough Little Fen, offences for which lay clerks John Kirkby and George Murray were also fined at various times.[31] When John Gotobed, minor canon of Ely, died in 1593 he left more than seventeen acres of land, four mares, two colts, three cows, five calves and two steers.[32] Robert Murray died in 1594, eight years after giving up his minor canon's stall at Durham Cathedral, leaving a plough, malt, corn sown and stored, wool worth nearly £7, a bee-hive, cattle including eight cows and four calves, a mare and foal, eighty-two ewes and lambs, eighteen rams and ninety-one pigs, suggesting that he was rather more than a small-holder. Thomas Humble, lay clerk of the same cathedral, bequeathed ploughing tackle, hay, eight oxen and eleven pigs.[33] Other choirmen indulged more modestly in gardening, presumably to produce vegetables for their own consumption or for sale. When Richard Base of Chichester leased a tenement and garden in 1562, for example, he found his property to lie adjacent to the garden of another lay choirman, Gilbert Adlington.[34]

A majority of cathedral lay clerks came from labouring, artisan or craft backgrounds and it was the humble origins of these men, some of whom had managed to get themselves ordained in the 1630s, which formed a common theme of Puritan attacks in the 1640s. A petition from the inhabitants of Norwich (included in papers relating to the impeachment of Bishop Wren) complained of the insufficiency of Robert Horne, minister of St John Timberhill, who had been a labourer in masonry before he became a lay

---

[28] J. Saunders, 'English Cathedral Choirs and Choirmen, 1558 to the Civil War: an Occupational Study', Ph.D. thesis, Cambridge University (1997), pp. 64–7.

[29] P. K. Orpen, 'Schoolmastering as a Profession in the Seventeenth Century: the Career Patterns of the Grammar Schoolmaster', *History of Education* 6 (1977), pp. 183–94.

[30] WSRO MS Ep III/4/6, fol. 56v; Ep III/4/11, fol. 173r.

[31] W. T. Mellows and D. H. Gifford (eds.), *Peterborough Local Administration. Elizabethan Peterborough: the Dean and Chapter as Lords of the City*, Northamptonshire Record Society 18 (Northampton, 1944), pp. 127, 132, 152, 76, 118.

[32] Ely Consistory Court Probate Materials C:20:176, fols. 176r–177r, Cambridgeshire County Record Office, Cambridge.   [33] DCD original wills and inventories 'Robert Murraye' (1594); 'Thomas Humble' (1623).

[34] WSRO MS Cap I/27/1, fol. 37r–v.

clerk. The petition carried on to complain of William Alsey, who had previously been a tailor, and John Souter, formerly 'a poore labourer, a filler of bobbins with learning'.[35] Puritan propagandist Richard Culmer recorded of the minor canons of Canterbury that one was a 'priested weaver in a canonicall coate', one a 'late tobaccopipe-maker' and another a 'late taylor, servingman and butler to the deane'.[36] Many choirmen (and particularly the laymen) chose not to abandon their trades on taking up their cathedral posts. Service in a cathedral choir was, after all, only a part-time occupation, leaving ample opportunity to pursue other trades, provided that the hours worked could be flexibly arranged. The accounts of the feoffees and governors of Peterborough's city lands include payments from William Ellis (lay clerk c. 1611–c. 1634) 'for olde woodde lefte at the repayringe of the bridge', a payment to Ellis for 'pinwood' and a further sum 'for the cariage of a loade of sand from William Ellis his house to the churche', suggesting that he may have run some sort of building supplies business. Minor canon Robert Townsend, meanwhile, illegally sub-let a house to more tenants than it could decently accommodate, forcing them to steal wood in order to keep warm.[37] Complaint was made that services at Rochester Cathedral were handicapped because 'certain of the singing men be pursers of the Queenes ships'.[38] Simon Moss, a lay clerk of Norwich Cathedral, was dismissed in 1604, 'for that he had erected an alehowse without license within the precin[c]t of this churche', although he was reinstated on his submission four years later. Roger Rugg, a vicar choral of Wells, was similarly ordered in 1591 to 'surcease from keeping an ale house and from selling of ale any longer'.[39] The will of William Cooper (lay clerk of Ely, 1542–80) mentioned chests and tubs 'in the shopp', suggesting that he probably engaged in retailing of some other kind.[40] Brian Crosby has shown that choirmen employed by Durham Cathedral between c. 1608 and the Civil War practised a variety of trades: George Barcroft was an innkeeper, John Davies an apothecary, Nicholas Sheffield a carpenter and Richard Smith a barber. William Cokey, also of Durham, was a pawnbroker on a large scale. On his death in 1634, he was owed more than £180, including 20s by lay clerk Henry Palmer 'for which a rug is pawnd' and a similar sum by choirmaster Richard Hutchinson 'upon a pawne'.[41]

Almost all studies of cathedral choirmen from the sixteenth century to the present day have emphasised the painful inadequacy of the stipends which they were paid. The poverty under which the singingmen laboured, it has frequently been said, actively discouraged high-calibre musicians from joining cathedral choirs, making it virtually

[35] Oxford, Bodleian Library, MS Tanner 220, fols. 119r, 120r (transcript generously provided by Dr Ian Atherton).

[36] R. Culmer, *Cathedral Newes from Canterbury: Shewing the Canterburian Cathedrall to bee in an Abbey-like, Corrupt and Rotten Condition, which Cals for a Speedy Reformation, or Dissolution* (London, 1644), pp. 2, 19.

[37] W. T. Mellows (ed.), *Peterborough Local Administration. Parochial Government from the Reformation to the Revolution 1541–1689: Minutes and Accounts of the Feoffees and Governors of the City Lands with Supplementary Documents*, Northamptonshire Record Society 10 (Northampton, 1937), pp. 30–1, 64; Mellows and Gifford (eds.), *The Dean and Chapter as Lords of the City*, pp. 71, 90, 97.

[38] WAM Muniment Book 15, fol. 124r.

[39] J. F. Williams and B. Cozens-Hardy (eds.), *Extracts from the Two Earliest Minute Books of the Dean and Chapter of Norwich Cathedral, 1566–1649*, Norfolk Record Society 24 (Norwich, 1953), pp. 41–2; Historical Manuscripts Commission, *Calendar of the Manuscripts of the Dean and Chapter of Wells*, 2 vols. (London, 1914), vol. II, p. 321.

[40] Ely Consistory Court Probate Materials C:17:70, fol. 170v, Cambridgeshire County Record Office, Cambridge.

[41] B. Crosby, 'The Choral Foundation of Durham Cathedral, c. 1350–c. 1650', Ph.D. thesis, 2 vols., Durham University (1992), vol. II, pp. 16, 41, 106, 114; DCD original will and inventory 'William Cockey' (1634).

impossible to attain high standards of music or behaviour. The prebendaries of Winchester Cathedral admitted in 1637 that the choir's stipends were 'so small that we can hardly get men of an indifferent ability to accept of the places, or to continue in it when they are admitted'.[42] Archbishop Laud, meanwhile, wrote to Norwich Cathedral to state his belief that a failure to increase choir stipends would leave the minor canons 'destitute', would 'utterly overthrowe the quire service' and would make it impossible for the cathedral 'to reteine either voices or skill'.[43] In more recent times, Peter le Huray concluded that while the impact of Puritanism was one cause of a 'decline in musical standards', there was 'some other and equally potent cause . . . [namely] inflation'. Over the long term, le Huray believed, the fact that 'standards of musicianship and conduct were often found wanting' was 'hardly surprising'.[44]

Strictly speaking, it may be true to say that the stipends of cathedral choirmen in the period under discussion were grossly inadequate to support standards of excellence in musical performance. However, failure to consider evidence of the additional sources of income to which most choirmen had access can lead the researcher seriously astray in his or her bid to understand how cathedral music functioned at this time. It needs to be recognised that some of the primary sources which seem to indicate significant poverty among choirmen or disastrously low standards in the performance of liturgy contain their own hidden agenda and are difficult to interpret. The anonymous Caroline tract quoted near the beginning of this essay is well-informed and factually accurate, but is also a highly partisan piece of writing which needs to be read in the context of Laudian attempts to give a higher status to cathedral worship if it is to be properly understood. Similar understanding needs to be given to other authors who took up their pens to defend the choirs in the sixteenth and seventeenth centuries. Church music at this time was viewed not so much as an art form, but as an expression of theological truths. As such, the fate of the choirs was inextricably bound up in much broader battles being fought between different factions of the church in England. Mention of the singingmen was more a way of scoring propaganda points than a carefully reasoned analysis of their socio-economic problems and the fact that choirmen were able to earn extra money to supplement low stipends was just one of the things which writers launching an attack on sacrilegious 'Puritan' influences in the Church wilfully ignored.

This is not to deny that a few singingmen genuinely suffered desperate poverty. Richard Mason, vicar choral of Wells Cathedral, 'dyed so poore and left his wife in such poor estat that she could not paye for his grave, ringyng the bells, and other requisites for his funerall' in 1612. Mark Holdred, minor canon and Master of Ely Grammar School (1598–1604), was imprisoned for debt, while in Wales, in 1625, 'John Price, clerk, one of the singing men at St Assaph, was buried within night, by reasons of debts and executions'. In Durham, rising food prices following a failed harvest, probably in 1592, were enough to push lay clerk William Harrison beyond his means and he was forced to petition the dean and chapter for a loan of three pounds, in consideration of 'his present great need, occasyoned as well by reason of the mayteyning of his great chardge of

---

[42] W. R. W. Stephens and F. T. Madge (eds.), *Documents Relating to the History of the Cathedral Church of Winchester in the Seventeenth Century*, Hampshire Record Society (London, 1897), p. 21.

[43] Simpson (ed.), *Registrum Statutorum*, pp. 420–1.

[44] P. le Huray, *Music and the Reformation in England 1549–1660*, revised edition (London, 1978), pp. 39, 41. For a similar analysis, see W. Woodfill, *Musicians in English Society from Elizabeth I to Charles I* (Princeton, 1953), pp. 135–44.

familie, as also by the present dearth of victualls'.[45] However, this sort of poverty was not typical. Such acute want was the result of unusual personal misfortune or recklessness, not inadequate stipends. Probate evidence, for instance, throws up examples of choirmen who were wealthy to put alongside those who are known to have lived in poverty. John Gibbs, Master of the Choristers first at Westminster Abbey and then at St Paul's Cathedral, left £610 in liquid assets alone on his death in 1624. Richard Base, a lay singingman, was in a position to bequeath his heirs a number of houses in Arundel and Chichester in 1570, while Thomas Harrison, the lay clerk and petty-school master of Durham, left his two sons £100 each and his two daughters £80 in 1582.[46] Another source, meanwhile, claimed in 1634 that lay clerk Richard Jackson of Bristol was 'reputed to be able to dispend £200 *per annum*'.[47]

The majority of choirmen, of course, were neither as poor as the unfortunates nor as rich as the fortunates, but occupied the middle ground where earned income from the cathedral and (for example) a curacy or a small shop was generally enough to make ends meet, with perhaps a little to spare. Comparative analysis suggests that a choirman's stipend by itself cannot have been considered a living. Most lay clerks earned in the region of £6 13s 4d a year (a sum which remained unchanged despite continuous, and sometimes acute, price-inflation in the period covered by this essay), whereas even an unskilled labourer might hope to take home between £7 and £10. Minor canons were a little better paid, earning about £10 a year in the late sixteenth and early seventeenth centuries, but even this put them on a par only with a semi-skilled worker and decidedly near the bottom of the clerical income scale.[48] Despite this, while cathedrals occasionally complained of problems recruiting singers of quality to their choirs, on the whole even the poorer institutions found it possible to fill vacant stalls without undue difficulty. The conclusion must be that while the stipends on offer were insufficient to support men in full-time service at a cathedral, they were attractive enough when understood as payment for approximately four hours work a day, with the opportunity to 'moonlight' for another employer the rest of the time.

One consequence of this was to make cathedral music a trade in which the employees had considerable power to dictate their own conditions of employment. Many choirs suffered badly from absenteeism among the choirmen, a reflection of the governing chapters' inability to enforce attendance. Prebendary Robert Swift of Durham wrote to Bishop Pilkington in 1568 to complain that, of the minor canons, George Winter was 'contynewally absent' and Thomas Pentland, John Brown and Thomas Matthew were 'aweay on Sundayes and holydayes' (precisely the days on which a full choir was most needed) 'so the quere dekayeth'.[49] Priest-vicar Godfrey Blaxton of Chichester spelt out the reality of the situation with even greater clarity in the course of an episcopal visitation in 1622. If

[45] *Calendar of the Manuscripts of the Dean and Chapter of Wells*, p. 364; D. M. Owen and D. Thurley (eds.), *The King's School Ely: a Collection of Documents Relating to the History of the School and its Scholars*, Cambridge Antiquarian Record Society 5 (Cambridge, 1982), p. 4; D. R. Thomas (ed.), *Y Cwtta Cyfarwdd: 'The Chronicle Written by the Famous Clarke, Peter Roberts', Notary Public, For the Years 1607–1646* (London, 1883), p. 104; DCD Miscellaneous Charter 3247.

[46] London Guildhall Library, MS 25,626/4, fol. 241v; WSRO Dean's Peculiar Probate Register (STD II) vol. II (MF 229), fols. 58r–60r; J. C. Hodgson (ed.), *Wills and Inventories from the Registry at Durham*, Surtees Society 112 part 3 (1906), pp. 93–4.

[47] Historical Manuscripts Commission, *Fourth Report of the Royal Commission on Historical Manuscripts. Part I. Report and Appendix* (London, 1874), p. 143.

[48] For the basis of these assertions, see Saunders, 'English Cathedral Choirs and Choirmen', pp. 160–1.

[49] WAM Muniment Book 14, fol. 54v.

he were bound to full residence at the cathedral, he stated, then 'the service of the quier is rather a servitude . . . the wages & maynteynaunce but smale if not helped by some other benefice, as we have ever been'. Addressing his bishop directly, he wrote that

> for myne owne particulare, I freely professe to your Lordship that I cannot *sanâ conscientiâ* leave both my [parochial] cures of soules to singe in the quier, where is noe sutch chardge. And I hope that your Lordship, with the Deane & Chapter . . . will not enjoyne me to sutch a continuall attendaunce, but that I shall have that liberty which I have ever had, to attend my course in the quyer for my weeke & give all attendaunce at other tymes which I can . . . Which, if it may not be, rather then I will be non resident from both my cures, let me have my stall wages & other dues to me . . . payed to me . . . & I will noe longer be an unprofitable member of the church, but will rathar resigne.[50]

This was the *quid pro quo* which enabled cathedral choirs to continue functioning when there was no will to find the money to pay the choirmen properly. The singers insisted on the freedom to take other work and, if necessary, to give their primary loyalties to an economic community outside the cathedral. The cathedral chapters, in exchange, were implicitly absolved from many of their pre-Reformation paternalist responsibilities towards the choirmen, and were no longer obliged to pay a living-wage. While chapters were frequently sympathetic in cases of misfortune, coping with poverty resulting from a failure to find additional employment became, ultimately, a choirman's own responsibility.

Viewed in this light, choir stipends were perhaps not unreasonable. Choirmen were paid as if they were still the celibate priests of earlier centuries. A single, somewhat ascetic choirman content to live in the cramped quarters which went with his post might just about have survived on his bare stipend, even in the 1630s. A man married with children and obliged to find more suitable accommodation, however, could not and was not expected to do so. To make ends meet, the vast majority of choirmen found additional employment – it was a matter of necessity. In their favour, though, was the fact that a choirman's job in the reformed Church of England was not the full-time occupation it had once been. The liturgical changes of the Reformation had drastically reduced the choirs' duties, meaning that, in effect, choirmen were now paid a part-time salary for a part-time job. Thus for some choirmen, singing was now no more than a sideline which fitted in conveniently with their other commitments, allowing them to capitalise on musical skills and still keep fingers in other pies. For the majority of choirmen, a post in a cathedral choir was a more significant part of their budget, offering a reliable income for relatively light duties and the freedom to supplement that basic stipend from other sources of income. Like modern lay clerks, cathedral choirmen of the early modern period were not full-time 'professional' musicians and to get a complete picture of their working lives we should see them as fully integrated members of the urban societies in which the cathedrals were situated. The majority of choirmen were born, brought up and worked as members of a town or city community, and while they may have had close connections with the islands of legal and political independence which the cathedrals represented, they never ceased to be part of wider society. For many reasons, including economic ones, the cathedrals could hardly have functioned any other way.

[50] WSRO MS Ep I/20/10, answers of Godfrey Blaxton.

CHAPTER FOURTEEN

URBAN MUSICAL LIFE IN THE EUROPEAN COLONIES: EXAMPLES FROM SPANISH AMERICA, 1530–1650

EGBERTO BERMÚDEZ

The process of Spanish settlement in America was primarily an urban enterprise. New cities were founded and existing ones rebuilt in the early sixteenth century and urban institutions such as *cabildos* and *audiencias* were established to regulate the social and economic life of the colonies (see Illustration 14.1).[1] In early colonial society, Spanish settlers, government agents and military officers coexisted with a few black African slaves and an immense Amerindian population which in a few decades came into full contact, sometimes conflicting and violent, with mainstream European culture. Moreover, these urban societies and their culture were the main contexts in which economic relationships between the city and the surrounding territories were formed.[2]

Colonial administration in America was consolidated in the period between the promulgation of the *Leyes Nuevas* of 1542 and the *Ordenanzas* issued by Philip II in 1573. Political and legal rationalisation was achieved during this time by the reorganisation of the *Consejo de Indias* (Council of the Indies) and the Crown took control of the church administration through the *Regio Patronato*. This climate of reorganisation witnessed the growth and expansion of the urban frontier and the subsequent foundation of city institutions which had an impact on musical life and which thus created a market for professional musicians.

State control of the church was reinforced by the Counter-Reformation programme which was used as a powerful ideological tool by Philip II to establish his Universal Monarchy. The prestige of the church as the cultural centre and as the fundamental axis of the Spanish monarchy's policies were factors which helped to strengthen musical activities both in Spain and in America.[3] The regulations issued at the Council of Trent in 1563 proposed a systematic use of images, theatre, music and public festivities as a medium of propaganda. Thus art, music and spectacle were not to be experienced solely by the elites

---

[1] *cabildo* – municipal council; *audiencia* – an advisory body to a regional chief executive in the Spanish colonies.

[2] For a general historic overview see G. Pendle, *A History of Latin America* (Harmondsworth, 1969); M. A. Burkholder and L. L. Johnson, *Colonial Latin America*, 3rd edn (Oxford, 1998); S. J. and B. Stein, *The Colonial Heritage of Latin America* (London and New York, 1970); L. S. Hoberman and S. M. Socolow (eds.), *Cities and Society in Colonial Latin America* (Albuquerque, 1986). See also R. Stevenson, *Music in Aztec and Inca Territory* (Berkeley, 1968); *Music in Mexico: a Historical Survey* (New York, 1952).

[3] The details of these demographic, economic and political processes are discussed by J. Reglá, 'La época de los tres primeros Austrias', in J. Vicens Vives (ed.), *Historia Social y Económica de España y América*, 5 vols. (Barcelona, 1974), vol. III, pp. 3–317.

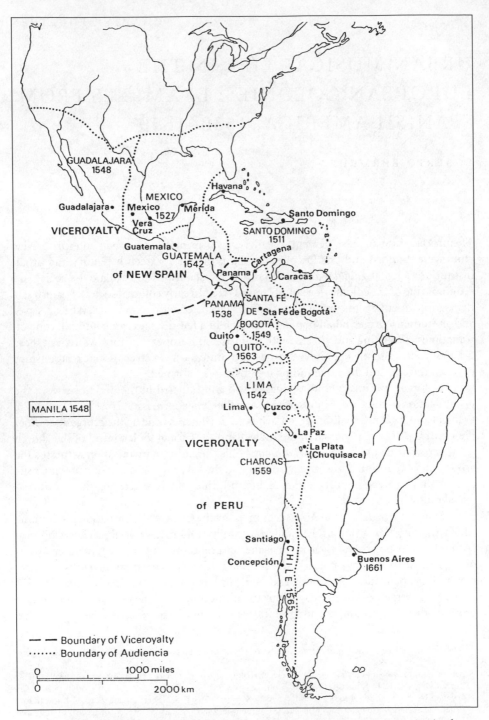

14.1   Urban centres, *audiencia* districts and vice-royalties in Latin America in the
       sixteenth and seventeenth centuries; F. Morales Padrón, *Historia general de
       América*, 2nd edn (Madrid, 1975), p. 391.

but were also to be used as a tool to indoctrinate the masses in the Catholic faith. This conversionary zeal and the propagandistic use of music paved the way for the development of the religious villancico, a form that in spite of its courtly origins gained popular acceptance in Charles V's reign and was included in the Counter-Reformation programme of Philip II.[4]

This chapter will explore the musical culture that developed in Spanish-American cities during 150 years of colonisation. Many documents have survived from this period, including music manuscripts, church records, legal and administrative accounts, notarial documents and historical narratives. These allow us to examine many aspects of musical culture in both sacred and secular contexts. Moreover, the source survival is sufficiently rich so as to allow an examination and comparison of these myriad aspects of music history in a variety of urban centres: the colonial cities initially founded in the region of Tierra Firme (Spanish Main), relatively marginal communities (socially, culturally and geographically) such as those in the Nuevo Reino de Granada (Santa Fe de Bogotá, Tunja and Cartagena), and culturally more fertile societies such as Mexico City (former capital of the Aztec empire and from 1521 capital of the vice-royalty of New Spain) and Lima (capital of the vice-royalty of Peru).

Owing to its strategic situation (between the unknown South American mainland and the settlements in the Caribbean islands of Santo Domingo, Cuba and Puerto Rico) the region of Tierra Firme (covering the northern coast of Colombia, Venezuela and Panama) was intensely urbanised. The earliest cities to be founded were Santa María la Antigua (1513), Panama (1518) and Santa Marta (1525). During the first phase of colonial administration, members of the lesser nobility and middle classes were usually appointed as governors of these earliest urban settlements. They imitated the ceremonial trappings of the upper classes and thus artillery, banners, flags and fanfares on trumpets, drums, fifes and other wind instruments were used by them as symbols of prestige and power whenever they appeared in public (see Illustration 14.2). These elements were present at the arrivals of new governors in Santa Marta in 1528 and 1535, and in the expedition to the Rio de la Plata in 1535 (to found Buenos Aires) the musicians present included Spanish, Italian and French musicians performing on drums, trumpets and fifes.[5] Music was also performed for the governors in the privacy of their own households and most maintained a group of minstrels who played instruments like the harp, pipe and tabor, bagpipe and the Moorish xabeba. In 1514, for example, such a group was present in the retinue of Pedrarias Davila, a nobleman from Avila who was governor of Castilla de Oro.[6]

The societies based in the new Spanish-American cities offered unusual opportunities for social advancement to professional musicians who would otherwise have been, in a purely Spanish context, of lower status. For example, the drum and trumpet players who came to Santa Marta in 1535 who had accompanied Gonzalo Jiménez de Quesada in

[4] P. R. Laird, *Towards a History of the Spanish Villancico* (Warren, MI, 1997), p. 19.
[5] Juan de Castellanos, *Elegías de Varones Ilustres de Indias*, 4 vols. (Bogotá, 1955), vol. II, pp. 328–9, 412–13; P. Boyd-Bowman, *Indice Geobiográfico de cuarenta mil pobladores españoles de América en el siglo XVI*, 2 vols. (Mexico, 1968), vol. II: 1520–1539, pp. 140, 179, 220, 257, 395, 398–9, 404; J. Friede, *Los Welser en la Conquista de Venezuela* (Caracas and Madrid, 1961), p. 341 and plate 19.
[6] E. Bermúdez, 'Historia de la Música en Colombia. Música Indígena, tradicional y Cultura Musical durante el periodo colonial. Siglos XVI al XVIII, Bogotá', unpublished MS, 1995, p. 173; Castellanos, Elegías, vol. II, p. 329, and R. Stevenson, 'La música en la catedral de México: El siglo de fundación', *Heterofonia* 100–101 (1989), p. 15.

14.2   Military music – fife and drum; British Library, Add. MS 15217, fol. 35v.

the founding of Santa Fe in 1538 became permanent residents in the town and ultimately achieved a relatively high social status for they obtained land and free Indian labourers.[7]

Middle-class royal officers and members of the lesser nobility stationed in the cities who were involved in establishing the new administration maintained the native traditions of Spanish music-making with which they were familiar, employing minstrels in their households or playing themselves as amateurs. In 1509, one of the conquerors of Tierra Firme was described as a *hidalgo* (untitled noble) with the learning and social graces of a Renaissance courtier as well as an 'accomplished vihuela performer'.[8] Similarly, the middle-class citizens who settled in some of these new cities enjoyed singing and playing like their counterparts in the Spanish cities back home. 'Romances' and 'coplas', to be accompanied by the vihuela and guitar, were often sung by these individuals and, despite royal prohibition, printed booklets containing this repertory were exported to America.[9] These cheap publications were present in Santa Fe in 1548 and in Tunja in 1552 along with jew's harps which were probably sold to the native Indians (and were still being sold, for example, in Mexico, in the later sixteenth century).[10]

[7] J. Friede, *Documentos Inéditos para la Historia de Colombia*, 10 vols. (Bogotá, 1960), vol. IX, p. 66, and J. I. Avellaneda, *La expedición de Gonzalo Jiménez de Quesada al Mar del Sur y la creación del Nuevo Reino de Granada* (Bogotá, 1995), p. 241.

[8] B. de las Casas, *Historia de las Indias*, 3 vols. (Mexico and Buenos Aires, 1951), vol. II, p. 374, and Bermúdez, 'Historia', p. 175.   [9] I. Leonard, *Los libros del Conquistador* (Mexico, 1959), p. 88.

[10] Bermúdez, 'Historia', p. 177; ARB, Histórico, 3, fol. 229v; 4, fol. 172r. Leonard, *Los libros*, p. 325, and J. Sarno, 'El tráfico de instrumentos y libros musicales de España al Nuevo Mundo a través de los documentos del Archivo General de Indias de Sevilla: notas para el comienzo de una investigación', *The Brussels Museum of Musical Instruments Bulletin* 16 (1986), p. 103.

In the light of these examples, it is not surprising that guitars and vihuelas were the main types of instrument exported to the New World. In 1523, for example, thirty guitars and thirteen vihuelas were taken by a merchant to Santo Domingo and Puerto Rico.[11] There are references to their use in instrumental pieces and as accompaniment to the vocal music sung by the inhabitants of Nueva Cadiz de Cubagua and Margarita, wealthy cities built in the 1520s on two small islands off the coast of South America which were economically reliant on the rich pearl banks surrounding their shores.[12]

The *conquistadores* (military conquerors) and their families were very fond of luxury goods – including musical instruments such as virginals or harpsichords – the possession of which was an indication of social status. These instruments are known to have belonged to individuals in the coastal cities of Colombia in 1542 and later in Tunja and Santa Fe.[13] In 1582 Francisco de Olaya, heir of one of the most important conquistadores of Santa Fe, owned a 'clavicordio grande de dos ordenes' (probably a 'double virginal').[14] Two more instruments of this type are found in Tunja as late as 1613. Some of the members of the elite had other instruments such as harps and vihuelas and these were also occasionally owned by those who inhabited the lands outside the city (a vihuela, for instance, is found in a country home in Iza, located to the north-east of Tunja).[15] The middle classes also possessed and played the musical instruments popular at that time as can be seen from the following examples. In Tunja in the 1570s some functionaries, such as notaries, possessed vihuelas, guitars or other stringed instruments and one of them requested a rebec and a 'good guitar' which was imported by merchants from Spain in 1576. Artisans and other professionals also possessed and played musical instruments: in 1580 a silversmith bought a guitar and a tailor owned a guitar and some books which included an edition of Alciato's *Emblems*.[16] In Cartagena in 1574 even a physician of probable New Christian ancestry possessed a harp and he himself indicates that he used it to accompany his own singing and that of his black female slave.[17]

It was not only the laity who participated in private music-making; the clergy also took part in this activity. Thus in Santa Fe in 1631 two vihuelas were purchased by two priests, one of whom was the curate rector of the cathedral. In 1633 another of the cathedral officers owned a guitar and a harp and in the same year one of his colleagues also had these instruments in addition to a vihuela and a lute. The ownership of such instruments was common amongst members of the higher echelons of the ecclesiastical hierarchy. For example, at his death in 1688 the archbishop had in his home a positive organ, several organ pipes, a harpsichord and a vihuela.[18]

---

[11] Sarno, 'El tráfico', p. 101.   [12] Castellanos, *Elegías*, vol. I, p. 597.

[13] Archivo de Protocolos de Sevilla, *Catalogo de los fondos americanos del Archivo de Protocolos de Sevilla* (Seville, 1932), vol. III, p. 61.

[14] AGN, Notaria 1a, 12, fol. 312r. A double virginal made in 1581 was found in Cuzco, Peru and was donated to the Metropolitan Museum of Art in 1929. It is possible that the instrument had been in Cuzco since the early sixteenth century and is likely to have been similar to (or may even have been) the instrument mentioned in the above quotation. See L. Libin, *Keyboard Instruments* (New York, 1989), pp. 14–15. See Beryl Kenyon de Pascual, 'Clavicordios and Clavichords in Sixteenth-Century Spain', *Early Music* 20:4 (1992), pp. 611–12.

[15] ARB, Histórico, 14, fol. 8v; AGN, Testamentarías, Boyacá, 14, fol. 759r, and Juicios Civiles, Boyacá, 3, fol. 175v.

[16] ARB, Histórico, 8, fol. 72v; Histórico, 10, fols. 42r, 278r, 481v; Histórico, 13, fol. 19r; Histórico, 14r, fol. 147r; AGN, Juicios Civiles, Boyacá, 3, fol. 175v.

[17] AGI, Justicia, 38, 1, fol. 9r, and Salamanca, University Library, MS 2208, Lib. 2, Cap. 9, fols. 149v and 351v.

[18] AGN, Notaria 3a, 32, fols. 118r, 39r and 208r; Conventos, 69, fol. 575r, Anexo Eclesiástico, 2, fol. 81v.

Owing to the presence of a larger middle class (consisting of merchants, traders and artisans), Santa Fe seems to have been a more open and flexible society than Tunja. One manifestation of this was the fact that a much wider variety of citizens from all social groups (including native Indians and people of African descent) possessed musical instruments. In 1574 and 1609 carpenters are documented as owning a vihuela and a small viol and in 1614 a free mulatto tailor (i.e. the offspring of black and white parents) owned a guitar which came into his possession in the dowry of his wife, who was of the same caste.[19] In 1633 a Christianised Indian, who belonged to several confraternities, owned a guitar.[20] Members of these social groups were sometimes even able to purchase expensive instruments and a transaction in which a blacksmith purchased a 'clavidordio' from a merchant at great cost exists from 1584.[21] Some of these citizens were taught to play their instruments by music and dance masters.[22] A music master is documented in Santa Fe in 1585 and dancing masters were in Tunja and Pamplona before 1571 and in Santa Fe in 1631.[23] Members of the upper classes also seem to have been taught by competent amateurs. A contract from 1629 made between two wealthy residents of Santa Fe stipulates that one individual was to instruct the other in plainchant, polyphony and performance on the harp.[24]

The presence of diverse ethnic groups in Spanish-American society offered many possibilities for cultural interaction between Amerindians, Spaniards and African slaves. In 1532 Indian chieftains visited the Spanish governor in Acla as part of the exploratory voyages to the Urabá Gulf and were lavishly received. During this encounter, a group of African slave musicians belonging to the governor were made to sing, dance and play on drums, cymbals, a frame drum and a flute. Male and female members of the Governor's household who witnessed the reception also sang and danced, possibly accompanied by the same instruments and thereafter all the Indians danced in their own fashion. At the end of the evening the slaves performed their own form of acrobatic dancing.[25]

A sizeable number of African slaves was already present on the Colombian coast around the same date. In Cartagena in 1546 male and female Africans were lured by musical means to hear the morning church services.[26] By the 1570s the slave population in the city was probably very high, for in 1573 the authorities prohibited them from wantonly congregating in the streets to perform songs and dances accompanied by drums; instead their behaviour was to be regulated and they were to meet only at specified times and in particular places.[27] Similarly in Santa Fe the Indian traditions, their songs, dances and feasts had been severely repressed since the establishment of the *Real Audiencia* in 1555. However, Indian music and dances did continue, for in 1591 a patrol reported that male and female Indians had been caught drinking, singing and dancing in the house of a barber in a manner comparable to the non-Christian Indians.[28]

The first cathedrals of South America were established in the cities of the northern coast of Colombia and Panama in the 1510s, and in the next two decades some were

[19] AGN, Juicios Civiles Cundinamarca, 10, fol. 434r; Notaria 1a, 31, fol. 338r; Notaria 3a, 4, fol. 167r.
[20] AGN, Notaria 3a, 37, fol. 67r.   [21] AGN, Notaria 1a, 11, fol. 232v.
[22] G. Saldivar, *Historia de la Música en México (Epocas Precortesiana y Colonial)* (Mexico, 1934), pp. 161–3.
[23] Bermúdez, 'Historia', p. 178, and U. Rojas, *Corregidores y Justicias Mayores en Tunja y su provincia desde la fundación de la ciudad, 1539–1817* (Tunja, 1962), pp. 111–13, and AGN, Notaria 3a, 33, fol. 161r.
[24] AGN, Notaria 1a, 41, fol. 6r.   [25] Bermúdez, 'Historia', p. 241.
[26] R. Stevenson, 'The First New World Composers: Fresh Data from Peninsular Archives', *Journal of the American Musicological Society* 23:1 (1970), p. 99.   [27] Bermúdez, 'Historia', p. 56.   [28] *Ibid.*, p. 232.

founded in Santa Marta, Coro, Cartagena, Quito and Popayán. In terms of their ecclesiastical organisation and financial provision for the performance of the liturgy all followed the Spanish model. These early churches took time to be completed and the development of their musical life was often slow. To a certain extent this was owing to the establishment of strong local government bodies (*Audiencias Reales*) and the implementation of the Counter-Reformation programme. In 1537, for example, the cathedral of Cartagena was already a bishopric see but it still only had a thatched roof building. Its *chantre* (precentor) was Juan Perez Materano (*c.* 1505–1561), a musician who was compared to Josquin by his pupil Castellanos.[29] Between 1541 and 1545 he became a canon, treasurer and dean and in 1559 he obtained a royal privilege to print a book he had written on polyphony and plainchant (*canto de órgano y canto llano*). Had it actually been printed, this book would have been one of the first publications on music in the New World.[30] In 1546 Cuzco Cathedral owned a number of books of plainchant and polyphony but the office of chapelmaster was not formally established until a few decades later.[31] Initially the cathedrals were staffed by immigrant Spanish, although native Indians soon began to be appointed as instrumentalists, as in Mexico Cathedral in 1543 (Illustration 14.3).

The cathedral of Santa Fe has one of the most complete music archives in the Americas, which provides a great deal of evidence concerning the sacred repertory used there in the period under consideration.[32] The earliest music, probably in use in the late 1570s, consisted of Masses and *Magnificat* settings by Cristóbal de Morales as well as *Magnificat* settings by Rodrigo de Ceballos.[33] Music for Vespers (mostly by Spanish composers, including the only known works of Gutierre Fernández Hidalgo) and Compline (mainly anonymous) survive from about 1625.[34] The only known complete version of the *Magnificat* settings of Ceballos also survives in this archive. It was copied around 1830 and is evidence of the continued popularity of this repertory until the end of the colonial period.[35] Several complete and fragmentary European printed editions also formed part of the earliest repertory, such as Francisco Guerrero's 1582 *Liber secundum Missarum*, Tomás Luis de Victoria's *Motecta* of 1583 and Palestrina's *Hymni totius anni*. The edition of 1584 by the Spanish composer Nicasio Zorita contained hymns, motets and Masses and this was the ideal liturgical complement to the books mentioned above. The plainchant repertory of the cathedral appears to have been renewed between 1606 and 1613 when thirty-two volumes were copied and printed chant books were imported from Spain.[36] The polyphonic repertory of the cathedral was renewed and augmented when, in a transaction involving the Colegio del Patriarca in Valencia, single parts in manuscript and bound (probably printed) volumes of polyphony containing music by well-known Spanish and Italian composers were brought to Santa Fe in 1626. Compared

[29] *Ibid.*, pp. 81–2, and Castellanos, *Elegías*, vol. III, p. 18. [30] Stevenson, 'First New World', p. 98.

[31] Stevenson, 'La música en la catedral de México', pp. 14, 16, and 'Cuzco Cathedral: 1546–1750', *Inter-American Music Review* 2:2 (Spring–Summer 1980), pp. 1–3. For the cathedral in Tunja see Castellanos, *Elegías*, vol. III, p. 245.

[32] R. Stevenson, 'The Bogotá Music Archive', *Journal of the American Musicological Society* 15:3 (1962), pp. 292–315, and *Renaissance and Baroque Musical Sources in the Americas* (Washington, 1970).

[33] Found in choirbooks LC1. I use here my own classification for the choirbooks, see Bermúdez, 'Historia', pp. 111–15.

[34] Choirbooks LC2 and LC3. Some of it may have been written by Alonso Garzón de Tahuste, Fernández Hidalgo's pupil and successor who worked at Santa Fé cathedral. [35] Choirbook LC4.

[36] J. Restrepo Posada, 'Los libros corales de la Catedral', *Boletín Cultural y Bibliográfico. Biblioteca Luis Angel Arango* 5:10 (1962), pp. 1257–61, and AGN, Fabricas de Iglesias, 10, fol. 924v.

14.3 Singers and wind players at church, *c.* 1600; Felipe Huamán Poma de Ayala, *Nueva Corónica y Buen Gobierno*, Copenhagen, Royal Library, MS 2232, p. 666.

to the collections at Mexico, Puebla and Guatemala, the repertory of Latin polyphony at Santa Fe was modest, probably because it was formed under stringent economic conditions.[37]

Between 1573 and 1590 the performing forces at Santa Fe cathedral chapel were very modest. In 1581, between seven and ten adult singers and at least four choirboys from the seminary college, in addition to the organist, were employed.[38] Around the turn of the century some instrumentalists are mentioned (see below). In 1605 the new archbishop, Lobo Guerrero, increased the income of the cathedral and appointed four choral chaplains and singers. Between 1609 and 1633, however, there were only five singers, all of them priests: one was described as a *tiple* (falsettist), another fulfilled the tasks of succentor and chaplain and yet another performed all these duties plus that of acting chapelmaster. This situation remained unchanged until around 1648, the time of the arrival of chapelmaster José Cascante (*c.* 1620–1702).

Cathedrals assumed an importance in New World cities for obvious reasons. However, even parish churches became prominent musical centres in some urban contexts. In 1575 the Tunja parish church of Santiago, despite being physically unfinished, was said to be the most important of the kingdom and one of its vicars, Castellanos, indicates that he had voices and instruments at his service.[39]

Once the Spaniards had begun to colonise the New World several distinct social groups – which were often in conflict – emerged. *Criollos* were individuals born to Spanish parents in the New World; *peninsulares* were Spaniards born in Iberia; and *mestizos* were illegitimate sons born to Indian women and Spanish soldiers or *conquistadores*.[40] *Mestizos* were often harassed by Spaniards on racial grounds. For example, Gonzalo García Zorro (*c.* 1548–1617), a *mestizo* son of a conquistador, was nominated to become a canon in Santa Fe in 1580. Initially rejected for the post by the cathedral *Cabildo* (council) on the grounds of his racial origins he only took possession of his canonry in 1599 after a long legal battle.[41] This conflict arose because of issues related to class and status interests; it also reflected internal conflict in the church itself, between the cathedral chapter and the episcopal or archiepiscopal authorities.[42]

The growth and prosperity which occurred in the first two decades of Philip II's reign in the mid-sixteenth century created a positive climate for the development and expansion of ecclesiastical urban musical activities both in Spain and the New World.[43] The clergy became more influential in the establishment of social and cultural institutions in the Americas. A strong and thriving church offered musicians improved professional, social and economic opportunities. The American careers of the Spanish composers Hernando Franco (1532–85) and Gutierre Fernández Hidalgo (1543–1623) exemplify the mobility, dynamism and opportunities available in Spanish musical spheres which were a direct consequence of this expansion. Franco arrived in Mexico in 1554 with his patron who had been instrumental in helping him gain a musical education in Segovia and Salamanca. Franco became chapelmaster in Guatemala around 1571

[37] Stevenson, *Renaissance and Baroque*, pp. 65–106, 131–7, 210–20.   [38] Bermúdez, 'Historia', pp. 102–4.
[39] Castellanos, *Elegías*, vol. IV, p. 442, and AGN, Fabricas de Iglesias, 10, fol. 934r.
[40] See also Burkholder and Johnson, *Colonial Latin America*, pp. 195–6.
[41] J. Restrepo Posada, *Cabildo Eclesiástico, Arquidiócesis de Bogotá* (Bogotá, 1971), pp. 35–8.
[42] García Zorro's case was not the first of its type; for others see R. Stevenson, 'Quito Cathedral: Four Centuries', *Inter-American Music Review* 3:1 (1980), p. 21, and *A Guide to Caribbean Music History* (Lima, 1975), p. 53.   [43] Reglá, 'La época', pp. 124–30.

and then went on to reach the same position in Mexico in 1575.[44] Fernández Hidalgo came to America after having worked for ten years in the collegiate church of Talavera de la Reina, his home town in Spain. He arrived at Santa Fe in 1584 and subsequently worked, until his death, as chapelmaster, composer and teacher of counterpoint, chant and composition in the territories of modern Colombia, Ecuador, Peru and Bolivia.[45] At some of the cathedrals in which he worked, Fernández Hidalgo's superior musical abilities caused conflict. In Santa Fe he proved superior to chapelmaster García Zorro and made some harsh comments on his musical abilities when testimonies were gathered during his fight to maintain his canonry. These comments were exploited by the authorities in order to undermine García Zorro's prestige as son of one of the most respected *conquistadores*. That they did this was also a reflection of power struggles within the church itself, mentioned above.[46] When Fernández Hidalgo worked at Quito Cathedral in the late 1580s, he helped to reorganise the cathedral chapel after Lobato's dismissal in 1583.[47] He also helped out in similar ways when he was employed in Cuzco and La Plata.[48] In Lima, Fernández Hidalgo worked briefly at the cathedral and at the Nuestra Señora de la Encarnación convent, whose outstanding musical activities were praised in chronicles written between 1605 and 1639.[49]

Organ-makers and players were certainly present in Santa Fe and Tunja in 1595–96 and 1631, and around 1614–15 an organ is also recorded at the church of Santiago in Tunja (bought from the Monasterio de la Concepción of the same city).[50] In addition to organists, players of shawms, sackbuts, flutes, curtals and other wind instruments played an important role in Spanish religious music and as such developed their own tradition in the New World.[51] In the late 1580s and 1590s services were celebrated at Tunja's main church using voices and instruments and in Santa Fe cathedral Indian *ministriles* were employed.[52] The systematic introduction of *ministriles* into the area came about largely through the establishment of schools at the Indian *doctrinas* (settlements, usually attached to cities, where a church and school for religious indoctrination was established) and missions managed by the Jesuits. Indians and free or enslaved Africans and their descendants were to become the church instrumentalists par excellence during this period. The cathedral, churches and convents in Santa Fe also had African and Creole slave *ministriles* at their service. In 1632 and 1636 slave players of shawms and sackbuts performed at the parish church of San Victorino and the Franciscan convent, and in 1651 the duties of the slave who played the curtal at the cathedral included playing in the morning services on major feast days and on the previous day at Vespers.[53] The music of *ministriles* (particularly shawms) was also part of the academic ceremonial in the recently founded Santa Fe university. In 1639 the parade organised for the inauguration of the

[44] D. Lehnhoff, *Espada y Pentagrama: La música polifónica en la Guatemala del siglo XVI* (Guatemala, 1986), pp. 99–103.

[45] E. Bermúdez, 'Estudio Introductorio', 'Gutierre Fernández Hidalgo. Opera Omnia', unpublished MS (1998), pp. 2–5.   [46] Stevenson, 'First New World', pp. 99–100.   [47] Stevenson, 'Quito', p. 26.

[48] Stevenson, 'Cuzco', p. 4, and Bermúdez, 'Fernández Hidalgo', pp. 2–4.

[49] Bermúdez, 'Fernández Hidalgo'; see also F. García, 'En busca de música colonial sacra en los Conventos de Monjas Limeños', *Boletín de Música. Casa de las Américas* 56 (January–February 1976), pp. 3–4.

[50] AGN, Notaria 2a, 59, fol. 102r, and Notaria 3a, 1631, fols. 1–7, and Fabricas de Iglesias, 10, fol. 925r.

[51] For instrumentalists in Colombia and Bolivia see E. Bermúdez, 'The *Ministriles* Tradition in Latin America. I. South America, 1. The Cases of Santa Fé (Colombia) and La Plata (Bolivia), Seventeenth Century', *Historical Brass Society Journal* 11 (1999), 149–62. For the Spanish tradition see K. Kreitner, 'Minstrels in Spanish Churches', *Early Music* 20:4 (1992), pp. 532–48, and D. Kirk, 'Instrumental Music in Lerma *c.* 1608', *Early Music,* 23:3 (1995), pp. 393–408.   [52] Bermúdez, 'Historia', p. 106.   [53] Bermúdez, '*Ministriles*'.

Dominican university of Santo Tomás contained two groups of *ministriles* on horseback with a full set of shawms and kettledrums who played alternately in antiphonal fashion.[54]

Besides churches, seminary colleges were important cultural institutions in Spanish America and were founded in most cities in the 1570s and 1580s following the instructions issued by the Council of Trent. They employed a rector and several teachers who taught students who intended to become ecclesiastics and included musical instruction as part of their syllabi. In the Colegio Seminario de San Luis established in Santa Fe by Archbishop Luis Zapata de Cárdenas in 1582 for example, students were instructed in grammar, the Indian language (*Muisca*), polyphony and plainchant. As they were sponsored by the archbishop they were also bound to serve at church on major feasts. The political conflict between the archbishop and the *Real Audiencia* affected the college when some students complained in late 1585 about what they considered to be excessive musical duties at the cathedral. Those students were children of *conquistadores* and settlers in the smaller cities in the surroundings of Santa Fe and also young members of the retinue of the *Oidores* (members of the *Audiencia*). It is possible that their parents or tutors viewed their musical commitments as an act of repression by the church authorities in this case represented by Fernández Hidalgo, who was appointed rector of the college upon his arrival in the city in 1584.[55]

Upon the arrival of the Jesuit order and the new archbishop, Bartolomé Lobo-Guerrero, in 1599, the college was reorganised and refounded in 1605 as the Colegio de San Bartolomé. Under the Jesuits, lessons in polyphony and plainchant were maintained and the participation of students at the cathedral services was increased. In the following decades music played a prominent role in the life of the Colegio as is shown by the accounts from 1616 to 1633 which contain payments for singers, shawms, drums and trumpets at major feasts and at the performance of plays with music such as *La Fabula de Orfeo* performed in 1625.

Music education at these colleges was only offered to Spaniards; Indians, Africans and all mixed castes were excluded. The Trent Council regulations were intended to maintain an elite culture and the Jesuit education system emerged as the ideal means by which to achieve that goal. However, in the *Ordenanzas* of 1573 the Crown provided a framework for separate music instruction for these latter groups in *Pueblos de Indios* (urban settlements exclusively populated with Indians), *doctrinas, reducciones* and *misiones* (urban settlements under the sole jurisdiction of the missionary orders).

Although the Franciscan, Dominican and Augustinian friars were in charge of the first attempts at conversion of the *Muisca* population of the territory of Santa Fe and Tunja, the arrival of the Jesuits in the late sixteenth century transformed those tentative approaches into a systematic campaign. By 1606 the Jesuits were managing important *doctrinas* such as Fontibón and Cajicá near Santa Fe and later on, after the establishment of a college in Tunja in 1608, Duitama and Tópaga. The existing legislation of 1573 allowed them to use singers and minstrels of high and low instruments (*música de cantores y ministriles altos y bajos*) to support the conversion programme in Indian towns. The Jesuits firmly believed in the power of music in conversion and frequently used it for this end; in their missions and in Indian towns under their control, the Indians were taught to sing plainchant, polyphony and to play instruments, and they were regularly permitted to perform at church services and festivals. From 1606 onwards Jesuits in

[54] *Ibid.*, and Bermúdez, 'Historia', p. 195.   [55] Bermúdez, 'Historia', p. 103.

charge of Indian towns asked for six *cantores* (musicians) and a music teacher to be provided in each of the *pueblos* to participate in church services, while the law only provided three or four who were exempt from paying the tribute imposed by the Crown.

In 1643 a report from the Jesuit Provincial indicates that in Fontibón an organ, singers and instruments were used in the three polyphonic Masses celebrated weekly. Indeed, inventories of the parish church made in 1639 list a set of viols and cornetts, curtals and three complete sets of shawms. The chapel consisted of a master of music and five *cantores* and none of the choirboys and only one of the instrumentalists is mentioned by name. In Tópaga, another *doctrina* located in the area which became the frontier of expansion for the future missions, a report of 1646 made by the Jesuit priest in charge mentions several musical instruments, including rebecs, viols, soprano lutes, vihuelas and harps (as well as the wind instruments mentioned above). However, it was not only the Jesuits who promoted music for reasons of conversion in their towns and *doctrinas*. In 1639 in Cerinza and Toca (near Tunja and Duitama), the *encomenderos* who obtained *encomiendas* (land, including Indian inhabitants) allowed them to be managed by the Franciscans who encouraged *cantores* to work in these areas under the same conditions as those working in the churches in the *doctrinas*.[56]

In addition to cathedrals and seminaries, convents and monasteries were an important part of the urban musical fabric in certain New World cities. By the second half of the seventeenth century, in Lima and Santa Fe, the convents and monasteries consolidated their musical activities by employing musicians (singers and instrumentalists) attached to the cathedral, who could perform only under special permission. Confraternities (*cofradías*) established both in convents and in churches were also an important source of employment for musicians, usually on a freelance basis. The confraternity of Saint Lucia at the cathedral of Santa Fe included both Indians and freemen or slaves of African descent amongst its membership, and that of Our Lady of Loreto (an Italian Marian devotion established at the Jesuit church in 1625) regularly employed musicians to perform at their feasts and had important Spanish and Creole city notables as members.[57]

Public festivities and plays were important urban cultural events in early modern Spain. They were often organised in connection with the celebration or commemoration of royalty; they were powerful tools of propaganda and made use of a variety of media including allegories, mottoes, sculpture, painting and vocal and instrumental music. Burgundian ceremonial traditions were brought into Spain during Habsburg rule and those same traditions were rapidly implemented in American towns; at the same time the traditions developed in native America began to be assimilated into Spain and Europe.[58] In this context, the Burgundian-style entries and pageants served as a political materialisation of the relationship between the cities and the monarch both in Europe and America.[59]

The urban centres in Spanish America also celebrated events in the life of royalty. In 1556 on the occasion of the proclamation of Philip II as king, the authorities of Tunja

---

[56] Bermúdez, '*Ministriles*', p. 2.   [57] Bermúdez, 'Historia', pp. 187–8.

[58] See A. Sommer-Mathis *et al.*, *El teatro descubre América. Fiestas y teatro en la Casa de Austria (1492–1700)* (Madrid, 1992) and H. Trevor-Roper, *Príncipes y Artistas: Mecenazgo e Ideología en cuatro cortes de los Habsburgo 1517–1623* (Madrid, 1992).

[59] R. Strohm, *Music in Late Medieval Bruges* (Oxford, 1985); Kreitner, 'Minstrels'; and L. Pérez, 'Juglares y ministriles en la procesión del Corpus en Daroca en los siglos XV y XVI', *Nassarre. Revista Aragonesa de Musicología* 6:1 (1990), pp. 85–177.

organised public rejoicing which included jousting, tournaments and processions. Later the same events were again organised headed by the *conquistadores* or *encomenderos* dressed in festive attire including 'masques'. Similar celebrations occurred in 1601 and 1606 to celebrate the accession of Philip III and the birth of his son, the future Philip IV.[60]

Royal funeral services and other occasions of mourning were also important public events. Those held in Santa Fe in 1559 for Emperor Charles V were celebrated with great solemnity as were those in honour of Queen Mary Tudor, wife of Philip of Spain, who died in 1558. Surviving accounts indicate that singers were involved in these events and in 1612 a procession with 'abundant music' and a play were part of the solemnities which commemorated the death of Margaret of Austria.[61] In Santa Fe this event was the subject of a detailed chronicle which describes an elaborate and flamboyant pageant containing the basic ceremonial elements (which had also been staged in Brussels and in other Spanish cities) including the performance of music by Morales and by the local chapel-master Lázaro del Alamo. In Lima, the music of Morales was also part of the repertory employed in the services dedicated to Margaret.[62]

Other public festivities flourished in the more secular and less austere cultural climate of the New World cities. In 1561 the Spanish inhabitants of Santa Fe attended 'bullfights, jousts, masques and Carnival feasts' and a similar entertainment along with *saraos* (dances) was organised in 1583 for the reception of the prelates coming to a council called by the archbishop. The festivities included theatrical performances (*comedias*), probably the first to be performed in the city.[63]

Perhaps the most important of all religious festivals occurring in any of the cities was that of Corpus Christi which was usually celebrated with a pageant which included *tableaux vivants* and masked dances, and many professional musicians participated.[64] In 1585 the council of Tunja organised Corpus Christi celebrations in which the members of the guilds of trades, with their standards, patron saint and dances, were involved. The Indians and people of African descent were also required to participate in Corpus Christi celebrations; in those of 1590 in Tunja, Indian and African dancers participated and the merchants of the main street and other trades organised torch dances.[65] Such festivities were celebrated with greater pomp and circumstance in richer areas of the New World. In Mexico for instance, the first Corpus Christi procession took place in 1526 and continued late into the nineteenth century; it included dances and also music performed on a platform assembled in front of the cathedral for the final *auto sacramental* (theatrical performance with a religious theme).[66] In 1538 Corpus Christi was celebrated in Tlaxcala with music and dance, and a spectacular display with aboriginal costumes and feather-work was also staged at the celebrations for Easter.[67] In Peru, Cuzco and Lima from the mid-sixteenth century, Spanish and Indian dances as well as *tableaux vivants* and *autos*

---

[60] Rojas, *Corregidores*, pp. 29, 236–9.
[61] E. Ortega Ricaurte (ed.), *Libro de acuerdos de la Audiencia Real del Nuevo Reino de Granada 1557–1567* (Bogotá, 1947), p. 139; Bermúdez, 'Historia', p. 194.　　[62] Stevenson, *Aztec and Inca*, pp. 200–3.
[63] L. Fernández de Piedrahita, *Noticia Historial de las Conquistas del Nuevo Reino de Granada (1688)*, 2 vols. (Bogotá, 1973), vol. I, p. 70, and J. Manuel Groot, *Historia Eclesiástica y Civil de Nueva Granada*, 2 vols. (Bogotá, 1956), vol. I, p. 324.
[64] K. Kreitner, 'Music in the Corpus Christi Procession of Fifteenth-Century Barcelona', *Early Music History* 14 (1985), pp. 153–204.
[65] U. Rojas, *El beneficiado don Juan de Castellanos cronista de Colombia y Venezuela* (Tunja, 1958), pp. 132–4, and ARB, Actas del Cabildo, 11 de junio de 1590.
[66] M. Ramos Smith, *La danza en México durante la época colonial* (La Habana, 1979), p. 19.
[67] Stevenson, *Aztec and Inca*, p. 159.

sacramentales were performed for Corpus Christi and other feasts.[68] Villancicos or *chan-zonetas* were often composed for performance before street altars in the Corpus Christi processions and were also performed in various urban churches at Christmas Matins. Their simple musical structure, with popular rhythms and vernacular texts, appealed to a wide audience and they were often used to convey doctrinal ideas to the lower classes and the Indian, African and Creole slave populations in an easy and relaxed fashion.

The presence of Indians parading in the streets wearing native costumes and featherwork was a familiar sight in the colonial cities; but this was merely an exotic element introduced into an urban culture that was mostly shaped by the Spanish, who were the dominant cultural group. Whenever the Indians wanted to celebrate their feasts, which included pageants and parades, they were severely repressed by the Spanish church and civic authorities. In Peru the *taqui onqoy* phenomenon in the mid-1560s well illustrates how a Messianic Indian movement used music and dance elements to recruit followers before finally being dismantled by the authorities in the early 1570s.[69] In the district of Santa Fe something similar occurred in 1563 when the Ubaque chieftain held a festival which coincided with the winter solstice. The pageant included groups from the different Indian towns wearing ritual costumes and masks accompanied by musical instruments (whistles, flutes, wooden and conch shell trumpets, jingles and bells) with organised dancing and the singing of laments using ritual language.[70] Although the authorities had granted permission for this, they started an official enquiry about its proceedings.

As we have seen, music was an integral part of urban culture in Spanish-American cities in the period under scrutiny. The scheme in which it functioned was modelled on Spanish practice but the American circumstances gave it a distinctive character. Acculturation changed some of the schemes while others were maintained. Change and continuity were to become explanatory patterns for Spanish culture and its American versions. In the sixteenth century, urban music-making in Spain and in the Americas was a fully integrated part of European mainstream culture. Following the progressive political and economic decline of Spain, by the end of the seventeenth century it was already a backward and very conservative culture by European standards. In America this process was even more pronounced and by the end of the colonial era, cultural norms were far behind European models. Obsolete musical forms, musical instruments and contexts became identity markers for the culture of peasant, Indian and mixed-race populations of most areas of the Americas, and today these traits of colonial urban musical culture are used as banners for cultural reconstruction and affirmation.

---

[68] G. Lohmann Villena, *Historia del arte dramático en Lima durante el Virreinato, I. Siglos XVI y XVII* (Lima, 1941), pp. 7, 12 and particularly Chapter II.

[69] J. Carlos Estenssoro, 'Los bailes de los Indios y el proyecto colonial', *Revista Andina* 10:2 (1992), pp. 353–404, and P. Duviols, *La destrucción de la religiones andinas durante la Conquista y la Colonia* (Mexico, 1977), pp. 133–45.

[70] AGI, Justicia, 618, fols. 1395–1466. I would like to thank Eduardo Londoño, Museo del Oro, Bogota, Colombia, for allowing me to see his unpublished transcription of this document.

INDEX